SONG OF THE SKYLARK I
Foundations of Experiential Religion

Gabriel Gomes

UNIVERSITY
PRESS OF
AMERICA

LANHAM • NEW YORK • LONDON

Copyright © 1991 by
University Press of America®, Inc.
4720 Boston Way
Lanham, Maryland 20706

3 Henrietta Street
London WC2E 8LU England

All rights reserved
Printed in the United States of America
British Cataloging in Publication Information Available

Library of Congress Cataloging-in-Publication Data

Gomes, Gabriel, 1946-
Song of the skylark / Gabriel Gomes.
p. cm.
Includes bibliographical references and indexes.
Contents: 1. Foundations of experiential religion.
— 2. Meditation : teachings and practices.
1. Spiritual life. 2. Experience (Religion) 3. Meditation.
4. Buddhism—Docttines. I. Title.
BL624.G645 1991
291.4—dc20 91-7893 CIP

ISBN 0–8191–8222–2 (v. 1)
ISBN 0–8191–8223–0 (v. 1 : pbk.)

ISBN 0–8191–8224–9 (v. 2)
ISBN 0–8191–8225–7 (v. 2 : pbk.)

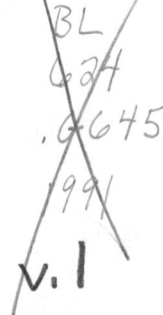

 The paper used in this publication meets the minimum requirements of American National Standard for Information Sciences—Permanence of Paper for Printed Library Materials, ANSI Z39.48–1984.

To the memory of my father,
fons et origo,
Louis Lalmon Gomes

Copyright Acknowledgements

Grateful acknowledgement is made for permission to reprint excerpts from the following works:

From *The Holographic Paradigm and Other Paradoxes* by Ken Wilber. Copyright © 1982 by Ken Wilber. Reprinted by arrangement with Shambhala Publications, Inc., 300 Massachusetts Ave., Boston, MA 02115.

The Gospel According to Zen, by Robert Sohl and Audrey Carr. Copyright © 1970 by New American Library. Used with permission.

Thomas Merton: *The Way of Chuang Tzu.* Copyright © 1960 by the Abbey of Gethsemani. Reprinted by permission of New Directions Publishing Corporation.

The Buddhist Tradition: In India, China & Japan, edited by Wm. Theodore de Bary. Copyright © 1972 by Random House, Inc. Used by permission of the publisher.

The Way of Life, Lao Tzu, translated by Raymond B. Blakney. Copyright © 1955, 1983 by Raymond B. Blakney. Reprinted by arrangement with New American Library, a Division of Penguin Books USA Inc., New York, New York.

Garma Chen Chi Chang (Chung-Yuan), *The Buddhist Teaching of Totality.* University Park and London: The Pennsylvania State University Press, 1971, pp. 219, 222. Copyright © 1971 by The Pennsylvania State University. Reproduced by permission of the publisher.

Reprinted with permission of Macmillan Publishing Company from *Mysticism East and West* by Rudolf Otto. Copyright © 1932 by Macmillan Publishing Company, copyright renewed 1960.

Wing-Tsit Chan, trans., *A Source Book in Chinese Philosophy.* Copyright © 1963 by Princeton University Press.

The Practice of Zen by Garma Chen Chi Chang (Chung-Yuan). Copyright © 1959 by Garma Chen Chi Chang. Reprinted by permission of Harper & Row, Publishers, Inc.

Sufism, by A.J. Arberry, Unwin Hyman Limited. Copyright © 1950 by A.J. Arberry. Reprinted by permission of the publisher.

Zen Flesh, Zen Bones, compiled by Paul Reps. Reprinted by permission of Charles E. Tuttle Co., Inc., Tokyo, Japan.

The Zen Teaching of Huang Po, translated by John Blofeld. Copyright © 1958 by John Blofeld. Reprinted by permission of Grove Press, Inc.

Manual of Zen Buddhism, by D.T. Suzuki. Copyright © 1960. Reprinted by permission of Grove Press, Inc.

All biblical citations are from *The New English Bible with the Apocrypha.* New York: Oxford University Press, 1971.

Contents

Preface ix
Introduction 1

Part I: The Oblivion of Time

1. Unawareness 9
2. Unreality - Illusion 21
3. Duality, Split Mind, and Conflict 29
4. Conditioning and Human Bondage 37
5. The Wheel of Life 47
6. The Oblivion of Time 55

Part II: Mind-Frames

7. Basic Assumptions 63
8. Experiential Religion on the Causes of the Human Condition . . .69
9. The Construction of Consciousness 91
10. The Construction of Reality 107
11. The Construction of Self 119
12. The Human Paradox 129

Part III: The Way Beyond the Oblivion of Time

13. The Failure of Other Approaches 141
14. Nonattachment 147
15. Desiringlessness 163
16. Emptying the Mind – Stopping the World 171
17. Leaving Self Behind 181
18. The True Self 195
19. Experiencing Oneness 211
20. All-Embracing Awareness 233
21. Completeness and Liberation 249
22. Love and Compassion 279

Part IV: One Who Shows the Way

23. The Way of the Founders 289
24. The Way of the Masters 305
25. The Master-Disciple Relationship 333

Part V: Discovering the Way

26. Meditation: The Path of Self-Realization 349
27. The Nature, Aims, and Forms of Meditation 353
28. The Process of Formal Meditation 369
    Bibliography 391
    Index 403

Preface

The inspiration for writing this book came from my "discovery" of Eastern religions. Although born and raised in Bangladesh amidst a Muslim majority and in a predominantly Hindu culture, having grown up as a Roman Catholic, I had no real appreciation of the Eastern religions. In those days Catholicism instilled in us a sense of religious superiority that set us apart from others. So when our teachers, who were mostly Hindus, told us that like Christianity, Hinduism had a trinity, we saw this merely as an attempt on the part of polytheism to appear as an equal to privileged monotheism. Little did I then realize that our stance was an age-old ploy insignificant minority groups usually adopt to maintain their identity and independence in the face of social pressures to conform to the cultural norm. So we did not take either Hinduism or Islam very seriously. As for Buddhism, I was so unfamiliar with it that I had difficulty spelling "Buddha" even after finishing my formal studies. Imagine, then, my shock when, after going through the seminary and teaching theology for several years, for the first time I encountered Eastern religions with open eyes. They spoke to me across the ages with such freshness, depth, force, and immediacy that they completely transformed my idea of religion. My previous prejudices vanished like mist in the morning sun. I realized then that sometimes you have to go very far away in order to discover what was very near to your heart.

At this time also, reading Western interpreters, particularly many in academia, I was appalled by their lack of understanding of these religions, especially of their "higher traditions." This conviction sparked the present undertaking.

As I began to articulate my views, I came across other Western interpreters, some of whom followed the experiential path but who were ignored by the academics, who did truly understand. Although initially I wanted to present a "correct" interpretation of these religions, soon I came to realize that they were self-consistent, organic wholes and that in order to do justice to them I had to undertake a full-scale study of their main tenets. As I also discovered that such views were not absent from Western religions but that on the deeper, transpersonal, level a profound unity—together with acknowledge diversity—existed among them, my project took on the character of a new paradigm of religion—one that existed alongside the usual, conventional model but addressed the higher, transpersonal dimensions of the individual. Rather than using the much misunderstood term "mysticism," I decided to call it "experiential religion."

Another fortuitous "discovery" provided the title of this book. Many years ago I had read Theodore Roszak's *The Making of a Counter Culture,* which contained an adaptation of Chuang Tzu's story which Roszak called "The Skylark and the Frogs." Upon reading it a second time, I knew I had the title of my book. However, I realized that to suit my purpose, I had to change the ending. In this modified form the story is nothing less than an analogue of Plato's Allegory of the Cave. The recasting also served as an allegory of my entire work. In my version, the story runs as follows.

There once lived a society of frogs at the bottom of a deep, dark well from where they could see nothing of the outside world. Moreover, their lives were pretty paltry. After much drudgery they could manage to find only tiny grubs and mites; and half of this meager subsistence was snatched from them by the Boss Frog, who ruled mercilessly over them.

One day a skylark flew down, sat at the edge of the well, and began to sing of all the marvelous things that existed outside—abundant food, marvelous rivers, lakes, and ponds in which frogs could frolic and gamble, vast oceans, limitless sky, horizons beyond horizons until everything melted into boundlessness.

This incident created a stir among the frogs. As the skylark kept returning to sing its song, the Boss Frog finally hit on an interpretation to offset the agitation. He told the frogs that what the bird was singing about was actually a place where frogs go after they die. This assurance calmed the frogs and they settled back to their hard lot. However, one day a philosopher frog told them that the skylark was actually singing about how they could convert their well into a beautiful place if they overthrew the Boss and made the necessary changes. Inspired by the philosopher, they conspired and overthrew the Boss, and transformed their well into a modern utopia.

Still the skylark returned to sing its song. Now, however, the skylark was pronounced mad and the frogs were instructed not to pay any attention. Hearing this, the skylark flew away and with vines and twigs made a ladder, brought it over, lowered it down the well, and this time began to sing about how the frogs could use the ladder to climb out of the well and find out for themselves what the skylark was singing about. Then it flew away.

Slowly, with much fear, anxiety, and hesitation some frogs started to climb the ladder. But others croaked, "You are crazy to try to get up there! It simply is too steep. If you persist, you will fall and break your neck!" Others reasoned with the climbers: "You have obligations and responsibilities. You should attend to your work down below and not follow every crazy idea that comes along your way." Upon hearing such talk, some got discouraged and gave up; others started doubting their capacity to climb; some began to think that the ladder would not hold up; others lost their faith in the Great Beyond; and still others succumbed to their friends' remonstration and ridicule even before they got started. However, there were a few brave frogs who, ignoring these importunities and holding firmly to the vines, with gaze fixed straight ahead, slowly began to climb. After much difficulty, but with patience and endurance, they were finally able to climb out of the well and behold for themselves the Great Beyond and experience for the first time the limitless vista of effortless Being. In joy they exclaimed, "Now we know what the skylark was singing about!" In ecstasy, they began to dance and sing the skylark's Song of the Great Beyond.

Meanwhile, some of the frogs in the well who had heard of the skylark's song but were afraid to use the ladder to climb out and discover for themselves what it was about, began to imagine the Great Beyond. They concocted theories and entire world views about it and began to teach them in their schools and colleges, to chant them in their worship centers, and to worship the Great Beyond. As the churches grew prosperous, the ladder and the Great Beyond were declared forbidden territory. But a few brave frogs could always be found who would defy all prohibitions, set aside their own doubts and fears, and take to the ladder in order to experience for themselves the Great Beyond. The skylark had flown away but its song remained; and for those who could hear, it reverberated in the narrow confines of the well.

Initially, my work was going to be only an intellectual enterprise. Little did I then know how it would change my life. I hope that for those who read and put it to practice, it will serve as a ladder of ascent and a basis for personal discovery of the wondrous Great Beyond.

This book (together with its companion volume, *Song of the Skylark II: Meditation: Teachings and Practices*) has been over a decade in the making. I started getting the germinal ideas as early as 1974. But it was not until the fall of 1979, when Marymount College gave me a sabbatical, that I composed the bulk of the work in the idyllic setting of a solitary house nestled in the woods of Vermont. Every summer thereafter I returned to that house, graciously made available by the owner, my friend Carol-Rae Hoffmann of Philadelphia, to add further refinements. By the end of the summer of 1986 the work was completed. But it required a great deal of revision. Marymount again came to the rescue with another sabbatical in 1987-88.

A work such as this, written over such a long time, needed the help and encouragement (in addition to that of Marymount College) of many friends and colleagues. Sue Bowen, Sr. Ellen Marie Keane, John Lawry, Richard Stojda, and Frederick Strath gave me much encouragement. Julius Vande Kopple, Jeff Gold, and Father Joachim Snyder helped me with the computer. William Darden lent his expertise in proofreading several chapters. Patrick and Sonya Munroe provided much assistance and encouragement. William Drumin of King's College, Wilkes-Barre, commented on some pages. Karen Honeycutt, of Berkeley, California, did a splendid job in preparing the camera-ready copy. I am grateful to them all for their assistance and encouragement. Above all, I am grateful to Caroline Whiting for her expert editing and proofreading. This book might not have seen the light of day without her felicitous improvement of my English and her deft deletion of unnecessary repetitions.

Introduction

Although religion has been studied from a variety of approaches, yielding vast and exhaustive works, these studies appear inadequate because they operate under a misconception of the nature of religion. Assuming that the highest development of which human beings are capable is the personal stage, they believe the corresponding personal form of religion to be the highest and judge other forms in terms of this criterion. As a result they fail to acknowledge stages of development beyond the personal that pertain both to the individual and to religion. However, the accumulation of evidence pointing to the existence of transpersonal stages throws into question the conventional view of religion.

The guiding assumptions of the present study are: just as there are stages of human development, so there are corresponding stages of religion; transpersonal stages of religion correspond to transpersonal stages of human development; just as no account of human nature can be complete without taking the transpersonal into consideration, so no account of religion can be complete without delineating its transpersonal stages. These stages usually are either not recognized or receive only tangential treatment. However, I maintain that there are two fundamentally irreducible but complementary aspects of religion, the personal and the transpersonal, which may be called, respectively, conventional and experiential religion. Each addresses different stages of human development. While the former is primarily preoccupied with the separate self, the latter is mainly concerned with expansion, unification, and integration beyond the personal. Each has its own presuppositions, starting points, methods, practices, and goals. Each addresses different levels of the individual and different stages of consciousness and reality.

Now, if the personal is the apex of human development, then the conventional model is the only valid form and experiential religion is an anomalous appendage. But if the opposite is true, then conventional religion is the lower and experiential religion the higher.

One of the most momentous developments of recent years is the recognition by many Western psychologists that human growth does not come to a halt at the personal stage, but that there are transpersonal stages which represent the highest stages of human growth and development. Until recently, Western psychology tended to explain manifestations of the transpersonal in the form of mystical phenomena in reductionist terms. Since one feature of such experiences is a breakdown of normal boundary conditions, many psychologists explained them as abnormal, pathological, or regressive to the preconscious, infantile stage in which such boundaries do not exist. However, humanistic and transpersonal psychology, as well as meditation research, have contributed to a wide recognition that such phenomena cannot be reduced to the prepersonal or the personal stage but must represent distinct stages, higher than the personal. Although these transpersonal stages may appear strange or unfamiliar, nevertheless they are part of human nature. Instead of viewing the personal stage as the final and optimal, many now recognize it to be an imperfect and transitional stage and the transpersonal to be the optimal state of psychological health, growth, and well-being.

I propose that although human development is normally thought to come to a stop, for reasons that will become subsequently clear, at the personal stage, nevertheless it is not the highest stage of human development; indeed, full human growth is not possible without realizing the transpersonal stages. Nor is it possible to understand fully either human nature or the nature of religion without observing the distinction between the personal and the transpersonal. Furthermore, any attempt to reduce one to the other creates a distorted view of the nature of religion. Thus, taking conventional religion as the only valid model, many writers have questioned whether Buddhism is a religion at all, when a recognition of the transpersonal stages reveals it to be one of the highest forms of religion. Since a full exposition of the transpersonal dimensions of religion is not available at present, a systematic study of them will provide a more accurate picture of the nature of religion.

Furthermore, this knowledge will offer a choice to those who cannot follow conventional religion, who find it meaningless, or who stand at various stages of dissociation from it. It will help them see that even though conventional religion may not, experiential religion may well provide them a context for discovering life's meaning and realizing its purpose. Instead of believing that religion has no place in their lives or that their choices are limited to blind adherence, indifference, or hostility to a conventional religion, they will see that an alternative is available. This alternative can fully engage their minds and hearts, transform the way they see and experience themselves and the world, and enhance their lives. This book has been written for those who have developed a healthy, mature, integrated ego, who have reached the limit of the personal stage of growth and exhausted the resources of religion based on faith alone. Such readers are not satisfied to remain on the personal stage but are ready for the transpersonal stage of development, for which experiential religion alone can be a pathway.

At its original stage, virtually every religion was primarily experiential. But after it settled down into the cultural framework, religion became conventional as it accepted the cultural construction of reality for its self-understanding and developed corresponding conceptual, normative, and organizational structures. As the personal aspect of human development became the focus of social and individual life, conventional religion became its servant.

Within this framework, conventional religion came to conceive God as a Transcendent Other, who is summoned to save the ego from the vissicitudes of life and bring it safely to the other shore of existence. To provide the ego security and survival, conventional religion developed faith and worship, a code of behavior, institutions, and systems of action directed toward the world. Thus it came to emphasize faith rather than the experience of the object of faith. When conventional religion speaks of experience what it refers to is an experience of faith and its presuppositions—doctrines, rituals, worship or prayer, codes or action, and individual or group responses to them. These presuppositions do not constitute a direct experience of what is believed; rather they only support the subjective state of the believer, for their reference point is not the reality itself but the mental and emotional constructs of the individual or the group. From faith, instruction, and childhood conditioning, the mind forms a mental model of God; and that is what the individual experiences, not God as "he" is. Since faith in or belief about an idea, image, or mental picture of God is derived from one's religious and cultural values and is a projection of personal and collective experiences and associations, especially of authority figures, it has little or no relationship to the reality of God. God is not the primary object of this experience, nor does conventional religion aim to lead anyone to it, at least in this life. Rather, it aims to save, protect, and serve the ego and its needs.

On the other hand, experiential religion aims to help the individual transcend the personal, progress through the transpersonal stages, and arrive at a direct realization of God or Reality as Such. To reach this ultimate goal, you may begin with faith but the final standpoint is not one of faith. Rather, it is a direct experience of what is initially believed. From first to last, therefore, experiential religion is concerned not with faith, doctrine, worship or organization, but with direct experience, to which faith acts as a presupposition in much the same way as a hypothesis acts in a scientific inquiry. And, although experiential religion may start with ideas or images, in the final stages it leaves them behind and arrives at a direct experience not of any idea or image, but of God or Unconditioned Reality itself.

Of the nature of this experience I shall have much to say in Part III. For the present it is sufficient to state that, first, experiential religion is concerned with your experience, not anyone else's. While the experiences of founders of religion and masters who followed them are important, they are so only as guideposts and pathways enabling you to arrive at your own realization. Their experiences are not substitutes for yours, and they will not save you from yourself. Your life is the laboratory in which you must test, in the crucible of your experience, the validity of the truth they opened up.

Second, this direct experience does not occur from any particular point of view or within any conceptual framework. It does not consist in selectively attuning oneself to some things and shutting out the rest. Nor is there any distancing from what is experienced, as there is in ordinary experience, which is always filtered through some medium. For this reason experiential religion is not so much concerned with "ordinary" experience as with the direct experience of whatever is, beginning with ordinary experience. The term I shall use for this is *awareness*.

Initially I shall define awareness as the ability of the mind to perceive itself, its states, modes, moods, activities, and events directly and exactly as they are. In other words, awareness is one's ability to see things directly, without anything filtering the seeing or intervening or creating a distance between the seer, the seeing, and what is seen. Awareness is the direct experience of what is going on, while it is going on, exactly as it is going on. For example, if you are upset, awareness consists in your directly experiencing the upset, while and exactly as you are upset, without your attention getting caught up in the feeling of upset. If you recall the upset after the event, if you deny it, deal with it through some thought, programmed reaction, or judgment, or if you do not notice it at all, you are not aware.

Note that I am differentiating awareness from consciousness. Most writers, however, do not observe this distinction but use the term *consciousness* to include awareness. Because this lack of distinction may cause confusion, I am reserving the term *consciousness* for the ordinary waking state (except where I am presenting the views of others) and awareness for the direct experience of what is. One of the few who explicitly adheres to this distinction is Swami Nisargadatta Maharaj, who says, "Awareness is the primordial original state, prior to the concept of space-time, needing no cause, no support. It simply is.... Consciousness is with a form, a reflection of awareness against the surface of matter. One cannot think of consciousness apart from awareness....But there can be awareness without consciousness" (Balsekar 13).

According to this statement, consciousness is the programmed mind, which forms part of the subject-pole in separation from the object-pole, or the world.

Within this dualistic framework, it operates according to the way it is programmed, through concepts and models, and on contents and objects. Thus you are usually conscious not of nothing but of something: a sunset, a butterfly in the meadow, your stomach growling. Your consciousness *is not* the stomach growling or the butterfly but *is of* it. By its very structure, then, consciousness is oriented toward and requires a world of objects maintained in separation from it. Such a duality is essential to its existence. If the world of objects were removed, consciousness would collapse.

On the other hand, in its essential nature beyond conditioning and construct, awareness is the Unconditioned State. It is not separate from anything, and so nothing can be its object or content. Although in the ordinary state we get the impression that awareness requires objects or that it is a dimension added to consciousness (so that, in addition to being "of something," it is further removed from the world than consciousness), in fact, the opposite is the case. When you become aware of the sunset, you do not step back from, but on the contrary step out of, your separate self and become identified with the sunset. Nothing comes between your mind and the sunset, or whatever it is that you are experiencing. The ordinary separation between consciousness, the object, and the experiencing subject is transcended in the unity of this direct experience. Far from creating another separation, awareness overcomes the separation inherent in consciousness and regains the mind's original unity with Reality. In the oneness of awareness things are experienced exactly as they are, and neither the experience nor the experiencing subject is perceived as separate from them. When and insofar as there are objects in the mind, awareness does not change them. Rather, they are revealed in their true state, just as they are. As a result, at the initial stage, when focused on ordinary experience, awareness appears to have objects. But, unlike consciousness, it is not tied to any object or content but can function without it.

It follows that from beginning to end experiential religion is concerned with awareness. Anything that does not lead to or is not a part of awareness cannot be considered a part of experiential religion. Although both ordinary experience and conventional religion are thus excluded from its essential nature, nevertheless experiential religion is not unrelated to either, since its first step involves directly experiencing conditioned existence. And it shares a common source with conventional religion. Its constant concern, however, is awareness.

Third, the question of the content of experiential religion has in a real sense already been answered: its content is everything and nothing other than itself. For in the Unconditioned State, there is nothing that is not identical with awareness. We could say, therefore, that experiential religion is concerned with pure awareness or with whatever is, just as it is.

The starting point of experiential religion, however, is awakening to your actual condition and seeing how you truly are. Accordingly, a four-step process, as well as the context in which you realize this awakening, form the heart of experiential religion: First, you must awaken to the actual condition of your life, which is also the actual condition of all human life. Second, you must awaken to the cause of this condition and directly experience how you cause, confirm, maintain, and reinforce your condition. Third, you must directly experience the possibility of freeing awareness, and thus yourself, and see in what it consists. Fourth, you must take the actual steps to bring it about; and fifth, you must find or create the appropriate context in which this realization will occur.

Parts I-III of this volume will explore the first three steps, Part IV will deal with the context, and Part V will outline the path that leads to liberation or absolute freedom.

Part I

The Oblivion of Time

I see no other single hindrance
such as this hindrance of ignorance,
Obstructed by which mankind
for a long time runs on and circles on.

- Buddha, *Itivuttaka Sutta*

Chapter 1
Unawareness

Have you ever asked yourself, "What is happening in my life and how is it happening? What does life amount to? Where am I going? How am I really? Who am I? Why am I here? Does life have a meaning or is it all 'sound and fury, signifying nothing'?" Have you ever directly faced yourself and asked such questions, taking a long, hard look at yourself with unblinking, non-judgmental eyes that do not look away, try to hide or cover up, avoid, excuse or explain away what you discover about the actual condition of your life? In sum: How does your life appear to you when you awaken to and directly see your actual condition exactly as it is, no more and no less? Such questions involving awareness of your actual condition pertain to the beginning of the journey of experiential religion.

According to experiential religion, when you directly experience your life the way it actually is, you discover that it has six main characteristics to which others can be reduced. By exploring its sources in Hinduism, Buddhism, Taoism, Judaism, Christianity, and Islam, in Part I shall present what experiential religion has to say about these characteristics, which circumscribe the human condition.

Although their perspectives differ, and not all these characteristics are equally emphasized by or found in all, nevertheless a remarkable unity of viewpoints on the human condition emerges from the sources of experiential religion. This unity is due in no small part to the fact that these sources see exactly how we weave our lives through the thread of time, create our condition, and program our lives in the same way in spite of diverse cultures and epochs. Such a common perspective beyond the surface diversity suggests that there is truth in what the sources of experiential religion report. Moreover, their viewpoint is backed up, as I shall indicate when appropriate within the limits of this study, by insights from nonreligious sources. These insights further confirm the perspective of experiential religion.

According to this view, the most ingrained and encompassing characteristic of the human condition is that human beings are unaware of their condition.

And being unaware of this unawareness, they assume or believe that they are aware. However, even though you are conscious, you are not aware of your condition. From moment to moment you do not directly experience yourself, your consciousness, or your world as they actually are. Unawareness covers your conscious, waking hours like a blanket, but since you do not ordinarily experience any state other than what is under it, you fail to see your condition. As a result, believing that you are aware, you continue to live in a cycle of reinforcements of this condition by everything you think, feel, and do.

This insight is variously expressed by the sources of experiential religion. Hinduism and Buddhism, which most extensively developed it, call it "ignorance." By this term they do not necessarily mean a lack of objective knowledge. There is plenty of objective knowledge around, but its advance has not brought an increase in awareness. On the other hand, "ignorance" does not mean unconsciousness; in fact, ignorance is a particularly virulent *dis-ease* of consciousness. It means the inability of consciousness to directly experience its own nature, processes, states, modes, moods, activities, and the nature of reality exactly as it is, beyond any conditioning or construct.

According to Hinduism and Buddhism, but especially the latter, this unawareness is so central and pervasive that all other characteristics of the human condition either emanate from or relate to it as their fountainhead. It permeates all aspects of human life, consciousness, reality, and identity (Prabhavananda and Manchester 1: 17).[1] The Buddha underscored its pervasiveness when he declared, "I see no other single hindrance such as this hindrance of ignorance, obstructed by which mankind for a long time runs on and circles on" (Conze et al. 70). Nothing is exempt from its grip. From beginning to end, and beyond, human life runs under its hypnotic spell, putting us in a culturally and personally induced trance-like state from which we seldom awaken in a lifetime. As long as we remain under it, like the air we breathe, we do not notice it.

According to Hinduism, ignorance means that, first, we are unaware of the nature of Reality as it is. Since Hinduism signifies the true nature of reality by the terms *Atman* (the Self) and *Brahman* (Godhead—to be explained later), what it means by unawareness is that we do not know nor are we aware of the truth that *Atman* is what we truly are and that *Brahman* is the nature of things just as they are. Our ordinary beliefs about our true identity and about the nature of reality are mistaken. What our perception discloses to us is how things *appear*, not how things *are* in themselves. So we become unaware of the actual state of what we believe to be real. This unawareness prevents us from directly experiencing anything as long as this condition persists. And every time we think, feel, or act from it, we reinforce our unawareness.

While Hinduism approached this insight into unawareness from the ontological point of view, early Buddhism regarded even the Hindu view of unawareness as part of unawareness. For it rejected the view of a substantial entity existing by itself, separate from the world we ordinarily perceive. The later Buddhist tradition, i.e., Mahayana, went further, teaching that we are unaware not only of our actual condition but also of Reality as Such, thus becoming trapped in our condition. As Yasutani Roshi states, "We live bound and fettered through ignorance of our true nature" (Kapleau 1: 29). And Philip Kapleau Roshi comments: "Our sufferings are rooted in a selfish grasping and in fears and terrors which spring from our ignorance of the true nature of life" (Kapleau 1: 16).

While remaining silent on the ultimate ontological issue, early Buddhism emphasized psychological unawareness, declaring that unawareness pervades the actual condition of our consciousness, self, and world. Indicating a direct cause-effect relationship between unawareness and conditioning, the Buddha declared, "Ignorance is the condition of all conditioned things" (Conze et al. 159). By this he means that unawareness is built into the very fabric of conditioned existence; whatever is conditioned is unaware. And since conditioning is basic to the human situation, the very nature of our actual condition is to be unaware. On the one hand, all programming traps awareness and makes us unaware; and on the other, unawareness leads to further programming. Awareness becomes lost in the contents which conditioning forms in consciousness. As the latter itself is formed through conditioning and its contents constitute our world, our consciousness, as well as everything in our world and every aspect of ordinary human life, makes us unaware.

Second, unaware of the fact that we are not who we believe we are, we become unaware of the Self we truly are. This unawareness makes us believe that the ego is something real, permanent, substantial, and exists by itself. According to Hinduism, ignorance consists in our mistaken identification with the ego as our true Self. For Buddhism, the ignorance consists in our unawareness of a lack of ontological status of both the Self and ego, and our belief that the ego is a separate, substantial, self-subsisting, permanent entity, when in fact this impression is derived from our identification of it with the characteristics of the body and mind or personality *(skadhas)*. For both, this predicament traps us in a double-bind: Identifying with what is not our real Self, we come to disbelieve in the latter and believe, instead, in the unreal one. As we get caught in the meshes of the latter and its drives, motives, activities and world rule our life, we become unable or unwilling to extricate ourselves from the web which binds us more tightly as time passes.

Third, we are unaware of the structure of consciousness, its states, activities, and contents. According to the Buddha, consciousness is formed and functions by grasping or fixating attention on objects. This fixation causes attention to become invariably lost, rendering us unaware. But without this fixation of attention, consciousness could not function. So, as long as there is a single object to which consciousness is attached, it remains unaware (Conze et al. 70-71). Since consciousness is formed by programming, which causes it to be unaware, and is maintained by programmed contents or objects in which awareness becomes trapped and lost, the very origin, form, functioning, and maintenance of consciousness make us unaware. Every act of perception is initiated and carried out in unawareness. And as long as this situation prevails — as long as consciousness remains programmed and continues to function according to programming — we remain unaware. Thus we are unaware not only when we are not conscious, but also when we are conscious, but remain unaware of our unawareness. To be conscious is simultaneously to be unaware. And as consciousness is pervaded and controlled by unawareness (since our reality and self form its contents), as long as it remains tied to and operates within these parameters, even when we try to become aware, we manage to entangle ourselves further in the meshes of unawareness.

Unable to see it for what it is, we come to love our condition and to consider ourselves happy. As a result, according to Buddhism, we create our own suffering, become attached to it, and refuse to let go even when someone points it out to us. This condition is illustrated by a parable: Once there lived a rich old man who had a marvelous house. However, it had only one door, its pillars were rotten, and its foundation unstable. Then suddenly the house caught fire on every side. Unaware that the fire was pressing upon them and pain and suffering were imminent, the man's children kept on playing in the house, paying no attention to their plight. Assuming that nothing was amiss, they refused to believe their father when he kept calling them to come out of the house. Only by conjuring up a trick was he able to get them out. Even then they were oblivious of their situation, happy in their unawareness (Burtt 142-143).

This parable makes clear, among other things, how in their unawareness people assume things to be otherwise than they are and then go on living as though they are aware of their actual condition. As a result, the text goes on to conclude, they endure much suffering. Absorbed in attachment, greed, desire and its pursuit they "neither apprehend, nor perceive, are neither alarmed, nor fear, and are without satiety, never seeking escape, but in the burning house of this triple world are running to and fro, and although they will meet with great suffering, count it not as the cause of anxiety" (Burtt 145). Being unaware, people come to assume their situation to be as natural as the air they breathe.

Because our consciousness does not directly perceive what we think, feel, and do at the exact moment we do them, we become fixated on repeating the same things without any awareness. Thus, like Socrates, Hinduism and Buddhism (particularly the latter) hold that we become subject to moral failure due to our lack of knowledge or unawareness. But, unlike Socrates and subsequent advocates of moral cognitivism, they hold that the root of moral failure or evil is due not so much to a failure of objective knowledge as to the inability of our minds to see directly and to clearly comprehend what we think, feel, and do at the precise moment we do it. And once we become habituated, repeated actions condition our mind and dispose us to act accordingly, creating a pull that becomes harder to break. As people devote their lives to securing, maintaining, and enhancing themselves and their world, their actions perpetuate their unawareness. Thus unawareness becomes the condition of all conditioned things, pervades and rules every moment of conditioned existence, and becomes the actual condition of our lives.

Taoism points out some consequences of this predicament when it says that through unawareness, we make our life the very opposite of Tao or the way things actually are in their original state prior to or beyond any conditioning and construct. Swimming against the current and being unaware of it, we fail to see what is good for us. Even our seemingly good actions recoil on us and harm us or others. For example, in our drive to make greater profit, we strive to preserve food by coating it with chemicals and carcinogens or by treating it with radiation, which endanger or destroy the very lives the food was intended to preserve. We contaminate our food and environment and then wonder why there is an increase of cancer.

The Taoist who developed this theme most poignantly is Chuang Tzu. According to him, through unawareness we create the very condition we try to avoid even when it is aimed to free us from the problems created by unawareness in the first place. Thus we make life a problem. To illustrate how unawareness leads to self-destructive behavior, he tells us the story of a man who was so disturbed by his own shadow and displeased with his own footsteps that he resolved to get rid of both. He got up and began to run, but for every step he took there was another step, and his shadow was right there with him. In a further effort to get away, he ran faster and faster until he dropped dead (Merton 2: 143). Thus, instead of making us face our condition, unawareness causes us to misconstrue it, even driving us to solve our problems by avoidance. As sociologist Philip Slater has also observed, our efforts ultimately aggravate our condition. Being unaware and becoming fixated in our belief that we are on the right track, we tend to redouble our efforts, which leads to fatal consequences. So amazed was Chuang Tzu at the depth of human unawareness and the complexity of problems to which it leads that he once exclaimed, "Are men living in this world really so ignorant?" But he knew that believing that we are aware when we are not, we become locked in unawareness and are seldom able to see the truth for ourselves. Only when we awaken to it do we see how our life has been governed by a mistaken belief (Chan 189).

While the inward orientation of the East led it to emphasize unawareness as a central trait of the human condition, the outward orientation of the West led to a preoccupation with the consciousness of oneself as an individual separate from others and the environment, and action directed toward transforming oneself, society, and the environment. Correspondingly, it came to emphasize individuality and personhood as the highest values and the primacy of religion based on faith. From such beliefs arose a view of the human condition in terms of a fall into duality, division, split mind, and conflict. Nevertheless, an emphasis on unawareness is not altogether lacking. For, a central theme running through the Old Testament is human unawareness, expressed in terms of forgetfulness. According to many prophets, especially Hosea, central to our condition is that we are unaware of God and our actual condition. This forgetfulness overshadows our consciousness and relationships. Thus the prophets never tire of reminding the people of their unawareness and infidelity, and the need to awaken to their condition. All history appears in this respect as a consequence of our unawareness of and separation from God, the actual condition of our life, and what we strive to become in this sleepwalking state.

This theme of unawareness as a sleepwalking state is explicitly developed by the Kabbalah. According to it, in childhood, on a deeper level, we sense the presence of the spiritual world, but when we become full-fledged members of society, we forget the other and come to regard the phenomenal world as the only reality. Once identified with it, we experience the Fall, become locked into the three levels of natural existence, and thereafter live in a sleepwalking state.

The lowest of the three levels is the vegetable state. It is ruled by the law of eating and excreting, waking and sleep. In this condition, which governs most lives, most people live and die without being aware of what controls them, and that they live in reaction to what is done to them and what they do to themselves. They live a secure, regular, predictable life, mechanically doing the same things day in and day out with minimal disturbance from outer or inner worlds. Ruled by habitual responses, such people live a life, in the words of Albert Camus in *The Plague*, "without intimations" (9).

The second level is the animal realm. It is ruled by a great deal of drive, striving, and perseverance. It includes leaders of society and, generally, successful people who are driven by achievement, success, and power. However, they, too, live in unawareness (Halevi 44-48).

The third level is the realm of the ego, the state of the fully developed natural human beings. They, too, are confined to birth, life, and death without being aware of their condition and the higher realms of life (Halevi 70-71). Thus, as the Baal Shem Tov has stated, people in the ordinary state are like sleepwalkers. They are "almost wholly oblivious to the myriad celestial mysteries which lie at every step" (Hoffman 123). So natural human life passes from unawareness to unawareness into oblivion.

In the New Testament, the author of *The Gospel According to John* implies that the human condition is one of "darkness," which is his term for unawareness. It covers not only conditioned existence but also our original nature, which he calls "light" or state of awareness. Unaware of both, we identify with our condition; and believing that it represents the truth about our nature, we proceed to claim or believe that we are aware and become trapped in the unawareness of our unawareness. John calls this condition "blindness" which, for him is "*the* sin of the world," the womb of all sin. The more trapped we become, the more tenaciously we hold onto our point of view and claim that we see our condition as it really is. As a result, Jesus says, our "sin" or unawareness remains, since by acting on it we reinforce and maintain it.

A constant theme in the Fourth Gospel, this unawareness is personified in a sharply etched dramatic dialogue involving the cure of a man born blind. Jesus gives sight to the blind man, who becomes aware of his blindness, for an awareness of our blindness is the beginning of its cure. The religious leaders, however, who are really blind or unaware of their unawareness but insist that they are aware, refuse to recognize it, thereby confirming and reinforcing their unawareness. In the closing dialogue Jesus announces what the cure signifies by saying that he came "to give sight to the sightless and make blind those who see." They then ask him point blank, "Do you mean that we are blind?" Jesus replies, "If you were blind, you would not be guilty, but because you say 'We see,' your guilt remains." (*The New English Bible,* Jn 9: 1-41. Hereafter all biblical quotations will be taken from this translation.)

That unawareness is also a central theme of the other Gospels can be gathered, for instance, from the Parable of the Ten Foolish Virgins. It is a particularly revealing teaching story as it characterizes unawareness as a state of sleep from which arises, to use Carlos Castaneda's phrase, "the endless folly" of our lives. Actually, since the virgins were first awake and then fell asleep, Jesus intimates that, in the innocence of childhood and early adolescence, our actual condition at first is like the interval before we fall asleep, in which we struggle for a while to wake up and stay awake. However, unable to muster the effort necessary to arouse ourselves, we succumb to the forces of socialization, programming, habit, inertia, various internal drives, desires, and external pressures. We thus drop into unawareness and dream of reality rather than actually waking up and seeing it as it is. Thereafter, except for occasional interruptions by forces from "outside" or within, we pass most of our lives in unawareness, oscillating between blankness and thinking, with life in the grip of confusion, conflicts, nightmares, and bad dreams. Pervading our emotions, unawareness keeps us fixated in the grooves of conditioning, repeating the responses that created it. Thus we live out of the dead past and become absent presences in the world. Extending its hegemony over our lives till we die, unawareness prevents us from waking up and coming to a direct experience of our actual condition. That is the reason, at the end of the Parable, Jesus urges us to stay awake.

Elsewhere in the Gospels Jesus constantly reminds his disciples of their unawareness and the need to stay awake. Like Chuang Tzu, amazed at their unawareness, on one occasion he exclaims, "Have you no inkling yet? Do you still not understand? Are your minds closed? You have eyes: can you not see? You have ears: can you not hear? Have you forgotten?" (Mk 8: 17-18). Here we have a convergence of viewpoints among Hinduism, Buddhism, Taoism, Judaism, and Christianity.

As for Islam, it is the Sufis (Islamic mystics) who make unawareness one of their central teachings. According to them, in the state of unawareness even our knowledge turns out to be ignorance and prevents us from seeing that we are unaware of the realities of life. Like Chuang Tzu and Jesus, the Sufis frequently express their viewpoint through teaching stories. One version of the Sufi view of unawareness is expressed in the story which is entitled, "The Tree Unaware of its State: "Pointing to a freshly cut tree a Sufi noted that the human condition is like the branches of this tree. The branches are still happy and full of sap because they are unaware that they have been cut off. So long as they are in that state, you cannot convince them of what it truly is. "This ignorance, this severance, these are the state of man" (Shah 2: 72).

As usual, this story contains a variety of meanings. First, it says that we are actually cut off from God or the Source of our being but are unaware of it. Second, thinking that we are in touch with reality, we appear happy. So long as we remain in this condition, we refuse to listen to anyone who tells us that our condition is otherwise than what we imagine it to be. Thus locked in unawareness, we fail to see either our situation or the source of our problems. As a result, like the idiot boy in Jean-Paul Sartre's play, *The Flies,* we live in a state in which we are not even aware that we are unhappy. On the conscious level we claim to be happy; and if anyone tells us otherwise, we may feel insulted, become indignant or downright hostile and doggedly defend our claim in the face of evidence to the contrary. The truth must be shouted down, as the main theme of Ibsen's play, *An Enemy of the People,* indicates, leading him to conclude: "In reality we are as blind as any moles" (90).

Such a stubbornly defensive stance, however, only reveals what we attempt to hide, namely, an incipient feeling of our actual condition. We do not want to admit this feeling to ourselves because that would mean facing life's confusion, meaninglessness, or unhappiness lurking underneath the veneer of happiness. Refusing to upset or depress ourselves by acknowledging our condition, we draw a line of defense and vainly attempt to stave off the awareness by constructing and maintaining a level of surface calm and happiness and engaging in various activities, diversions and pursuits so that we will not have to face the feeling of dissatisfaction with life. But in moments of shock, crisis, or honesty, such a defense collapses, and we come face to face with our actual condition. We may then be frightened by what we discover, draw back in horror, put up another line of defence, and try to create a semblance of normalcy or happiness. Or we may again occupy ourselves with busyness or distractions as before, like the characters of Sartre's play *No Exit.*

So long as we remain engaged in such responses, we cannot be brought to a direct experience of our condition. According to the Sufis, our condition is like that of the wax in the honeycomb that knows nothing of the fire and guttering. Only when it is made into a candle and is lighted does it know. Similarly, we have no knowledge of ourselves in our present state. We think that we are alive, when in fact we are dead (Shah 2: 73). Thus the Sufis clearly hold that, first, because of our unawareness, we know neither our actual condition nor the true Self (explained in Chapter 18). As a result, cut off from real life, we feel empty and unreal. Although in our unawareness we think that we are alive, in reality we are more dead than alive.

Second, as Chuang Tzu has observed, only when we awaken to our actual condition by undergoing a transformation of consciousness, do we come to know our condition for what it is. Until we do so, we can have only a distorted view. As we cling to it we become "like a swimmer hampered every moment by his clinging clothes" (Shah 2: 254-255) – attachments, desires, expectations, limiting beliefs, viewpoints, preconceptions, judgments, habits. As we refuse to grow beyond the egoic stage, our life becomes increasingly stunted and crippled. Wanting others to conform to our limited and distorted view of reality, we project our internal states outside and create a society and environment that become equally as stunted, crippled, conflict-ridden, destructive, and pervaded by unawareness as our own. This situation is illustrated by the story of a well-meaning old woman who found an eagle perched on her window sill. Thinking that it was a strange bird and feeling sorry for it, she first snipped off its crest, then cut its crooked beak straight, and finally clipped its oversized wings. Then, thinking that it looked more like a bird, she set it free. But now it was unable to fly (Burke 65-66). Thus our society becomes engulfed in unawareness and, in the words of Roger Walsh, "trapped in individual and shared cultural illusions" (3: 31). The Sufis characterize this condition as a state of sleep. As Hakim Sanai puts it, "Everyone in the ordinary world is asleep" (Shah 2: 190). Elsewhere he elaborates: "Humanity is asleep, concerned with only what is useless, living in a wrong world" (Shah 3: 1).

Taught by the Sufis, Gurdjieff made their teachings his own. As explained by his student and associate, P.D. Ouspensky, Gurdjieff said, "Man is asleep. In sleep he is born, in sleep he lives and in sleep he dies. Life for him is only a dream, a dream from which he never awakes" (Walker 25). As Kenneth Walker explains, we live in a sleepwalking state in a world inhabited by people who move about in a twilight of consciousness, imagining themselves to be awake. It is our consciousness itself that makes us unaware. Its very make-up puts us in a state of what Ouspensky called elsewhere "waking sleep" from which we occasionally wake up, only to fall back into it again. And he believed that the chief obstacle to our waking up to a higher state of consciousness is our mistaken belief that we are already awake (38, 43).

Among modern writers, Henry David Thoreau clearly perceived and characterized the human condition as a state of sleep when he said, "we are sound asleep nearly half our time" (570). This unawareness prevents us from seeing our actual condition. As a result, he says, "for the most part, we are not where we are, but in a false position. Through an infirmity of our natures, we suppose a case, and put ourselves into it, and hence are in two cases at the same time, and it is doubly difficult to get out" (566). We are not only unaware, but unaware of that fact; and in this state, we believe or suppose that we are aware. Thus we become locked into the double bind of unawareness, its denial, and the counter claim of awareness, from which no escape is possible as long as we remain in it. Agreeing with this view, Erich Fromm says, "The average person, while he thinks he is aware, actually is half asleep" (Fromm et al. 108). Thus unawareness and a mistaken belief about our condition render us sleepwalkers through time, which is the historical condition of humankind.

Our entire life, then, comes to be spent under the control of unawareness, so that we seldom directly experience our actual condition. From beginning to end, our life passes from unawareness to unawareness into the oblivion of time. Only occasionally, when we make the effort and peer outside, do we notice our situation. But fear, confusion, the demands and preoccupations of life, habituation, and the very structure of our consciousness, self, and world make us assume cover again and continue to live in our accustomed unawareness.

The very first step of experiential religion consists in directly experiencing this condition exactly as it is. Unless we do, we will remain trapped in the illusion of being aware. And this will prevent us from taking further steps in the journey of awakening that is experiential religion.

---

[1]Departing from the MLA method of citation, otherwise used throughout, in cases of multiple works by the same author, I have adopted a modified course. According to this method, the first number in the entry after the name of the author and before the colon refers to the number of the work cited in the bibliography, while the number(s) following the colon refer(s) to the page number(s) in the work.

Chapter 2
Unreality - Illusion

Once you become aware of your unawareness, you discover another basic fact of the human condition, namely, that you are not as in touch with things as you believe you are. As you come to see your life and world directly, you realize that they are not quite what they had appeared. You begin to see that most of the time you live in a fantasy world populated by thoughts, opinions, arguments, fears, desires, wishes, memories, fantasies, judgments, and your inner dialogue. These mental contents color your world and give it the texture it assumes in real life. And it is through them that you peer out toward the world and others. You see that the ordinary view of what is real and what life is all about is largely a belief system held together by these and other factors, interwoven by a network of programming and held up by a consensus within a larger framework called "reality." As you survey this, you come to realize that what you call "the real world" is largely a socio-cultural and personal construction with which you identify. In taking your construction for the way things are, you build up an illusory picture of the world, and in identifying with it you become trapped in its folds. Thus, according to experiential religion, a fundamental illusion permeates human life at its very core and affects the way we perceive, what we perceive, and how we think, feel, live, and act.

Although their explanations differ, both Hinduism and Buddhism agree that what we believe to be real or "the real world" is illusory, *maya*. Stated in this way, the term *maya* is subject to misinterpretation, not only in the West — where anyone who holds such a view is likely to be labeled world-denying or other-worldly — but in the East as well. In his book, *Zen and the Art of Motorcycle Maintenance*, Robert Pirsig tells us that his teacher in India repeatedly explained that the world is illusory. Finally, one day Pirsig asked if the bombs dropped on Hiroshima were illusory. Apparently, neither Pirsig nor his Hindu teacher understood the teaching of Hindu scriptures — *that our illusions cause us to create our realities.* The same illusions that led to making and dropping these bombs have locked us, worldwide, into spending hundreds of billions of dollars on "defense." Our "defensive" weapons are now capable of killing not only those whom our illusions tell us to be our enemies, but also ourselves and all human life on this planet, several times over.

And there is no end in sight. For our illusions keep us in the grip of fear, of the desire for power and dominance. Since everyone is in the same game, conflict, strife, and killings go on unabated. Is it any wonder that Hinduism and Buddhism consider the core of the human condition to be a fundamental deception that turns into a self-deception? It is necessary, therefore, that we carefully examine such a central aspect of the human condition.

Besides meaning "illusory" and "unreal," *maya* also denotes "magical," "deceptive," "things being otherwise than they appear," "a game." Hindu teaching on the unreality of the world is perhaps best expressed in the *Vedanta*, epitomized by Shankara. According to Ramana Maharshi, the teaching can be reduced to three statements: (i) *Brahman* (Godhead, Reality as Such, That other than which nothing exists, or things just as they are in their Unconditioned State beyond any conditioning or construct) alone is real; (ii) the universe is unreal; and (iii) *Brahman* is the universe. These three statements must not be taken separately, however, otherwise the meaning of Hindu teaching will be lost. Taken together they mean, as Ramana Maharshi states, "when the Universe is perceived apart from Brahman, that perception is false and illusory. What it amounts to is that phenomena are real when experienced as the Self and illusory when seen apart from the Self" (Osborne 16). Similarly, from the Buddhist point of view Yasutani Roshi observes, "Broadly speaking, the entire life of the ordinary man is nothing but a *makyo* (illusion)" (Kapleau 1: 38). Such statements make it clear that, for Hinduism and Buddhism, the world is not unreal in the sense that it does not exist. Nor are their statements to be construed, as is often done, as an expression of philosophical idealism. How, then, are we to understand them?

First, according to Hinduism, our claim to perceive reality as it is is *maya*, mistaken or illusory, because what we call "reality" is in fact a construction or belief system which the mind projects or superimposes on what is (Prabhavananda & Manchester 1: 68-69). What we perceive as phenomena, objects, or things is not the way reality or the world is in itself, but what filters through our perceptual apparatus and is perceived by the programmed mind. It is not that this construction presents to us only a small portion of the vast cosmos, but what we perceive is distorted through perceptual information-processing, model construction, interpretation, evaluation, and judgment. Thus any construction or condition distorts reality. Since we live in a conditioned state (and every conditioning creates distortion and normal consciousness is formed through conditioning), it follows that in this state we can form only distorted pictures of reality. None of these can reveal Reality as Such, which is beyond all conditioning and constructs. As a result, whatever appears to us is not reality as it is, but remains only our version of reality. (Philosophically speaking, it may be noted, everyone is an idealist, including especially those who claim to be realists!)

Now if we stayed here and recognized our construction for what it is, there would be nothing deceptive or illusory about it. But we believe that what we perceive is the way things are. Then we proceed to assume that what we perceive is the natural state, and hence necessary, final, and the only way things can be. This belief is what makes our version of reality *maya,* that is, illusory or unreal.

Maya, then, signifies a misconstruction of reality resulting from identification of our version with Reality in itself. This identification, which is also a category mistake, makes the unreal appear Real or our reality unreal, as we misunderstand its constructive nature. Thus misunderstanding the nature of both, we invert the real order and fall into the fundamental, all-encompassing illusion *(maya)* that envelops our reality, consciousness, and selves. Such is the nature of *maya* which makes us believe, in the words of Henry David Thoreau, "that is, which appears to be" (349). It not only makes us set our reality on "purely illusory foundation" (349), but also creates a double fixation, as we "suppose" our construction to be Reality as it is, identify with and become encased in it, and come to believe Reality to be remote or unreal. Thus we become twice removed from reality and remain fixated in our illusion (566). On this point Hinduism clearly agrees with Plato, whose Allegory of the Cave neatly portrays the human condition as *maya* – our belief that we see reality in itself when in fact, chained by conditioning, we see only our cultural and personal constructs, the shadows of how things are in themselves.

According to Hinduism and Buddhism, then, at the core of the human condition, along with unawareness, is this illusion in which we become trapped in the process of growing up. However, this deception is ours; we put a veil on ourselves and then declare that there is no veil. Our reality becomes illusory not only in what it hides but also in what it reveals and in what we do to reveal it. As reality comes to us veiled, our minds become enveloped in a hypnotically induced trance and our behavior becomes a game. For the rest of our lives our reality plays tricks on us; that is, we play tricks on ourselves. As we seek solutions to the problems created by this reality, we find they ever elude us. Hence the meaning of *maya* as a game. Everything in a world we ourselves create becomes a game; the framework and rules we make bind and govern our lives; the game becomes deadly serious. As Lama Govinda has observed, this is the creative aspect of *maya:* Our cultural creations, all our endeavors – our drive to find identity, self-worth, meaning and fulfillment through success, achievement, acquisition of wealth or power, manipulation of others and the environment –

fall under this category. Since anything conditioned or constructed is *maya* in this sense, all that we are, all that we create, and what we call "the real world" is a game.

An illustration will clarify how our illusions, fantasies, and beliefs create and hold together the picture of what we believe to be real. Things in themselves do not produce fear; nor do people threaten our survival or come with the label "enemy." But if I believe (illusion) them to do these things, my fear will color my world and induce me to give it a fearful or negative interpretation. I will see others and the world as the cause of my fear or feeling of threat; and I will be on guard, suspicious of people, reserved or withdrawn, worried, and anxious. In fact, it is I who make myself afraid as my mind creates a model of reality glazed with fear, projects it onto others, and then claims them to be its source. Internationally, of course, the entire world lives by fear and distrust, and the idea of enemy is its creation. Fear of survival, loss of power, dominance, resources, or advantage make us build elaborate defense systems and believe others to be our rivals or enemies. In reality they are human beings just like ourselves, having the same sort of beliefs about us as we do about them.

As a result of the illusions of fear and aggression world-wide, we have created bombs, the arms race, armies, defense departments, and a generally hostile world. Similarly, our illusion of greed creates our realities: Wanting more and bigger things to satisfy our fantasies of identity, power, fulfillment, happiness, and self-importance, we have created a business world that vies to satisfy our wants and in turn creates more wants (greed) through advertisement. It fills us with the profit motive (greed) so we will produce more and different things to keep the engine of greed turning. Thus we have created a production-consumption cycle in a runaway economy which controls much of our lives. And the very thought of its slowing down sends us into a paroxysm of fear. If you carefully examine your picture of reality, you will find nothing in it that is not pervaded by illusions.

Carlos Castaneda's don Juan observed that our reality is "an interpretation we make" (4: 24). We make the description we learn from society our own, substitute it for the world, and then attempt to conform the world to it. Thus we come to perceive not the world as it is but our description of it. Since we believe it to be the world, we lock ourselves in the bubble of our description and become trapped in a vicious circle from which we rarely emerge in a lifetime (1: 263-265; 2: 8, 299; 3: 100, 246).

Confirming this view, Chuang Tzu declared that what we perceive as the real world is a description learned in the process of socialization. Only upon awakening, do we come to see that what we thought to be reality was only our made-up version. Thus Chuang Tzu said, "Finally there comes a great awakening, and then we know life is a great dream. But the stupid think they are awake all the time, and believe they know it distinctly" (Chan 184, 189).

Second, not only *what* we perceive, but also the *way* we perceive is illusory *(maya)*. Since all programming distorts perception, and the very structure of consciousness consists of programming, distortion is built into the very structure and functioning of consciousness. That this distortion, which is another meaning of *maya* or illusion, is caused by the normal perceptual process is confirmed by psychology. As Roger Walsh observes, "The mind continuously creates a largely unrecognized stream of thoughts, images, fantasies, associations which distort our awareness, perceptual process and sense of identity to an unrecognized degree." As our consciousness identifies with its content, "awareness is reduced and distorted, resulting in an unappreciated trance state." For most of the day we remain immersed in this state and conduct our affairs, believing that we are dealing with reality This distortion, he goes on to add, is described in various traditions as *maya* or illusion (1: 22-23). Buddhism calls the fantasies or distortions resulting from programming "a fault of vision, a magical creation" (Conze et al. 161, 211). As Lama Govinda observes, "The tacit presupposition that the world which we build up in our thought is identical with that of our experience (to say nothing of the world as such) is one of the main sources of our erroneous conception of the world" (1: 136).

Modern cognitive psychology also maintains that what consciousness responds to directly is its constructs, programming, processes and contents. As Fromm puts it, "most of what the person is conscious of is a fiction — while that which it represses (i.e., which is unconscious) is real" (107-108). As we perceive and interact through layers of programming and mental contents our contact with reality is always mediated and never direct. Most of what we believe to be real is a set of constructs and contents which arise from our need to survive and to interact with others and with the environment. As a result, we come to spend most of our life amid fabrications of our own mind, chasing fantasies or shadows and taking them to be, or trying to make them and thus ourselves, real. Thus Fromm concludes, "The average person's consciousness is a 'false consciousness,' consisting of fictions and illusion, while precisely what he is not aware of is reality" (109).

In regard to the self, *maya* becomes self-deception and puts us in a double illusion as we identify with ego, believe it to be our true Self, and attribute to it the latter's characteristics (Prabhavananda 40). We become twice removed from reality — from the Self and the world — and settle down to being less than what we truly are.

In the Old Testament, the sense of the illusoriness of our condition is clearest in Qoheleth. Like Castaneda's don Juan, Qoheleth calls our situation folly. He sees the ordinary individual pursuing illusions, mistaking them for realities and becoming a victim of his/her own conditioning (Qoh. 10: 2-3). Yet like Camus' Meursault in *The Stranger,* who sees that in the face of death all of society's ideas of what is real and important become equally meaningless and unreal, and like don Juan himself, who sees death equalizing society's values and relative viewpoints and rendering its description of reality unreal, Qoheleth declares that wisdom and folly are equally empty, for death equalizes them (Qoh. 9: 30). Thus they declare that, like waking up from a dream, when you awaken to the actual condition of life, its illusory character becomes apparent.

From the Kabbalist perspective (not unlike that of modern psychology), Baal Shem Tov declares that the ordinary consciousness is full of illusions and deceptions which are formed when it imposes division, order, and separation on things. This situation makes the real appear illusory, while what we believe to be real is actually illusory. To illustrate the illusory character of our perception, Baal Shem Tov tells the following story: There once was a king who built a palace and placed himself in the innermost room. When his servants came to pay him homage, they could not approach him because of the devious maze leading to the inner room. Finally, however, the king's son came and showed them that the partitions were not real but were magical illusions (Hoffman 122).

The point of view of the New Testament is best expressed, as already explained in the previous chapter, by *The Gospel According to John,* which declares that unawareness makes us fall into the fundamental illusion from which arises the disorder that circumscribes our life. In his *First Letter,* John calls it "the original lie," the primal deception.

Although Christian mystics do not dwell on this point, nevertheless a contemporary practitioner, Bernadette Roberts, does point out that because in the ordinary state we do not directly experience reality but only think about it, all our views about reality are illusory. Our thoughts, which are disconnected from the real world, become illusory because the self colors its perception with desires and wishes, and makes the world appear what it is not. But we have no notion of this condition until we experience the nonrelative state and see in retrospect that what we thought to be the real world was only a thought. Until we become awakened, then, we have no way of recognizing the illusory character of ordinary waking consciousness (1: 100). Thus Roberts corroborates the views of Chuang Tzu, the Sufis and the other traditions.

The Sufi perspective is conveyed not only through the stories discussed in the previous chapter but also through the following story told by Idries Shah in his book *The Sufis:* A man once hurt his leg and had to walk on crutches. As he found them very useful for walking and for many other purposes, he not only continued to wear crutches regularly but also taught everyone in his family to use them. Thus crutches became a normal part of their life. Soon the whole town adopted their ways. After having used crutches for many generations, few people could walk without them, confirming their necessity. However, when the few who had started to walk without them pointed out that crutches were unnecessary, the cripples replied that this was merely a figment of their imagination. By this time the cripples were becoming blind as well because they refused to see the truth (Shah 3: 353-354).

Like Jesus' teaching, this parable illustrates how unawareness makes us blind not only to our actual condition but also to reality, leading us to build up an illusory picture of what is real. Once we accept our condition as the truth, we proceed to believe it to be normal, natural, necessary, and final. Thereafter, if someone points out that our condition is not what we imagine it to be, we refuse to believe it and declare the assertion itself a fantasy. Afraid of facing the truth and anxious to avoid upsetting the regular rhythm of our lives, even if it makes us suffer, we turn reality into an illusion, creating an inverted picture (Shah 3: xxvii).

According to experiential religion, then, the sweep of *maya* is total. It covers every aspect of our life and thought, identity and reality—in fact, the entire realm of conditioned existence. Through unawareness we identify our constructs to be reality as it is and fall into the fundamental illusion that defines our condition. Once we fall into these mistaken identifications, we remain spellbound, generating problems that clog our lives.

Although this viewpoint that what we believe to be real is actually an illusion or distortion may appear farfetched at first, as I shall show in Part II, it is actually supported by psychology, sociology, and other Western disciplines. Thus, far from being other-worldly or world-denying, the concept of *maya* expresses one of the profound truths about the human condition—that our reality is a construct and not what we believe it to be, that it is we who construct and maintain it by our belief and consensus that this is how reality is in itself, and that by believing that this is the only way things can be, we have created a deadly game.

Chapter 3
Duality, Split Mind, and Conflict

When we experience our actual condition as described in the last chapters, we awaken to our separation from what is. Cut off from the Source and set adrift in a stormy sea we ourselves create, we keenly sense the separation. A feeling of not being quite real or quite at home in the world descends on us. Restless and dissatisfied, we try to set things right, but in spite of our attempts to overcome it, the separation remains. We feel claustrophobic, bored or angry at some anonymous force that, we believe, put us in this situation, unaware that we have done so ourselves. "Raging against the dying of the light," as Dylan Thomas put it, we find that we are in conflict with ourselves and our environment. As don Juan remarked to Castaneda, "Your problem is that if you are not bored with the world you are at odds with it (1:129)." Similarly, pointing to our limited, conditioned existence as the source of our restlessness, Achaan Chah says, "We human beings are constantly in combat, at war to escape the fact of being just that much. But instead of escaping, we continue to create more suffering" (Kornfield & Breiter 42).

We may try to get the restlessness and discomfort out of our system by aggressive or competitive behavior, channeled into achievement, success, and power or manipulative games. In the process we may generate a lot of things that may dazzle the imagination, but our condition remains as before. Believing in progress, we increase our activities, but the restlessness and dissatisfaction lurking beneath the surface remain or even increase.

In a panic, we may then drive our proverbial boat at astonishing speeds, only to find that we are still in the same directionless sea, cut off from things as before and unable to overcome our condition. Feeling our efforts to be futile, we may internalize the anger and become depressed or despondent, feel empty or lonely, and withdraw to a corner of the stormy sea. The terror of not being alive may make us crave something that would make us feel real and significant. Our terror sets off other chain reactions, and we dash off again.

As we come to live in a world cut off from Reality as Such, separate from persons and things, dissatisfaction and restlessness grow, and our life becomes enveloped in internal and external conflict. According to experiential religion, such conflict is another basic characteristic of the human condition, resulting from a triple separation. The primary one is our separation from Reality as Such, our true nature or Self. Cutting ourselves off from what is, we create a second separation as we form a dualistic structure of reality, the polarity of self and the object-world; while the third separation is formed by the arrangement of a world made up of separate, individual persons and objects. As the outer, so the inner: within ourselves we experience a split in body and mind; and a mind split into conscious and unconscious spheres, reason and emotions. Out of this triple separation arise fragmentation, dissatisfaction, restlessness, conflict, and confusion. To overcome these negative qualities, we set ourselves off to create a world that becomes a materialization of our inner states, that sets the trajectory of our life. The sources of experiential religion focus on one or another aspect of humankind's state of being lost at sea.

The *Bhagavad Gita* emphasizes conflict as a basic condition of human life, symbolized as a battlefield. In this state we project outward the conflict raging among our inner forces, creating a corresponding world. Life becomes a battleground in which the self is split into identities or self-images, desires, emotions, and drives that fight against one another and against the outer forces of society and environment. Becoming aware of this situation within himself, the warrior Arjuna realizes that these conflicting forces have made his life a battlefield, in which those who are opposing him are the very ones with whom he is identified. Feeling that in battling and overcoming them he would be cutting out the very things that made up his self and world, Arjuna is overcome with terror, confusion, and despair.

This theme of conflict as a basic characteristic of the human condition is, then, very ancient and very modern. It would be tempting to demonstrate the centrality of this theme by analyzing modern literature, but that is not possible here. It is sufficient to note that if you examine some of the prominent modern writers, such as Melville, Hemingway, Wolfe, Kazantzakis, Hesse, Mann, Camus, Kafka, and Sartre, you will find them describing life as such a battleground. They portray human beings as cut off from the sources of their being. Having lost their moorings, they are adrift at sea, directionless and purposeless, except for what their own striving can create. At the threshold of the twentieth century, the philosopher Friedrich Nietzsche expressed this condition in his famous "Parable of the Madman." Psychology and psychoanalysis also bear witness to this same condition. Freud found conflict to be fundamental to the human condition and pinpointed its source: the split mind at the level of the second order of duality. At this level consciousness becomes organized as the subject-pole in separation from the object-pole and becomes split within, differentiated by the unconscious. The Buddha discovered the same truth, and, in accordance with the Indian terminology, called it *dukkha*. He gave voice to his discovery in what is now called, "The Sermon at Benares":

> Now this, monks, is the noble truth of pain *(dukkha):* birth is painful, old age is painful, sickness is painful, death is painful, sorrow, lamentation, dejection, and despair are painful, not getting what one wishes is painful. In short, the five groups of grasping *(skandhas)* are painful. (Burtt 30)

According to the Buddha, then, our actual situation is *dukkha*. This term is usually translated as "suffering," or, as above, "pain." Now what does it mean? Does it mean the physical sensation of pain itself in such events of life as birth, old age, sickness, and death, which the Buddha mentions? Or does it mean something else? If it denotes physical pain, then the Buddha's observations are rather obvious. You do not have to be enlightened to see that, and enlightenment will not free you from the physical sensation of pain. Nor are all human beings (or the whole of human life) always in physical pain; whereas the Buddha is saying that all of conditioned existence, even our moments of happiness, under the sway of dispositions, is pervaded by *dukkha*. He goes on to say, moreover, that there is a way to be completely free of it.

As even astute and knowledgeable observers miss the point of Buddha's teaching, a close examination of it is necessary. To begin with, by *dukkha* the Buddha does not mean physical pain but psychological and ontological suffering. A distinction must be drawn between the physical sensation and the psychological and ontological condition of suffering. The first is inherent in our having a body with nerve centers that react to painful stimuli. As long as we have a body, we cannot be immune to this physical pain. As a psychological state, on the other hand, suffering is our mental and emotional reaction to the physical sensation and originates from a feeling of being trapped in our world and life-situation, and our struggle to get out of or avoid it, or from our desire to have something other than what we experience in the present moment. This psychological reaction of the programmed mind has ontological roots.

On the ontological level, *dukkha* issues as our reaction to being cut off from Reality as Such; to being conditioned and trapped in our constructs and the web of life we spin around them; to settling down to a separate world of our own making; and to being less than what we are. Moreover, it is our reaction to the illusory condition of life. Since these reactions make up the human condition, suffering is equated with and is seen as inherent in every reaction and embraces the whole of conditioned existence. Hans Wolfgang Schumann is correct when he says that *dukkha* means "whatever is subject to the cycle *(samsara)* of becoming and passing...in other words everything that is unliberated" (41). And as Jack Engler points out, this meaning of suffering is tied to our normal attempt to remain at the stage of the separate self and world, which is seen as pathogenic or a point of fixation and arrested development (1: 47).

On this ontological level, the state of being cut off from the Unconditioned creates a sense of insufficiency or not-enoughness. Since that precisely is the structure of conditioned existence, whatever we experience in this state, we experience as insufficient unto itself. Thus, the core of *dukkha* is the insufficiency of conditioned existence, its inability to be permanent and self-subsistent, to be the foundation of its own being and consciousness, to be the true identity and the goal of existence, in separation from Reality as Such, and thereby satisfy our ontological hunger.

So *dukkha* is this insufficiency of everything we experience, create, and encounter from moment to moment. That is why to be conditioned is to suffer or experience life as unsatisfactory. Anything that is conditioned or constructed, anything that arises from and is subject to conditioning is subject to or constitutes *dukkha*. That is the reason it embraces "conditioned genesis," that is, anything that arises from and is subject to conditioning, the separation from the world and the split mind that emerges with self-consciousness. That is the reason the Buddha did not deny that we experience moments of pleasure or happiness, but he saw that even these moments are pervaded by *dukkha*. For, even in these moments we react to rid ourselves of the discomfort and dissatisfaction resulting from separation and the feeling of not being at home in the world.

On the psychological level, the core of *dukkha* is the mental and emotional reaction to the feeling of insufficiency or not-enoughness we experience from moment to moment. Since consciousness functions by grasping and fixating on objects, which are its attempts to make things permanent and substantial, *dukkha* is inherent in its very structure. Moreover, consciousness necessarily reacts out of programming, which constitutes its very content or inner circuitry and mode of operation. And since any programming is necessarily reactive, the very structure and functioning of consciousness is made up of reactions that form the core of *dukkha*. To be conscious is to experience *dukkha*. Thus it ranges over the entire human life and consciousness.

As to the nature of this reaction, the Buddha mentions negative programmings, which are instances of *dukkha*, "contact with things unpleasant," or having what we don't want, and "not getting what one wishes," or not having what we want. These states are caught, in the words of Tarthang Tulku, in a "cycle of expectation and disappointment" (1: 104). Thus, the core of the psychological reaction is desire and grasping or avoidance. Because we are dissatisfied with our actual condition, we attempt to get rid of it or make it other than what it is. And, just as the feeling of insufficiency encompasses whatever we experience from moment to moment, so dissatisfaction lies at the very core of all our ordinary psychological states and responses to the world, to others, to life and our condition.

Because we experience the present moment as insufficient, the mind reacts. It wants to hold onto and repeat or prolong the stimulus experienced as pleasant and to resist, push away or avoid what is experienced as unpleasant. Hence desire, grasping, and attachment are at the core of the programmed mind and cover the entire range of its operation. That is the reason the Buddha says that the *skandhas* — form, feeling, perception, drives or will, and consciousness — are forms of grasping. The very structure and operation of our bodily and mental processes and states create *dukkha* by grasping at and fixating on objects. Whatever form we perceive, whatever feeling arises, the entire perceptual process, our drives, latent tendencies, will, and the entire programmed mind operate by reacting, grasping, and attaching to or avoiding the primary order of sensations that impinge or register on them. That is the reason all programmed reactions, according to the Buddha, are forms of grasping, desire, and avoidance. And since they encompass the entire conditioned existence, all conditioned states are *dukkha*.

Furthermore, not getting what we want and getting what we don't want characterize our entire life. We are always dissatisfied with the present, not quite at home in it, because we are cut off from it and wishing, as Stephen Levine puts it, to be elsewhere, wanting things to be other than they are. Our whole life seems to consist of waiting for something to happen, or wanting to get something (of which we are not quite sure), something that will remove the unsatisfactoriness of the present and reveal the purpose, significance, sufficiency, or completeness of life. But, like Godot of Beckett's play, *Waiting for Godot*, the fulfillment never comes.

As Tarthang Tulku observes, "Even though we are not very happy, we continue to behave in the same way, hoping that the future will somehow be different, and finally — life is over" (1: 107).

Moreover, there is *dukkha* even when we get what we want or think we want. We are so caught up in getting that we become more interested in the process than in having the object. We seem to become disappointed after we get it. As Levine points out, our gratification occurs in the process of moving from not-having to having, instead of the having itself. The satisfaction consists, not in the possession of the object, but in the cessation of the painful desire or overcoming the discomfort of not-having. When we go beyond this point of satisfaction, we get bored and want something else (100-103). We are so used to not having that when we do have what we want, we feel a letdown. I remember as a child I always felt a sadness or disappointment when we arrived at a destination. I was always more excited by the journey and wanted it never to end. Or, because of our self-defeating, negative programming, even when we have within our grasp what we want, we fail to take advantage of it. We mess it up, become unhappy with, reject, miss, or lose it in the end. As Krishnamurti has said, "The tragedy of man is not that he never finds what he seeks, but that he always finds exactly what he seeks, and no more" (Needleman 1: 144). Fundamentally, because what we usually want is not Reality as Such but a limited object, which is a substitute, we are bound to be dissatisfied even when we have attained it. Thus dissatisfaction is present in the very getting of what we want and in the satisfaction itself. As we grasp at momentary states in the effort not only to form a stable self and world but to make them permanent, we turn life into *dukkha*.

This inability to accept change, which results in *dukkha,* includes ordinary unhappiness, neurotic conflicts, unstable and borderline personalities, and dissociated and contradictory ego states (Engler 1: 46-47). It is also evident in the physical symptoms of *dukkha* the Buddha mentions: birth, old age, sickness, and death. Being unable to accept these states, we try to deny, avoid, or turn them into something else. What these mental reactions are we learn from psychology. Briefly, it may be said that birth is *dukkha* because it is "the primal experience of chaos, of being trapped, of separation" (Deikman 1: 7-13). Old age can be *dukkha* in the sense of the loss of power or self-importance; in the absence of someone to love, of someone who needs and wants you; or in the sense of having failed in life, resulting in regret, remorse, despair, or depression (Erikson 269), as well as in the apprehension of approaching death. The inability to accept sickness, physical or mental, and "the schizoid condition of life" (May 24) are themselves instances of *dukkha*. Moreover, according to Freud, Rank, and others, all human strivings and achievements, even culture and civilization, are a consequence of human beings' attempts to avoid death and make themselves immortal. In Ernest Becker's terms, *dukkha* results from an apprehension about or terror of death and the sense of finality for a self-consciousness that does not want to die (15-24). According to Becker, this terror arises with self-consciousness and pervades all human life and activity. For modern human beings, so conscious of their individuality, the din of the drumbeat of death is constantly in their ears. Everything they are and do are under its sway.

For the Old Testament, again, conflict is central to the human condition. It sees the source of this conflict in the primal duality or separation that rends asunder conditioned existence from its moorings in Reality and sets it in vortices, rudderless and spinning away on its own momentum. The Old Testament expresses this teaching through the story of the Fall, which is presented as the primal human act of separation from God, the experience of an inner split, and the setting up of a world along dualistic lines—a world in which the individual, split also from his/her fellow human beings and the environment, experiences further dislocation, conflict, and strife within and without. And history is nothing other than the story of what humankind does, individually and collectively, after the Fall.

According to Edward Hoffman, from the very beginning the Kabbalistic tradition has observed that not only is ordinary consciousness split, full of conflicting thoughts and desires, but the entire individual self is also split into two opposing forces of lower and higher natures, which keeps it is in a state of constant war with itself. And this inner conflict is basic to the human condition (92-93).

The New Testament has observed this conflict with particular keenness. According to St. Paul, conflict not only encompasses the entire human condition but it also has cosmic overtones; that is, it reaches all the way to the primal separation from God. In the human realm everyone experiences the split and separation when s/he first becomes self-conscious (Rom 5: 12). In each individual there is an inner split between what Paul calls "the lower nature" and "the Spirit;" that is, between conditioned existence or the separate self and its reality-construct, and the higher Self. As long as human beings live according to the lower nature, they will suffer from the ravages of separation, and their life will become torn by conflict from top to bottom (Rom 8: 5-13). Moreover, from this duality in nature and the split in consciousness there arises a duality of desires which are in fundamental conflict with one another, turning the split-mind into a battleground of conflicting forces (Gal. 5: 16-18), as the *Gita* and the Kabbalah have also noted.

A similar note is struck by *The Gospel According to John*, in which the author depicts a fundamental conflict raging between the forces of light and darkness, which are his terms for the higher and lower states in ourselves. Although in itself the Light, which is the *Logos* or the true Self, has no unawareness, in our actual condition it is covered over by darkness or repressed by the conscious mind. In this state, as we proceed to organize our world, the mind plunges into unawareness and turmoil and becomes topsy-turvy: what is light appears as darkness, while darkness appears as light. Not only does repression split the mind and cause conflict; the attempt to live in darkness, that is, in unawareness of our true Self or the Light, and according to the forces of the programmed mind, also turns the entire life of the individual into a conflict between these two realms.

Agreeing with Paul, John says that the conflict envelops not only the individual, but also society and history. The entire socio-political-economic-religious fabric of our world is coated and glazed in this unawareness and conflict. It even reaches beyond—to the entire created order, that is, to the collective unconscious and the transpersonal states up to the very limit of primal separation. And John presents his entire Gospel as a gigantic, cosmic struggle between the unconscious forces on the one hand (the negative cosmic energies and the corresponding dark forces [the devil]) and the forces of Awareness (Jesus) on the other—both in and outside the individual.

The Sufis, too, see the conflicting character of our actual situation as a consequence of our primal separation from God and our attempt to make ourselves Real on the basis of our constructs. In this state, as El Mahdi Abbassi once demonstrated, even when you try to help an individual, something in him/her frustrates that aim (Shah 2: 65). Our mind becomes engulfed in conflict due to a contradiction between the desires of ego and those of the Self. Becoming unaware of what we most need in order to be ourselves, we strive for the very opposite and our life becomes unworkable. As we become attached, whenever we try to overcome the original condition, we become further entangled in frustration, conflict, and contradiction. Such is the trajectory of human life.

Chapter 4
Conditioning and Human Bondage

When you directly experience your actual condition as described in the last chapter and find that in spite of your best efforts to change, you seem unable to free yourself from this pattern of life, you experience two other closely related basic characteristics of the human condition: conditioning and bondage.

According to experiential religion, whatever is not Unconditioned, whatever is limited, constructed, and finite, is programmed. And not only is conditioning as pervasive as the other factors already discussed, it also immediately affects every aspect of your life—your perceptions and relationships. Having formed everything you consider to be yourself, conditioning now dictates all your responses. You are one big mass (or mess) of programming—a prefabricated, prepackaged deal. (Maybe that is why we like packaged deals!). Nothing in you or your world is free from the formative influence of conditioning. Your self, individuality and uniqueness, from the deepest to the most superficial of your wishes, desires, wants, needs, thoughts, feelings, ideals, beliefs, values, and goals, are all formed and ruled by it. Your consciousness is nothing but a network of programming. As the inner, so the outer: society and its institutions, culture, civilization, the whole of what you consider real—all are a result of programming. From cradle to grave, and even beyond, all human life is under its grip. In fact it begins before birth, when the central nervous system of the foetus is fully formed. So central and pervasive is it that everything else—the entire human condition itself—can be seen as its consequence. Emphasizing conditioning and the need to awaken to it, Idries Shah says, "In order to approach the Sufi Way, the Seeker must realize that he is, largely, a bundle of what are nowadays called conditionings—fixed ideas and prejudices, automatic responses....Man is not as free as he thinks he is" (3: 134).

First, according to experiential religion, whatever is conditioned, limited, finite, constructed, and separated from Reality as Such is bound. So conditioning is bondage. It sets us on a determined track of responses to stimuli and makes us ignore the rest. Repeated responses form patterns of brain waves, which bind us as they determine our thoughts, feelings, and behavior. And we become further bound as we respond to the world and others as these patterns dictate. As character is a sedimentation of these patterns, character formation is bondage. Since no one is without set patterns or character, no one is free from bondage. To be conditioned is then to be trapped and imprisoned in a world of our own making.

Both positive and negative programming determines and fixates us in grooves of responses, which we reinforce every time we exercise them. And the more it is reinforced, the stronger the fixation becomes. Thus, positive programming of such qualities as love, trust, and compassion bind us to set responses to people and situations just as much as do negative programmings. However, it is fear, anger, stress, depression, anxiety, and other negative internal forces that cause the greatest harmful mental and emotional fixation and suffering in our life. We become unaware, not only of things outside these fixed patterns, but also of the programmed reactions themselves and their objects. Thus, both states limit, fixate and bind us as we stay within their parameters, seeing the world through them, and reacting accordingly. Recognizing this, the Sufis hold that most people are enslaved by their desires, drives, greed, hypocrisy, isolation, illusion, and delusion (Shah 3: 309-310).

Second, as programming forms habits, to be habituated is to be bound. Habit is an insidious and crippling form of bondage. It is arthritis of the mind. It responds to mulishness in us — our tendency to tread the familiar path, to stay within the safe and secure fold until awareness, freshness, sensitivity, and openness are pressed out of our lives. It regulates our lives, thoughts, feelings, actions, and consciousness, and makes us repeatedly elicit the same responses. The more we respond out of habit, the more tightly we become bound and the more fixed, determined, and predictable our lives become. As time goes by we take the path of least effort or resistance and are simply dragged along by the tide of habit and inertia, which are expressions of the death wish, carrying us into oblivion. Occasionally we may feel the urge to break free of the shackles of habit and become free and spontaneous, like children. Occasionally we feel like beginning all over again. But as the years go by, the weight of accumulated conditioning and habits appears massive, our mind wavers, and we are unable to muster the desire and strength to throw them off. Our forlorn longing for freedom gradually grows evermore faint in our hearts as we slink back to our habitual ways and eventually go to seed.

Third, our awareness is constantly being trapped and lost in our thoughts, fantasies, internal dialogue, and stream of consciousness. In short, all programmings and contents of our mind trap and imprison us. That is the reason we are unaware. Our mind takes a dive amid its objects and swims along its programmed channels without seeing what it is doing. To become aware, we have to raise our head above the waters of both conscious and unconscious spheres and free awareness from the structures and forces of our programmed mind, reality and self. To be unaware, then, is to be bound by both conscious and unconscious forces.

The source and locus of this bondage is the entire programmed mind, both conscious and unconscious. This is repeatedly stated by Hinduism and Buddhism. Thus, *Maitri Upanishad* says, "Mind is indeed the source of bondage" (Mascaro 104); and *Srimad Bhagavatam*, "the mind causes physical bondage" (Prabhavananda 103). Buddhism not only teaches that the programmed mind is bound but also emphasizes the mental factors that give rise to conditioned existence and bind human beings to it (Conze et al. 66-67). Thus the entire network of programming that encompasses the human condition keeps us bound to mental contents or objects and repeatedly impels us to experience various states as we go through life.

Fourth, we are bound by outer forces: our world, culture, society, way of life, associations, relationships, duties, responsibilities, institutions, rules and norms, the whole of reality, which are the objects of the inner forces. The *Maitri Upanishad* expresses it well when it says, "To be bound to things of this world: this is bondage" (Mascaro 104). Expressing a similar view from the Christian perspective, Linda Sabbath says, "the source of slavery is our dependence on the external world for our happiness" (41). However, both these and other sources emphasize that this bondage is internal. It is not the world or matter as such that causes bondage but the world that is constructed by and forms the content of the mind. There is not the slightest trace of bondage or problem anywhere except in the human mind—in the way it is constructed and programmed. Human beings get caught in everything they spin within and around themselves.

Fifth, this mental bondage consists in identification with its contents or objects. This is clearly stated by various sources of experiential religion. Thus the *Srimad Bhagavatam* declares, "Man, by identifying himself with the mind and its modifications, attempts to satisfy his desires, and straightway he becomes bound" (Prabhavananda 292). Underscoring that the mind binds itself to the object world through identification, the Buddha says that as long as there is an object in consciousness, it identifies with it and remains bound (Conze et al. 71). Similarly, Wei Wu Wei observes, "As long as subject is centered in a phenomenal object, and thinks and speaks therefrom, subject is identified with that object and is bound" (2: vii). Thus, as long as there is a single programming or object with which the mind identifies and to which it becomes attached, we will remain trapped and bound. Since ordinary consciousness is nothing but a network of such programming and contents, to be conscious is to be bound.

The all-encompassing sense of bondage is clear from the Kabbalah which holds that bondage, symbolized by the Israelite condition of slavery in Egypt, covers the three states that make up our normal life — vegetable, animal, and the separate self. As Halevi states, "Most of mankind is in bondage and lives in the vegetable state of eating, sleeping and propagating" (117). The animal man is subject to drives, desires, attraction and repulsion, and the need to dominate (118). Incorporating these states, the natural self is ruled by the desires of ego, animal drives, and vegetable, mechanical rhythms of life, and suffers their effects in a fragmented world: in exile, conflict and isolation (Halevi 64).

Sixth, attachment is bondage. To be attached is to be fixated on some object; and this fixation, which is usually both mental and emotional, is bondage. On the mental level, attachment fixates and binds us to self-images, judgments, ideas, values, viewpoints, constructs, and the like. As we view reality through these we become separate from it. On the emotional level, fixation to programs, especially to negative programs, produces, in the words of Ken Keyes, "addiction," which is "emotion-backed demand or desire for something you tell yourself you must have to be happy" (2: 4). Such addictions produce fixations and separating emotions that prevent our growth, blocking our ability to think, feel, see, act, experience, or be in any way other than the way they dictate. And the stronger the addiction, the greater the entrapment. Moreover, when the individual fixates on an object, attachment tears reality into opposite camps, detaching us from one half, and locking us in the other, and causing split mind, conflict, and unawareness.

Seventh, desire is bondage. According to Hinduism, desire both arises from and creates further bondage. Thus the *Ashtavakra Gita* states, "It is bondage when the mind desires or grieves at anything" (Johnson 125). And earlier we saw the *Srimad Bhagavatam* stating that any attempt to satisfy desire causes bondage. For Hinduism and other sources of experiential religion, any movement of the mind motivated by desire and any attempt to satisfy it are signs of and lead to further bondage. This topic will be discussed in Part II.

Eighth, the separate self is both made up of and lead to bondage. As the *Ashtavakra Gita* puts it: "Where there is 'I', there is bondage" (Johnson 125). This entrapment encompasses not only the realm of the ego but also of the super-ego, id, and even the higher, archetypal self. We are bound not only by the things with which we identify and to which we are attached, but also by the things we repress. Ordinarily, therefore, as growth comes to a halt at the stage of the separate self, our normal state is seen by the sources of experiential religion as a state of arrested development. This idea will be discussed in Part II.

Ninth, bondage of will. In the New Testament, the Gospels disclose the bondage of the will, especially through the "miracle stories." These stories depict our enslavement by the inner forces, which produce split and conflict, leading to a paralysis of will and an inability to change. This bondage is clear from the story of the Gadarene demoniac in whom multiple conflicting selves or identities brought about complete internal chaos and self-destructive behavior. When Jesus asked him, "What is your name?" "My name is legion," he replied, "there are so many of us."

Many modern writers have also keenly discerned how we become bound and ravaged by inhuman, irrational, demonic, or destructive forces, when they emerge to the conscious level and take control of our life or personality (May 123). In his Doctor Faustus, for instance, Thomas Mann portrays how the demonic element enslaves us and brings about our destruction.

St. Paul especially emphasizes the bondage and paralysis of the will. According to him, as we attempt to live within the world we create, we become prisoners of various internal and external forces which come to rule our life. Signifying that the bondage is internal, Paul says, "Scripture has declared the world to be a prisoner in subjection to sin" (Gal. 3: 24). Thus our sins or negative programmings trap us. As we become fixated on them, they become the law that rules our emotions by triggering negative responses: "While we live on the level of our lower nature, the sinful passions evoked by the law worked in our bodies" (Rom. 7: 5). And as we become attached to our desires, they come to rule our life (Rom. 6: 12). The result is a split mind and a life full of strife and craving; a life ruled by passions, desires, confusion, and delusion (Gal. 5:19-21; 1:21-26); and above all, by bondage, impotence and paralysis of the will, where the bondage comes to be centered (Rom. 7: 14-23). Other internal bars further extend the outer walls of our prison, which is the entire fabric of society, with its programming, values, and beliefs (Gal. 3: 23; 4: 8).

Many modern commentators on the human scene have also noted the same phenomenon. Quoting Leslie Farber, Rollo May says that this is the age of "disordered will." The problem modern humans face is no longer deciding what to do, but deciding to decide. A feeling of omnipotence on the one hand and impotence on the other has created an inner feeling of emptiness which has thrown into question the very basis of the will itself and the ability to decide. The very things that give us the feeling of omnipotence — our scientific and technological achievements, cultural creations and constructs — imprison the will and make us feel powerless. And the more powerful or monstrous the creations, the stronger the bondage and the consequent feeling of omnipotence and impotence (15, 184-189). The will oscillates between omnipotence and impotence and becomes paralyzed, inducing "a state of feelinglessness, the despairing possibility that nothing matters, a condition very close to apathy" (27). This produces a cleavage or "schizoid condition." As a result, we are rendered unable even to decide to bring about a fundamental change in our condition (27).

Not only does Paul agree with this analysis, he goes further and points out that this problem is endemic to the human condition. It rules all human life and holds sway over the entire species "from Adam to Moses" to now. All are powerless and suffer from bondage (Gal. 3: 24).

Tenth, bondage of action. In the conditioned state, every action arises from and causes further bondage. This is especially true of every action resulting from habituation. As the *Gita* declares, "Man is a prisoner, enslaved by action, dragged on by desire" (Prabhavananda & Isherwood 1: 58). For, at the core of all such action is the law that rules it: the Law of *Karma* or causality which explains the basic mechanism of action-reaction or programming that causes bondage. As the *Brihadaranyaka Upanishad* declares, "According as a man acts, so does he become. A man of good deeds becomes good, a man of evil deeds becomes evil" (Prabhavananda & Manchester 109). Similarly the Buddha states, "All that we are is the result of what we have thought: it is founded on our thoughts, it is made up of our thoughts. If a man speaks or acts with an evil thought, pain follows him...If a man speaks or acts with a pure thought, happiness follows him" (Burtt 52). By "thought" the Buddha means a programmed reaction of the mind, triggered by internal or external stimuli. Thus all that we are is a result of programming; everything we do arises from, confirms and reinforces our programming. It forms a chain of bondage or a cycle of repetition in which we live like wound up, mechanical dolls. Our mental reactions program us and in turn we react accordingly. These reactions are ruled by *karma*.

As the word *karma* itself means "action" or "behavior," the law of *karma* is what governs human behavior. In essence, it says that every action, mental as well as physical, has a reaction or determining effect on our consciousness. Our present behavior is a result of programming from past experiences. Ordinary activity consists in replaying or repeating of past responses, activated by a present stimulus. What we call action is, therefore, a reaction. And we always react from out of the past in a chain of responses that may go back, especially in cases of our ingrained or deep-seated habitual patterns, not only to our childhood events, of which we have no memory, but also to the evolutionary past and to the formation of the reservoir of what is presently known as the universal collective unconscious. Or, as the Buddha stated, our present condition is a result of conditioning in previous lives, that is, in youth, adolescence, infancy, the chain link of programming reaching all the way back to the depository of racial memory, the universal collective unconscious, and the origin of the species. Once the programming is set, what we do ordinarily, automatically, habitually, or repeatedly is strictly governed by this law of programming. And this latter is bolstered by the law of conservation: whatever is programmed is programmed to maintain itself unless deliberate, conscious effort is made to change it. (This is a cognate, on the psychological level, of Newton's First Law of motion.) Since our present programming will prompt future behavior, given similar circumstances and stimuli, we can predict what we will do in the future. We will lead determined, predictable lives unless we make an effort to stop and get off the track.

It is clear that this law of *karma* is in agreement with such psychological views as behaviorism in stating that all our actions are a result of past programming; that so long as we respond according to it, none of our actions is free; and that to talk of freedom as long as we discharge programmed responses is indeed illusory. Where it does differ from behaviorism is in the proviso that we can be free if we make an effort to break the chain and arrive at the Unconditioned State. In the present, conditioned state, however, our actions are normally triggered by programming and are not and cannot be free. As our present response reinforces and strengthens the programming, our bondage grows stronger. Our future responses will be even more automatic, determined, and predictable than they are at present, and, for that very reason, will appear more natural to us. We will behave even more like a well-oiled machine, more bound by our past than we are now. Thus, as conditioning creates bondage, unless we make an effort to break the cycle now, we will continue to do the same things, think the same thoughts, and repeat the same emotional responses over and over again until we die. Such repetition of conditioned-reaction is called "rebirth."

There is a tendency among Western writers, and many in the East as well, to assume a necessary connection between *karma* and rebirth and to take the latter in a literal sense to mean, exclusively, birth in the next life, popularly known as reincarnation. Such an interpretation is mistaken on several grounds. First, initially these two ideas were separate, and the latter may have been older than the former (Embree 62). Second, although they fit together, rebirth is a consequence of *karma* or causality, which is of vaster scope and generality. It is concerned with all human actions and their formative effect on human consciousness. Third, in the context of *karma* as the law of conditioning, rebirth essentially refers not to physical, but to psychological, rebirth. It refers to the repetition of conditioned reaction as a consequence of programming and habituation. Since whatever is programmed is programmed to maintain itself, rebirth is our invariant tendency to trigger reactions automatically according to the way we have been programmed.

Thus our experiences sow seeds or program consciousness with tendencies, dispositions, and habits which give birth to mental, emotional, and behavioral fixations. And we go round and round triggering programmed responses over longer and shorter cycles that resemble a wheel—the wheel of samsara or conditioned existence. Once trapped in it through identification, strapped through attachment, propelled by desires and impelled by drives, we cyclically repeat the same reactions and come to believe them to be part of our nature (and thus create *maya*). Rebirth or repetition of programmed reactions is, therefore, a sure sign of bondage.

Although you come to see this imprisonment when you directly experience your actual condition, the vast majority of people do not, precisely because their awareness is trapped. Unawareness and the automatic operation of ordinary consciousness prevent them from directly experiencing their programming or bondage. In addition, because in later years they have no memory of the actual process by which they come to be programmed and bound, when it becomes automatic, they come to assume that they live in a free and natural state. Such beliefs, which are themselves products of programming, prevent them from seeing their actual condition. Unaware of their actual condition and unable to see their lives exactly as they are, they continue to live in bondage, mechanically responding to people and situations out of habit, believing that they are free. The awakening shows how illusory, indeed harmful, is this belief, for it only serves to reinforce their bondage by making them accept their condition willingly, preventing them from seeing their bondage and doing something about it.

Others are conscious of this bondage—some, especially many modern writers and artists, very keenly—but are unaware of its source. So they, too, do little more than witness the fact and protest against it. In fact, the entire tragic vision of life arises from a consciousness of human bondage. However, this tragic sense derives almost invariably from the fact that deprived of a direct experience of its formation and maintenance, they come to believe that its sources are outside: in material things, technology, relationships, circumstances, socio-economic-political forces, irrational or demonic spheres, nature, cosmic forces, or fate. As a result, it appears gigantic. In this belief people are aided by the mechanism of projection and the external orientation of consciousness. So they are unaware of how they spin a web of conditioning and habits around themselves and then forget the fact and come to live under the control of something they themselves create. Thus they get caught in the meshes of their own net. They lock themselves in a self-created prison, throw away the key, and live in bondage. Consequently, they see that joined to the battle, human beings prove unequal; their struggle appears tragic and futile—"foul, futile, and a barren boon," says Sartre in his play *The Flies*. Or it may appear, as it did to Camus, like the situation of Sisyphus—condemned to push the boulder, bondage, or burden of life to the top only to have it roll down so that they have to start all over again. Although other writers see the human bondage differently, the final result is the same: unable to free ourselves from it, we are consigned, like Sisyphus, to repeat the cycle of responses in thought, feeling, and behavior. We get up in the morning and go to work, where we do the same thing day in and day out or over longer periods; return home, have dinner, watch television, go to sleep; and get up to start the process all over again.

The sources of experiential religion emphasize, however, that although in the conditioned state bondage is as real as programming, in a deeper sense it is an illusion and not anything real in itself. It becomes real when we identify with our reality-construct and bestow on it the characteristics of Reality as Such and act from that belief. Our belief makes our world the way it is and binds us to it.

These sources also emphasize that you need to awaken and recognize these states in yourself, if you want to begin the journey of experiential religion. Unless you directly experience your conditioning and bondage, you will not take other steps on your long march toward freedom.

Chapter 5
The Wheel of Life

When you awaken to your condition and find that you are trapped in a world of your own making, running on programmed tracks and repeatedly making the same responses to set conditions, your life appears very much like a wheel in which you are caught. As it turns over and over again, you experience various stages and states that encompass your life.

Unaware of how life got to be the way it is, you may start out feeling that your condition is normal, natural, and necessary. As you sink into the flow and are dragged along by the current of conditioning, habit, and inertia or compulsion, your behavior becomes very predictable and mechanical; your thoughts, feelings, and responses to people and situations become automatic and repetitive. Day in and day out you do the same things that make up the regular span of your life and that appear little different from, to use B.F. Skinner's phrase, that of "a radish or a rat."

Occasionally you may feel trapped or claustrophobic; you may feel the walls of your cage lined with identification and attachment, fear and anxiety, desire and delusion. You are afraid of the dark forces within, the social forces without, the unknown beyond, of breaking out and experiencing the chaos, nothingness, loneliness, isolation, despair that you believe such a break would bring in its wake. So you resort to delusion. You hope things will get better; you believe that you are not in a cage, that you are progressing and going somewhere; or you blame others for your condition. However, these responses are never satisfying. You may then project your anger and dissatisfaction outside, and, propelled by the desire to overcome your difficulties, you go to the next stage.

Feeling restless, you want to break out of the cage. Although you have accepted its limits by becoming a full-fledged member of society, you find that the walls are elastic. Endless variety and expansion are possible. So you put in a great deal of energy and expand the walls. However, since you are driven by anger for being put in the cage, blaming anonymous, outside forces for your condition, you project the anger against them. Setting yourself at odds with everyone and everything, you express it in aggressive, competitive behavior. But it does not bring an end to your condition. The walls still remain, and so do separation and bondage.

Desire and dissatisfaction may then drive you to the next state. You may try religion. But being good or holy does not work either. A role or mask cannot overcome bondage; it is good only for hiding things. As did the Puritans, you may turn salvation into success, achievements, work, aesthetic pursuits, fine taste, cultural refinements. As this effort does not bring a fundamental change, a creeping feeling of inner vacuity throws you into the vortex of the next state.

Now, as the full force of your bondage dawns, a feeling of futility and meaninglessness descends over you. You feel completely boxed in, separated from everyone and everything significant. Isolated and lonely, you find yourself unable to generate any fundamental change or movement in your life. However, such feelings do not last long. Desire sets you to do something about your condition.

Next, you may resort to cultivating virtues, asceticism, a moral character, a good image. You may become an upright and solid citizen, do good, become a self-sacrificing person. These substitute gratifications do not work either. As Chuang Tzu has said, neither these nor duty nor manipulation can save you from unhappiness. A feeling of dissatisfaction and a gnawing feeling of having failed in life and the futility of trying to change may make you resigned to your condition. You may sink back into the flow again — back to where you started.

Although you experience such states through various stages of your life, you develop a style of your own. One of these states becomes your home base of operation, your launching pad, so to speak. You may start at the first one I described, the animal-like state in which, according to the Kabbalah, most of us live. From there you go through the others and return to it, only to start the process all over again. The same would be true if you started out from a different base.

Cut off from Reality and trapped in our own constructs, then, we go round and round in our cage, looking like gerbils, although in our case the cage has many layers, stages, endless variety, and is very elastic. Nevertheless, it remains a cage. As it rolls, the cage resembles a wheel, whose cyclic or repetitive motion comes from programming. Once the wheel is set in motion, we react primarily to those stimuli that activate the programmed contents as we go from one state to the next. Others simply pass by unnoticed, without registering anything. We become blind to anything except what the cyclic patterns of our conditioning allow. When they press the programmed keys — of love, hate, fear, anger, anxiety, likes and dislikes, wants and needs, desires and attachments — we react predictably. As we get stuck in the grooves of programming and repeat the same responses over and over again, our lives become closed, narrow, and unsatisfactory. We become computer-like, mechanically playing the programmed tapes when stimuli hit the keys. When external stimuli do not, internal ones — memory, fantasy, regret, argument, inner dialogue — keep triggering the cycle, fearful that without it, we will cease to exist. So the stream of consciousness goes round and round in vortices. Because our responses do not bring about the desired state, we continue to elicit them or their variations over and over again, like scratching a wound to make the itch stop.

The cyclic patterns are repeated during the course of a day, over longer periods, over a lifetime. If you observe yourself carefully, you will notice that, starting from the particular state that is your characteristic style, you go through thoughts and feelings peculiar to the others and then return to your original state. Over a longer period, for instance, your cycle may be some action, plan or project you have in mind, or your relationships, job, environment. Not only do your responses to them exhibit a cyclic pattern as you go through the states, but right in the midst of one state, your mind will go through responses characteristic of the others.

Although the patterns in the cage are cyclic, the cage itself may not be stationary. It moves, as you look to the future or make plans, giving you the impression of linearity, time, and forward motion or progress. This is particularly true if you take a longer span of a lifetime or the history of a nation, society, culture, or civilization.

The wheel or cyclic view is not opposed to the linear view. For, as you go through life or observe the history of a nation or civilization, you do not notice the wheel or its internal motion, since your consciousness is rivetted to the external, object world. Rather, as you notice only the external, forward or meandering motion, you see the course a nation takes over a period of time, which gives you the forward notions of time, history, and progress. If a culture, such as the West, is primarily oriented toward the outside environment, it will develop a future-oriented outlook, will be given to planning, and will notice the linearity of time, causality, and history. The wheel will be seen to move forward, thus creating the wheel of progress. In such a case, the wheel may resemble a steamroller. On the other hand, if a culture is mainly inner-directed, as is the East, it will notice the cyclic motion inside. The wheel of culture will barely move, creaking along in its meandering course like an oxcart, from which the Hindus probably got the symbol of the wheel representing human life trapped in programmings and constructs that make up its world.

So Hinduism and Buddhism have sought to portray this state by using the wheel as its symbol, calling it *"samsara,"* or closed circle, where conditioning feeds conditioning in an endless succession. Other religions have also observed this cyclic character of the human condition. Chuang Tzu, for instance, conveys a vivid feeling of it through so many of his stories, showing how people get trapped in the very thing they devise to get out of their situation. In the Bible, Qoheleth points out how human life goes "round and round and returns full circle," and how humans go "chasing the wind," running after illusory fulfillment or substitutes which do not bring an end to their plight. He speaks of how loneliness can drive a man to seek possessions in order to end his loneliness and dissatisfaction, only to reap a harvest of greater isolation, loneliness and dissatisfaction. Thus he is kept strapped to the wheel, going full circle. And according to the Kabbalah, the life-cycle of "the natural man" is called "Gilgul or the Wheel of Transmigration," which makes the individual repeat the cyclic pattern not only over many lifetimes but also in shorter spans of time within the same lifetime (Halevi 48). However, since it is Buddhism which has developed this perspective most fully, in what follows I shall present its viewpoint as representing experiential religion in general.

Chogyam Trungpa (2: 131-133; 4: 23-40), Lama Govinda (1: 234-241), John Blofeld (2: 119-122), and others depict the Wheel of Life, *samsara,* or conditioned existence formed by the "twelve chains" of programming that drive the habit-patterns and keep us going in circles, in six compartments, representing six states which we experience as we go through life. These states are those of the gods, the titans or giants that the Kabbalah calls "the animal state," the hungry ghosts, the hell, the animal ("the vegetable state" according to the Kabbalah), and the human (what the Kabbalah calls the "natural self"). At the center of the Wheel are a cock, a snake, and a pig symbolizing, respectively, craving and greed, aggression and aversion, and unawareness and delusion. These core negative traits trap us in the Wheel and provide the driving energy to keep it, and thus ourselves, going. In the outer rim of the Wheel, beyond the six states, are the twelve chains of "dependent coarising" that cause the programming. We reinforce and maintain these chains as we go through the six states that make up our conscious life.

As Trungpa explains, these states represent different styles of preoccupation, thought and internal dialogue, emotional attitudes, and behavior which you develop toward yourself, others, and the environment. Although you may go through all of them during the course of a day, your personal standpoint is rooted in one state, which provides "a style of confusion, a way of entertaining and occupying yourself so as not to have to face your fundamental uncertainty, your ultimate fear that you may not exist" (4: 24).

The inner working of these repetitive, cyclic patterns show that when you are in one state, you have an incipient, unconscious fear of the opposite, imbedded in the very fabric of your outlook, consciousness, and behavior. Thus, when you are in the god realm, you feel an unconscious threat of impotence, emptiness, isolation, loneliness, and despair characteristic of its opposite – the hell state. In the human state you have an unconscious fear of the opposite, the state of the hungry ghost. If the animal state is your style, the opposite state haunts you.

Furthermore, these states, and indeed the entire Wheel, work through projection and introjection. What you fear you project outside, and it becomes part of your reality. As you internalize it, it becomes the substance of your experience of the next state. So through the entire cycle of "birth and death" or the rising and passing of these states, the programming gets complicated and you fail to notice the cycles of repetition that make up the tangled skein of your life.

Let us now see how these states work. Suppose you are in the god state. Your consciousness is dominated by the feeling of power and omnipotence – the feeling that you can do anything. According to Trungpa, you are absorbed in yourself and hung up on various goals not only in the material but also in the aesthetic and the spiritual realms. In the first, you are absorbed in being wealthy, powerful, successful, a high achiever, influential, important, and famous. The second is signified by preoccupation with art, music, various social and cultural refinements. In spirituality, you may aim at happiness, fulfillment, or seek spiritual highs, being holy or fanatically religious, seeking paranormal powers or collecting the latest spiritual teachings. You run from one thing to the next, gilding your cage, creating more chains with which to bind yourself. Unaware that you are creating more bondage, you lose track of where you are going. Even though you attain your goals, they do not end your separation and bondage. The feeling of insufficiency *(dukkha)* arises even before you attain your goals. Upon attaining them, as you get bored, desire, dissatisfaction, and restlessness drive you to the next state. Thus in the midst of your preoccupation with the god state, the threat from the hell state surfaces in the form of disillusionment, disappointment, or despair. So the Wheel turns. As it does, you may be thrown into the hell state.

You may, however, switch to another state, if you feel anger rather than despair or impotence for not getting what you wanted out of life. It all depends on how you react to your situation. Let us say that you get angry and switch to the giant *(asura)* state – the state of those with a gigantic ego. You are then preoccupied with elemental drives, ambition, achievement, power and aggression. As a war rages within and without, you become restless and constantly at odds with yourself, others, and your situation. To be rid of this feeling, you may project it outside and be driven by the desire to succeed, to dominate and control others – acquiring and controlling an ever vaster empire with a ruthlessness that may appall many and engender fear in others; dealing your opponents out or destroying them; or transforming the environment into a veritable imprint of your enormous ego. Such are the people at the top of their professions, be they the titans or tycoons of business and industry, or the leaders in the arts, sciences, and government (Halevi 47). Or internalizing and repressing the aggression, you may become very defensive and be on guard. Everyone and everything seem to threaten your position, possession, or attainment. You become absorbed in struggling to maintain and improve yourself. A fear of the animal state lurking in the back of your mind drives you to be better than everyone else, to avoid the state of the herd. Insecure and anxious, hounded by the fear of failure, you are driven to further achievement. Further anxiety and fear of failure ensues.

In this predicament, you may succumb to fear and give in to the animal state or switch to the dominant feeling of the human state. If the latter is triggered, you will be dominated by the desire to grasp at anything you think will bring you happiness. Above all, you will be driven by higher ideals — intellectual, ethical, and religious — that you believe will make life meaningful. The belief that multiplying desires and pursuing their satisfaction will bring fulfillment and make life exciting, interesting, and significant, will impel you to search for such experiences, situations, or relationships as you expect will bring this about. But you discover that instead of giving you what you wanted, they increase your dissatisfaction. Desire and fear of the opposite — the hungry ghost — begin to gnaw at your heels.

To mute the pain and frustration of not finding what you wanted, you may sink into the animal state — into unawareness, delusion, inertia, and stupor. As you sink into the flow and are carried along by the tide of habits and automatic responses, you become oblivious to what is around you. Fearful of exploring new ways, you plod along without veering away from your programmed path, mechanically reacting to people and situations. Fear of disapproval, rejection or threat of punishment keeps you within the limits defined by society. Afraid of being out of step, you become reserved, preoccupied with keeping everything under control. You fear that repressed feelings — anger, irritation; the demonic, dark, irrational forces of the unconscious; and uncontrollable drives and tendencies — will erupt and throw you into chaos, will overwhelm or destroy you, or bring displeasure, rejection, or ridicule. Meanwhile a gnawing feeling of wanting to live, a hunger to possess everything, stemming from a feeling of not being alive, of living only a phantom life, begins to germinate and grow.

If you are in the grip of such a feeling, you will find yourself in the state of the hungry ghost or the consumer society. In a sense, this is part of the ego state — the state of acute self-consciousness. Pervaded by the triple terror — of existing, not existing, and not being alive while existing — you become filled with an insatiable hunger to live, a desire born of the illusion of ego. You are driven to consume everything: material, sensual, aesthetic, spiritual. But consumption only fuels the fire of hunger, desire, and longing. The more you want and strive for satisfaction through production and consumption, the more unfulfilled your desire remains. And the more your dissatisfaction, frustration and restlessness grow, the more you are driven to satisfy them.

In such a predicament, you may be thrown into a feeling of the impossibility of satisfying your desires. Their contradictory nature may make you persistently feel powerless to do anything about your situation and may lead you to feel that life is futile and hopeless. Filled with despair and seeing no way out, you may feel an urge to withdraw into yourself. This will make you suffer from greater separation, isolation, loneliness, and emptiness. These are, of course, the dominant features of the hell state.

In this state you experience your separation and bondage very keenly. For the essence of hell is separation from any living contact with reality, entrapment in a world or situation void of meaning, and an inability to do anything to overcome the dissatisfaction and bondage. The result is a sense of separation and exile that never ends, as Camus pointed out. Judging from the witness of modern writers and artists, hell may seem the predominant state of modern humans. So conscious of themselves and their individuality, they live in a world devoid of meaning, direction, or purpose, save what they can create from their uncertain resources. But seeing that it is wiped out by death, in the silence of God and indifference of the universe, they suffer from a keen sense of exile and isolation. So, feeling powerless to do anything significant about your condition, you may give up the struggle and become depressed, despondent, or indifferent. Unwilling and unable to feel or to commit yourself to anything, you numb yourself against openness, vulnerability, self- surrender, and healing contact with others. A paralysis of will develops as you experience a schizoid condition of omnipotence and impotence—the condition of modern *homo sapiens* (Trungpa 2: 121-148; 4: 19-40; May 24).

These, then, are the six states we experience as we go through life. One reason that we remain trapped in the Wheel is that it does move and we do not stay in one state forever. Then there is what Joseph Chilton Pearce calls "the ace up the sleeve"—the hope that things will get better (1; 114). For, if you really go to the bottom of the hell realm and directly experience it to the very end, if you see the futility of trying to overcome the separation and bondage, all the while keeping yourself trapped in the Wheel, you can take steps to unstrap yourself and become free. But instead of doing that, you keep creating more things which trap and bind you further, increasing your separation and keeping the Wheel turning even more, while creating the illusion of freedom and control.

As it turns, so does your life, from one state to the next, going full circle and returning again to your home base of *dukkha*. Then you are impelled to lurch forward in your tied-up condition, as did the cock in D.H. Lawrence's story, *The Man Who Died,* to set the Wheel moving again.

Chapter 6
The Oblivion of Time

It hit me like a thunderbolt. I had just passed the bend around the High Court in Dhaka, Bangladesh, on my bicycle one balmy afternoon, when suddenly a vast tapestry opened up before me. In it I saw hundreds and thousands of people rushing in different directions going to their work — the scene resembling, I was to learn years later, Grand Central Station in New York City during the rush hour. As the scene further opened up and its details came into clear focus, I saw people pursuing various professions, getting married, building homes, raising families, growing old and dying, and passing into the oblivion of time, with nothing left of them except the debris of their striving. From this portrait of ordinary human life there came a flash of realization like a thunderbolt that left me dumbfounded: Were my life to become no more than what I saw, I might as well end it right there. As if bleached in excessive sunlight, as the scene went colorless, the ordinary human life I saw became devoid of meaning. Bewildered and frightened by such a realization — for I was only eighteen years old, a whole life lay ahead of me, and the thought of suicide was too violent, and personally and religiously too repugnant — I became confused, disoriented and close to despair.

The vision I saw that day revealed ordinary life to be small, vacuous, insignificant. The life of an individual appeared no more substantial than the gasp of a dying moment. And every moment, every hour, every year, millions of such individuals were being born, dying, and passing into oblivion. It occurred to me that so long as life is centered on and lived for the self, time invariably wipes it out as though it never existed, like waves erasing footprints on the seashore. Each moment appeared as a dying of the self without a trace; each moment cancelled it before it could come into existence or become real. It was as though each moment shouted at this phantom trying to materialize itself, "You are nothing. You can never be. Look! I vanish before you can lay hold of me and be born. You are a contradiction that can never cross the threshold of nothingness!"

Seeing conditioned existence passing in this way into the oblivion of time, I was in a quandary. On the one hand, ordinary life was utterly void of meaning and there was no sense of continuing it; and on the other, I did not want to give it up. I saw life as an impasse, with no way out, and did not know what to do. When I came to the United States, the vision followed me here, as if to remind me from time to time of life's passing and its impasse, my predicament and that of every human being caught in the grip of time, trapped in a world of his/her own making and suffering from the ravages of separation from Ultimate Reality.

Conditioned existence is inherently time-oriented. Space and time frame human life; they also form the context of its being and the content of its becoming. Time forms an integral part of normal life and a necessary dimension of ordinary consciousness, as it consists of programming and contents that are formed and exist only in it. Yet the space-time continuum is constructed out of the filtered contents of consciousness. Thus on the one hand time forms both the context and fabric of ordinary consciousness, reality and self, and makes all conditioned existence time-bound and subject to its oblivion; and on the other hand, being itself a construct of consciousness, time ceases as consciousness is destructured or transcended (Ornstein 1:98-106).

The sources of experiential religion are witnesses to this oblivion of time to which all conditioned existence is subject. For Hinduism and Buddhism, anything that is born or comes into being is under its sway, since anything that has a beginning must have an end. Everything that is subject to time is subject to its double oblivion: Time itself is in constant process of oblivion, and everything that arises in time meets the same fate. Nothing in the phenomenal world is exempt from it. This is true as much of the ego as of the universe as a whole.

According to Hinduism, since creation is only a movement in the mind of Shiva or the true Self, as movements arise and cease, so all creation, manifestation, becoming, or relative states come into being and pass away. As Nisargadatta Maharaj states, the entire universe exists only in consciousness; and whatever is an appearance in consciousness must end (Balsekar 10). Dependent on space-time modalities, all manifestations are subject to their oblivion, for in their absence no manifestation can arise in consciousness (Balsekar 16). As no manifested or relative order has absolute existence, whatever comes into being, is subject to time. It is part of non-Being, and hence *maya*, and creates suffering. Eliade is therefore correct when he states that there is a direct line between maya, temporality, and human suffering, and that suffering is a result of humans striving to create themselves and find the meaning of existence within a world conditioned by time (xviii-xix). For nothing that comes into being, that is temporal and historical, is free of the dissolution, illusion, or unreality, and fundamental anxiety and despair that arise in a consciousness confronted by this fact.

It is Buddhism, however, that made the impermanence of all conditioned existence one of its central teachings. What the Buddha meant by *anicca,* usually translated as "impermanence," is that change constitutes the very fabric of the phenomenal world. Conditioned existence is an ever-changing process in which one thing arises and passes, and another follows. In this constant process all things are interlinked and interconnected, making the universe an interpenetrating whole in which each thing exists in relationship to all, and all with each thing. In this undivided wholeness things and events constantly, simultaneously arise, pass, and transform themselves. There is nothing permanent, no substantial entity that exists by itself, behind or separate from this ever-changing process. As all conditioned things or events are in a state of constant becoming and passing away, there is nothing to which you can attach. The only constancy is change. The Buddha saw in this impermanence the key not only to understanding conditioned existence and how we cause ourselves to suffer by grasping at fleeting moments of experience, but also to freeing ourselves from its grip. He saw how in this state, seeking permanence so as to stave off the oblivion of time, every human being grasps for and attaches to the contents of consciousness and reaps for him/herself nothing but *dukkha,* thus ensuring oblivion.

Chuang Tzu likewise saw constant change as the universal process of nature. He observes that the conditioned world is the world of relativity, punctuated by alternate rhythms, in which opposites produce and contain one another. Thus he says:

> There is nothing that is not the "that" and there is nothing that is not the "this"... Therefore I say that the "that" is produced by the "this" and the "this" is also caused by the "that." This is the theory of mutual production. Nevertheless, when there is life there is death, and when there is death there is life. When there is possibility, there is impossibility, and when there is impossibility, there is possibility. (Chan 182-183)

For Chuang Tzu, these opposites are not only interlinked and inseparable, they also produce each other (Chan 183). Out of life comes death; out of death comes life. Everything that is born is not only going to die; but the moment of birth is the moment of death. The moment that is born dies and passes into oblivion. Nothing of it remains. Birth and death are inextricably linked as two movements of the same dance. There can be no dance if one step is not followed by another. There could be no dance of life if it did not come to be and pass away. Thus birth and death are two moments of the dance of the manifest, conditioned world.

Perhaps because of its emphases on individuality and temporal and this-worldly orientation, the Western world is, on the one hand, more acutely conscious of the oblivion of time, from which arises its anxiety, restlessness, and relentless drive to transcend time and attain immortality through a transformation of nature and lasting cultural accomplishments. On the other hand, sensing a failure of this project, it becomes further riddled with anxiety, dissatisfaction, and restlessness that propels it to greater achievements that will endure the test of time. This apprehension is true not only of the early formative period of the West but also its later, twentieth-century manifestation. As a Greek myth tells us, Gaia (earth) arose from chaos and then gave birth to Uranus (sky). These two produced the Titans, among whom was Kronos, who castrated his father Uranus and became king. Kronos proceeded to devour his offspring, but Zeus escaped this fate, overthrew Kronos and the Titans, and himself became king of the gods. Clearly, this story tells us how human, this-worldly concerns are framed and formed by time (Kronos), which became the dominant force in the created order. But time devours its own children. Not only time itself, but everything that is produced in or subject to time, every human accomplishment, is subject to this fate. It is only by passing beyond the oblivion of time that Zeus attains the divine status or immortality and becomes the father or source of the gods. Thus, only by transcending time can you hope to attain immortality or the divine realm. Unable to sense this dimension of immortality, in the twentieth century, the West has become even more acutely riddled with anxiety and desperation, restlessness and the drive to extricate itself from this condition, as twentieth-century art, literature, and philosophy clearly attest.

As heir to both the biblical and Greek perspectives, Western religions exhibit this two-fold concern — a consciousness of time and a need to transcend it. On the one hand, their temporal orientation has given them a future orientation and optimistic outlook (omnipotence) and, on the other, has given rise to a sense of oblivion that has generated a sense of futility (impotence). We get the latter perspective in the Old Testament from Qoheleth, who is keenly aware that in the face of oblivion, man's attempt to seek permanence is futile. In the New Testament, St. Paul attests to both concerns when he says that everything in this world and subject to time passes away, while Spirit abides forever.

So we see that, being the matrix of conditioned existence, time defines the basic character of the human condition. And everything within its parameter passes into oblivion. In its grip the entire human condition becomes unsatisfactory, insufficient, and a problem unto itself, which nothing within its domain can ever resolve.

The above characteristics circumscribe the main features of the human condition. The first step of experiential religion consists in awakening to it and seeing life exactly as it is. When you do so, you discover the basic characteristics herein discussed. Unless you directly experience the entire human condition in all its depth and breadth in your own life, so that it becomes a living reality encompassing all spheres of your consciousness, you will not touch the first base in reality or the first step of experiential religion; and the other steps will remain closed to you.

This first step is the first act of transcendence or freedom. In itself, of course, it is not sufficient to free awareness from entrapment or to overcome your separation from Reality and free you from bondage to your constructs, but it is the beginning without which the others cannot follow. Once you make a thorough exploration of the first, you will be ready for the second step, to a discussion of which I now turn.

Part II

Mind-Frames

The moon was asked:
"What is your strongest desire?"
It answered: "That the sun should vanish,
and should remain veiled forever
in the clouds."

- Attar in *The Way of the Sufi*

Chapter 7
Basic Assumptions

The second step of awakening with which experiential religion is concerned, as stated in Part I, consists of directly experiencing what has made you the way you actually are and how and why you continue to be in your present state. In other words, the central task of the second step is to discover the causes of the human condition—to discover how they have shaped and continue to shape and maintain the very fabric of human existence in general and your condition in particular.

The reason for this step is clear. Since at each moment you create and maintain your condition, each moment offers you an opportunity, in Yokio Mishima's apt phrase, "to recreate existence instant by instant" (44), *if* you have a direct experience of the process. Unless you see the causes in actual operation and see that, as Ken Keyes puts it, it is you, and not anyone or anything else, who causes your condition (2: 70), you will not do anything to bring about a fundamental change in your life.

As long as you think that the world or outside factors are responsible for your condition, you will remain bound by that belief and will continue to give the world and others the power to control your life. But when you directly experience that it is you who make your self, consciousness and world the way they are and thus cause your condition, and that you make yourself powerless by projecting the cause outside, you come in touch with and regain the source of the real power for change within. As you see that since it is you who are doing it to yourself, you realize that you have the power to undo it, to free yourself and recreate existence in the here-now. Awareness is that power. It is the key that opens the door of your prison, the door to transcendence. It is the lever which, when turned, can bring a complete revolution in your life and end your exile from what is.

This step is both theoretical and practical. Although theoretical knowledge is necessary, by itself it is not sufficient to move you to take the steps necessary to bring about an end to all your problems. Hence, although this discussion will take a theoretical turn, its aim is entirely practical: to provide you with the knowledge of how you cause and maintain your condition so that recognizing it, you will proceed to a direct experience of how it actually occurs and take steps to disentangle yourself and become free.

Without this theoretical understanding it will be very difficult for you to identify in your experience the causes and the process whereby you create and maintain your condition, and what you need to free yourself. Thus, without it you fail to grasp the relevance of the second step and will run after patchwork solutions or quick fixes.

Such solutions are available in abundance. We are constantly applying them. They do not and cannot work because they treat only the symptoms but fail to remove the causes. Consequently, as Camus noted, they will appear elsewhere in new guises and often, as Jesus observed, in worse forms than the first; or they will become multifarious, like Hydra's head. It is essential then that these causes be rightly understood and directly experienced in your life. Otherwise you may run after "easier" solutions or packaged deals that keep you hanging on forever for solutions that never come. Meanwhile, the impact of the first step of awakening dissipates; and you become disillusioned and discouraged from seeking real solutions that bring about a total change. Such a negative reaction may make you succumb to cynicism, pessimism, resignation, despair, or make you sink into various diversions and escapes. Or, still left hungry and thirsty for answers, you may be kept tethered to the consciousness circuit. Blessed are those who hunger and thirst! But it is no good running around in circles, driven by desire and thwarted by delusion and unawareness.

The answers that can finally resolve human problems rest on some fundamental assumptions about reality, consciousness, and self that form the foundation of experiential religion. These premises are verifiable not only in your and others' experience, they are also indirectly confirmed by sources outside experiential religion. Although not explicitly stated by any of the sources, they form its working bases and are essential to the validity of its claims. If these assumptions are unfounded, so is experiential religion. It is therefore necessary to state them explicitly and present their confirmation. Accordingly, in this Part, I shall first state some of the major premises, then describe what the sources say about how we cause and maintain our condition, and finally present their confirmation from nonreligious sources.

The following are among the salient assumptions that govern experiential religion:

(i) Our reality, consciousness, and self are constructs, not Reality as it is.
    (ia) Since our consciousness is a construct, it cannot perceive Reality as Such.

Basic Assumptions

- (ib) Since ordinary reality is a construct, and all constructs are objects of consciousness, so is ordinary reality.
- (ic) Since the self is an object among other objects and exists only in consciousness, it has no reality except as a mental construct.
- (ii) The whole of our constructed reality is severed from Reality as Such. This severance is primary duality. Within it there is a further duality between consciousness or the subject-pole and the world or the object-pole; and our perception of the world as consisting of separate, individual objects forms a third level of duality. Duality is then a construct, having no direct connection with Reality as Such.
  - (iia) Whatever is constructed, conditioned, or programmed cannot be the full, unrestricted, natural state. What we experience and believe to be the natural state has been constructed from some of the possibilities inherent in the lower states of nature.
  - (iib) Reality as Such is the unrestricted, unconditioned, undifferentiated, natural state. Our belief that our present condition is natural, necessary, or final is a fundamental mistake.
- (iii) We are not ordinarily aware of the constructive nature or the process by which our consciousness, reality, and self are constructed and maintained.
- (iv) We construct our reality by imposing our category system or conceptual framework on the datum of experience, interpreting it according to what the category system tells us it is, and then identifying and assuming it to be reality as it is.
- (v) Once constructed, we build up our world through identifications, solidify it through attachment, and maintain and extend it through desire.
- (vi) Since all constructs are in and of the mind itself, the source of all our problems and suffering is the programmed mind; they exist nowhere except in it.
- (vii) Duality is the core problem of the human condition. Being constructed or conditioned is the fundamental problem. What is constructed is severed from, and becomes a barrier to, Reality.
- (viii) All human problems originate from this severance from Reality and identification with dualistic constructs.
- (ix) As long as the triple constructs remain the foundation, and identification, attachment and desire the framework and operating principles of the human condition, no final resolution of any of the fundamental human problems is possible.
- (x) Such a resolution requires a transcendence of all conditioned states and constructs, and a realization of the state in which they can never arise or exist.

(xi) Such a state must necessarily be unconditioned. No conditioning or construct can ever enable anyone to reach it.
(xii) This state must necessarily exist; and its existence is presupposed by dualism and the constructs themselves.
(xiii) We can experience this state only directly or not at all. This direct experience is neither ordinary knowledge nor intuition but is something "ontological," that is, it is none other than the Unconditioned State itself, so that there necessarily is an identity between the experiencing mind, the experience, and the reality experienced.
(xiv) It is possible to go beyond all conditionings and constructs and experience this Reality directly.
(xv) To do so we must transcend our programmed mind.
(xvi) We can free ourselves, and only we can do so, since it is we who form the triple constructs and maintain our separation and bondage.
(xvii) Many claim to have freed themselves; the experience has brought about a resolution of the fundamental human problems in their lives; and these claims appear genuine.
(xviii) This realization is not anything unnatural but the realization of our true identity, the ultimate unfoldment of what we truly are.
(xix) This realization is the ultimate purpose of human existence.

Although not all the sources of experiential religion will agree with all the premises or the way I have stated them, nevertheless they share a broad unity of perspectives which can serve as the basis for my subsequent exposition. The main differences concern dualist and nondualist traditions in the way they view reality, in their approaches and levels of realization, conceptualization of experience, and framework of exposition. As a result, what dualists call "nature" nondualists regard as "conditioned state" or "construct"; and what the former believe to be "supernatural," the latter regard as "true nature," "the Unconditioned State," "Reality as Such," or "Reality just as it is beyond any conditioning or construct." Consequently, while the former view God as supernatural, the latter view "him" as the Unconditioned State of Reality as Such. The former state further that since the Supernatural is beyond nature, humans can in no way realize it by their own effort. Viewing the same state as the true nature beyond all constructs, the latter assert that Unconditioned Reality can in no way be realized within or by any construct or conditioned state. In their own way, therefore, both are saying the same thing.

There are, however, profound differences of attitudes, approaches, and consequences. Thus, viewing the ultimate state of realization to be a permanent relationship with God, dualists misunderstand the nondualists' assertion that the ultimate realization is an identity with God. For this equation appears to them as blasphemous. In fact, nondualists neither equate the creature with the Creator nor say that the creature becomes the Creator, since no creature or conditioned existence can become the Unconditioned. Rather, what they assert is that the realization consists of a revelation of the Unconditioned in conditioned existence as the true identity of each individual—as the only identity other than which nothing exists.

Another difference is that seeing the Unconditioned as the true nature of each, beyond any conditioning and construct, nondualists find nothing inconsistent in actively aiming to realize it. On the other hand, regarding it as completely separate from nature, dualists take a passive attitude toward this realization.

This same contrast is carried over to the question of self-transformation in the two traditions. For if the ordinary world, consciousness, and self are our constructs, we can deconstruct or transform them or form alternate constructions. But if they represent nature as it is, it does not appear that we can change them; or any fundamental change appears as tampering with and doing violence to nature. Since the dualist traditions take the latter attitude, they are opposed to active self-transformation. On the other hand, since nondualists take the former stand, they advocate an active approach toward self-transformation in order to bring themselves into harmony with the true nature. However, the situation is reversed when it pertains to change in the external world or the rest of nature, including the physical (or biological) and psychological dimensions of humankind. Thus, believing that the phenomenal world or conditioned existence is natural and possesses finality, dualists take it seriously and adopt an active approach toward its transformation. On the other hand, viewing the Unconditioned State as the true nature, nondualists do not invest the external, phenomenal world with the same seriousness; rather, they set their face toward internal, self-transformation.

Along the same line, viewing the Unconditioned as the true nature, nondualists do not see its realization as a denial of or alienation from the world. But believing this goal to be beyond nature, dualists regard its pursuit as an attempt to deny our nature, escape our task on earth, and alienate ourselves from our times.

There are, of course, many other differences, some of which I shall discuss later. In the chapters that follow, I shall present, from religious and nonreligious sources, a confirmation of those premises that deal with the constructive nature of ordinary consciousness, reality, and self; and show how we create and maintain our condition and its attendant problems. A confirmation of the rest of the premises will occupy the subsequent parts of this work.

Chapter 8
Experiential Religion on the Causes of the Human Condition

As we now turn to the sources of experiential religion for an explanation of the causes of the human condition, we find that they confirm many of the premises. While it is nearly axiomatic for many of the sources to hold that our consciousness, reality, and self are constructs, they do not give a systematic account of how we construct them. However, they are clear on one thing: duality in its various forms, starting with separation from God or Reality as Such, is the primary cause of the human condition.

The Construction of Reality, Consciousness, and Self

In the Hindu tradition, the *Chandogya Upanishad* explains that out of its seamless, undifferentiated garment, *Brahman* or pure, All-embracing Awareness constructed primary duality as it projected the universe out in order to mirror or look at itself (Prabhavananda & Manchester 68-69). And the *Srimad Bhagavatam* declares, "This objective world, which is recognized by the mind and perceived by the senses, is only a projection of consciousness" (Prabhavananda 40). Such statements can be understood in two ways: The first refers to the creation of the manifest order out of the Unmanifest. In this sense all forms are manifestations or finite dimensions in and of the infinite, unmanifest Consciousness — movement, change, or manifestation in the mind of *Shiva* or in *Brahman*. Everything is frame upon frame of God. In the second sense, it refers to how we construct our reality. Once the primary duality is created, ordinary consciousness imposes its conceptual framework or category system on the data of experience, interprets it, and then judges what it has thus perceived to be the real world (Prabhavananda 156). What we perceive as the world is a construct expressed, as we saw in Part I, in terms of maya. Ramana Maharshi calls it thought (Bercholz 13), while to Nisargadatta Maharaj it is a manifestation in consciousness (Balsekar 10). Confirming the sixth premise, the *Maitri Upanishad* says further that not only is the programmed mind the cause, but the entire human condition and its problems are in and of the mind only (Mascaro 104). As the human mind creates its world, it sets in motion the Wheel of Conditioned Existence — its cyclic or repetitive patterns of reactive thought, feeling, and behavior.

One Buddhist perspective on the creation of duality is seen in the doctrine of *anicca*. According to it, since reality is a dynamic whole, existing in a process of constant transformation in which everything flows into and interpenetrates everything else, there is nothing solid, permanent, separate from, or behind this process. In the drive to organize his/her perception and form a stable or permanent world and self, the child separates him/herself from it and creates a stable, permanent world. Our consciousness therefore creates the dualistic framework and organizes the objective world in separation from the subjective pole. As the Buddha declares, "All that we are arises with our thoughts. With our thoughts we make the world" (Quoted by Walsh & Vaughan 15). Conditioned existence is thus constructed and maintained by thought or the programmed mind.

Similarly, according to the *Tao Te Ching*, in the original state, which is the state in which all things actually are at all times, there is "the Nameless" or formless, unconditioned, and undifferentiated reality of Tao. Out of it primary duality or "heaven and earth" is first created. This primal polarity then becomes the framework and source of the multiplicity of forms. The creation of the primary polarity as well as the phenomenal world is a result of our imposition of "names," categories, or constructs on the data of experience (Chan 139). Elaborating on this view, Chuang Tzu says that we create our condition and reality by separating ourselves from the Tao. We perceive what is real according to the way people describe it to us. And we learn this description as we become conditioned and socialized into the consensus reality of culture. He states, "Things become so-and-so because people call them so-and-so" (Chan 184).

The Old Testament view of duality as the source of the human condition is crystallized in the story of the Fall. According to this story, the state of Adam prior to the Fall or the creation of duality represents the natural state of humankind prior to or beyond duality. If we view this state of innocence as the preconscious state of the infant prior to the rise of self-consciousness, then in essence the story depicts how we create our condition or dualistic world from the actual, undifferentiated state of harmony and unity with all things. With the rise of self-consciousness there occurs a split in this unity, a differentiation of consciousness from the world. This split is the primal experience of the Fall. As self-consciousness develops, we experience a further split: an inner split between the conscious and the unconscious, between good and bad, right and wrong, things permitted and prohibited; and an outer split or separation among human beings, between ourselves and nature. As we react to our world from the split mind, we project it outside to create a correspondingly split world. Thus our world comes to mirror our mental state. As Norman O. Brown has noted, "Here is the fall: the distinction between 'good' and 'bad,' between 'mine' and 'thine,' between 'me' and 'thee' (or 'it'), come all together — boundary between persons; boundaries between properties; and the polarity between love and hate"(2: 143). For boundaries arise, as Ken Wilber observes, with consciousness of oneself as a separate entity, which gives rise to the primary boundary between 'I' and everything that is 'not-I' (2: 75-76). Thus the experience of oneself as an 'I' is the experience of a boundary, separation, or the fall. At its very core 'I' is a dislocation, aloneness, and alienation, which are consequences of the Fall. And every time we use the term 'I' to assert or appropriate anything to ourselves, we declare our actual, fallen condition.

Similarly, according to the Sufis, the most fundamental source of the human condition is our severance from God or Reality as Such. This severance is primary duality. Unaware of this cleavage, we proceed to organize our reality-construct in separation from God, inverting the real order and becoming bound to our construct.

Identification

According to the sources of experiential religion, this entire process is made possible, initiated and carried out through unawareness, which is a fact as well as a cause of the human condition. According to Hinduism, unaware of the projective activity of consciousness and its primary orientation toward what it has projected, we come to believe the world to be "out there" and so perceive it as such, independent of the projection. Thus becoming subject to a dual unawareness — of the nature of Reality and our constructive activity, and unaware of our unawareness — we mistakenly identify our world of experience as reality, become attached to it, and thereby become bound (Prabhavananda 49).

Going beyond Hinduism, Buddhism explains this process in terms of "dependent coarising," or a mutually conditioned chain of twelve causes in which unawareness appears as the root which pervades and influences all others (Conze et al. 66). As stated in Part I, unawareness not only prevents us from seeing the process by which we create and maintain our condition, but also makes it possible. Pervaded by it, the child proceeds to take her first step in constructing a world through mental patterning or "*karma*-formation" (which is the second link). Events and experiences program our mind with rudimentary, unconscious memories, impressions, dispositions, and tendencies, which form patterns. These patterns forge the third link. Consciousness now becomes constructed through the formation of perceptual schemata or models — making consciousness a network of these models linked together by dispositions, tendencies, brain patterns, and other programmed states and objects. Perceiving according to the way it has been programmed, consciousness organizes reality or the object-pole (beginning with the construction of solid objects) in separation from itself, the subject-pole. Thus we construct the fourth link, "body and mind," or the basic, dualistic framework of our world.

The fifth link, perception or sensory awareness, now gets programmed along these dualistic lines, beginning with the sixth link, contact with sensory objects or the primary stimuli. The senses perceive according to object-construction, concepts, and linguistic identification or labels. Upon contact with objects, there arises the seventh link, feeling or sensation of pleasure or unpleasure which now accompanies every experience of an object. This sensation gives rise to the eighth link, "craving," or the tendency to react to the sensation with desire or avoidance: We desire those things that give pleasure and avoid those things that appear unpleasant. Once mental and emotional reactions program our consciousness, they form its superstructure so that we come to perceive the world according to their dictates. As craving splits our world into the dualistic lines of approach and avoidance, it leads to the ninth link, "grasping" or attachment. We tend to hold onto those things that we desire in order to prolong pleasurable momentary states and avoid unpleasant objects and states.

However, since these states do not last, the mental and emotional fixations that grasping causes program the tenth link, "becoming" or creating or filling a world with objects that we believe will give us satisfaction and repeating those states and feelings to which we are driven by our mental and emotional fixations. As we repeatedly go through them, we create *samsara* or the Wheel of Life that circumscribes our life. So "becoming" conditions the eleventh link, "birth" or rise of repetitive thoughts, feelings, and behavior, want, and desire that make up the vortex of *samsara* in which we go round and round. As we thus create and maintain our world or conditioned existence, we cause and maintain the twelfth link — our condition of *dukkha* (Conze et al. 66).

Other Buddhist texts reflect a similar view. Thus, *The Lankavatara Sutra* states that the idea of a world made up of separate, individual objects is formed out of the mind's perception of things in separation from one another (D.T. Suzuki 2: 130). According to *The Awakening of Faith*, with the emergence of the ego in separation from the object-pole and the centering of the subject-pole around it, the entire system of our world becomes fully formed and operative (Hakeda 53, 47). As this happens, says *The Lankavatara Sutra*, consciousness becomes fixated not only on the dualistic framework and the world it constructs, but also on the causes that led to the original construction (Suzuki 2: 131-141). And the entire system is reinforced and maintained, as Zen master Tsung-mi observes, by thought activated by programming and external stimuli (de Bary 193).

According to the Old Testament story of the Fall, having separated from and projected God outside the created realm and closed the gate of our world behind us, we become trapped and bound as we identify with our construct and believe it to be our natural state. As the Kabbalah explains, in childhood and youth we sense the presence of the higher realm. But having identified with the natural world in the process of growing up, as we become adult we forget the upper country from which we came. Its memory is lost as desire, survival, and comfort become paramount. As a result of this separation from and unawareness of the higher reality, and identification with our fallen condition, we become enslaved to cyclic existence and suffer the consequences as we try to find fulfillment in this fallen state (Halevi 59-71).

As discussed in Part I, Sufism explains this process of conditioning and construction through "The Story of a Man with Crutches." The following story, again taken from Idries Shah, amplifies the point. There once lived an ideal group in a far-off land where the lives of the people were rich and full. However, it was discovered that their country was to become uninhabitable for a time. So the leader of the people planned an escape to an island where they had to undergo a transformation and suffer many privations. To reduce the pain resulting from the new condition and the memory of the former state, they were made to forget the past almost entirely. Yet their stay on the island was meant to be temporary, since they were to return to their original home where lay their destiny. Although there were some on the island who possessed the knowledge and skills necessary to make the return, the leaders found that the effort to do so was a heavy and unwelcome burden. So they decided to remove their burden by declaring that there was no burden. But, to make it acceptable to the people, they first proved that there was no homeland, and so no need to build ships for the return, and they ridiculed those who said otherwise. They then proved that the island was the only home they ever had; and, to secure their inverted picture of reality, they began to ascribe to the island all the attributes of their original home (3: 1-11).

This view, similar to that of the Kabbalah, holds that unaware of our "original home" or Reality as Such, we become cut off from it. As we proceed to organize our world in this condition, we forget our original state.

The story also illustrates the third step, according to experiential religion, namely that, once the dualistic structure is erected, becoming the mental framework for perceiving things and organizing our world, we identify as and attribute to it the characteristics of Reality as Such. We then proceed to believe it to be natural, necessary, and final. Thus, in spite of the suffering we endure, through unawareness we come to believe the island or our actual condition to be our natural state and then proceed to ascribe to it all the characteristics of our original home or Reality as Such.

Thus we invert the real order and fall into the primal illusion of believing both to be otherwise than they are. This mistaken identification makes our condition, in the words of Hakim Sanai, "upside down in relation to reality" (Shah 3: xxvii). And our construction becomes what other Sufis call "a closed world," "a prison of deceptions" (Shah 2: 106), as we become bound to our constructs. As Idries Shah puts it, we create our own cage with invisible bars. And because we claim to see things straight and declare that there are no bars and no cage, we become trapped in our condition. As a result, we find that, as Thoreau stated, "for the most part we are not where we are but in a false position. Through an infirmity of our natures, we suppose a case, and put ourselves into it, and hence are in two cases at the same time, and it becomes doubly difficult to get out" (566).

Thus we fall into the fundamental illusion *(maya)* described by Hinduism, creating our entrapment and bondage to our reality-construct through belief and identification (Johnson 121, 35, 84). We then proceed to identify with the entire network of programming and come to believe the programmed states — fear and anger, aggression and aversion, love and hate, anxiety, boredom, frustration, and the rest — to be a necessary part of being human. This identification leads us to believe that if we got rid of them, we would lose part of our nature, or that our condition would be abnormal. The stronger our identification and the more negative our programmings and self-image, the more tenaciously we hold on to them. As identification becomes more fixated and solidified, any action or response based on it only confirms and strengthens it.

Attachment

According to experiential religion, thus fallen and bound, we set out to make our world stable, secure, and permanent by attaching to everything with which we identify. So attachment is born essentially from the drive to consolidate and secure our world. For this reason consciousness lives by attachment. It attaches to all its contents, that is, to everything it perceives to be real, and in relationship to which ego can be assured of its survival, identity or expansion, and permanence. As Ram Dass observes, "Each of us is living in our own universe, erected out of our projected attachment" (1: 79). And *The Lankavatara Sutra* states that the world is such because of attachment to the habitual functioning of the dualistic mind, constructed out of the impressions in the universal collective unconscious (Suzuki 2: 129).

Attachment, however, makes our world impenetrable and ourselves stolid and loaded down, inhibiting flexibility and change. According to Buddhism, on the emotional level attachment causes fixation in repetitive, circular patterns of programmed reactions through projection and introjection. As we keep repeatedly recycling the same responses, we get stuck in the grooves of our programming, becoming disconnected from reality. Like an artist repeatedly trying to produce a perfect picture he thinks will put him in touch with reality, we trigger responses that have no relationship to what is, here and now. Our life takes on an air of emptiness and sterility. To attach, then, is to suffer. What was summoned up for survival now becomes death-dealing. In Freudian terms, starting out as eros or "life instinct," attachment turns into *thanatos* or "death instinct." So, while identification locks us in our present condition, attachment encumbers us with baggage, slowing us down, and eventually stopping our growth. Our thinking turns delusive and action becomes contradictory, as we become trapped and loaded down by attachments. Although there is no way out as long as we hold onto our present state, nevertheless we cling to the hope that our constructs will magically turn into Reality. So the *Srimad Bhagavatam* declares, "As the mind is allowed to cling to the world and the objects of the world, attachment grows, and there comes delusion" (Prabhavananda 53). And Swami Rama and others observe that attachment is the most basic obstacle to growth (*Yoga and Psychotherapy* 175, 182).

Desire

According to experiential religion, having cut ourselves off from Reality, as we become strapped to our condition and settle down, we feel an unreality about it and an emptiness or lack within. Dissatisfied and restless, we feel we need room to breathe, expand, and free ourselves from the deadening effects of identification and attachment. So we project our feelings outside and convert them into the energy which turns the Wheel and creates a world in which, we hope, such feelings will no longer be present. Like Prospero, we summon desire out of separation and lack; we use entrapment and dissatisfaction to fashion a world, to create new objects and forms with which to enhance ourselves and consolidate our gains. Summing up this process, the *Ashtavakra Gita* says, "Desires alone are the world" (Johnson 125). Desire becomes the driving force which keeps the Wheel turning and ourselves going in order to possess more, new, or different things, experiences and relationships. Thus we strive to fill and expand our world in the hope of becoming Real, overcoming separation and bondage and the feelings of unreality and incompleteness.

It is not, therefore, surprising that the Buddha singled out desire as the cause of *dukkha:*

> Now this, monks, is the noble truth of the cause of suffering: the craving, which tends to rebirth, combined with pleasure and lust, finding pleasure here and there, namely, the craving for passion, the craving for existence, the craving for non-existence (Burtt 30).

The Buddha states that the cause of our actual condition is *tanha,* translated as "craving." Elsewhere it is stated simply that desire is the cause (Burtt 148). In what sense is desire or craving the cause of the human condition?

Basic to craving is a constant, gnawing feeling of wanting or desiring something. The focus of this desire is not any particular object you may want today or tomorrow. Rather, it is an inchoate, amorphous general feeling that something is amiss, that there is a lack, and that you must have something or be somewhere other than where you are now. If you observe this feeling carefully, you will notice that it is an insistent, recurring, trapped sensation smoldering in the back of your mind that nothing relieves. This feeling of an essential lack that drives you to want this or that might be called "desiringness" or "wantingness." Chogyam Trungpa calls it a "psychological hunger" (1: 40), and Tarthang Tulku a "hunger at some fundamental level" (2: 287). It is as both a psychological and an ontological hunger that the Buddha saw in craving the cause of the human condition.

On the psychological level, craving or desiringness causes "rebirth" or repetitive triggering of the same thought, feeling, and behavior that lead us to create and maintain our condition. The feeling of a lack and dissatisfaction drives us to change or get rid of our condition by wanting the next moment of experience in the hope that it will have what the present moment lacks. But as each succeeding moment of experience is found insufficient unto itself and fails to relieve our condition, we get caught in the Wheel of wanting and having that spans our entire life. As Levine points out, "At the root of our conditioned mind is a wanting, which consists of the dissatisfaction with what is and the urge for the next moment to contain what this moment does not. When there is wanting in the mind the present moment feels incomplete. Hence the hunger of wanting cannot be satisfied" (13).

Moreover, deep down we are afraid that were we to get what we want life would be over. So used are we to not-having and striving for some goal just out of reach that we become afraid that if we had all we wanted, there would be nothing to live for because there would be nothing to strive for. Life would lose its challenge or interest, and we would lose the will to live. On the other hand, we also suspect that if we got what we wanted, it would not end the craving because it is not what we really want. So we would rather not have it — yet. For, on the deeper level, what we really want is something that will rid us of the discomfort of the dissatisfaction stemming from not-having, and from the ultimate separation. Since nothing that we can have or get can ever do that, every experience is insufficient and unsatisfactory at its core and creates further dissatisfaction.

On the deeper level, the cause of this psychological hunger is the ontological hunger — the hunger to be complete, Real, to BE absolutely and unconditionally. On this level, the cause of our condition is separation in its triple form — from Reality as Such, from others and the world, and from being in a world of separate things — and the sense of unreality or emptiness and incompleteness resulting from it. From this feeling arises the drive (already present in infancy) to reach out, expand, explore, possess the world, and thus become Real.

But having separated ourselves from Reality and thus experienced our reality-construct to be insufficient, we feel that completeness or fulfillment lies neither in what we experience in the present nor in Reality as Such but in our mental model of how things should be. So we attempt to make reality conform to our preconceptions, expectations, desires, wishes, or ideas. As Stephen Levine puts it, *dukkha* is caused by "our inability to accept, and the consequent attempt to avoid, push away or change our actual condition, which is not found quite satisfactory because it does not conform to our mental image or model of how we want things to be" (100-101). As a result of our mental image of things, events, or people, we constantly try to change our situation, either because we do not have what we want or because we have what our mental picture tells us we don't want. So we crave to be elsewhere than where we are, we want reality to be other than what it is; we set out to make reality and ourselves something more than what we experience from moment to moment. But in the attempt to make what is fit our mental model of reality and completeness, we try to add something extra to what is; we change it, render it something other than Real, and thereby ensure the insufficiency of conditioned existence and our inability to overcome the feeling of insufficiency. Thus the ontological hunger, the source of further wanting that gives rise to the cycle of repetition, creates *samsara*, the human condition, and maintains it.

Thus, while the expressions "craving for existence" and "craving for non-existence," in the psychological sense, mean wanting the present to be complete and sufficient unto itself, and avoiding, resisting, or not wanting what we experience in the present moment; on the ontological level, they indicate the hunger for complete and unconditioned existence, for Reality as Such. Not only is the source of desire the hunger not to be unreal, incomplete, or dissatisfied; it is also the impetus to be rid of the reality that fails to make us real and complete. At bottom, it is a hunger to be rid of the hunger and find its resolution in final fulfillment. Craving consists of the opposite pulls present in every desire that arise from the split mind trapped in its constructs. In not-wanting what is and wanting what is not (thus wanting to be and not to be at the same time), we avoid the very thing that could make us real, and we do the very thing that ensures the opposite. This contradiction reinforces the dissatisfaction at the core of every desire, and drives us to repeat the process, confirming and maintaining our condition, frustrating our desires, and striving for a reality and completeness which we both want and sabotage at the same time.

Moreover, as Hinduism points out, our attempt to find fulfillment in the world cannot help failing. Desire keeps us frustrated not only because, in the Freudian sense, the social fabric collides with our desires so that we cannot get what we want, but more fundamentally, because dissatisfaction is built into the very nature of desire itself. For it stems from the core unreality and incompleteness which arise from our severance from Reality as Such. Our attempts to free ourselves from this condition by satisfying our desires only reinforce and perpetuate it.

As the *Laws of Manu* and the *Mahabharata* point out, attainment of its object not only increases desire so that its fire cannot be quenched by any object, it also increases our identification and attachment as we extend them to the objects and to desire itself. This situation gives rise to further desire, rather than bringing the hoped-for satisfaction (Johnson 114, 52). As we become dissatisfied or bored with what we have, our incipient sense of unreality and incompleteness impels us to want more or different things, thus turning our desire into desiringness, which causes us to turn the Wheel of our programmed life and repeat the cycle. As it expands our world, makes us fill it with new, different, and an endless variety of things, we get the heady feeling of movement and progress, of gaining ground, going somewhere. As this cycle reinforces, maintains, and enhances our world, we become further bound and are, as the Upanishads say, "whirled along the rushing stream of muddy waters of the three conditions of nature [i.e., unawareness, desire, and delusion] and become unsteady and wavering, filled with confusion and full of desire" (Prabhavananda and Manchester 1: 100).

In such a predicament, filled with the terror of not-existing, we increase our desires in the hope of creating a sense of reality and meaning, of being alive and gaining a permanent foothold in the shifting situation. But this increase only guarantees a perpetuation of the condition and its consequences. As Ram Dass remarks, "Knowing that none of them will last, you figure that enough of them with small enough spaces in between will keep the rush going. Rush after rush after rush. But it's like building a house on sand—you can't stop because it gets a little frightening if you stop. If those spaces in between get too big, there is depression, confusion, disorientation, anger, loneliness, self-pity, unworthiness" (2: 23). So the conquest of illusion by pursuing the objects of desire remains illusory *(maya)*.

Taoism, too, has noted the same insatiability at the heart of our desires. Although nowhere explicitly stated, the *Tao Te Ching* fairly brims over with the realization that because of primary duality and our unawareness of that original act of severance, we move down the path of grasping, desire, striving, and self-assertion. With these we fashion a world contrary to Tao, although it is Tao wherein lies our fulfillment. Grasping makes us miss Tao by separating us from it and fixating us on objects. And by leading us away from it, desire always leaves us unsatisfied and frustrated. So the *Tao Te Ching* states: "Doing spoils it, grabbing misses it." So "when we try and try, the world is beyond the winning" (Blakney 2: 117). All our striving is, therefore, useless, since it cannot bridge the chasm we ourselves create by our belief that there is a chasm. Thus striving both assumes and maintains our separation from Tao.

More explicitly than Lao-tzu, Chuang Tzu teaches that since whatever we construct causes a separation from Tao, nothing we do can put us in touch with it. Unawareness obscures both the reality we construct and Tao in our minds. As a result, our attempts to reach it within the limits of our constructs, through desire and striving, only generate problems "like malignant tumors."

Moreover, desire makes us obsessed with what we are not, blind to our condition and fixated in doing the very things that will set us apart from what we are, ensure our being what we are not and confirming our condition (Merton 2:154). Or, unable to find satisfaction in the world we create, we may become attached to our desires and their objects. Instead of our controlling the objects, they now control us. So we become bound by a world we seek to master (Merton 2: 134).

The Old Testament intimates that our desires become insatiable because they arise from duality, split mind, and the consequent setting up of our world in separation from God. As we experience the consequences of this dislocation in terms of inner and outer conflict, alienation and isolation, we project them outside; and they become the embodiment of culture, society, institutions, and the driving forces of history. However, all our striving to overcome the separation through or within history is a tale of failure; and our efforts yield a harvest of further dissatisfaction, restlessness, conflict and division. To get rid of this harvest, we attempt to create further history. Our failure shows that history is an illusory project, for we do not know that the goal of our striving—the end of separation—means the end of history as we know it. We, the historical animal, thereby become dissatisfied animal, perpetuating dissatisfaction as we strive, leaving history behind us as the debris of our striving, marching through time into oblivion.

The Sufis express a similar view by showing how pursuit of the object of desire causes frustration and dissatisfaction. Unaware of the source of our feeling, we become restless and employ further desire to overcome our restlessness. With the original aim of desire forgotten, we now become enmeshed in the problems created by desire. The effort to solve the new problems generates further problems, like Hydra's heads. Thus, our efforts to overcome our entrapment set the Wheel turning, which traps us even further. So the harnessing of desire to free ourselves from the effects of attachment and identification only exacerbates our condition. This predicament is conveyed in the following story: There was a king who was thirsty but did not know the nature of his condition or its cause. When he expressed his thirst, his servants forthwith produced lubricating oil. While the oil relieved the king of thirst, it produced extreme discomfort. Then his doctor prescribed pickles and vinegar, which only added stomachache and watering eyes to his condition. When he finally reasoned that he must be thirsty, his attendants gave him rose-water and syrupy wine. As he drank it, he did not feel better—only added indigestion to his condition (Ornstein in Tart 2: 387).

The reason for our inability to solve our problems or find fulfillment through pursuit of the objects of desire, according to the Sufis, is that by its very nature desire is insatiable. Thus attainment only fuels the fire of the next round of desire and sets in motion the Wheel of Life (Shah 2: 66).

Furthermore, according to experiential religion, conflict and contradiction are at the very heart of desire and craving. This is clear from Hinduism, which points out that the world we create is a projection of our desires. But desires arise from the sense of lack and the resulting dissatisfaction. The existence of the world, then, requires the sense of lack and dissatisfaction. But in striving to find fulfillment in this world through satisfying our desires we fall into the contradiction of trying to be rid of something which presupposes, depends on, and maintains the very sources and conditions it is supposed to remove. In effect, our striving amounts to holding onto our condition while at the same time trying to overcome it; it is like holding onto a can you are trying to throw away. Moreover, according to "the Structural Law," (which says that any problem that encompasses an entire structure and lies at its core cannot be resolved by or within it but only by something greater than or outside it), this contradiction at the heart of desire cannot be overcome by desire itself but only by something greater than or outside it.

Buddhism sees this contradiction in our constant striving for permanence within conditioned existence. In so doing we want to turn impermanence into permanence while holding onto its impermanence. In effect, we want to assure ourselves that separation and entrapment do not exist, while everything we do serves to perpetuate them. We are caught in a vicious circle as we seek to overcome the feeling of a lack through the very things which arise from or are created in response to (and whose existence depends on) that lack. So our striving becomes a self-annihilative, illusory project. Thus desire or craving is unsatisfactory in essence; and it creates a human condition that is experienced as insufficient, not-enough, or *dukkha*.

For its part, the Old Testament focuses on the schizoid condition and conflict in human desire, which arise from our drive to make ourselves the center of our world. Having separated ourselves and become lords of our own realms, we feel omnipotent on the one hand and impotent on the other. As creators of our separate reality, we feel omnipotent, seen in our drive to transform our environment into images of ourselves, imbuing it with our own designs and purposes (Gen 1: 28). But as this project fails to overcome our separation, we feel impotent to initiate any deep change in our personal and social life. When we redouble our efforts in the temporal and historical dimension, we become involved in a never-ending quest that encompasses our entire life.

In the New Testament this conflict is seen most acutely by St. Paul. We saw in Part I how, according to him, as the desires of ego, in conflict with one another and with those of the Spirit, repress and deny the latter desires, a conflict ensues on all levels of the split mind. Wanting to be free but afraid of freedom of the Spirit, we become unwilling to let go of our present fixations and cross the boundary staked out by the desires of ego. In the grip of these desires, as we strive to overcome the bondage and conflict, we become further split, trapped in conflicting desires. We are then driven to do the very opposite of what we really want, thus experiencing paralysis of our will. Feeling impotent, we seek to resolve the conflict by taking refuge in programmed responses. The result is further bondage and enslavement by both inner and outer worlds, conflict, and loss of will (Gal. 5: 16). Speaking of this situation in the first person, Paul says:

> I am unspiritual, the purchased slave of sin. I do not even acknowledge my own actions as mine, for what I do is not what I want to do, but what I detest. But if what I do is against my will, it means that I agree with the law and hold it to be admirable. But as things are, it is no longer I who perform the action, but sin that lodges in me...The good which I want to do, I fail to do; but what I do is the wrong which is against my will; and if what I do is against my will, clearly it is no longer I who am the agent, but sin that has the lodging in me. (Rom. 7: 14-20)

Of this conflict between the desires of the Spirit and the "law of sin" dominating "the body," or life situation, Paul says further:

> I discover this principle, then: when I want to do the right, only the wrong is within my reach. In my inmost self I delight in the law of God, but I perceive that there is in my bodily members a different law, fighting against the law that my reason approves and making me a prisoner under the law that is in my members, the law of sin. (Rom. 7: 21-23)

This "law of sin" is the law of karma as it pertains to negative programming of the emotions, desires, will, and consciousness. The result is that what ego desires is the very opposite of what the Self prompts us to do. Since such programmings rule our life and bind us to the world we create, they make us repress the desires of the Self and do, instead, what they dictate. Thus the nature of negative programming is such that it sets up a self-defeating cycle of reactions and makes us do, even when we want the opposite, precisely the things that will reinforce and maintain itself, ego, and the actual condition of life in response to which it was produced and in perpetuation of which it operates. For instance, if in childhood you developed a sense of inadequacy or a lack of self-worth in response to what others said, felt about or did to you, you formed a negative self-image, expressed in such negative judgments as "I can't do anything right," "I always mess things up for myself," "I don't deserve anything good," or "I'm worthless." Once formed, negative emotions (such as anxiety, fear, depression, and the rest) will be triggered when situations arise similar to the ones that led to their formation. Indeed, your programming will make sure that you set up or seek out occasions that will make you go through the cycle of reinforcing it and consequently your negative self-judgment, self-image, and the view of the world you formed in childhood. Once your life-situation is set up, you will continue to reinforce and perpetuate it, with the result that suffering will be ensured as you proceed on your course, with your programming continuing to spin the Wheel of Life set to recycle itself.

Desire and programming serve our negative and positive self-image and our self-judgment, which operate on a level inaccessible to our conscious experience. Not being real in themselves, they need, and constantly seek, confirmation and reinforcement from everyone and everything in order to ensure you a sense of identity, permanence, and self-worth (or worthlessness). That is the reason you constantly want, need, or seek acceptance or approval, and confirmation. When you receive approval, you feel good about yourself; when you do not, you feel rejected, lonely, abandoned, alienated, depressed, or withdrawn. To offset the negative and assure positive reinforcement, you constantly seek to have your identity or self-worth confirmed by being important, influential, powerful, and successful. So you repeat your programmed reaction in an attempt to bolster a sagging image in danger of disappearing. However, since your negative self-image and self-judgment are not anything real and are, moreover, set up in opposition to and denial of the real Self, in this endeavor you confirm the very things that make you feel empty, unreal, and incomplete; you repress and deny the very thing that could make you Real.

In such a situation, says Paul, the cross-fire of desires and contradiction in the will make you feel powerless to bring about any significant change in your life or to realize what you most deeply desire. This situation makes your claim to being free and in control of your life illusory (Rom. 7:20).

Some of the consequences of this condition are self-hatred and self-destructiveness. Hating what we do because we do not do what the deeper Self desires, we come to hate ourselves, our life, and what got us trapped in this predicament; we project our hatred and resentment outside and create a world full of anger, aggression, resentment, conflict, and destructiveness (Gal. 5:19-21). We may seek various means of escape by turning to sex, pleasure, entertainment, diversion, work, religion, and worship of social values (Rom. 1:24-26). Or, feeling hurt and powerless, we become despondent and indifferent (Eph. 4:19). As a result, life becomes futile and our mind becomes "plunged in darkness" or unawareness (Rom. 1:21). Full of craving, our desires become insatiable (Col. 3:5), and our minds become clouded by illusions and delusions (Eph. 4:19). Thus unawareness comes to prevail over the entire human condition; and we become as lifeless as stones (Eph. 4:20-21). Our bondage thereby becomes complete.

In a view remarkably similar to that of St. Paul, the Sufis also discern a contradiction in human desires born of the same duality in nature. As Farid ud-din Attar states:

The moon was asked:
"What is your strongest desire?"
It answered:
"That the sun should vanish, and should remain veiled forever in clouds." (Shah 2: 65)

The strongest desire of ego, here symbolized by the moon, forming its very core, is contradictory and self-cancelling. Unaware that the only light it can have is a borrowed one and that were the sun to hide behind clouds it would be impossible for it to shine, the moon wants to become the only source of illumination. But this only ensures the impossibility of its ever attaining what it wants. The strongest desire of ego is to be the Self, here symbolized by the sun, while being cut off from and appropriating the attributes and identity of the latter. It wants to shine on its own, to become a separate center of being and consciousness, the foundation of its own existence within the dualistic constructs, that is, in separation from the Self and in opposition to the world. Hence its strongest desire is contradictory, self-cancelling, and impossible to realize, for that would signal its own end.

The Separate Self

While some sources of experiential religion regard the ego as illusory and others as real, all agree that it is a construct, a transitional form of identity. The ego becomes the last cause of the human condition and the final point of our separation from Reality as Such when we identify with it as our true self and believe it to be the final form of identity or the highest point of human development.

According to Hinduism, we construct the self by identifying with the elements (Prabhavananda & Manchester 88), that is, with qualities, characteristics, and states of body and mind, external objects and mental contents. As we do so through unawareness, we come to attribute to ego the characteristics of the true Self and come to believe the latter to be unreal and the former real (Prabhavananda 40). This belief puts us in a worse situation. We attribute to ego contradictory characteristics, believing it to be a permanent entity that exists by itself (it does not), separate from others and the world (it is, but the Self is not). Thus we misperceive the nature of reality *(maya)*, invert its real order, become trapped in a double illusion twice removed from reality, and settle down to being less than what we truly are. Expressing the Buddhist view of this misperception and inversion, Jack Engler says:

We misperceive what is impermanent *(anicca)* as permanent; what is incapable of satisfying *(dukkha)* as satisfactory; and what is without substance or enduring selfhood *(anatta)* as substantial and having selfhood. In other words, owing to faulty reality testing we ordinarily perceive and experience ourselves and objects *just the opposite* of the way they really are. (1: 46; italics his)

As we let this self rule our life, in its drive to be real, it creates all the problems that define the human condition.

It is not surprising that following the thread of causality and going past the middle manager — desire — the Buddha came to see the ego as the root of what causes and maintains the human condition. And this is so because, according to the Buddha, the separate self is not anything real in itself.

It is a central Buddhist teaching that there is no separate, individual entity, existing by itself, corresponding to the terms I, self, ego apart from the *skandhas,* that is, personality traits: form (including bodily characteristics, talents, aptitudes, the name), feeling (including emotions, desires, hopes, dreams), perception, drives, dispositions, latent tendencies or will, and consciousness (including programmed states, habits, memories, experiences, values, beliefs, and thoughts). By identifying with these traits, we form the idea of a separate, individual entity existing by itself and remaining permanent through ever-changing impressions, patterns and reactions (Conze et al. 166). Thus the self remains a mental construct, having no reality other than as a concept or object of consciousness and acting as a reference point for gathering around and maintaining its sense of separation from the world (Burtt 140). Summing up this view, Seung Sahn Roshi says, "Man's discriminating thoughts build up a great thought-mass in his mind, and this is what he mistakenly believes as his real self. In fact, it is a mental construction based on ignorance" (Mitchell 134). Concurring with this view, Stephen Levine says, "The ego is a fiction, the outcome of the thinking mind trying to pull itself into the center as though it had a nucleus that was solid, stable and unchanging" (82).

According to Buddhism, this idea of a separate self arises in the wake of the creation of the dualistic structure, the separation of consciousness from the world, and the need to make one's world stable and permanent. Cut off from Reality and set apart from the world, feeling empty or unreal and incomplete, consciousness becomes imbued with the drive to become Real and to overcome these feelings. It forms the idea and strives to make it real by clustering its contents or objects around it as their focal point. As one text puts it, the self arises from the desire of consciousness to lay a foothold into reality by striving to create, through memory and attachment, with language serving as a key element, a permanent, unchanging standpoint from which to view the ever-changing phenomena of the world (Burtt 140; D.T. Suzuki 2: 60-61).

According to Chogyam Trungpa, the construction takes place when space is actively organized along dualistic lines into "I" and "other." By identifying with the "I," we consolidate our self as the effort to maintain this identity in opposition to the other. As the duality is created and held up by self-consciousness, there arises in us a need to constantly confirm our existence and to prove to ourselves our solidity or realness. Since there can be "I" only in separation from "other," ego requires and constantly searches for acceptance, approval, and assurance that it exists. As duality is not anything in itself real, says Trungpa, without the effort to keep up the separation it feels a constant threat to its flimsy structure. This effort to maintain the separation is the process of ego:

> The source of the effort to confirm our solidity is an uncertainty as to whether or not we exist. Driven by this uncertainty, we seek to prove our own existence by finding a reference point outside ourselves, something with which to have a relationship, something solid to feel separate from. (4: 19)

In the process of maintaining itself, therefore, ego also maintains (and must do so in order to be and remain itself) the dualistic structure, on which perforce it gets fixated. So the dualistic fixation comes from and is maintained by the fear of nothingness, and ultimately of death. In maintaining it, ego maintains the fear as itself and thereby assures its own nothingness.

This situation happens because the fear arises from, depends on, and is maintained by duality. As we become conscious of our separation from reality, with the rise of self-consciousness, and sense at a fundamental level an unreality and incompleteness, we are seized by the fear of not existing. Out of this arises a drive to exist, to be real and complete. To overcome this fear, what we want above all is lasting satisfaction, permanent Reality. Everything we do or strive for is to render the self permanent. But believing Reality to be unreal, we become afraid that identification with it would be the end of ego and so pull ourselves apart from it. And having assumed our reality-construct to be reality as it is and seeing it to be separate, we come to believe that separateness, solidity, and permanence constitute the very nature of reality and proceed to identify with everything we feel will make ego permanent. So all our striving is directed toward overcoming impermanence and death by forming a self that is permanent. We want to stop the universal process of the primary order and create a solid ground on which to stand and thus avoid change, and so death.

As Ernest Becker has observed, we try to be special, unique, immortal, Godlike, or find cosmic significance by summing up in ourselves all life or meaning. But seeing that ego's being what it is depends on its being separate also from the world, we become afraid that identification with it would also render ego unreal. So we strive to make ego the foundation of our existence by organizing the contents of consciousness and objects of our world around it and yet maintaining it as the foundation of our separation from them. But as these are created and maintained in separation from the Real, they are incapable of putting ego in touch with Reality or giving it the permanence we seek; on the contrary, they make it spin further and further away from the Real in the very attempt to reach it. When change presents us with things otherwise than what we believe they should be, we feel angry, defeated, and somehow empty and isolated. Thus we build up a life of frustration (Levine 10-12). As Tarthang Tulku observes, struggle, frustration, and conflict permeate the human condition because of man's inability to face existence as change (1: 1-15). And Suzuki Roshi states simply: "Because we cannot accept the truth of transiency, we suffer" (103).

Moreover, afraid of being rendered unreal by Reality and the world, and seeing that ego can be itself only in separation from both, we become involved, on the one hand, in a constant effort to support and secure the dualistic structure and the object-pole, and on the other, to prop up the entire edifice of consciousness in separation from the world. The effort, which is ego, solidifies and maintains the separateness but makes it feel empty, insufficient unto itself, and incomplete. Thus, in trying to make our self unique and keep it separate, to forge an identity, find meaning and fulfillment in the world we create, we try very hard to make ourselves unhappy. Since the essence of ego is the effort to maintain the separation from what is, which is also the nature and source of *dukkha,* the essence of ego is *dukkha.* You can see why the Buddha eventually found that the reason you experience life or each present moment not to be enough *(dukkha)* is because you experience yourself to be not enough, incomplete, unreal, or empty. To be a separate self is to make yourself unhappy. And in the effort to maintain it, you maintain your condition as *dukkha.* You can see why Buddhism says, "All human defilement, the whole human condition, have the false view of individuality at its root" (Conze et al. 168). Concurring with this, Wei Wu Wei observes, "All the evils in the world, and all the unhappiness, comes from the I-concept" (1: 68). And Lama Govinda concludes: "There is no illusion more dangerous, more inimical to life, than the illusion of ego; no illness deadlier than craving and clinging" (2: 211).

From this situation all our problems follow. Split within and established as the subject-pole, in its struggle to maintain itself and the dualistic structure, ego becomes engulfed in conflict, fragmentation, restlessness, and dissatisfaction; and, by projecting them outside, creates a corresponding world filled with anger, aggression, resentment, frustration, competitiveness, grasping, and greed, as well as fear, anxiety, stress, tension, insecurity, emptiness, and impotency. As the ego identifies with these negative programmings, they become part of its texture, its inner and outer reality. To cope with this predicament, ego employs various defensive strategies and manners of escape: Occupying itself with various diversions, activities, and goals in order to maintain a sense of continuity, permanence, and separateness as a wall against the invasion of the fear of nothingness, unreality and incompleteness, and to keep the dualistic structure from collapsing. Such strategies form the dominant characteristics or styles by which we move through the six states of existence constituting the Wheel of Life. But the failure of the efforts to be rid of dissatisfaction and maintain a real sense of continuity and permanence makes its desires insatiable and drives it to create more. Becoming fixated and bound to its condition, the ego keeps the Wheel turning and marches into the oblivion of time.

According to Taoism, as we set ourselves to create our world through desire and attachment, we make ego the point of origin and the convergence of all our problems by polarizing the world around it. So, for the *Tao Te Ching*, ego's desire is the cause of human suffering:

> I suffer most because
> Of me and selfishness.
> If I were selfless, then
> What suffering would I bear? (Blakney 2:65)

For Chuang Tzu, it is the will or self-assertion that is the source of human problems: "There is no deadlier weapon than the will!" It is not nature that does the damage, "it is man's own will" (Merton 2: 137). By setting out to create or possess the world, we pull ourselves apart from others through will and self-assertion, find a decreasing amount of satisfaction, and become enveloped in increasing isolation. The resulting hostility, conflict, and frustration create a world in which fulfillment becomes impossible (Chan 189-190).

As a result, according to Sufism, in striving to be Real, ego creates frustration, dissatisfaction, and a world of unrealized dreams. Split within and fragmented among many conflicting desires, and trapped and lost among their objects, we lose the direction and purpose of life; we succumb to illusory fulfillment and substitute gratifications; drawn by the currents of unawareness, habit and inertia and aided by loss of will, we move toward oblivion. So the Sufis conclude:

I fear that you will not reach Mecca, O Nomad!
For the road which you are following leads to Turkestan! (Shah 2: 93)

It remains now to present evidence from nonreligious sources, confirming the constructive nature of our consciousness, reality, and self, and showing how they are constructed and maintained.

Chapter 9
The Construction of Consciousness

One of the most momentous developments in Western disciplines is a growing recognition that our reality, consciousness, and self are constructs; that other constructions are possible; and that reality in itself cannot be identical with what we perceive or the way we perceive it. These realizations confirm premises (i), (iv), and (v) of experiential religion. They also indicate how, in the process of fashioning ourselves and our world, we give rise to nearly all the problems discussed above. On this newly emergent plane of reflection, there is a broad agreement between Western disciplines and experiential religion on the nature and causes of the human condition and what human beings do to confirm, reinforce, and maintain it, thus perpetuating their problems. In the next three chapters I shall present this confirmation from such Western disciplines as psychology, sociology, physics, and philosophy.

Four types of frames – physiological, psychological, cultural, and personal – interweave in the construction of consciousness. Each time a frame goes up, our consciousness and reality become narrower, more limited, and processed, creating a distance from Reality as Such. Once these frames are in place, what we perceive and how we perceive are dictated by the frames themselves, so that their limits become the limits of our consciousness and our world. It is not that each frame presents a smaller version of what is, but that it changes the nature of what appears within its limits by filtering things out through the sieve of its constructs. These constructs make consciousness select, limit and organize the incoming stimuli, form a perceptual schema or model in the central nervous system, and then interpret and judge it as real.

The Physiological Frame

As Robert Ornstein explains, by their physiological makeup our senses are designed to select, from the vast multitude of sensory stimuli reaching them, some data and exclude others, rejecting what has been judged as unimportant for the organism. The eye, for instance, is designed to exclude much of the data from the electromagnetic spectrum and to select and respond only to a tiny portion (1: 42-72). Moreover, even the selected datum that appears to us as a solid object, on the atomic level is nothing but a vast space composed of millions of atoms which are themselves nothing but vast spaces in which electrons move around their nuclei, held together by electrical forces (Capra 40-71). Solidity is, therefore, a construct; and so is what we call, on the gross perceptual level, a thing or an object. It is clear that by their physiological makeup our sensory apparatus prevent us from perceiving the world as it is. If we did, we would be overwhelmed and our survival would be at stake. So our physiological frame is designed to perceive selectively only those things as objects that will maximally contribute to our survival.

The Psychological Frame

This frame screens things out even further. According to cognitive psychology, as Charles T. Tart observes, before we become conscious of anything, all incoming stimuli go through various degrees of processing. Thus the programming of consciousness does not consist of merely passing along the incoming material from the senses but involves the constructive activities of comparing incoming data against previously learned material stored in memory.

Second, the programming consists of selecting for further processing only what is judged important by the organism. What is judged as not important does not register in consciousness. The judgment itself depends upon environmental and individual factors, which are themselves determined by our biological survival drive, psychological needs, and cultural programming. The selected data is then transformed, abstracted, and passed along to consciousness (1: 97).

Third, after the incoming material reaches the brain, from a single or repeated experiences it constructs a perceptual schema or model of the event or situation. In later situations, when the incoming stimulus reaches the brain, it activates this model, so that what we experience is this model, from which we interpret and judge what the situation is (Tart 1: 99). The model may modify prior programming or brain wave patterns. Tart calls it a generalization that we learned to form, according to some psychologists, by the time we were eighteen months old (Janis et al. 422). On the physiological level, according to Roger Sperry, Leon Festinger, Jerome Bruner and others, there is clear evidence that our brain forms a model out of the processed material reaching it and that, once formed, according to constructivists, it is what we experience as the objective world (In Ornstein 1: 31-32).

This construction begins in infancy with the organization of perception. At first the infant experiences no boundaries, no inside distinguished from outside, no subject separate from object, no duality between consciousness and world. Because there is no separation from anything, there are no things or solid, individual, permanent, separate objects or a world composed of them. There are only shifting fields of sensations and an undifferentiated unity (Buddha's impermanence) in which everything flows, linked with a succession of impressions, movements, and experiences. As Jean Piaget observes, "At first there is neither external nor internal world but a universe of 'presentations'...there is yet neither substance nor individualized objects nor even displacements...there are only global events connected with movements of the body proper" (240).

The survival drive prompts the infant to organize his/her sensations and form a stable world (permanence). This process begins with the development of preattentive processes, which store experiences in memory, focal attention, and pattern recognition (Neisser 46-93). Through these processes, as the infant begins to differentiate and recognize people and things by directing attention and movement and fixing his/her gaze on them, s/he severs the original unity and constructs duality. As perceptual syntheses and models are constructed, his/her brain waves fall into patterns and frequencies. Correspondingly, s/he begins to construct and recognize solid, separate, individual objects, out of which a stable world is formed.

With the next step, identification, this dualistic structure becomes fairly fixed. The degree of fixation depends on the firmness of identification or belief in its reality. However, insofar as s/he is fixated on it, the child will hardly ever come to question this assumption or be aware of its constructive nature.

Although the structure is fully in place and operative with model and object construction, generalization and identification, the programmings and models themselves are subject to revision and change when they do not match the incoming stimuli, that is, when new experiences require a modification of the earlier picture of the event, person, situation, or world. Fixation, however protean, means entrapment and loss of awareness. It is important, therefore, to note how this situation comes about and why it is inherent in the very structure of consciousness itself.

Once the dualistic structure is fairly complete, the child's response to the world and to duality itself, insofar as s/he is identified with and fixated on it, becomes automatic, that is, made without any awareness. This automatization occurs when an external or internal stimulus agrees with the model in the brain and poses no danger to survival. Thus, after the responses to familiar events become habitual, in any situation in which there is agreement between the model and the stimulus, our response involves no awareness. However, if there is no agreement, we notice the incoming stimulus until the model is revised, agreement is reached, and the new stimulus becomes part of the familiar world. Thereupon the responses again become automatic. For example, entering a smoke-filled room after you have been outdoors in the fresh air, you notice the acrid smell, but you become oblivious to it after getting adjusted to the situation. Explaining the phenomenon, Ornstein says that we tune out the occurrences by constructing a model of the external world and testing input against it. Agreement between the two is the basis of the stability and constancy (Buddha's permanence) that our consciousness seeks between itself and the world. Such an achievement is an important step toward survival, since a stable world no longer appears threatening or overwhelming, and thus needs no attention. Consequently, as the child's responses to his/her familiar world become automatic, they stay out of consciousness (1: 27-31).

Arthur Deikman points out that this habituation is a "magic means" whereby consciousness is able to process an enormous amount of incoming data, save us from being overwhelmed, and perform many tasks that would otherwise be impossible (1: 15-17). Now, while automatization enables us to navigate smoothly around our world, it is also one of the essential ways in which awareness becomes trapped and lost. There is a direct and proportional correlation between the two so that to the degree the responses of consciousness are automatic, to that degree awareness is trapped and lost. As its very nature is to tune things out and respond to familiar things automatically, loss of awareness is the core of automatization. And since it covers much of the process of consciousness, unawareness is inherent in much of the normal functioning of consciousness. This explains why we spend much of the day in a sleep-walking state. And it brings us to the fundamental paradox governing the dualistic programming of consciousness: The very process that was designed to make us conscious, renders us unaware. Moreover, the nature and functioning of consciousness, its object-pole or the world, and the dualistic structure itself—in fact, any construction—make us unaware, for several reasons.

First, as automatization involves self-cancelling of consciousness, were it not for incessant scanning for new stimuli or internal triggering of thoughts, automatization would lead to a complete loss of consciousness. In fact, the process of consciousness consists in constantly dying (automatization) and being reborn (scanning). Now this process, involving programming and reprogramming, is the way consciousness and the dualistic structure are constructed and maintained. So the very structure, operation and maintenance of consciousness make us unaware. So long as consciousness remains programmed — and it does so as long as it remains what it is — it cannot make us aware.

Second, the incessant scanning of the outer world in search of new stimuli, which gives consciousness its essential outward orientation and aliveness, and renews it, not only makes it inherently restless and distractible and so unaware, but also ordinarily prevents it from focusing on and becoming aware of itself.

Third, since the very nature of ordinary consciousness is to be conscious of something such that in the absence of any object consciousness ceases to function, the very nature of our consciousness and world, that is, the dualistic construction, entails entrapment and loss of awareness. Unawareness is, therefore, built into the very nature of dualism, since to maintain itself and the dualistic structure consciousness must fixate on and prop up the object-pole, in the process of which awareness becomes trapped and lost. As we saw earlier, this condition is what the Buddha meant by "ignorance."

Fourth, for the same reason, as long as there are models and programmings through which consciousness responds to stimuli, and thoughts or the stream of consciousness continue to be triggered, awareness will be prevented from rising to the conscious level. So an exercise of either of the activities by which consciousness maintains itself continues to ensure unawareness. In addition to making us unaware, automatization thus becomes an expression of what Freud called "the death instinct." Thus the attempt to ensure survival through automatization has the effect of putting us in a death-like state of unawareness in which we spend most of our life. This predicament explains what the Sufis and others mean when they say that people in the ordinary world are asleep or dead (Shah 2: 251; 3:xxviii).

In addition, with psychological programming, something extra is added, becoming part of our picture of reality and a permanent structure of consciousness. The psychological frame thoroughly transforms and supersedes the physiological one, determining our perceptions and our responses. As consciousness becomes coated with emotional layers and we respond accordingly, the psychological frame further narrows what the physiological frame allows. It makes us select and respond to those stimuli that fit the newly programmed models and repress, ignore, or screen out those that do not. As our present programming depends upon prior programming, which depends upon yet other programming, what we become conscious of depends on layers of programming, in which later ones reprogram the earlier ones along their own circuitry. So long as our consciousness remains a network of programmings that determine our responses, that is, in the normal state of consciousness, we perceive things through this emotional filter. We experience or respond not to what is just as it is, but to the emotional coating, modifying what is. Since past psychological and cultural programming conditions and determines what we experience in the present, this experience is not of the present as such but is a playback of past programming, triggered by present stimulus. This description is fully in accord with experiential religion, confirming the theory of *karma*.

Psychological programming is, then, the more immediate frame that produces positive and negative "fixed disks," models, or patterns of mental and emotional states, motives, and tendencies. We react to events, people, and the world at large according to these models, rather than directly by responding to a stimulus itself on the primary level. Since things in themselves do not have these qualities, it is our programming that makes those qualities part of our picture of reality. Thus we make ourselves happy or unhappy, sad or joyful, in obedience to the dictates of our programming. All our problems, then, are caused by and exist only in our mind.

As the psychological programming becomes part of our consciousness, we become insulated in it and rarely break out of the inner circuitry of stimulus-response, wired up by programming and reprogramming, to come to a direct contact with reality. This circuitry constitutes one of "the casements," of which Thoreau spoke, into which we put ourselves. Like a cocoon or what don Juan called "a bubble of perception," it envelops and forms a self-contained environment within which we live, unaware of reality beyond. Once fully formed and operative, its inner circuitry keeps functioning, confirming, recycling, and maintaining itself according to the Law of Conservation—whatever is programmed is programmed to maintain itself—independent of things in themselves; and we act as an instrument of its perpetuation. Thus trapped and held bound by our programming, we keep the Wheel of Life turning by the constant repetition of our conditioned reactions.

Two additional areas in which psychology confirms the viewpoint of experiential religion on the cause of the human condition are the programming of attachment and desire.

Along with identification, attachment is one of the key factors in the formation of a stable consciousness, world, and self. Central to the very first steps an infant takes to sort out changing, fluid impressions into separate objects in order to form a stable consciousness and world is attachment or fixation to stimulus. It requires learning to focus attention exclusively on individual objects of the immediate environment, particularly the mother's face. As the infant's vision gets focused, s/he is able to fix attention on persons and things, isolate one thing from another, and pursue it to the exclusion of all else. Once s/he learns such strategies, s/he attaches to them, and together with identification, builds up the dualistic structure of consciousness and world. Without this exclusive focus of attention, there would be no learning to isolate things and so no perceiving things in separation from one another and oneself in separation from the world, that is, no dualistic structure. Nor would there be the construction of fixed, solid objects, nor construction of a world composed of them.

Once developed, attachment works to stabilize and expand the infant's world by generalizing the responses from the earlier object to similar ones (Janis et al. 427-429). As the infant increasingly comes in contact with persons and events, not only does s/he extend attachment to them but, far more importantly, also to the models themselves and to his/her mostly emotional responses. As it expands, attachment acts like a thread, tying models together and forming a network of models. Thus attachment holds consciousness together, gives it a sense of stability and continuity, and maintains it in existence.

Consciousness, then, lives by attachment. It spreads its tentacles among objects — even among persons attachment is an object relationship — binding them together with programmings and thoughts and forming a world, and going back and forth, like a spider in its web. In so doing, attachment not only binds us to this construct but also to our programmings and gives rise to new ones, to which we become similarly bound. Thus it becomes a bonding factor, a principle of bondage. To the extent attachment is essential for the normal development of a child, to that extent it forms the chains in which normal life becomes and remains bound. Both attachment and bondage expand as consciousness expands to stabilize, secure, and incorporate more of the world into the child's domain.

While a lack of attachment leads to abnormal development, withdrawal, and lack of interest, active exploration, and social responsiveness; its normal development also produces negative programmings, such as fear, anxiety, insecurity and dependency, clinging and grasping, possessiveness and greed, mental fixations and emotional blockages. Moreover, the undertow of the active, dynamic side of attachment is the manipulative character of consciousness, which constantly strives to impose on things its own ideas of how they should be (Janis et al. 425-434). Attachment makes us cling to everything we believe to be real and important, that will make us grow, confirm and enhance our identity, and bring happiness and fulfillment. Clinging becomes essential both to keeping the world stable and overcoming anxiety or the fear of loss. But it also serves to guarantee their continuation in our life. Fear of the unknown and the unfamiliar drives us to cling to and remain within the fold of the known, familiar world. And the greater the fear, the more our energy and attention are devoted to increasing and multiplying attachments, thereby becoming the more entangled in them. This increases our fear, insecurity, and anxiety (Keyes 2: 5-14).

It is clear, then, that attachment leads to the programming of what Ken Keyes calls, as noted in Part I, "addictions" or fixations, expressed in terms of repetitive thought, feeling, and behavior. Clinging to familiar forms inevitably leads to fixation. As we become stuck in models formed in the past, out of which we perceive and respond to the present, and insist that the present conform to them, our responses always fall short of what is, which is always in the present. So they are incapable of putting us in touch with it. As such responses fail to give us the desired satisfaction, we become fixated on repeating the same past responses, getting trapped in them. Life becomes very routine; and our responses automatic, mechanical, repetitive, and fixed. Detached from the present and frozen in the past, we become unaware, out of touch with the moving river of life, and absent from the world. Consequently, such attachments signal a failure of and are the most basic obstacles to growth, not only within but especially beyond the personal stage. As the authors of *Yoga and Psychotherapy* state, when we cling to a familiar concept of reality and refuse to let go of a narrow and limited way of seeing ourselves, others and the world, we become locked in repetitive patterns that bring our self-growth to a grinding halt (Swami Rama et al. 152-154, 185-187). Psychology and experiential religion are in full agreement here on the effects of attachment.

Allied to attachment is the programming of consciousness with desire. Psychologists see the origin of desire in the reflex reaction of the infant to the sensation of comfort and discomfort, pleasure and pain. This presupposes a dualistic structure and cannot arise in its absence. For desire develops from focal attention, model and object construction, and the ability to fix attention on something and pursue it. But behind the programming of pleasure-unpleasure is a vague sense of a lack, a separation from and absence of what gives pleasure or poses a threat to it. Correspondingly, it implies a sense of an absence in ourselves and wanting to overcome it or wanting to be rid of something we have and wishing for something else. Thus desire gives consciousness its active, outward orientation and becomes the driving force for striving, reaching out and pursuing, and, in general, overcoming an absence or limitation and extending ourselves and expanding our world.

Yet desire also limits our world. As the child's activities become goal-oriented, things become split up into dualities of likes and dislikes, desire and avoidance, interest and disinterest, active and passive programming. Correspondingly, s/he comes to perceive things as divided into desirable or undesirable, satisfying or unsatisfying. As his/her goals become oriented and fixed on one half of this split world, s/he becomes geared toward obtaining rewards, satisfaction, fulfillment, or happiness in terms of those things that are defined as desirable, and avoiding or ignoring those that are not. His/her world becomes further limited as s/he confines him/herself to doing or avoiding things along these lines. Once this happens, s/he will hardly ever get out of this track of desire, pursuit, and avoidance, and experience the world afresh or in its totality, thus expanding his/her horizon.

When the programming of desire is complete and fully operative, consciousness becomes completely modified and ruled by it. Desire becomes the general headquarters issuing commands which the child faithfully obeys. As desire is an active force, the type of consciousness that develops under its domination is called by Arthur Deikman "the action mode." He defines it as "a state organized to manipulate the environment," having such characteristics as focal attention, striving, outward orientation, mastery, control. With the development of focal attention and emergence of the action mode as dominant, and having desire and striving as the motivating force, consciousness comes to perceive the world as desire dictates. To carry out this active stance the child develops "heightened boundary perception, object-based logic, powers of analysis, discrimination, exclusivity, and discursive and linear thinking," which is "for action, for acquisition and control" (In Ornstein 2: 68). Language serves the same function and further programs consciousness in the same grid, since "our words are from the object world, the world we made by separation, in the action mode" (1: 22-24). Along the same lines, consciousness becomes time-oriented, governed by succession, progression, causality and success (In Ornstein 2: 68).

It is desire, therefore, which puts this construction into a high gear, develops its higher functions, and maintains it through striving for goals and satisfaction. However, in giving consciousness this external orientation and channelling the child to find in the world identity, fulfillment and happiness, desire guarantees a failure of his/her efforts, yields dissatisfaction in their wake, and succeeds in perpetuating itself, the entire construction, and his/her condition. This truth is clear from the next frame.

The Cultural Frame

Beginning with socialization, three of the most important ways in which culture's consensus reality gets programmed into consciousness, forming its superstructure, are the child's ability to symbolize, use language, and think conceptually. Although the process of symbolization begins with the formation of perceptual schemata, active cultural programming begins when the child learns symbolic names. As models of these names are formed in his/her brain, the child begins to perceive the world according to their description. Reaction to symbolic names is then the crucial point of transition from object construction to the socio-cultural programming of consciousness. At this stage, as don Juan remarked to Castaneda, "everyone who comes in contact with the child is a teacher who incessantly describes the world to him, until the moment when the child is capable of perceiving the world as it is described" (2: 9).

Cultural constructs further limit and channel consciousness according to their codification of reality. As Tart explains, culture encourages certain possible experiences and suppresses others for the child's construction of a normal state of consciousness which helps to define and reinforce, and is effective in culture's particular consensus reality (1: 33-34). As Jerome Kagan observes, at age two the child learns the words "good" and "bad," which are codifications of the split mind of culture. Learning from parents and significant others through positive and negative reinforcements, identification and imitation, the collection of attributes and actions s/he eventually comes to regard and internalize as good and bad make up the indoctrination into culture's dominant values, beliefs, motives, goals, rules, approved and disapproved behavior, assumptions, deceptions and defenses, self-image and self-judgment (Janis et al. 443-447). Such programming makes consciousness further fragmented, narrowed, conflict-ridden and neurotic. It becomes programmed with anxiety, fear, aggression, frustration, stress, guilt, shame as s/he struggles to stay within the limits of what is culturally approved and to mold him/herself into the cultural model of what is good, to cultivate what is liked or accepted, and to avoid what is labeled bad, disliked or disapproved (Pearce 1: 65-75).

As consciousness becomes coated with these traits, they act as the immediate filter for screening the world, allowing to register in consciousness only what agrees with their models and processing out those that are incompatible. Putting more layers of programming on consciousness, culture transforms and modifies earlier frames; removes the child even more from a direct contact with reality; dictates what and how s/he will perceive; and increases his/her involvement in and bondage to an abstract universe of socio-cultural design. As s/he internalizes it, s/he becomes insulated in its constructs. Driving a wedge between his/her desires and social demands, it causes a greater split in consciousness as s/he represses the former and molds his/her consciousness along its approved dualistic lines. As Joseph Chilton Pearce observes:

The child's initial programming is masked, inhibited, and finally dominated by the process of acculturation so that it comes to be non-existent. In its place culture emerges as the meta-program and he shapes his experiences along its description of reality. Once this meta-program takes over his perceptual apparatus, it becomes his only mode for interacting with reality. (1: 21-22)

It is, however, with the full use of language and abstract, conceptual thinking that the child fully internalizes the cultural construction and makes the transition to what Pearce calls "the word-built world." Thereafter, to paraphrase Ludwig Wittgenstein, the limits of language becomes the limits of his/her world. As language codifies the cultural construction of reality, in being programmed by it, his/her consciousness comes to be limited to the linguistic frame. And the world that language delimits, in cultures that are dualistic and in which the action mode predominates, is also invariably dualistic. This fact is shown by the structure of a language in which the subject is separated from the object and connected by a verb (action). Not only does the subject-object dualism of language further confirm and reinforce the dualistic structure, it also contains the assumption that things exist as separate, individual entities independent of consciousness. Explaining this feature, Lawrence LeShan says:

> Any sentence is a picture of a state of affairs and this state of affairs includes a description of how things basically are. The sentences in our language all include the idea that things are out there, separate from here, and have qualities that go on without any help from us. Every time we use a sentence, we are trained a bit more in believing that this is true and that any other way of describing and understanding reality is an insane one. (2: 39)

Moreover, the logic of this language is linear, successive and discursive, progressing from thought to thought. As the focus of consciousness shifts to this conceptual, discursive world and the child gets perceptual models from it, its category systems and abstract thinking program his/her consciousness and determine what s/he perceives as real. As s/he learns the language and is able to think and operate according to its rules by manipulating its abstract, conceptual networks through which cultural transactions take place, the child becomes domesticated in this, in Pearce's terms, "semantic universe," and perceives and interacts with its elements, systems and pathways (1: 54-74). Because this world-picture forms the immediate world of experience within which the child develops and functions, s/he comes to assume that s/he is dealing with objective reality, existing independently of consciousness, when in fact s/he has become insulated in an abstract world constructed and maintained by his/her own culture and consciousness.

According to sociologists Berger and Luckmann, this internalization of the cultural construct provides the child with a stable, secure, and organized environment. Seeing that survival depends on it, s/he represses his/her own desires and wishes and internalizes those that are held up by society; and seeks to fulfill them according to culturally defined and approved ways. Thus the cultural construct becomes his/her subjective reality and regulates the form and function of his/her consciousness. This programming closes off the possibility of realizing that this reality is a construct and that other constructions are possible (19-20).

Because the social construction presents itself as a coherent and ordered world, the child comes to believe it to be also objective reality, outside of which there is only chaos and nothingness. The fear and anxiety over functioning in any other setting, coupled with the fact that once it is programmed, s/he automatically perceives and responds to things according to the dictates of this construction, and the sheer massiveness, pressure, and pervasiveness with which it imposes itself — all lead him/her to assume it to be normal, natural, necessary for survival, the only reality there is, and therefore final, normative and binding (Berger and Luckman 40-51). As s/he thus becomes enclosed in this construct, all his/her subsequent attempts at transacting with reality by dealing with, in Pearce's phrase, "the word-built world" only recoils on him/herself as s/he remains within the parameters of that construct. By taking this construction for reality, s/he builds up the assumptive world, identifies with and immerses him/herself in it, and in the process hands over the control of his/her thought, feeling, behavior, desire, and life to society.

Once this happens, the individual's desires begin to multiply without finding any real satisfaction, for the survival of society depends not on the satisfaction of desires but in multiplying them and keeping him/her dissatisfied. Otherwise s/he will cease to strive and maintain the social construction. Because these desires arise from and depend upon dissatisfaction, the fact that neither they nor the reality in which s/he tries to find satisfaction represents Reality as Such and because they are largely symbolic, by their very nature they are designed to keep him/her dissatisfied and perpetually hungry and thirsty.

In this sense, then, the entire process of acculturation is largely an internalization of the process of desire and striving held up by society. A society becomes "advanced" or "developed" to the extent to which it is able to induce into its members artificial desires, needs, and wants, and to provide goods and services that will give temporary relief but keep them essentially dissatisfied and hungry for more. It fills them with a sense of incompleteness and inadequacy, and then offers glittering promises and symbols of power, success, and fulfillment, which purport to satisfy the inner hunger without actually doing so. Thus the more developed a society, the more its members are filled with a multiplicity of desires and needs which it cannot satisfy. As Pearce has noted, culture survives by a circular system of feeding and feedback that is a clear instance of the Wheel of Life: It survives by insulating us against fear, anxiety and the terror of death; and yet by inducing desires and keeping us striving to satisfy them without actually doing so and convincing us that the failure is ours and not that of society, it keeps us in the grip of fear and anxiety, tension and stress, guilt and shame, negative self-image and self-judgment, dissatisfaction and striving. It first fills us with the hope that things will get better if we work harder. Failing that, it convinces us that neurosis is a normal human condition and then offers defenses that become our life goals. In pursuing the latter we ensure the survival of culture, our split mind, dissatisfaction and striving, goaded by the belief that were we to stop striving to satisfy our desires, there would be nothing worth living for. This fear makes us seek further defenses on the one hand and increase our striving on the other (1: 80-121). The resulting dissatisfaction and frustration keep the wheel of culture (progress) turning and ourselves bound to it, having first fallen into the fundamental illusion *(maya)* that it constitutes the real world and identifying it as our natural condition.

Thus bound, as time goes by, we become increasingly entangled in the web of programming in cultural constructs. And the older we get or the more we progress toward becoming a full-fledged member of society, the more tightly we become bound. As a result, by the time we reach adulthood we are, in Tart's phrase, "maximally bound within this consensus" (1: 34). The stronger our bondage, the more unaware we become and the less we notice it. And the more our responses become automatic, the more we come to believe our condition to be natural and become immersed in it. Thus the cycle (Wheel) repeats and maintains itself. Moreover, in internalizing the cultural construction, we also internalize its neuroses, conflicts, and problems. So man the social animal becomes also the neurotic animal.

The Personal Frame

Beyond psychological and socio-cultural constructs, which become part of our personal frame, elements of personal history, background, and associations enter into and further limit and modify our personal construction of consciousness. Some of these are family, parents, upbringing, education, relationships, personal needs, wishes, likes, interests, desires, hopes, dreams, etc. Forming the actual shape of our consciousness, these make up the more immediate frame. And the entire system is maintained by thoughts.

At any one time the range of our consciousness is the range of our thoughts. As Ornstein states, "More than any other factor, thoughts are the foundation of normal consciousness. We maintain and refresh our personal construction through continued thought" (1: 38). So once our consciousness is constructed, thoughts and internal dialogue—reassuring, reproving, arguing, agreeing, approving, cautioning, justifying, and, in general, keeping the incessant commentary on everything going—reinforce and maintain it. As don Juan tells Castaneda, "We maintain our world with our internal talk...We renew it, we kindle it with life, we uphold it with our internal talk...Thus we repeat the same choices over and over until the day we die, because we keep on repeating the same internal talk over and over until the day we die" (1: 262). This internal dialogue, or what Pearce calls "roof-brain chatter," constantly shifting, in Swami Vivekananda's phrase, "like a drunken monkey," from one thought or association to another, keeps the need for constant stimulation, and thus itself, alive and running.

This internal triggering of thoughts and the incessant scanning of the external world for sensory stimuli are the two ways in which consciousness maintains itself. They produce thoughts, which are the actual range and running of consciousness. Detached from reality, drifting on their own momentum or association, thoughts are propelled by their own onrush or impelled by consciousness, which is afraid that if it ever stopped, it would cease to exist. So long as they keep running, they hold the dualistic construction firmly in place. All our perceptions are thus dictated, directed, projected, accompanied by, and filtered and seen through the film of our thoughts.

Pearce explains how thoughts, projected outside in childhood, get internalized in adult life and form the roof-brain chatter. He says, "As part of language development and exploration of his world, a child talks out his world. He talks to himself out loud and unconcerned, verbalizing his exploration of reality" (1: 122). This is the internal dialogue projected outside, so to speak. This talking out the world gets repressed and internalized from the pressure to use language only for communication with others and only in socially accepted ways. Such pressure disapproves of children expressing their views, especially in company, so as not to offend or embarrass others, or for fear of what others will say or do. So, in order to be accepted, liked, approved, and not to be rejected, frowned upon, ridiculed, shunned by or isolated from others, the child represses and internalizes his/her talk and learns the hypocrisies, deceptions, and duplicities of adult life. This situation creates further split, confusion, and conflict within.

"One may smile and smile and be a villain," says Shakespeare. Or one can smile to another but think, "I hate you! I want to wring your neck!" "Hi, how are you?" "I'm fine!" says the grownup, while inside s/he may be saying, "I'm lonely, depressed. I feel abandoned." Or s/he may be a seething hot bed of pent-up emotions, a volcano ready to erupt but kept from it with all the defenses society has instilled. Such defenses, of course, do not always work. I once saw in the subway a girl who, after taking off all her clothes, made her fingers look like claws, and kept charging toward other passengers. It was as if, like a threatened, cornered, wounded animal, breaking through her defenses and repressions, she was coming out of her lonely cage and making a last desperate attempt to break through the cages of others, to contact and relate as a human being.

Thus the social construction of reality gets completely internalized and becomes the content or object of consciousness and the substance of its insulated and isolated running conversation with itself. By the time the child becomes an adult, it continues uninterrupted in his/her waking hours, keeping him/her in the grip of culturally induced hypnosis and making him/her a sleepwalker going through the trance called life. Talking to ourselves inside our head now acts as our way of establishing normality and stability. It forms our private world, hiding our shame, inadequacy, guilt, regret, hurt, pain, insecurity, and depression, continuously triggered by the mind so as to keep itself going. In this world of privacy we learn to hide from the world because otherwise, we believe, it will reveal what our self is really like and we will meet rejection, disapproval, ridicule, and isolation, which we judge to be worse than death. So, in fear and shame we consign ourselves to the deathlike state of isolation we fear and attempt to avoid.

To be a self is, then, to have something to hide, to have and want privacy; and the most private is this running chatter. Being a self means having this continuous monologue that gives us a sense of ourselves as separate entities, witnesses to our thoughts, and thus a sense of continuity and permanence. Imagine millions, even billions, of us walking around with tapes of this running chatter in our heads, passing each other, sometimes without even noticing, so absorbed are we in this trance. Occasionally we open up a little slit and vocalize a few of these thoughts, which are not actually what we want to say but what we believe others want to hear. We hope what we say will be acceptable, will make our world familiar, will make others think we are a nice person; will confirm our existence or identity; or will at least relieve the deadening isolation. All the while, however, what we want to say remains locked up inside, removing us further from any direct contact. So we continue as human beings, each isolated and insulated from the others and trapped and lost in our private world of thoughts. Unaware of our plight, cut off from Reality, but spinning reality out of our thoughts, we become split, isolated and disconnected within and from anything that is real, vital, and alive. Such is the construction and condition of the adult personal consciousness and life. *Life?*

Chapter 10
The Construction of Reality

As mentioned in the last chapter, one of the most profound developments in the latter half of the twentieth century has been a growing recognition, as Erwin Schroedinger has noted, that science does not describe reality as it is (as it was once thought), but as it appears through a construct or framework, held together by a network of theories, laws, and experimental results. Lawrence LeShan calls this perspective "the new view" and says that, according to it, "a human being does not discover what is out there, but – to a large degree – creates and maintains it, that he is the organizer of, and responsible for, the reality in which he lives" (2: 4-5). This view is gaining ground among those who are in the forefront of some of the most advanced branches of Western disciplines, especially physics. With Plato's Allegory of the Cave in mind, Arthur Eddington says of this new development: "The frank realization that physical science is concerned with a world of shadows is one of the most significant of recent advances" (quoted by Wilber 1: 41). In light of this recognition, to continue to take our construction for reality, says Sir James Jeans, as did earlier systems of physics, from the Newtonian mechanics to the old quantum theory, is a fundamental mistake. This is a second order of development, for it represents not only science, but also other disciplines, indeed consciousness itself, becoming aware of the nature of its own activities.

In the wake of this development, the ordinary view that what we perceive and the way we perceive it is the way reality is in itself, cannot be maintained. In this chapter I shall develop the argument, by presenting evidence from psychology, physics, and philosophy, that this view is mistaken and that what we believe to be real is a construct.

The evidence from psychology has previously been presented. Because consciousness is not focused on itself nor constructed to perceive itself but the incoming stimuli, we do not see the process by which it constructs models, imposes them on events or data, and then interprets and judges them to be out there, thereby giving an independent status to the object-pole. Since consciousness does not see itself to be part of this framework, we come to believe that it mirrors reality. But this belief is untenable. If consciousness, the subject-pole, is a construct, then of necessity reality, the object-pole, is likewise a construct. For, if consciousness is the capacity of a system to respond to stimuli, which are the basis for interpreting as real that from which they are received, then what we perceive as real is that interpretation, which is a construct. Any object is an interpretation from the model constructed out of data received in the brain and projected to be out there. And what we perceive as the objective world is a system of interpretations, or of models or objects interpreted to be out there, internally held together by a system of programmings and externally by a consensus that that is what reality is in itself.

Now this reveals a crucial fact about the dualistic construction of consciousness and world. First, the subject-pole of consciousness and the object-pole of reality are correlative and interdependent. They are not absolute entities existing by themselves, independent of each other. As is the case with all relative entities, the structure of consciousness depends upon the structure of the world, and the latter on the former. Their polarity depends on the organization of the subject-pole of consciousness in separation from and opposition or relationship to the world. And this construction makes perception possible. Thus, essential to consciousness is the object-pole separate from it; and essential to the latter is its being the object of consciousness. It follows that, as will become clear in Parts III and V, since duality depends upon consciousness holding the poles apart, were you to remove or transcend one pole, the other would collapse, leaving reality as it is.

Second, the poles are simultaneously constructed. Since it is the model that determines what and how we perceive, both consciousness and reality are not only constructed from these models; they also go up simultaneously as the models are formed and a network created through programming. For, since consciousness is essentially a system of models held together by programmings, and the world is a system of interpretations out of the totality of stimuli and data received and judged to be real according to the models, they are not only constructs and relative to each other, each is constructed at the same time as and is dependent on the other. And both are reduced to perceiving, which is a mind-spin, apart from which neither structure can stand.

Karl Pribram has sought to show how our brain constructs reality. As Marilyn Ferguson explains his view, the brain functions as a hologram, abstracting and interpreting frequencies from the realm beyond space and time, and storing the image constructed not in one area but, like a hologram, throughout the brain. She writes: "The theory, in a nutshell: Our brains mathematically construct 'concrete' reality by interpreting frequencies from another dimension, a realm of meaningful, patterned primary reality that transcends time and space. The brain is a hologram, interpreting a holographic universe" (in Wilber 4: 5).

Pribram explains that constructing the image hinges on transforming the data received into frequencies. The frequency domain is the primary order of the universe, of which physical reality and the brain are expressions. What appears in the perceptual field as the observable universe is not the primary realm but what is abstracted from it by the brain's neural interference patterns. Thus our world of solid objects consists of images constructed or "read out" of the frequency realm and represents one state of the universe. It is a "special case," the boundaries of which depend upon the brain's constructs (in Wilber 4: 27-34).

In physics, David Bohm has a similar view. Called "the holonomic theory," it maintains that the primary order of reality is "the holomovement," also called "the implicate order." It is the undefined totality of movements of vibratory energy that fills what we call empty space and is the ground of what is manifest. From this implicate order, the entire universe of matter and form, which he calls "the explicate order," is constructed through a process of abstraction. This occurs when a small, "quantized" wavelike excitation is created in the vast background of energy, the implicate order (1: 183-184; Weber in Wilber 4: 51). The basic process of this universe is that whatever is manifest or unfolded is enfolded in the implicate order; and "in the implicate order the totality of existence is enfolded within each region of space (and time)" (1: 172). Thus "what is always a totality of ensembles, all present together, in an orderly series of stages of enfoldment and unfoldment, ... intermingle and interpenetrate each other in principle throughout the whole of space" (1: 183). So he concludes: "The entire material world, with its separate things, space and time, are therefore constructed by us" (1: 178). He adds that this view is sustained by theories unconnected with the holonomic one — the far more solid grounds of relativity and quantum theories:

> Relativity and, even more important, quantum mechanics have strongly suggested (though not proved) that the world cannot be analyzed into separate and independently existing parts. Moreover, each part somehow involves all others: contains them or enfolds them. (Quoted by Weber in Wilber 4: 190)

On the basis of relativity and quantum theories, other physicists concur. Fritjof Capra, for instance, points out that one consequence of relativity theory is that space and time are not separate but are inseparably connected to form a four-dimensional continuum. And a fundamental consequence of quantum mechanics is that the way we perceive can no longer be separated from what we perceive (quoted by Weber in Wilber 4: 219). What we perceive on the sensory level as discrete, individual objects on the one hand and our scientific picture of reality on the other are both constructs. Science gives us models of reality, which do not tell us how things are in themselves but provide "approximate descriptions which are improved upon in subsequent development in successive steps" (1: 27). It selects a group of phenomena and builds a model to describe it. Since this involves neglecting others, the model will not give a complete description of reality. So "all these models are approximations which are valid for a certain range of phenomena. Beyond this range they no longer give a satisfactory description of nature" (1: 28).

Espousing a similar view, in his *Masks of the Universe,* Edward Harrison says, "the universe in which we live, or think we live, is mostly a world of our own making" (1). Each age has formed such descriptions, pictures, or masks of the universe. These universes "are models of the Universe...Each universe is a self-consistent system of ideas, marvelously organized, interlacing most of what is perceived and known. *A universe is a mask fitted on the face of the unknown Universe"* (1-2; italics his).

Others have used different metaphors not only to describe the view that the universe as we perceive it is a construct but also to emphasize the distinction between it and the universe as it is. Thus using the metaphor of map-territory, Ken Wilber says that what we ordinarily perceive is the map, which is a symbolic representation of the territory or reality as it is. Neither sense impressions nor science presents us with the territory, but only a map (1: 41-42).

Using the metaphor of net, after Novalis, Arthur Eddington says that just as the net is not the ocean nor the fish caught in it the only fish there is, but what is caught depends upon the mesh; so the scientific theories do not present the world as it is but as it is able to be ordered, analyzed, represented, interpreted, and predicted by the scientific method. Only what gets caught in the scientific net is pronounced real. Science attempts to make the mesh increasingly finer, to catch as much as it can. It would be a fundamental mistake, however, to believe that the scientific net or what gets caught in it is the entire ocean of reality. That would be mistaking the net for the ocean.

The reason for this is, as Eugene Wigner says of microphysics (but it is equally applicable to science as a whole), that it studies relationships among observations, not among observables (quoted by Pribram in Wilber 2: 28). Even more pointedly, G. Spencer-Brown observes:

> What is commonly now regarded as real consists in its very presence, merely tokens or expressions. And since tokens or expressions are

considered to be *of* some (other) substratum, so the universe itself, as we know it, may be considered to be an expression of a reality other than itself...the world we know is constructed in order (and thus in such a way as to be able) to see itself...But *in order* to do so...whatever it sees is *only partially* itself...In this condition it will always partially elude itself. (104-105; italics his)

Pointing out that things in themselves are beyond scientific constructs so that none of them can tell us what it is, Bohm says simply, "What the universe *actually* is, is unsayable" (quoted by Weber in Wilber 4: 87; italics his). This is a view with which Harrison concurs (as Kant did before him) when he says, "What it [i.e., the Universe] is in its own right, independent of our changing opinions, we never know" (1).

From his unique perspective, but sounding this time very much like a scientist, Castaneda's don Juan says that our familiarity with the world forces us to believe that we live in a world of objects "existing by themselves and as themselves, just as we perceive them" (4: 33). But in reality "there is no objective world, but only a universe of energy fields which seers call the Eagle's emanations" (4: 108). What we perceive as the world "is an interpretation we make" through alignment of emanations inside the human cocoon with those outside (4: 24, 108).

Both in this perspective and in the emergent scientific construction, the entire universe appears as an undivided whole in which everything is interconnected, interpenetrating everything else. There are no separate entities existing independently of one another. On the subatomic level the view of separate entities appears to be an abstraction. This outlook is supported not only by the holographic imagery, but far more significantly, by quantum, bootstrap, and other theories circulating at present. Expressing both holonomic and quantum points of view, Bohm says:

> The idea of a separately and independently existent particle is seen to be, at best, an abstraction furnishing a valid approximation only in a certain limited domain. Ultimately, the entire universe has to be understood as a single undivided whole, in which analysis into separately and independently existent parts has no fundamental status. (1: 174-175)

Consequently, "in the implicate order of undivided wholeness, everything is enfolded into everything, intermingling and interpenetrating each other throughout the whole of space" (1: 184). The universe is an undivided whole in which each part contains the whole; and everything interpenetrates everything else, effectively constituting its infinite multidimensionality (1: 189).

Fritjof Capra explains how the concept of solid objects was shattered by atomic physics while at the same time revealing the basic oneness of the universe. Quantum theory showed that as we penetrate matter, we find that there are no solid, isolated building blocks in nature. Rather, nature appears as a complicated web of relationships between the various parts and the whole. And relativity revealed that mass is not a substance but a form of energy, the basic character of which is process. Thus a particle is a process involving the energy which shows up as the particle's mass. So, quoting Henry Stapp, Capra concludes: "An elementary particle is not an independently existing un-analyzable entity. It is, in essence, a set of relationships that reach outward to other things" (1: 53-57, 66-67, 125).

This is also a conclusion of bootstrap theory. Summarizing it, Capra says it "not only abandons the idea of fundamental building blocks of matter, but also accepts no fundamental entities whatsoever." On the contrary, it views the universe as

> a dynamic and interconnected web of relations in which particles are dynamically composed of one another, such that every particle consists of all other particles. None of the properties of any part of this web is fundamental; they all follow from the properties of other parts, and the overall consistency of their mutual interrelations determine the structure of the entire web. (In Wilber 4: 114-115)

Capra goes on to emphasize that the central feature of the emergent paradigm is "the fundamental unity and interrelatedness of the universe and the intrinsically dynamic nature of its phenomena" (quoted by Weber in Wilber 4: 226). It follows that although we ordinarily believe that our world is made up of separate, individual objects, in fact these are constructs:

> The universe is one interconnected whole, and this whole, this process forms patterns. We discern these patterns and in everyday life we separate them and regard them as isolated objects; and then we say there's no connection between these objects. But in doing so, we have already made an approximation and we have left out the connection which was initially there. (Quoted by Weber in Wilber 4: 228, 231)

Within the scientific explanation itself, the problem of adequate evidence in scientific proof implies, on the one hand, that the universe is an undivided whole in which everything is interconnected with everything else and, on the other, that the boundaries set up by scientific explanation are frameworks constructed by the mind to impose order on phenomena and make sense out of the data of experience and experimentation. The ingredients of scientific explanations and the world that appears through their interpretation and is confirmed by experimental results are held up by scientific consensus. Within this context, the problem of explanation is deciding what constitutes adequate evidence for establishing the validity of a scientific claim, theory, or law beyond any doubt, uncertainty, disproof, or contrary evidence. Any attempt to gather adequate evidence that amounts to certainty seems to involve circularity or infinite regress. The problem is usually solved pragmatically: At one point the scientist simply decides that the evidence s/he has gathered is sufficient, based on previously established knowledge, theories or laws, which are themselves established as valid as a result of a decision based on prior knowledge, laws, theories, and so on. Now, although this is a perfectly sound procedure, it clearly indicates that the boundaries thereby created are all mind-made and are already in place when the scientist poses the question or the problem. Reality does not come with such boundaries but lies beyond them.

This transcendence of reality over the framework of proof or explanation is implied by the frameworks themselves. This implication is clear from the decision that conveniently settles on what to take as adequate evidence. In itself the evidence does not come with this cut-off point. Since it does not add up to certainty, it could conceivably imply all of reality as part of the evidence. This consequence also appears to be an import of the logical theory of implication, which says that a true statement implies all true statements. Since such statements are logically infinite, the decision as to what to count as adequate evidence shows that the evidence, and consequently the explanation, are constructs not to be found in reality in itself; and that reality is an undivided whole in which everything is in touch with everything else, so that if you touch one point, you touch all points. In such a situation, as Zen master Shen Hui said, "One word is sufficient to reveal the whole truth," unless you decide to put up boundaries on evidence for the sake of your theories and explanations, which are themselves boundaries.

An important consequence of this implication is that in introducing the decision into the explanation, the subject becomes part of the very structure of the explanation thought to be object, unconnected or unaffected by the subject, observer or experimenter. This conclusion demonstrates the untenability of the separation of the subject from the object. The dualistic notion of a completely objective explanation breaks down under the very assumptions and procedures that were set up to confirm it! This consequence again points to a unity or nonduality and an interconnectedness of the universe. It also shows the constructive nature of the dualistic assumptions that the self is separate from the world and that the latter consists of discrete, individual entities unconnected with one another.

Moreover, implicit in the emergent scientific view is a confirmation of the premises of experiential religion that other constructions are possible and that Reality as Such lies beyond all constructs. LeShan explicitly draws this conclusion when he says that each culture is a map or world-picture. Constructions other than one's own are not only possible, but they are a fact. What we have, therefore, are alternate realities, no one of which is a complete map of reality. None works completely. So he concludes, "None of the valid systems of organizing reality is closer to *truth* than the others; each is a different way of perceiving and reacting to what *is*" (2: 36; italics his).

Mathematics and logic indicate that the entire realm of ordinary knowledge works by putting up frames which reality in itself does not have. These frames, without which we cannot know anything in the dualistic or action mode, are not only constructs, they themselves, on the one hand, imply that we cannot know Reality as Such through or within any frame or through any ordinary method of knowledge, and, on the other hand, point to it. That what we perceive or know as real depends on the frames is clear from mathematics and logic, which tell us that we cannot prove anything without setting up a framework. The frame itself is not and cannot be proved within itself but must be assumed, although it can be proved in a more comprehensive system, which itself must assume, and cannot prove, all its basic elements, and so on. This fact, which is a form of what I have called "the Law of Construction," is a cognate of Gödel's Incompleteness Theorem, which states that "any complex deductive system must have at least one premise that cannot be proved within that system without contradicting itself. So every system assumes principles whose internal consistency is as open to question as the system itself" (Bohm, quoted by Weber in Wilber 4: 190). It follows that nothing can be proved in an absolute sense because every proof assumes propositions all of which cannot be proved within it and because no absolute frame over Reality is possible. Such an idea is a contradiction in terms. Therefore, Reality as Such cannot be known within any framework, system, condition, or construct. And yet all frames and systems presuppose a greater reality than themselves and so assume reality to be wider than what can be proved within them. The larger the system or frame, the greater is the reality assumed to be there. The ultimate or primary framework or construct, therefore, presupposes a reality that lies beyond it. Thus primary duality assumes Reality as Such, out of which it is created, by putting up the dualistic frame.

Consequently, all frames or constructs assume and point toward Reality as Such, and suggest that no frame can ever reach or enable anyone to attain it.

Logic is in a similar situation. For instance, as Alfred Tarski has shown, no formal definition is possible except in a formal, limited language. Since a definition is itself a frame, this means that we need a frame to construct another frame. And as logical paradoxes have also taught us, we better make the first frame larger. This means, again, that any system presupposes or requires a context larger than itself for its validity. Since every system is a construct, it follows that every construct requires something other than it for its construction and validity. Now, either this "something other" is a construct or something beyond all construct. If the former, it would lead to infinite regress; if it is not, this "something other" is beyond all construct. While regress can work hypothetically or notionally, this will not do in the case of all constructs, especially those that pertain to reality as a whole or primary reality-constructs, such as primary duality. Thus, just as a particular construction of reality presupposes and points toward the reality out of which it is constructed, so primary reality-constructs presuppose and point toward Reality beyond all constructs. All primary constructs, forms, or systems presuppose and require something other which is not a construct, form, or system and which they can neither circumscribe nor describe or explain but yet toward which they point. And by the same token, they declare themselves to be constructs, requiring the beyond to prop them up. Since they can describe only what is within their parameters, they cannot tell us what is or is not outside all frameworks. Because of this, completeness lies outside all systems and frameworks. Every time we try to study or measure reality, we assume a limit and at the same time what lies beyond, so that our attempts to limit all truth or reality within a system simply fall apart. The very rigor of Western modes of inquiry shows that every time we try to put the genie in a bottle it gets out. In itself there is no limit to truth or reality; no framework or boundary. They are all our own creations and serve useful purposes, to be sure, but beyond that they become prisons when we take them for Reality and become attached to and spellbound by them *(maya)*.

The two important conclusions of modern science that what we perceive as real is a construct and that our observable universe is not how the universe is in itself can be traced in Western philosophy all the way back to Plato. In his Allegory of the Cave, Plato not only clearly shows that the world of appearance is not reality as it is, but also that the former is a construct, held up by cultural consensus. Becoming bound to it in the process of growing up, we do not see its constructive nature, assume it to be the only reality there is, and become unaware of Reality as it is. In this state our minds can perceive only through the network of its programmings and constructs and only what they reveal, not Reality as Such, which is open only to a direct vision.

In the modern period, it was Immanuel Kant who saw the two central points clearly. In the *Critique of Pure Reason,* he set out to demonstrate the constructive nature of the phenomenal world by arguing that our minds or "pure reason" can perceive only through its categories and interpretative schemes and only what they reveal about the world. Pure reason imposes its categories, or frame, form, and order on the perceptual field so that what we are thus able to perceive is only what filters through them. As the limits of these categories are the limits of its world, pure reason is incapable of going beyond its categories and the phenomenal world and knowing noumenon or reality as it is. As to how this latter could be known, Kant had no clear idea.

In line with Plato and Kant, modern constructivist philosophers, such as Nelson Goodman, hold that what we call "the world" is constructed by the mind through its activities and symbolic language. Unlike Plato, who believed that Reality as Such could be directly experienced, and Kant, who believed in it but thought that it could be neither known nor experienced by reason, and more in line with modern empiricism, Goodman believes that there is no noumenon or Reality as Such independent of human mental activity. We simply construct our world by assuming and operating on other constructs or worlds as given and with the help of symbol systems (see Bruner's discussion in *Actual Minds, Possible Worlds,* 95-105). Indicating how we get these systems from culture in general and science in particular, Willard van Orman Quine says that the conceptual scheme of science is a tool for interpreting and predicting future experience in the light of past experience in which physical objects are conceptually introduced as constructs and mediant realities between laws, theories, and the data of experience. We obtain these objects and our belief in them as realities from our cultural posits (44). Thus this view confirming the constructive nature of what we believe to be the real world is fully in accord with experiential religion.

It is not possible to present here further confirmation of the constructive nature of the ordinary view of reality from other nonreligious sources. What has thus far been shown confirms many premises of experiential religion, namely that what we ordinarily believe to be real is not how Reality is in itself; that both the ordinary and scientific views are constructs, as are dualism and our belief that reality consists of discrete, independently existing individual objects; that beyond such constructs, the universe exhibits a fundamental unity and undivided wholeness in which things and events are interrelated and exist in mutual interpenetration, forming a dynamically interconnected web. Furthermore, these nonreligious sources also hinted at the possibility of other constructions and the impossibility of knowing Reality within any construct, category or framework, and showed that primary frameworks or reality-constructs, forms, and systems ultimately presuppose, point toward, and depend on it.

Having discussed the constructure nature of reality and consciousness, I shall now turn to show the constructive nature of the separate self.

Chapter 11
The Construction of Self

Evidence from psychology demonstrates beyond any doubt that the separate self or ego is a construct. Hence there is no need for me to present extensive evidence here.

Psychologists Gordon Allport and Theodore A. Sarbin both agree that the self, or the consciousness of oneself as a separate, individual entity, is an inference made by the mind when it becomes conscious of a separation from others and the environment. They add that the child's name contributes to this sense of being an independent, permanent entity that remains identical with itself and unchanged through the changing flow and rhythm of life (Allport 1: 113-114; Sarbin in Gordon & Gergen 181-183). Allport says further that we postulate for ourselves a permanent personality through "the dovetailing of the successive moments of consciousness with their imbrication of temporal reference and content" through which "we arrive at the conviction that we do somehow possess consistent personalities surrounding the momentary conscious core" (2: 159).

According to Allport, then, the self is only a reference point for consciousness, formed by overlapping successive moments of itself on the constantly running programmed tapes or internal dialogue, producing an onrush of thought and creating an impression of permanence. Pointing to the process of this construction, the authors of *Yoga and Psychotherapy* state that the substance of the self is formed from past impressions. From these impressions arise programmings and habit patterns. The momentum of these impressions in our thoughts and the repetitive responses resulting from habit patterns create a sense of continuity over time. These become fixed and congeal into "the consistency and solidity of 'I'" (Rama et al. 184). Similarly, Ken Wilber defines the self as "the sum of all one's possible personae," and says that "the ego itself is built and constructed by the learning and combining of various personae into an integrated self-concept," which makes "the core of ego...a thought-self, a self-*concept*" (3: 33, 31; italics his). Surveying the evidence, D.T. Suzuki concludes: "The psychologist informs us that 'I' is non-existent, that it is a mere concept designating a structure or an integration of relationship" (in Fromm et al. 63). Summarizing the evidence from psychology and Buddhism, Jack Engler says that the sense of self evolves developmentally out of our experience of objects and interactions. It is "an internalized image, a composite representation," which is not only "constructed out of our experience with the object world," but is *"actually being constructed anew from moment to moment ... by a selective and imaginative 'remembering' of past encounters with significant objects in our world"* (1: 22; italics his).

It is clear, then, that the separate self is only a thought, a concept, a sense, an image or representation, constructed as a reference point around which consciousness identifies and attaches its contents or objects and its network of programmings and characteristics. This subjective organization gives rise to the sense that it is a stable, solid, permanent pole in relationship to and separation from others and the world. Identification provides the ground for building up the reference point; attachment supplies the cement for solidifying and maintaining it as the subject-pole in separation from the object-pole; while desire serves to expand its world and maintain it and the dualistic structure. It is, therefore, nothing other than a mass of identification and attachment, imbued with the desire and drive for self-expansion, locked in the mental framework of conditioning and constructs, and holding them up.

Now, since the self is only a thought, it exists only in the mind — and only when we think about it. It does not have any permanence or independent existence, nor is it anything apart from consciousness. It is, in fact, one of its contents. However, since we believe it to be in itself something real, our belief is illusory. So it is not difficult to see why behaviorists refuse to talk about it, convinced that there is no such thing. Similarly, after asking the question "what makes a person the person he is?" and surveying the field in search of something existing by itself to which it would point as the answer, the philosopher A.J. Ayer concludes that neither space, nor time, nor the body, nor anything with which we ordinarily identify, constitutes the self. All we can find are a set of properties. And these do not add up to a substantial entity called "the self," existing independently of them (176-187). This position is identical to that of the Buddha and many of the sources of experiential religion.

Now, if the self is a construct, how is it constructed? Since its construction and various stages have been well documented, a few highlights of the main steps will be sufficient for our present purpose.

The same drive that leads the infant to construct a stable consciousness and world also moves him/her to organize the self. Out of undifferentiated unity, the self is formed through a process of differentiation from others and the environment. When perception and consciousness are organized as the subject-pole and a stable world as the object-pole, having become separate from reality, at its very root consciousness senses a fundamental cleavage. From this split arises, on the unconscious level, a sense of nothingness or unreality, incompleteness and insignificance in the face of the world. Thereupon it becomes seized with separation anxiety, fear of nothingness, and death or non-existence. To overcome them, the survival drive impels consciousness to form a stable and permanent reference point for its contents or objects, endows it with reality and independent existence, and maintains it in separation from others and the world. At the root of the drive to be a self is this "life instinct," this heroic urge of life to recover what was lost in the organization of consciousness in separation from the world.

This self-creation begins, already at six months, according to Sarbin, with a differentiation of objects and persons. At this stage, however, both are perceived as objects, instruments to manipulate for survival and the reduction of fear, tension, and discomfort. This perception of everything as objects is a very significant development, as the first self-concept formed is that of an object, "me," one which will cling to the self, never to be lost.

The formation of this object-self is possible with the development of the principles of stability—identification, attachment, grasping, and possessiveness—and expansion—desire, motor ability, manipulation, control—and memory, time, symbolization, and language.

Differentiation-identification-attachment-differentiation, so the process of building progresses: from the environment, between objects and persons, and within oneself as the individual goes through the various stages of development. The differentiation between objects and persons leads to the development of attachment and identification, through which one further stabilizes the world, solidifies the dualistic structure, and builds up the sense of the self as a permanent entity separate from others and the world. The child identifies with objects and persons differentiated from the environment, and, by attaching to them, forms the sense of a stable self. Similarly, identification and attachment to possessions leads to the development of possessiveness and "the acquisitive instinct." Thus clinging, grasping, possessiveness, and greed become programmed into the very makeup of the self. That is the reason, according to psychologists, that identification and attachment precede the object-self, "mine" before "me," and the latter develops out of the former (Deikman 19). Thus, in constantly referring to things and persons as "mine," the sense of the object-self as something solid, continuous, and objective is formed. This construction also gives the self its sense of being a permanent center or organizing principle around which to build up one's life. It is in this sense that the authors of *Yoga and Psychotherapy* say, "I-ness is no more than the sum of one's attachments. It is defined by the totality of those objects, persons, and thoughts with which he is entangled. This is the stuff of which one's identity is made" (Rama et al. 182).

Generalization extends this sense of self to the contents of the child's consciousness and to objects and persons of his/her world. Memory further adds to the sense of solidity, continuity, and permanence by overlapping successive events and experiences. As Allport observes, the sense of continuity with the past is created by overlapping significant moments in consciousness and with the future by overlapping moments of planning and imagination, fantasy and expectation, and selective attention to thoughts (2: 159). But if this is indeed the one sure criterion of identity and personal existence, as Allport contends, then the self is entirely a creation of the past. Concurring with this conclusion, Ken Wilber states that ego is "thoroughly based on the past," and is "in essence, nothing but a bag of edited memories" (1: 136).

It follows that, since the past is not anything real in itself except in our present thought, formed out of memories, the self is likewise real only in the mind and as our present thought. It cannot be anything outside the mind. Insofar as we identify with it, not only does this identification fail to create a sense of reality but because of that very fact drives us relentlessly in search of an identity that can never be fully attained but is always just out of reach. Because it is based on and its reactions come out of the past, they are always behind the times and out of touch with the present. To be a self is to be stuck in the past, out of step with reality, and out of tune with things. None of ego's actions can put it in touch with Reality or make it Real. Detached and absent from reality, the self perpetuates this condition as it becomes attached to and absorbed in its own games, which stem ultimately from a self-consciousness afraid of death. Absence is thus both the origin and the mark of the self.

However, the survival drive or "the life instinct" impels the child, and later the adult, to overcome the sense of a lack and the fear of not-being by giving rise to the principles of expansion. Motor ability serves to extend the child's sense of power; while manipulation aids in the development of the ability to organize and control, and later in life to strive to fit others and the world into its idea of reality and to confirm and maintain itself. As Deikman explains, manipulation is associated with attachment; while motor ability is associated with desire and intention, with "a 'need' to escape and expand, a need for power, to control, and a fear of helplessness." It expands the child's sense of power and manipulation over the prior experience of helplessness (1: 13). Motor ability sends the child crawling, hurtling, and tumbling toward the object from which s/he is separated. In this separation and pursuit are born intention, want, desire, and desiringness. Here we see again that the very origin and essence of desire lie in this separation and sense of lack. Absence or unreality is both the background for the formation of the self and its deepest layer. But it prompts the child to summon desire in order to set up the life-project of overcoming it. Such developments give the self the appearance of a cyclone, with an empty center, swirling with desire and attachment in an effort to make itself real and to find meaning.

The development of symbolization and language ability provides a greater consolidation and expansion of the child's world. But absorption in creating a word-built world makes the self further removed from reality and increasingly a product of thought and memory.

A continuous reference of things and persons in his/her environment to "mine," "me," and the use of the term "I," leads the child to shift from "me" to "I" as the center or pole around which everything in his/her world becomes organized, and to infer that "I" is a continuous, permanent entity which remains unchanged through the changing events of life. With the development of the ability to use abstract and conceptual thought, the final stage of the separate self becomes fully formed.

Allport observes that this separation at the heart of the self is the most momentous development because it enables the child to differentiate him/herself from others and the environment, and to perceive events as significant to him/her as an autonomous being (1: 112). However, in spite of this transition from "me" to "I," from the object to the subject self, the self does not thereby turn into pure subjectivity, that is, a reality founded on itself and existing by itself. As Deikman explains, it remains an object of consciousness. He writes, "'Mine' leads to 'me' (the object) and 'you' (the object) and finally to 'I', whose shape and meaning are ruled by the possessive mode" (1:19).

This self not only represents the farthest point of separation from what is, but, emerging under pressures of socialization, it also experiences an internal split from which arises its sense of incompleteness and a conflict in all its inner and outer dimensions. As Freud explained, nothing brings about the internal split in the child more than the demands of society imposing its desire and control. As the desires of society run counter to those of his/her own, the child resolves the conflict by repressing his/her own and internalizing, identifying, and attaching to those of society in order to survive and be accepted, loved, and liked, thus expanding him/herself. However, in so doing, s/he internalizes the split and conflict, over which ego is thrown as a moat of reconciliation so as to create a sense of normalcy and to enable one to function as a member of society.

Out of this dislocation, split, and conflict develop negative and positive self-images. These self-images are formed as a reaction to negative judgments, disapproval, threat, and ridicule, on the one hand; and a desire to please, to be liked, loved, approved, and have one's identity confirmed on the other. Thus, if parents constantly scold the child, using such negative judgments as, "You are bad, stupid, or clumsy," "You can't do anything right," "You are a worthless bum," or "You will never amount to anything," s/he will form negative self-judgments and self-concepts—what Harry Stack Sullivan called "bad me," and "no me." From then on s/he will not only perceive him/herself as these judgments and concepts dictate, but will also create occasions so as to perceive him/herself as such, thus confirming and maintaining his/her negative self-concept. However, as these are painful to face, they will invariably be repressed and become part of the unconscious. From there they will exert their control over his/her desires, drives, and thoughts, trigger negative feelings or emotions, prompt behavior, and dominate and terrorize his/her life. And on the conscious level s/he will project a positive self-image in the hope of gaining others' acceptance, approval, love, or esteem and thus counter the effects of the negative one. S/he will try to have others confirm the positive image by doing what is acceptable or pleasing to them, even though it goes contrary to his/her own desires and wishes.

Now, while the positive image will push the individual to have others' approval, the negative, especially if it is the stronger one, will create or set up occasions so as to have itself confirmed, thus creating a seed-bed of conflict between fear and desire, and resulting in frustration, resentment, anger, regret, depression, or guilt. The degree of dominance of the positive over the negative will spell the health of the individual. However, if we are to believe the transactionalists, it is the negative self-image—"I'm not OK"—that usually prevails. In either case, the fundamental split and the consequent source of conflict within will remain. As Hermann Hesse noted in *Demian,* "Such fissures may come together again, but in the innermost recesses they continue to seep and bleed" (15). For their source is none other than the core of ego itself.

This contradiction at the heart of ego is a function of its separation from Reality and the object-pole, and interaction of identification, attachment, and desire. Upon its emergence and establishment as the center around which the subject-pole, the entire dualistic structure itself and the above-mentioned pillars that hold them up solidify, the self becomes the center of separation from what is. As the individual identifies with it, s/he proceeds to believe and thus experience, and consequently strive to maintain this separation as his/her very being. Getting its sense of itself from this separation and maintaining it in order to be itself, ego becomes unreal, illusory, and incomplete at its very core.

Feeling this separation and unreality at a fundamental level, ego is seized by a fear of non-existence or death. So, at the core of ego is a sense and a fear of nothingness or emptiness translated on the empirical level as survival anxiety. This fear is the core of all fears.

Now the survival drive impels ego to overcome the feeling of separation and unreality and the fear of death by becoming Real, permanent, immortal. Filled with a desire, drive, or hunger for the Real, ego wants to be the permanent Self or God. But sensing that attainment of the goal requires its death, dissolution, or transcendence as a separate center of being and consciousness, ego is seized by a fear of the Real. Fear creates resistance. Thus at the core of ego is a desire for, fear of, and a resistance and opposition to and separation from God or Reality as Such. This resistance, this effort to keep itself separate from God, is the essence of ego. To be or to strive to be a separate self is to be a holdout against God. It is saying "No!" to God. In Christian terms it is the "No!" of Lucifer. Hinduism and Buddhism call it *"ahankara."*

Thus, wanting to be and yet filled with the fear of being God because that forebodes a dissolution of its sense of itself as something separate, ego wants and resists God at the same time and embarks on the task of becoming Real or the foundation of its own existence in separation from and opposition to Reality as Such. It wants to be, in Sartre's phrase, *ens causa sui* — to create itself out of nothing so as to overcome its nothingness. However, this desire not only does not overcome its nothingness; it ensures it. Furthermore, it renders its project contradictory because, in effect, it wants to be and not to be at the same time.

In this predicament, finding its craving to be Real, blocked by fear and resistance, and yet filled with desiringness, longing, and the urge to live, ego casts its desire on the only other object that it believes could make it real and embarks on possessing the world. However, since its sense of itself depends on its being separate from the universal process and the object-world, in striving to be real in relationship to the world, it keeps itself separate for fear of being rendered nothing also by the world. So it finds that it cannot *be* the world but can only *have* it. As Ken Wilber explains, ego's self-creative project turns "the desire to be All into the drive to possess all." But "in place of *being* everything, one merely desires to *have* everything. That is the basis of all substitute gratifications, and that is the insatiable thirst lying in the soul of all separate selves" (3: 106-107; italics his). Unable to be the All by possessing all and to find the identity, satisfaction, or fulfillment it seeks in what it possesses, ego turns itself into "the hungry-I" as it becomes filled with the insatiable desire that can never be quenched. For, in trying to be the foundation of its own being and consciousness within the dualistic structure by appropriating the world and yet keeping itself separate from it, ego again negates the very thing it tries to affirm. It tries to be both the object-pole, or real, and the subject-pole, or separate self, at the same time — Sartre's *en-soi-pour-soi* — that is, not to be what it is trying to be. So again it renders itself nothing as the project of self-creation in the direction of the world is also blocked.

We come up with the same result if we view ego as itself. Being a concept, ego remains an object of consciousness. By keeping itself separate from other objects, ego makes itself neither a subject nor an object nor anything real. And in attempting to be a subjectivity, on the one hand, it tries not to be itself, that is, a concept, but remains so by keeping itself separate and hence nothing. On the other hand, the attempt to be real by possessing and identifying with things and yet keeping itself separate, it also remains a concept or nothing. Thus its attempt to become real is blocked both from the subjective and from the objective side. And so it reduces itself to a perpetual striving and unquenchable desire that can never be satisfied but perforce remains unfulfilled and unreal or nothing.

Thus the project to create itself out of nothing and within the dualistic structure reveals the double-bind that is ego: By striving to be and yet holding on to its not-being, ego renders itself contradictory and cancels itself out. As Richard DeMartino explains:

> In this predicament, in having itself ego does not have itself, since it can have itself only as an object. Nor does it have the world, since as subject ego separates itself from it. Thus, the only way it can have itself, makes it not to have itself; and the only way it can have the world makes it not-itself or not to have it—thus rendering itself nothing...It is precisely this—the dichotomy of its subject-object structure—which constitutes the inherent existential ambiguity, conflict, and, indeed, contradiction of the ego in ego-consciousness. Bifurcated and disjointed in its unity, it is delineated by, but cannot be sustained or fulfilled in itself...Having and not having, at once bound to and conditioned by, and at the same time separated and cut off from, itself and its world, the ego is rent by a double cleavage, split within as well as without. (In Fromm et al. 144-145)

We now see how the core of ego is framed by the double blockage and the triple terror. Having become and wanting to remain separate both from Reality and the object world because its sense of itself depends on this separation, yet feeling unreal and incomplete because of this very separation; wanting to overcome this separation and yet afraid of being rendered unreal or nothing by Reality as Such or by the object world, ego becomes filled with the triple terror: the terror of not-being or death and of being rendered dead by Reality and the world; the terror of existing in a self-created isolation from which there is no escape because it both wants and resists Being; and the terror of not being alive or real by remaining separate from the Real and the object world. Framed by the fear of death and trying to avoid it, ego makes itself dead in life and assures the very death to avoid which it sought to be permanent and the foundation of its own existence.

This is the quandary at the heart of the separate self. Wanting Reality and yet being afraid, and so resisting and holding out against it, ego makes itself an empty striving, a wanting that can never be realized. Resisting the very thing it wants, ego never IS. And in holding itself aloof from the world it craves, ego misses the world. Nothing that it does can make it Real. All efforts to make it so turn futile. Thus it is neither here nor there, neither this nor that; rather, it is caught in the limbo of the living-dead, of not-being and becoming no-thing. In trying to be here, ego winds up in escape. In trying to be there, it renders itself empty, unreal, nothing, and nowhere. In front is a great abyss and sure annihilation; behind, the door is shut. Sitting on a narrow ledge with nowhere to go and no way out, separated from everything and fixated on itself, ego is forever exiled from reality. Wanting to be born but being afraid, it becomes enfolded and stuck in the cocoon of self-imposed limitation: unable to go forward or backward, unable to cut loose, unable to be born. Such is the contradiction and impasse that is ego. That is why its life-project cancels itself out, its desires are contradictory, and its attempt to overcome this contradiction nullifies itself—managing only to make desire insatiable, giving rise to the feelings of insufficiency, incompleteness, and dissatisfaction that keep it bound to its world.

It follows that as long as ego remains ego, so too will remain the dualism of self and the world, our feelings of unreality and incompleteness about ourselves, our bondage to the world we create, and the drive to make our ego real so as to overcome our separation and bondage. All ego's striving to free itself will only bind it further and keep the Wheel of Life turning and turn life into an impasse. In this predicament, wanting reality and yet being afraid, fearing oblivion and attempting to be rid of it, the ego ensures the very thing it fears and marches into the oblivion of time.

Chapter 12
The Human Paradox

In the effort to free itself from the contradiction in which it becomes inevitably embroiled, ego creates a world and strives to find identity, completeness, and fulfillment within it. But in so doing it becomes caught in a paradox that encompasses the entirety of human life and comes to an impasse. In this chapter I shall briefly examine how this paradox and impasse come about.

Simply stated, the human paradox (I am using the term *paradox* in a nonphilosophical, colloquial sense) is that as long as we remain separate from Reality as Such, we cannot realize what we most deeply desire within the triple constructions of reality, consciousness, and self. All attempts to do so within these parameters frustrate our desire, push life to an impasse, and into the oblivion of time. Not only does reality frustrate desire but—since we create our reality—we frustrate ourselves in the very attempt to satisfy our desire. Now, what is it that we most deeply desire? And how do we know it?

According to experiential religion, what we most deeply desire—I have been stating it all along—is to realize the purpose of existence, which is none other than to realize the true Self or identity with Reality as Such and manifest it in our very being: in our thought, feeling, behavior, and daily living. We want to end our separation and exile from Reality, our bondage to our constructs; we want to become absolutely free. We want to overcome the split within and become whole, complete, and unconditionally one with all that is.

The paradox results from the core contradiction that is ego. For what creates it is our attempt to realize the purpose of existence within the reality, consciousness, and self we construct in separation from Reality as Such. As we want to be Real and complete without crossing over the conditioned state, we render our situation contradictory and block the path to realization. By casting our desire on the world and striving to find fulfillment within it, we end up maintaining our condition and turning life into an impasse. For, as our world is made up of a multiplicity of limited, separate, individual objects, when our deepest desire is cast on them, it becomes split into a multitude of corresponding desires. This multiplicity is one of the reasons our desires are never satisfied, for it prevents us from having one all-embracing desire and the Reality that corresponds to it.

Moreover, as we keep spinning our desires to create more things, becoming preoccupied with pursuing more numerous and diverse objects, we become unaware of our deepest desire and the Reality toward which it is directed. Detached from Reality and cast on the world, as our deepest desire is splintered into limitless, conflicting, contradictory desires, it creates in us an insatiable hunger for the Real. On the empirical level this hunger is manifested in the form of insatiable desires, the nonfulfillment of which causes dissatisfaction and frustration. So these latter signs indicate the limitlessness of both the desire and the Reality, which alone can satisfy it and of which it is an expression.

Furthermore, being finite, limited, and separate from both desire and Reality, the objects we pursue can give us only momentary satisfaction, so that the permanent underlying dissatisfaction is never overcome, even when the objects are attained. Since what we most deeply desire is a permanent state of satisfaction, which only a limitless reality, complete and perfect in itself, can provide, no string of momentary satisfaction or possession of limited, finite objects can create that state. For even an infinite number of finite objects can never add up to that infinite Reality but remain finite in essence.

Since we already *are* that Reality, in trying to become Real in separation from it by pursuing objects of desire, in effect, we try to be or attain something other than what IS. In effect, our striving amounts to our trying not to be Real, or not to be, while in fact wanting to be Real. Such striving render us other than and false to ourselves.

Moreover, in attempting to find satisfaction of our desires in the objects of the world, we seek substitutes for Reality. But since no substitute can turn into it, our striving succeeds in doing the very opposite of what we want. Speeding away from the very thing we want, we reap frustration and dissatisfaction and render our desires insatiable. Thus, the human paradox is that no matter what we do, we can never attain what we most deeply desire within the dualistic constructs.

This paradox can be logically explained. As we have seen, Gödel's Incompleteness Theorem, logical paradoxes, and the Law of Construction imply that any problem that originates from, is endemic to, involves the essence of, or encompasses the entire structure, cannot be resolved by any element from within but must come from a context larger than itself. A resolution that encompasses this larger context requires a still larger, self-consistent context, and so on, or else a contradiction will result. So, if being constructed or conditioned is itself the problem, it can never be resolved within any construct or conditioned state. Now, since the human paradox encompasses the entire dualistic structure and ultimately arises from being constructed and conditioned, it cannot be resolved within the dualistic or any other construct, context, form, or condition. Nothing in the human condition can resolve the problem that is the human condition itself. Its resolution can come only from a realization of the Unconditioned State of Reality as Such.

Expressing a similar view, Ken Wilber says that each person wants only Atman or the original oneness but under conditions that prevent its realization, since s/he wants it on the foundation of his/her separate, isolated selfhood. The reason is that, although the individual wants real transcendence, because it requires a death or dissolution of ego, s/he is at the same time terrified of it and resists it. Afraid of death or cancelling him/herself out in the process of realizing transcendence, says Wilber, s/he turns life into

> the fundamental dilemma: above all else, each person wants true transcendence, Atman-consciousness, and the Whole; but above all else, each person fears the loss of the separate self, the 'death' of the isolated ego or subject. All a person wants is Wholeness, but all he does is to fear and resist it (since that would entail the death of his separate self). Atman-telos vs. Atman-restraint. And there is the fundamental double bind in the face of eternity, the ultimate knot in the heart of the separate self. (3: 102)

Furthermore, Wilber says that since each person wants transcendence but does not want to let go of the separate self, his/her attempts to realize it within the dualistic structure prevent the realization and lead him/her to accept symbolic substitutes. In so doing, the individual believes and accepts the substitutes as fulfilling the wish to be the *Atman*. But since the substitutes are not the real transcendence, instead of satisfying the wish, our striving creates dissatisfaction, makes desires insatiable, and tethers us to the pursuit of substitute gratifications, while the insatiable desire continues unabated and remains the sign of our wish to be the *Atman* (3: 100-103, 167-173).

An answer to the question "How do we know that we have this desire?" should now be clear: According to experiential religion, we know it from our dissatisfaction and restlessness, from the insatiability and limitlessness of our desires, and from the fact that nothing can kill or still it. It is also clear from the experience of those who have unified their desires. For when unified, the desire is experienced as a pull from Reality as Such that accepts no substitute. It is as if when our head stops spinning from running after a thousand things, our vision becomes clear. From being fragmented, contradictory and insatiable, as our desires become unified and all-embracing, they experience the pull, which takes on the center stage of our life, pushing the substitutes to the periphery. Then we clearly see for the first time that our deepest desire and its object are one and the same. So when our head stops spinning, we feel the full force of the desire and know that nothing other than our life becoming a full embodiment and revelation of the Unconditioned can still the desire. Thus desire and dissatisfaction serve us notice that we cannot find the Self in any object, in anything other than the Self itself, since nothing other than the Self can be the permanent state of satisfaction. So long as we seek anything else, the paradox will remain. Since that is precisely what people ordinarily do, the entire human life, caught in the Wheel, turns into the paradox, the signs of which pervade the human condition.

The *Srimad Bhagavatam* expresses the paradox for Hinduism when it says, "Man struggles to find happiness and to end his misery in this world, but he never attains this goal so long as he remains within the states of his consciousness" (Prabhavananda 143-144). The reasons for this, Swami Ajaya tells us, is that the objects of this world give only momentary satisfaction in the midst of a state of dissatisfaction and restlessness, for the source of happiness does not lie in objects but in a state of mind independent of them (16-17). Since what we want is satisfaction as a state of being, we can never gain it from any object. For all objects remain separate from and cannot become part of consciousness (or separate subjectivity) or turn into the Self (or pure Subjectivity), the very nature of which is satisfaction and from which satisfaction arises as our essential nature. Thus, as the state of satisfaction we want is infinite, it can arise only from the Self that is infinite. Since no object can ever be the infinite state, nothing other than the Self can be the Being which constitutes the state of satisfaction or complete happiness. Moreover, being relative, all objects and relationships remain other than or separate from, and so can never turn into the identity or subjectivity that is Reality as Such. So, not only are they incapable of providing the satisfaction that constitutes our identity, they also prevent us from seeing the real satisfaction we nevertheless desire through all substitute gratifications.

For the same reason, real satisfaction cannot be attained in any relative state of consciousness, but must be in the Awareness that is identical with Reality as Such and constitutes our essential identity. In other words, such satisfaction is possible only in the Unconditioned State of Reality, Awareness, and Self. Thus when we cast our desire toward the object world in the hope of finding such happiness, we get caught in the paradox, with the result that our desires become insatiable without finding any lasting satisfaction.

Buddhism clearly expresses the paradox in "The Buddha's Pity," which says that caught in its net, everything we do yields the opposite of what we intend. Instead of freeing us, all our actions, desires, and strivings bind us to our world.

Pointing out how these strivings cause suffering, the text says that the Buddha "saw the men of the world ploughing their fields, sowing the seed, trafficking, huckstering, buying and selling; and at the end winning nothing but bitterness." Our daily activities, prompted by the desire for gain, yields pain and frustration. When we try to disentangle ourselves from them, we create further *dukkha:* "Eager to escape sorrow, man rushes into sorrow, from desire of happiness he blindly slays his own happiness, enemy to himself; he hungers for happiness and suffers manifold pains." This is because "though they longed for happiness, they made for themselves no *karma* of happiness; though they hated pain, they willingly made for themselves a *karma* of pain" (Burtt 135, 240-241).

In Taoism, Chuang Tzu shows an acute sense of this paradox, which forms the crux of his writings. He observes, for instance, that the world values money, reputation, achievement, long life. When people find that they lack these things, they go into a panic or fall into despair. They become so concerned for their life that their anxiety makes life unbearable, even when they have what they think they want. Craving enjoyment, people make themselves unhappy. The rich make life intolerable by driving themselves to get more and more and in so doing alienate themselves and make it impossible to find the very satisfaction they crave. The ambitious drive themselves after honors, but in the process become filled with anxiety about the success of their plans and exhaust their real life in service of shadows created by their insatiable desire. Afraid of death and attempting to grab life, those who desire long life miss real life by becoming absent from the here-now and falling into the very death they sought to avoid. Summing up the matter, Chuang Tzu says, "The birth of a man is the birth of his sorrows" (Merton 2: 99-100).

In the Old Testament, the most clear expression of the paradox is to be found in Qoheleth. In expressions strikingly similar to those of the Buddha and Chaung Tzu, the author says that he saw a lonely man toiling endlessly and, never satisfied with his wealth, denying himself the good things of life in the process (Qoh. 4: 7-8). So he concludes: "The man who loves money can never have enough, and the man who is in love with great wealth enjoys no return from it" (Qoh. 5:10).

In the New Testament St. Paul neatly expresses the paradox in his observation of a contradiction in the human will: As humans repress their desire for the true Self and project their refracted desires on the plane of the object-world, they become caught in a paradox which leads them to do the very opposite of what they desire. This causes an impasse and paralysis of will. As a result, they become powerless to do anything effective toward their real fulfillment.

Stating the paradox for the Sufis, Rumi says, "Mankind has an unfulfillment, a desire that he struggles to fulfill through all kinds of enterprises and ambitions"

(Shah 3: 137). Rumi is implying that humans' attempt to fulfill their deepest desire by pursuing objects of the world remains unrealized because, as Idries Shah points out, our endless desires are not the real one, which is shown by the fact that when objects are attained, our yearning is not stilled (3: 140). As long as this situation prevails—it will do so as long as there is ego—we cannot find ultimate fulfillment. Our life will continue to be one of longing and resistance to the Reality longed for, with the result that our life-project will turn into the paradox and impasse.

Nonreligious sources, too, have noticed the paradox. With a keen eye like that of Chunag Tzu, whose stories have inspired his own observations, sociologist Philip Slater states that society is riddled with paradox. He points out how, in search of security, we have become caught in a deadly arms race and have piled up weapons capable of destroying all human life on the globe, thereby making the world more insecure. In fear we create instruments that ensure and perpetuate our fears, for our creations are materializations of our fears and fantasies. As for control, he says that the more we attempt to control our environment, e.g., with pesticides, the more it gets out of control in terms of pollution and the havoc it causes to our health. The attempt to solve problems through technology aggravates them. Instead of solving the original problem, technology creates further problems so that soon we find ourselves attempting to solve problems created by technology as it attempted to solve the original problem. Thus our solution itself turns into a problem. As we spin away from the original problem, we lose touch with the environment and increasingly come to deal with our own constructs, which now begin to dictate our decisions. Thus the controller becomes the controlled, and the control gets out of hand. This inability to solve problems makes us feel powerless, which in turn prompts us to give the control of our lives over to technology. The frustration generated by our inability to control our own lives increases our passivity and the desire to hand over the decisions affecting our life to the power elite, who themselves look to technology for solutions. Thus our life comes full circle to the paradox and impasse (2: 9-11).

The paradox affects our thought, feeling, behavior, and entire way of life. As Ken Keyes observes, "Almost every way we were taught to work toward happiness only reinforces the feelings and activities that make us unhappy" (2: 21). In trying to change people and situations to fit our ideas of happiness and how things should be, we wind up confirming our original condition of unhappiness as we move away from what could give us the permanent state of happiness.

As for the self, everything it is and does reveals the paradox. Take, for instance, the paradox of survival and defense. In a real sense, ego is nothing but a mass of defenses, since it is only by setting up defenses and boundaries that the separate self-sense can be created and maintained. In attempting to create an identity by becoming cut off from reality, ego sees survival in terms of maintaining the separation from others and the world. However, this makes it feel isolated, alienated, lonely. But the attempt to escape these states by immersing itself in various diversions and pursuits aggravates its condition. To escape the isolation and emptiness of this survival game, ego may take to aggression or withdrawal, indifference or cynicism, thus ensuring the initial condition and threatening survival.

The same is true of ego's desire for privacy and exclusivity, since to be a self is to have something to hide. As the ego seeks more and more privacy, it finds less and less of it, for everyone gets into the same act. On the other hand, when it does get it, the ego feels alienated and lonely as it becomes separated from healing contact with others. As a result, the ego becomes more and more abrasive, restless, competitive, resentful, and angry. To overcome this predicament, it creates a world in which its relationships become correspondingly hostile, abrasive, fitful, sporadic, transient, shallow, and unsatisfying. So its action reinforces and traps it in the very condition to escape which it acted in the first place (Slater 1: 7ff.).

Our effort to find self-confirmation and enhancement yields the same paradoxical result. As Ken Wilber observes, "Looking for Wholeness in ways that prevent it, the individual is driven to create ever tighter and narrower and more restricted modes of identity" (3: 173). The drive to find an identity and self-worth feeds our insecurity. The more insecure we feel, the more we try to have our identity confirmed and enhanced by attempting to make people and situations confirm our idea of who we are. But this generates further insecurity and anxiety as we become unsure of people's reactions or as our attempts to control them backfire. Moreover, as our sense of self erodes, we seek ways to confirm it. But since in so doing, we project our insecurity, anxiety, and negative self-image, to which others react with avoidance, indifference, dissociation, manipulation, or hostility, our efforts accelerate the very erosion they seek to halt. Thus we become caught in the grid of repetition-compulsion or *karma,* bondage, and the Wheel of Life.

Thus in attempting to find fulfillment in the world by satisfying our desires, while simultaneously keeping ourselves separate from it, we invariably get caught in the paradox, like Ludwig Wittgenstein's "fly in the fly-bottle." Once in the bottle, we feel trapped and want to get out. First feeling restless, then angry, at outside forces which, we believe, put us there, again and again we bang our head against the bottle. Then feeling dizzy, we go in circles. Unable to get out, we withdraw into a corner, and in moments of rest devise various avenues of escape. But all our strategies take us full circle to the paradox and impasse of life.

As the self is, so is the culture. Cultures that regard the self as the highest value believe that the self is free and is neither imprisoned nor going in circles, but is making progress and is the master of its own fate. In such a situation the desire for mastery, power, domination, control, and manipulation of both oneself and the environment becomes the driving energy of culture. And this drive keeps the self going round and round. In cultures that do not have such beliefs the self has no such drive to change; it is carried along by its own inertia and confusion. Seeing the unreality of its bottled-up world and feeling no desire to change it, the ego seeks a purely mental escape. In the end, the culture as a whole remains bottled up and is far worse off in its poverty, misery, and human degradation. In this case, then, descending to the bottom, the fly just goes round and round, very much in the animal state, like a mule in a stupor, blinded by unawareness, plunged in delusion and self-deception, and driven by greed, craving, aversion, or inertia. It feels no need for improvement; no need to make the bottle comfortable or spacious or to try to overcome the problems that being bottled up creates. In either case, however, life remains trapped in the impasse and the paradox stays intact.

In spite of the fact that all our efforts to escape fail and must fail, there would not be the paradox were the desire to escape not an expression of the desire to be Real. And there would be no such desire if there were no reality that could satisfy it. The fact, however, is that the split mind and the consequent repression cause the desire to descend and become part of the unconscious from where it pushes to emerge to the conscious level. On this level the desire for Reality as Such is felt as a threat and repressed. Because of this it comes out in the form of a longing for liberation or completeness on the one hand, and on the other hand, the experience of the insufficiency of conditioned existence, with its attendant consequences. But we become afraid of chaos, death, and nothingness, of the impossibility of maintaining our present way of life if we allow this desire to dominate our conscious state. So we repress and deny its reality; we regard it as unreal, illusory, escapist, or neurotic to want or long for something outside our reality-construct; or to consider it mature, adult, tough, realistic, or modern to deny both the desire and the Reality. This attitude is regarded as the mark of the hero. It is also the source of man's tragic condition.

If we did not seek Reality, if our whole being did not long for it in its limitless, unconditioned state, if there were no such Reality, and if we were not that already "from the beginningless beginning," then our situation would not be so tragic. We could then say that the desire for it is escapist and the attempt to escape the desire by pursuing the above-mentioned strategies realistic. Then, tragic as our condition would still be, we could come to terms with and adjust to it. Such a scheme would certainly not resolve our condition but would make life "livable." Besides, we could then continue with our accustomed rationalization that our conflicts and suffering are a natural, necessary, or inescapable part of life; or that this makes life interesting, challenging, exciting, serious, and zestful. Or we could claim that conflict and suffering are necessary because without them, as Aldous Huxley remarked, there would be no art or literature. Such strategies would not carry life beyond the oblivion of time but would make it "bearable."

The fact remains, however, that encompassing all is the All which manifests itself as the deepest desire in human being to be the All so that in each the All can fully BE and manifest itself in Being and thus return to itself. The core of the tragedy is that we try to find ultimate fulfillment, which is necessarily transpersonal, within the limits of the personal. So our life remains bound, limited, meager, paltry, superficial, unsatisfactory. Our unconditioned nature, however, knows nothing of these states because it is limitless and complete, absolutely free, pure awareness and joy. Try as we may, we cannot cut out, rip apart, or root out our deepest desire, since it arises from the illimitable depth of our unfathomable nature. Nothing can kill or still this desire. No substitute can satisfy it. And so long as we seek its realization among objects of our world, nothing can stop us from wanting that fulfillment which is always just out of reach.

So we have come full circle to the fundamental paradox that sums up our condition, points to its causes, and shows the final consequences of a life lived in this condition.

I should emphasize that, if you wish to take the path of experiential religion, you must come to a direct experience of the fundamental paradox, ego as a contradiction, human existence as an impasse, and the futility of all your attempts to free yourself as long as you remain bound to your condition, consciousness, world and self. Only when this experience becomes a palpable reality in your life will you be ready to take the next step that makes up the heart of experiential religion. In that experience the final option of life opens up before you.

Part III

The Way Beyond the Oblivion of Time

Unless a man is born over again,
He cannot see the kingdom of God.

- Jesus, *The Gospel According to John*

Chapter 13
The Failure of Other Approaches

If the human condition, its causes, and consequences are indeed as I have depicted thus far, then what options are available to us? Is there any way that we can go beyond the oblivion that is the fate of us all if we remain within our constructions of reality, consciousness, and self? Is there a way that we can transcend conditioned existence and attain liberation or the absolute freedom of the Unconditioned? Or must we conclude that the desire for and belief in liberation is the great illusion, a projection of a consciousness unable or unwilling to face death and oblivion? Must we conclude that our deepest desire has to remain forever unrealized and that to do so is essential to being human, to keeping us alive and going? Or is there a way beyond the present condition, beyond the contradiction and the paradox—a way that denies nothing, is separate from nothing, and so includes everything? If so, how is it possible? How can we realize what we most deeply desire and so fulfill the purpose of existence? And in what does this realization consist? Running through and overshadowing all others, these are the central questions that face us now as they face every human being in his/her journey through time. The third step of awakening, making up the axis of experiential religion, consists in providing an answer to such questions.

To the first question—the options available—there are essentially three types of answers.

The first type denies the possibility of liberation and tries to adjust human beings to their situation by offering a variety of ways to mute the pain and despair of separation and bondage. The answers that fall within this type are almost as wide and diverse as are the ways in which people ordinarily live—from the semi-lives of the starved millions throughout the world to those who, being scarcely aware of their condition, succumb to compromises by which they descend to the adult world. Discovering that none of the strategies removes their condition, some may lower their expectations, adjust life goals to lower heights, and come to terms with life as they find it, which means succumbing to compromises — that bane of adulthood — becoming "realistic." Settling down to their bottled-up condition, they no longer want to escape, and slowly give up their desires and dreams. They limit themselves to the reality of the bottle or everyday life and just plod along, earning a living, raising a family, and settling down to the little joys and sorrows of life. Doing what is expected, they diverge little from the pattern set earlier when they were alive. They may fill their lives with various activities and experiences, diversions, and entertainment. Or they lose themselves in various roles in work, career, success, achievement, wealth, status, marriage, parenthood, relationships, or just keeping busy. Like Billy Pilgrim in Vonnegut's *Slaughterhouse Five,* "remembering the good and forgetting the bad," they may look for a fantasy escape. Or they may attempt to blot out the undertow of the feeling of being trapped, of having been passed by, by escaping to pessimism, cynicism, or despair. They continue to live with the gnawing feeling of unease, with the incipient cloud of the sadness of not having lived or of being the living dead. They may express their dis-ease with a vacant, listless, faraway look; with a bent body, a short step, and the unsure stride of one unopen to life.

Into this category also fall those psychotherapists and psychiatrists who seek to adjust people to their world by making them normal, functioning units of society. As Freud has argued in *Civilization and Its Discontents,* this attempt does not resolve the contradiction, paradox, and impasse that encompass the human condition.

While admitting the possibility of liberation, the second type of people believes that it can be attained by changing either the external circumstances or the internal programming. Those who advocate changing circumstances attempt to resolve human problems by either reforming or overthrowing the established order. The reformers throw themselves into various causes: fighting for justice, equality, and peace, and fighting against hunger, poverty, and human degradation. The others attempt to establish a new order through revolution. Neither brings liberation. Reform treats only symptoms but does not eliminate the causes that produce the ills of society. And revolution fails to see that *no* system or construct within the dualistic framework can liberate human beings but can only create further bondage.

Seeing the futility of ordinary ways of life, some people may rebel against their condition and struggle heroically to make life meaningful, knowing that it, too, will be futile in the end; yet seeing in this struggle, as did Camus, human dignity and a measure of meaning. Or, like Thomas Wolfe and Dylan Thomas, they may just "rage against the dying of the light" and "the approaching darkness." Or they may attempt to go on living (as Nietzsche said was the condition of modern man) by the unsteady, flickering, fitful flames of their own lives without any meaning, purpose, or direction save what their own creations can provide. Such creations, however, bring no real change in their condition.

The attempt to free ourselves by changing our programming has an initial similarity with experiential religion. One such approach is psychotherapy. In enabling us to face our situation, to see the neurotic games we play, to see the source of our bondage and how we cause and maintain our condition, and in helping us to disidentify, psychotherapy performs essentially the same task as the first two steps of experiential religion. As Arthur Deikman observes, "The activity of Western psychotherapy holds up a mirror to the patient's mind, showing him his mental life. In the process, he disidentifies" (1: 69). Thus psychotherapy and humanistic psychology help us attain a unity of body and mind, and perform a necessary and important, but intermediate, task of preparing us for liberation. As Deikman says again, "A second-level school is needed, to learn what you have never tried to know: the process of your thought, the way you lie and hide, and what is hidden — the secret workings of your fantasies, the forms of your fears" (1: 67). For many, this second-level school is necessary for integrating a fragmented life and developing a healthy, strong, self-trusting and mature ego, since only such an ego can take the next crucial step of experiential religion, or what Deikman calls "the third-level school." So the central task of the second-level school at the personal level is to prepare us for the third or transpersonal stage of growth. In Ken Wilber's phrase, its task is "to prepare a self strong enough to die" (3: 147).

Essentially the same is to be said of Arica, EST, Ken Keyes' "Living Love" method, TM, Subud, 3HO, Rajneesh, the Hare Krishna Movement, the New Age movement, and many others. Such movements have sprung up like mushrooms in the humid soil of human longing, left unsatisfied by our modern scientific (positivistic) world view. Insofar as they help us see our own programming and reprogram ourselves, these movements prepare the way for liberation. However, they themselves are incapable of liberating anyone. Thus the "enlightenment" EST offered was an insight into our programming, an experience that "we are a machine, that life is a game, and that ego is a point of view caught up in the game of its own survival" (Adam Smith 273, 276). Knowing that, we were to "create a space" or reprogram ourselves so that we could "change the quality of our experience," that is, we could play the game more smoothly, with less hassle or hang-up and greater enjoyment. For, as the EST instructors told you, if you attended a "guest seminar," or hard-sell, "You are now in a small box, feeling claustrophobic, paranoid, strung up in your games, and going crazy. EST will help you expand your box, create a space, and give you room to breathe so you can change the quality of your experience." This meant, however, you still remained in your box or bottle, still in your fixations, still caught up in playing games *(maya)*. The difference was that you now had learned to reprogram and so your box was more spacious, your fixations were looser, and your games more enjoyable. EST had no way of showing you how to get out of the programmed, boxed-up condition altogether.

Similarly, Ken Keyes first shows how we make ourselves unhappy through addictive programming. And so long as we continue to act to satisfy our addictions, we continue to suffer. Then he argues that since our problem does not lie in something outside but wholly in our addictive programming, the way we can be happy is by upleveling our programming from addictions to preferences. To accomplish this, he offers us a method of "twelve pathways," which basically consists in repeating counter-instructions to our mind or "bio-computer" whenever it triggers an addictive demand, until the new programming replaces the old.

While such methods can produce the aforementioned results, what Deikman says about the limits of psychotherapy applies to them also: They are incapable of taking us beyond programming and so are incapable of liberating us from bondage to constructs or overcoming separation from what is. The reason is that, as Daniel Goleman points out, they take mental contents and processes as factual and attempt to change the impact of the contents on the present, to break the hold of past conditioning on present behavior. They do not attempt to break free of conditioning by deconstructing and transcending ordinary consciousness (1: 172-174). Moreover, as Deikman remarks, they stand "on a plane whose basic dimension is the separate self. Discontent arises from that separate self, but the solution cannot be found because the ground of the separate self on which the therapist stands is not open to challenge" (1: 77). Since the separate self is itself the problem and the source of bondage, any method that does not enable us to transcend it is unable to lead us to liberation.

The third type of answer, which is essentially that of experiential religion, says that liberation is possible and that it does not consist in trying to change our outside conditions or getting us out of one type of programming into another, but out of all programmings and constructs. So long as we remain bound to constructs or programming and separated from what is, no liberation is possible. This answer, then, proceeds to show us how we can undo the process of our imprisonment and find a way beyond.

This third type rests on the premises of experiential religion outlined in Part II. While Part II was concerned with expounding the first few premises, Part III will concentrate on the rest.

Accordingly, this Part will consist in showing that liberation is not a pipe dream, a wild and crazy idea, a pie in the sky that you get when you die. Rather, it consists in directly seeing its possibility in the here-now. Indeed, it argues that it is already a reality right at this very moment so that it can be realized only in the here-now. Hence it is not something reserved for a select few, but is open to *you* and to everyone else; and this realization does not take you out of this world and its concerns but immerses you in the very center of life itself.

With this third, pivotal step of awakening, experiential religion parts company with other fields. It claims not only that constructs other than the existing ones are possible but that it is possible to go beyond all constructs. It claims that liberation consists in nothing less than this transcendence and in the realization of the Unconditioned State of Reality as Such. In claiming this, experiential religion also parts company with those who, while taking this claim seriously, regard this State as another construct. The claim of experiential religion, on the contrary, is that Reality as Such is beyond all programming, conditions, and constructs, none of which can ever enable anyone to arrive at it. What it is and in what its realization consists is the subject matter of Part III.

Accordingly, this step has three essential aspects: knowing how you can stop creating and maintaining your condition and break free of all conditioning and constructs; knowing in what a realization of the Unconditioned State consists; and knowing how you can live from this liberated state. Although these aspects will be presented separately in nine steps, no suggestion is thereby made that they have to be practiced or attained successively, or in the order in which they are here presented.

You will notice that each of these aspects represents the very opposite of a characteristic of the human condition and what causes and maintains it. For liberation consists in nothing less than doing the very opposite of the process whereby we create and bind ourselves to our constructs and thus create our condition. Once we know the process by which we become bound, we can take steps to become unbound. Essentially this consists in ungluing ourselves or breaking free and going beyond conditioning and constructs.

Since you become separated from Reality through creating the dualistic structure and becoming bound by identifying and attaching to it, it is obvious that the first essential step (not chronologically) is to disidentify and let go of it. This step, which makes transcendence possible, is called nonattachment.

Since, once separated and bound, desire reinforces and maintains our condition, a second necessary step—desiringlessness—is concerned with freeing us from desire and desiringness.

A third aspect is concerned with directly breaking free of programming and constructs by emptying the mind of thoughts and the inner dialogue that maintains the dualistic framework. Hence this aspect — emptying the mind — is the direct path to transcendence. What the mind is emptied of is its contents or the object-world, which controls and maintains the dualistic structure through providing sensory stimuli and producing thoughts or inner dialogue. So it must be stopped and transcended. Hence "stopping the world."

A final step in the process of undoing your imprisonment concerns "the Guardian of Duality," which must be slain or transcended; otherwise no liberation is possible. This aspect is therefore called "leaving the self behind."

Once you step into the process of undoing your imprisonment, you begin to see the Reality in which liberation consist. After exploring the above steps, therefore, I shall turn to a discussion of the nature of Reality as Such or the true Self; the experience or state in which it is realized; the Awareness in which you realize it; and the state of complete realization in which liberation is found. A final chapter will discuss the consequences of liberation in relationship to others and the world.

Chapter 14
Nonattachment

The term *nonattachment* is apt to conjure up visions of yogis lying on beds of thorns, going semi-naked, practicing extreme forms of fasting, or living in caves. Or it is likely to be confused with self-denial or giving up external things or activities, like meat, sex, or smoking. Although such prohibitions or behavioral restrictions are enjoined in many traditions as part of the training in nonattachment, nevertheless, without their becoming a way of cutting the psychological roots of craving and fixation, by themselves such practices are worse than useless, for several reasons.

One is that, instead of making us stop craving, such restrictions may actually increase it. That would make us worse off than before. Thus, while fasting, we may become preoccupied with thinking about food and long for the period to be over so we can go and gorge ourselves. Moreover, self-denial may create self-deception by making us believe that we are doing something holy, virtuous, or meritorious. Or we may conclude that we are better than others, when in fact we are feeding our ego. Or we may become attached to our point of view or become filled with pride in our superiority or accomplishment.

Furthermore, since no problem is outside our mind, giving up external things or activities may create the delusion that we are licking the cause of our problem, when in fact, we may be giving up one addiction but developing another, even worse one. That is why don Juan calls self-denial an indulgence. Chuang Tzu points out that self-sacrificing martyrdom is useless in making us happy. And the *Bhagavad Gita* observes that the abstinent run away from objects but carry their desires with them wherever they go (Prabhavananda & Isherwood 1: 42). Since attachment is in the mind, not in things, we carry it along with us wherever we are; and it may appear in stronger forms when we are deprived of gratification. Self-denial may also create self-deception by making us believe that we are free of desire or have uprooted craving, whereas the truth is that, as the Buddha found, it does not bring enlightenment or liberation from suffering.

Realizing this fact, as Edward Hoffman points out, the Kabbalah does not view "asceticism as a virtue in itself, but only as a path toward a greater goal" (97). For this reason Kabbalistic training in nonattachment consists in both prohibitions of certain behavior and development of psychological states through such ascetical practices as fasting and exposure of the body to extremes of temperature. Such practices are meant to be a preparation for purifying the body and developing mental control over the physical or for destructuring consciousness (97).

A similar situation has prevailed among Christian ascetics who have tended to view nonattachment in terms of self-denial or behavioral restrictions, such as fasting, abstinence from meat or sex, various ways of "mortifying the flesh" or bringing emotions under control, and practicing silence and solitude. Admittedly, in many cases their original aim has been forgotten and the practices have come to be seen as virtuous in themselves. Some of the practices may even have verged on neurotic self-torture. Nevertheless, originally they had been part of the path of purification, of removing mental and emotional fixations or negative programmings, and gaining control over body and mind.

For the same reasons nonattachment must not be confused with detachment, renunciation, or withdrawal from the world, although these terms are sometimes used interchangeably by the sources of experiential religion. For since the world is not anything outside the mind, it is illusory to try to withdraw by removing ourselves from the external conditions of life. In reality the only withdrawal from reality or the world possible is by becoming fixated on some construct or programming through attachment. To the extent there is attachment, to that extent there is withdrawal (which means we are ordinarily withdrawn from reality as it is). But since attachment is only in the mind, withdrawal is a purely mental escape. The opposite of this state is nonattachment, which removes our ordinary withdrawal or avoiding tendency so that we may come to a direct experience of reality.

This is a lesson which the warrior Arjuna learns in the crucible of life. In the *Gita*, Krishna tells Arjuna that since he is no other than the world and ceasing to act is itself a mode of action, it would be illusory to try to withdraw from the world or to stop acting. For, as Ramana Maharshi explains, if the world existed apart from us, we could possibly withdraw. But since it is in our mind or owes its existence to our thought, as long as the thought is not stilled and the mind emptied, it is impossible for us to be away from it (Osborne 78-92). Any attempt to escape will result in another attachment, which will bind us further to the Wheel. The question is not, therefore, whether we should withdraw or act, but whether we should act to create more bondage or free ourselves through nonattachment. And it is this latter course of action that Krishna urges Arjuna to take by revealing to him the secret of nonattached action—action that does not create but frees us from bondage.

The Sufis adopt a similar stance. Although for the early Sufis nonattachment meant, according to Annemarie Schimmel, the prohibition of certain behavior—some purely external—and withdrawal from the world (110-111), this is not how most later Sufis have understood it. Contemporary Sufism views such practices as temporary measures, assigned as needed during the formative period. It provides a context for training and the development of certain states of consciousness, removing the barriers that ordinarily impede the adept's self-growth, and opening up the mind to a direct experience of reality as a whole so as to gain a new point of view and a new orientation on life. As such, nonattachment is not essentially a physical withdrawal from the world or a giving up of external things but a state of consciousness that cuts through the separation and limitation inherent in the ordinary conditions of life in order to free the Sufi to develop to the fullest the state of the Perfected Man. This is clearly stated in a conversation between Sheikh Daggash Rustam and Raphael Lefort, in which the former characterizes the latter's desire to withdraw as "a primitive attitude, useless for the requirements of the present age," and implies that real nonattachment consists in developing those skills which enable the Sufi to be in the world without being limited, defined, conditioned, or controlled by it (105).

Explaining the view that the development of the community and the destiny of creation are interwoven with the destiny of the Sufi, and hence permanent withdrawal is impossible, Idries Shah likewise observes that the Sufi may withdraw or detach himself for a period from society but ultimately he is interlinked with the eternal whole (3: 33). For the Sufi, detachment is not in itself a goal but only a part of the dynamic interchange, useful only if it enables him to attain his goal, which is Self-realization (3: 394).

The Psychological Meaning

Nonattachment, then, is neither self-denial nor withdrawal nor escape but essentially a psychological and spiritual practice. As Robert Ornstein explains, psychologically it consists in removing "normal restrictions on awareness" so as to "destructure normal consciousness" (1: 135-138). This means that it is essentially concerned with removing limitations normally placed on consciousness by unawareness, identification, mental and emotional fixations, or attachment to mental contents, programming, constructs, habits, and dualistic thinking and goal orientation. This meaning is emphasized by all major sources.

This is clear in Hinduism. Thus, in his *Yoga Sutras,* Patanjali expresses the psychological meaning when he defines nonattachment as "self-mastery; it is freedom from desire for what is seen and heard" (Prabhavananda and Isherwood 2: 19). For the *Ashtavakra Gita,* nonattachment is not indifference nor suppression of our natural feelings but freeing ourselves from desire and emotional fixations, especially involved in seeking pleasure and avoiding pain (Johnson 121, 125).

The Buddha considered nonattachment so central to the cessation of *dukkha* or liberation that he set it down as the Third Noble Truth:

> Now this, monks, is the Noble Truth about the cessation of suffering, the cessation without a remainder of craving, the abandonment, forsaking, release, nonattachment. (Burtt 30)

For the Buddha, essential to nonattachment is complete freedom from any fixation on anything whatsoever (*Udana,* quoted by Schumann 40). On this deeper level, since we become fixated on mental contents or objects through identification and attachment, according to the Buddha, nonattachment is nothing short of disidentification with and breaking free of all fixation on every content of consciousness. When this happens, the very basis of thought and internal dialogue (which maintains the present programming and constructs and the desire to create more things to make ego real) ceases; and consciousness thereby becomes destructured (Conze et al. 45, 101). Transcending programming, objects, and constructs, awareness arrives at the Unconditioned State and becomes free of bondage, separation, and limitation. Thereupon *dukkha* entirely ceases (Burtt 69; DeBary 69). Thus nonattachment leads to a complete cessation of the causes of *dukkha* and a realization of the Unconditioned State, signified by *Nirvana.* For this reason, far from removing anyone from reality, for the Buddha, nonattachment clears from the deck of our mind everything that creates a sense of separation and enables us to directly experience Reality as Such.

Far from viewing nonattachment in terms of behavioral restrictions — he broke many of them — Jesus saw it solely in psychological and spiritual terms. As he once said, "A man is not defiled by what goes into his mouth, but by what comes out of it" (Matt. 15: 11). It is not external things that cause negative programmings, addictions or fixations, but what is "in the heart;" that is, their roots are entirely in mental reactions. This is where they have to be uprooted. Thus mere external practices are insufficient. An inner transformation is necessary. Seen in this light, Jesus' teachings are essentially concerned with transforming and destructuring consciousness. Essentially they constitute a path of nonattachment designed to enable us to break free of programmings, habitual fixations, and limitations, and to open a pathway to Self-realization. This theme of nonattachment is as much a part of his first proclamation as that of his later teachings. Thus "repent, for the kingdom of God is within you" (Matt. 4:7) is not concerned with enjoining penance, self-denial, or giving up something external, but turning the orientation of consciousness inward, which requires breaking free of mental and emotional fixations, attachments, and external orientation of the mind. Only such a radical clearing can enable us to see the Kingdom that is already within us. To bring about this shift and inner transformation, Jesus taught nonattachment to reward and punishment (the Beatitudes), to judgments, and the like. Especially, he taught ways in which we can break free of positive and negative programmings through nonattachment.

How to break fixation on negative programmings is contained in the famous injunction of "turning the other cheek" when someone strikes us. This is, of course, not to be taken in the literal sense. Rather, it means ceasing to act as our programming dictates. When we do not hit back or, in general, react, but do something other than what our programming dictates or do something that is prompted by the true Self, we stop reinforcing our negative programming and shift the action to an altogether different plane. Without this reinforcement, the programming weakens; upon continued practice, it eventually dissolves and disappears. Moreover, as we practice nonattachment, not only do we not get caught up in the other's view of reality, we do not also reinforce that view for the other and we offer him/her an opportunity for change. So, while hitting back is "doing," ceasing to react is "not-doing," or dissolving the fixation that locks us in our present programming, thus becoming free.

On the other hand, "loving your enemies" is concerned with removing the limitations imposed by positive programming on our natural qualities. When we love only those who love us or, in general, do only those things that will confirm and enhance our identity or our idea of how things should be; when we do what we like and avoid what we dislike, our world becomes correspondingly split into dualities and limited to what or whom we care for while we become indifferent to those we do not care for. Our reality, consciousness, and self thereby become narrow, limited, unsatisfactory, and conflict-ridden. Instead of reinforcing this programming, by acting contrary to it, we can break free of these limitations and allow our natural qualities to return to their limitless, undifferentiated, natural state. This process enables us to experience the unconditioned state of perfection — the state that *is* the heavenly Father — and thus become perfect as our heavenly Father is perfect.

Similarly, the Sufis emphasize nonattachment in terms of breaking free of mental fixations and emotional blockages as a step necessary for liberation. As

Idries Shah states, "The Sufi is an individual who believes that by practicing alternate detachment and identification with life, he becomes free" (3:26). For the Sufi, nonattachment is a state of consciousness, exercised toward all things, whereby the mind becomes free of ordinary restrictions due to programming and opens to experiencing the whole directly. Hence the alternation. As a Sufi master in India explained to a Western student, through nonattachment you can become free of anxiety and other negative emotions and the accumulated burdens of culture. Since what you ordinarily do to seek relief from them binds you further to your cultural conditioning, you cannot become free through your customary behavior but, as another master advised, "only through detachment from fixed ideas and preoccupations" (Shah 3: 351, 205).

Since one of the essential ways in which dualistic consciousness maintains itself is through action oriented toward goals external to the individual or the action, another essential result of nonattachment is the freedom from habitual fixation on such goals and thus a deactivation or deconstruction of the action mode of consciousness. This does not require us to stop acting or getting involved in the world but to stop acting in such a way as to prevent the world from controlling or defining us by dictating what we should be or do. When the world sets the agenda for our life or sets our goals, it defines us and controls our behavior; and when we continue to strive for external goals according to this determination, we continue to maintain our present constructions of reality, consciousness, and self. One of the important ways to become free of the causes that maintain our condition, therefore, is nonattached action.

Realizing this truth, the *Gita* teaches that the secret of nonattached action, which forms the basis of *karma yoga,* consists in acting without external goal orientation or attachment to outcome: "renouncing the fruits" and "complete giving up of all actions which are motivated by desire" (Prabhavananda & Isherwood 1: 40, 120). Similarly, don Juan turned Krishna instructs Castaneda to act "without expecting anything in return" (3: 233). What the *Gita* means is that when we are not attached to any goal, such as the desire for gain or the fear of loss, or to action, we can become free of goal-oriented activity and the chain of desire and striving that ordinarily binds us to the action that maintains our consciousness and world. Since the desire for gain and the fear of loss, or reward and punishment, are some of the main ways in which consciousness gets dualistically programmed, whenever we act on it we reinforce and maintain this programming. But when we stop acting on it, we become free of goal-oriented action, which is, according to Deikman, a pillar that holds up the action mode of consciousness. Thus nonattached action is intended to break this programming and free consciousness from being tethered to action motivated by desire. Since the goal of nonattached action is intrinsic to itself, such action stops reinforcing the dualistic mode, cuts the root of desire, and dissolves our fixation on external goals or results. As desire stops playing back the programmed tapes, for lack of reinforcement, in time the programming ceases.

As the focus of action is shifted from external goal orientation inward, its orientation shifts from the object-pole inward toward itself and consciousness begins to be destructured. Remaining focused on consciousness, action starts to dissolve mental and emotional fixations, attachments, and negative programming, i.e., bad *karma*, and purify our motives for acting. In the absence of these factors, the fixations that create ego-identity begin to dissolve. This disidentification enables you to transcend ego. The Self becomes clear. Penetrating deeper and passing through the transconscious states, as you arrive at Self-realization, a final shift of the source and center of action from ego to the Self takes place. Then you no longer act to satisfy ego's desires or to confirm and maintain it, for at this stage ego and its desires have been transcended. Rather, centered in the Self, all your actions arise spontaneously as its manifestations. So the *Gita* declares, "To unite the heart with Brahman and then act: that is the secret of nonattached action. In the calm of self-surrender, the seers renounce the fruits of action, and so reach enlightenment" (Prabhavananda & Isherwood 1: 41). Since to unite your consciousness with *Brahman* is to realize oneness with *Brahman,* when you act from that oneness, you act as God acts; and your action becomes a saving activity toward others and the world. All your actions are prompted by the desire to reveal, and is the revelation of, *Brahman.* Thus your action becomes a revelation of God in the world. This is the heart of the *Gita's* teaching on nonattachment.

A similar teaching is to be found in Taoism, expressed in terms of *wu wei,* not-doing. As the principle of nonattached action, it is designed to destructure the action mode. This is evident from the following passage of the *Tao Te Ching:*

> The student learns by daily increment.
> The Way is gained by daily loss,
> Loss upon loss until
> At last comes rest.
> By letting go, it all gets done;
> The world is won by those who let it go!
> But when you try and try,
> The world is then beyond the winning.
> (Blakney 2: 101)

In contrast to the action mode, *wu wei,* not-doing, is not the lazy man's way of doing nothing. It is not a way of lulling ourselves to sleep but a way of waking up by undoing the action mode through removing fixations, attachments, and identifications. It is a way of bringing to a stop our usual striving to find happiness, self-worth, meaning, status, success, or achievement by satisfying our desires. When we try to win the world by striving or grasping, or have people and situations confirm our identity or self-worth according to our ideas and expectations, we lose touch with reality. When we keep interacting with own ideas, we miss the very thing we sought: our true identity. We can never attain the world or Tao in this way because our attempt creates the impossible situation of first assuming a separation and then trying to overcome it. So it is by letting go of our identification, attachment, and striving that we "win" the world by realizing our unity with it. When we stop trying to possess all, the mind-spin stops, the orientation of consciousness shifts toward the Source, and we see that we are the All and there is nothing lacking in us. The way we can realize Tao, therefore, is through the nonaction mode of "daily loss" or letting go of everything in our daily activities that could cause separation until nothing but Tao is left.

So, far from being a withdrawal from action, *wu wei* is activity without wantingness, striving, grasping, or attachment. Such action is filled with clarity and stillness, void of fixation or stagnation, a stillness that is an active, dynamic process without separation or opposition between action and goal, being and becoming. Such a stillness is the very axis of Tao, which, as Chuang Tzu declares, embraces "all things without clinging to this or that way" (Chan 206). Since the axis "passes through the center where all affirmations and denials converge" (Merton 2: 43), in this state there is no duality between action and stillness; between the not-having and striving to possess which action implies, and the having, being, or fullness which stillness connotes. When you are not driven to act, striving to attain a goal, or fixated on something, you are at rest while acting because there is no anxiety about how it will come out or whether you will reach your goal. When the goal is already in the action, you can act, not from a lack or from a craving to get something, but from the fullness of Tao and as its manifestation.

Ultimately, then, *wu wei* is action which proceeds from and is a manifestation of Tao. When consciousness shifts from the dualistic to the nondualistic mode, which is the ultimate aim of nonattachment, and actions proceed from it, they become spontaneous manifestations of what is, in response to the actualities of the present. Free of confusion, conflict, or ideas of how things should be, we are able to see how things really are and respond in terms of what is most appropriate, constructive, or helpful, instead of imposing our will or mental model on what is. Since such actions are free from programming, habituation, models or patterning of brain waves, they produce no further fixation, attachment, or identification. This is "doing without doing."

Sounding very much like a Taoist sage this time, the mercurial don Juan tells Castaneda that his entire method can be summed up as one of nonattachment or not-doing: He says, "Everything I have taught you so far is an aspect of not-doing" (2: 238). For don Juan, since "doing" is the action mode that constructs the world, not-doing is its undoing by stopping the inner dialogue that upholds that view. In not-doing, our consciousness becomes destructured, our view of the world changes, and we are able to open up a clear space in which a new view of reality can dawn. And this leads to the ultimate realization.

The Spiritual Meaning

The spiritual meaning begins with disidentification with everything with which we identify and letting go of all our attachments and fixations. Disidentification opens a way to the ultimate stages of growth, with which the spiritual meaning is concerned. In this sense, nonattachment is a way of becoming free of all limitations, which requires disidentification with the personal stage, growth through the transpersonal, and arrival at the ultimate state of Being and Awareness.

The world with which we must disidentify is our reality-construct, the objects of consciousness, attachments, identification, desires, and preoccupations. Without this disidentification, destructuring of ordinary consciousness will not occur and the transpersonal stage of growth will be impossible. Since the so-called "real world" is a result of models, forms, and patterns formed in the past that detach us from reality, by disidentifying with it we remove the barriers separating us from reality and are able to be fully present to people and situations as they are in the here-now. To the extent that we have no fixation on any construct, object or the world, to that extent we are in direct contact with things. So nonattachment is a way of being fully in the world. Insofar as it takes us out of our fixations in the past and enables us to be fully in the present, nonattachment, as Ornstein observes, leads to the development of a totally present-centered consciousness (1: 138). Since reality is always and only in the here-now, nonattachment enables us to become centered in Reality as Such.

In the spiritual sense, nonattachment pertains to the transpersonal stage of growth. In addition to destructuring consciousness and disidentifying with the world, it requires us to disidentify with ego. For, when we remain identified with ego beyond the point of its maturation, not only are we prevented from transcending our limited identity and experiencing ever fuller and more comprehensive ones, but we also condemn ourselves to eventual stagnation. Essential to the spiritual meaning, therefore, is stepping out of our present limited identity, our present suit of armor that keeps us fixated in the separate self stage and prevents us from realizing our true identity. It is for this reason that, in the ultimate sense, as Ken Wilber, Swami Rama, and others emphasize, nonattachment is an essential principle of growth from the infant to the personal and through the transpersonal to the ultimate stage.

According to Swami Rama and others, at each stage of development there is a failure of the sense of self which forces the child to let go and sets the stage for redefining the new sense of self when it emerges. Self-growth occurs through such a failure of identification and attachment, and disidentification and breaking free of the fixation on the existing structure, thus opening oneself for the emergence of the new. Then there is a need to redefine and restructure the self through identification and attachment — only to be destructured again as the definition is found inadequate, which opens the way for the emergence of the next stage. In this way "a more comprehensive grasp of oneself and the world results. With time and the accumulation of more experience, each new 'I' in turn will be found to be lacking. Its limitations must be experienced and understood. It must be relinquished for a more inclusive and less restricted identity. The course of evolution is made up of innumerable such steps" (*Yoga and Psychotherapy* 182).

Espousing a thoroughgoing evolutionary view, Ken Wilber likewise maps out in greater detail the evolution of the self from the undifferentiated unity of the preconscious state of the infant to the transpersonal state of the final unity. In this state complete nonattachment of consciousness to all previous stages and forms enables their integration in the Supreme Identity. The core of Wilber's argument is that at each major stage of development a higher-order structure emerges in consciousness and the self identifies with it. When the next higher structure emerges, the self disidentifies with the previous construct and shifts its identity to the higher. This shift enables consciousness to transcend the lower structure and operate from and integrate it into the higher. In this way you are able to integrate all previous levels in the final unity of Consciousness as such. Since development can occur only through such nonattachment or differentiation, it is the key factor in the evolution of consciousness toward the ultimate. So, for Wilber, nonattachment is synonymous with growth, development, and transcendence (3: 79-81).

Although there are grave problems with this viewpoint, the essential point for our purpose is that nonattachment is the crux of self-growth. The gravest problem in Wilber's view is the assumption that differentiation and the emergence of a new structure are automatic. On the contrary, it appears that beyond the personal stage, they can occur either spontaneously or through a conscious effort. As Erikson has shown, although the possibility of failure exists at every stage, the failure to disidentify and to arrive at the next higher stage occurs at the personal stage in every human being who becomes identified with and attached to the current stage. Such an attachment prevents one from seeing the possibility of further growth.

This situation is exacerbated by the fact that society is founded on the separate self and the dualistic structure underlying it. As a result, personhood is perceived as the highest stage of development. Having no inkling of stages beyond the separate self, society is unable to recognize the transpersonal and so fails to provide the structures, framework, support, or guidance for transpersonal growth. Consequently, individually and collectively, no further growth is sought or even believed possible, not only because the maintenance and enhancement of ego become the individual's life goal, but also because survival becomes identified with it. Fear of rejection, isolation, or ridicule drives the individual to conform to, rather than disidentify with, society's fundamental norms and beliefs.

Barring spontaneous emergence (to be discussed in a later chapter), without conscious nonattachment from the personal structure no transpersonal structures can emerge and, consequently, no transpersonal stage of growth. It is not, therefore, surprising that transpersonal stages have usually emerged through conscious disidentification with existing structures of consciousness, reality, and self.

Although it is true that, as I have said, identification and attachment are necessary for the development of a healthy personality, the continuation of each stage beyond its maturation not only prevents further growth but actually causes personal stagnation, arrested development, and dissociation from reality. For, while life moves on toward greater expansion, such attachment fixates, traps, and confines us to repeating the responses we forged when the stage first emerged. We then find ourselves cut off from the ever-transforming process of life, bound to past forms, and separated from the realities of the present. And since that separation is the source of suffering, to attach is to suffer. Thus separation and attachment become the greatest barrier to transpersonal growth.

In the ultimate, spiritual sense, then, nonattachment is a dynamic process that enables us to successively break free of limited identities and grow to the fullness of who we are. It is a principle of the unconditioned, completely open state of being—a state free from identification, fixation, or attachment to anything in particular and a realization of identity with all things. Such nonattachment is not possible without realizing the Unconditioned State. Thus nonattachment entails the state of liberation. For, by removing all identification with limited forms, fixation on programmings, and attachment to constructs, nonattachment removes the very basis of bondage and separation. Removing all otherness, it enables us to realize absolute Oneness and completeness. As everything which creates separation melts away, we arrive at the completely open space of being and awareness in which nothing remains to prevent us from being identical with all things. Then you *are* what *is*. Not to be fixated on anything is to be boundless or omnipresent; not to be identified with any form is to be formless or infinite; and not to be attached to any moment in time is to be in every moment in time or eternal. Complete nonattachment is, therefore, complete identification with God or Reality as Such, which is the fullness of Being.

For this reason, Patanjali states that the highest kind of nonattachment is the knowledge of or identification with the Self, which brings to an end any desire for anything limited (Prabhavananda & Isherwood 2: 22). The *Gita* points out how nonattachment leads to union with Brahman (Prabhavananda & Isherwood 1: 27). And, according to Ramana Maharshi, ultimate nonattachment is complete disidentification with everything other than the Self: "Renunciation is the non-identification of the Self with non-self" (Osborne 40).

Realizing that complete nonattachment entails the Unconditioned State in which there is no construct, limitation, separation, fixation, bondage, or *dukkha,* the Buddha defined *Nirvana* or liberation in terms of it and considered the two to be synonymous: "Nirvana is where it is recognized that there is nothing but what is seen of the mind itself; where there is no attachment to external object, existent and non-existent" (Burtt 163).

Following the Buddha and with the aim of realizing the ultimate spiritual state of Buddhahood, Zen masters have particularly emphasized this spiritual meaning and have characterized it as the ultimate transcendence of all limitation, condition, construct, and qualification. It entails the Supreme Identity, which is realized by breaking free of our normal fixation on dualistic thinking. Thus we find the Sixth Patriarch, Hui-neng, summing up the essence of Buddhism in terms of nonattachment:

> From ancient times up to the present, all have set up no-thought as the main doctrine, no-form as the substance, and non-abiding as the basis. Non-form is to be separated from form even when associated with form. No-thought is not to think even when involved in thought. Non-abiding is the original nature of man. (DeBary 219)

According to Hui-neng, then, nonfixation on any thought (no-thought) is the direct path to ultimate transcendence; nonfixation or nonattachment to any form (no-form) the state of formlessness or *Sunyata;* and nonattachment to any object or thing (non-abiding) is the ultimate, Unconditioned State, which is the original nature of man. Since any fixation or attachment causes duality, limitation, and bondage, complete nonattachment is both the way to ultimate transcendence of conditioned existence and realization of the Unconditioned State of Buddhahood itself. That is why for Hui-neng, complete nonattachment is the very foundation of Buddhism.

It is for this reason also that Zen master Huang Po says that a realization of the Ultimate State rests on three kinds of disidentification: the letting go of the split between body and mind, of the dualistic constructions of self and the world, and of anything that is not the Void-nature of Reality. As this letting go removes all fixations and limitations, and enables us to arrive at the Void-nature itself, he instructs us to avoid attachment to anything:

> If you students of the Way wish to become Buddhas you need study no doctrines whatever, but learn only how to avoid seeking for and attaching yourself to anything. Where nothing is sought this implies Mind unborn; where no attachment exists, this implies Mind not destroyed; and that which is neither born nor destroyed is the Buddha. (Blofeld 1: 40)

Where there is no striving or attachment, no conditioning, construct, separation, or bondage is created. In such a state, nothing comes into being or passes away, so that the mind remains in its original, eternal, uncreated, unconditioned state of Buddhahood. Similarly, Huang Po's disciple master Lin-chi teaches that complete nonattachment is the absolutely pure, nonconditioned state of Buddhahood (De Bary 226-228). And, for master Takuan, it constitutes the ultimate state in which the mind is absolutely free from any fixation or limitation, and so is infinite and omnipresent, for "not fixed anywhere, the mind is everywhere" (De Bary 378). Void of any space-time coordinates, the mind returns to the state of infinity and omnipresence. Thus nonattachment is both the way and the state of completeness or Buddhahood.

According to Roshi Seung Sahn, this state is the 360-degree turn in which there is no attachment to anything, and so nothing can limit, bind, or condition you, and consequently no new attachment or fixation on anything is created. In this ultimate state you are, as the *Tao Te Ching* puts it, like "a good runner who leaves no tracks" (Blakney 2: 79). Meister Eckhart calls it the divine state of "pure disinterest" (Blakney 1: 21). According to Zen master Hakuin, in this state there is "neither attachment nor nonattachment nor detachment nor withdrawal," but being unconditioned, you live in the midst of conditioned existence without being fixated on (since there is nothing other than you), apart from (since there is no attachment), or a part of (for there is no otherness), anything. You live immersed in the conditioned world without being programmed, controlled, ruled, or limited by it, "like the waterfowl whose wings do not get wet even when submerged in water" (DeBary 391).

Similarly, according to Chuang Tzu, through nonattachment or not-doing you return to the primordial state of Nature (Chan 205). Being free from fixation on anything, in this state you are in complete unity with all things, and, transcending all duality and limitation, you travel in a "transcendental world...without any attachment" (Chan 206). With all hindrance, barrier, fixation, and separation having dissolved, you live, as the Buddha said, like a lotus in the mire, or muddy water, as expressed in the following Zen story:

> Tanzan and Ekido were once travelling together down a muddy road. A heavy rain was still falling. Coming around a bend, they met a lovely girl in a silk kimono and sash, unable to cross the intersection. "Come on, girl," said Tanzan at once. Lifting her in his arms, he carried her over the mud.
> Ekido did not speak again until that night when they reached a lodging temple. Then he no longer could restrain himself. "We monks don't go near females," he told Tanzan, "especially not young and lovely ones. It is dangerous. Why did you do that?" "I left the girl there," said Tanzan. "Are you still carrying her?" (Reps 18)

The title of the story, "Muddy Road," implies that in ordinary life we get muddied or confused through identification, attachment, or mental and emotional fixation. We become loaded down with the burdens of stress, anxiety, fear, tension, pressure, depression, frustration. Depending on the importance we place on them and the degree to which we are attached to them, we carry these burdens wherever we go. As we become completely nonattached, these burdens fall away; and we are able to walk the muddy road of ordinary life and do things we previously did without any of the mud or conditioning, burden, conflict, or problem clinging to us. Thus being free of their shaping influence and limiting conditions, we are able to see things just they are and, consequently, can respond to the needs of each situation without reacting.

Nonattachment does not, however, turn us into jellyfish. Spineless behavior follows from our attachment to being nice to people, from a self-concept that says that we have to say "yes" even when we want to say "no" — for fear of going contrary to our self-image as a nice person, losing others' good opinion, friendship or respect, or meeting their disapproval, rejection, or dislike. Such a stance is the very opposite of nonattachment which, by removing addictions, frees us from the fear of the opinion of others and anything else that could compel us to submit to others' manipulation. With nothing to cloud our vision, nonattachment enables us to see through people's games. Free of addictive interference, we are able to respond from the depth of ourselves and in the most constructive or helpful way to people's real needs instead of getting caught up in their manipulative needs and games. Thus, nonattachment frees us from any need to depend on or be subservient to others or let them run our life. Having no addiction in ourselves, we then become, as Ornstein puts it, a mirror in which others' manipulative games are exposed for what they are.

Nor is nonattachment an uncaring, unfeeling, or unloving attitude, as is sometimes thought. As the Zen story above indicates, nonattachment consists in caring, desiring, loving, and acting without being attached to any of these qualities. To love, care, or do anything that needs to be done but not to be attached to loving, caring, or any activity or its object—that is the secret of nonattachment. Such a state of being makes one fluid, spontaneous, open, and ever ready to respond to the realities of the present.

It should be clear by now why nonattachment is a central and all-pervasive principle of experiential religion, one without which liberation is not possible and which, when fully realized, brings complete liberation, but which cannot be fully practiced without being liberated. So central and pervasive is nonattachment that all other aspects of the third step can be seen as its various expressions. Hence the great emphasis placed on it by the sources of experiential religion.

Chapter 15
Desiringlessness

I have explained that we perpetuate our separation from what is and our entrapment in a world of our own making and that we cannot stop reinforcing and maintaining our condition by trying to satisfy our desires. To overcome our separation, therefore, we need to cut our desires off at their roots and transform and integrate their energies from the transpersonal levels. Hence the importance of desiringlessness as an essential aspect of experiential religion.

The term *desiringlessness* is apt to be misunderstood. Not only does it appear ungrammatical, but the idea of a state free of desire seems to go against the way our world is set up and the way we function, individually and collectively. So, in disbelief, panic, or bewilderment you may ask, "Does the term imply repression or sublimation of desire?" "How is it possible to get rid of all desire?" "How can I go on living without any desire?" "Would not life lose its meaning without any desire?" "What would the world be like without any desire?" "What's the use of giving up all desire?" Such questions rush out in torrents to stave off the thought of a life without desire and to keep your world the way it is. For the very basis of our idea of fulfillment and happiness is the satisfaction of desires—a course on which every life is set from infancy.

To begin with, as the *Bhagavad Gita* clearly indicates, desiringlessness does not consist in destroying, controlling, repressing, or sublimating our desires. Such strategies are useless, since they not only reinforce and maintain desires but also distort them, thereby giving rise to split mind, conflict, confusion, and destructive behavior. And certainly, they do little to help us to transcend them. As long as our desires remain, we take them with us wherever we go and whatever we do, creating a world riddled with conflict, contradiction, frustration, dissatisfaction, and further desiringness.

Rather, what the *Gita* teaches is the elimination of the very source of desire, so that with the source removed, the desires undergo a transformation, or they disappear. This does not require an elimination of all desire—if that were possible—but uprooting the craving and restlessness that arise from the feeling of a lack, and ultimately from the separation from Reality. It consists in removing the clamor and the panic that drive us to want something. Thus what ceases is the craving that gives rise to the drive and the compulsion that make us identify with our desires and their satisfaction as the way to find identity, meaning, and realization of life's purpose. When we dissolve our fixation, break free of our attachment, and stop striving to satisfy our desires, not only do the objects of striving drop off, but so does the striving itself. With that the entire cycle of wanting and striving comes to an end. Then nothing can make us turn the Wheel of Life and maintain our condition. We are thereby off the Wheel and free of our condition.

Furthermore, since desiringness arises from and is rooted in ego, desiringlessness requires the cessation of ego's striving to be real and complete as a separate center of being and consciousness. As long as desire persists, there will be desiringness, ego, and its longing and striving to be real and complete; and we will not be our true Self. We will feel a lack and try to fill it with possessions, power, status, success, achievement, relationships, and experiences. The state of desiringlessness involves not only the realization that no object can satisfy us and make us complete or Real, it also entails seeing the futility of striving and dropping the struggle. Unless all striving, even the striving not to strive, stops completely, the latter striving itself will become another object of striving. Then we will be tethered to its circuit and continue to turn the Wheel and maintain our world. When striving completely ceases, desiringness has no foothold on any object and so nothing to lay hold of and maintain itself. When every effort to fill the lack is exhausted and given up, the root of desiringness is severed; in time it withers and disappears. That is the reason Buddhism, for example, teaches that liberation from bondage and suffering is not possible without a complete cessation of desiringness:

> The cause of all suffering
> Is rooted in desire.
> If desiring be extinguished,
> Suffering has no foothold.
> To annihilate suffering
> Is called the Third Truth.
> For the sake of the Truth of Extinction,
> To cultivate oneself in the Way,
> Forsaking all ties to suffering,
> This is called Emancipation. (Burtt 148)

If the cause of all suffering is rooted in desiringness, then, of course, there can be no liberation from suffering without its complete cessation. But if desiringness itself originates from a deeper source, it will continue to produce its effects unless that source is removed. Thus, by the logic of its position, Buddhism is led to maintain the need to uproot not only desiringness but also its causes. When these are eliminated and all fixations on programming and objects are removed from consciousness, desiringness, together with the striving to make ego complete, comes to an end. Then there remains nothing in consciousness that could give rise to further desires. Thereupon suffering entirely ceases. This is the meaning of "stopping without rebirth" (Conze et al. 100).

Among Christian sources, the New Testament speaks of the need to cut off desires and fixations—plucking out the right eye and cutting off the right hand—in order to enter eternal life (Matt. 5: 29-30). St. Paul speaks of "crucifying" our lower nature, with its passions and desires, so that we can realize our spiritual nature.

Among Christian mystics, Meister Eckhart especially emphasizes desiringlessness in terms of what he calls "pure disinterest," as the way to arriving at the realization of oneness with the "formless essence" that is Godhead (Blakney 1: 21). This is, so to speak, Eckhart's way of backing into God. A way of picturing this is to imagine that you are at all times on the ground—grounded in God. But through dualistic constructs, desires, and strivings you attempt to lift yourself up from that ground and create a world in separation from it. Through nonattachment, as you stop this futile effort to lift yourself up and build a castle in the air, you wake up and see where you are, and slowly descend to the ground. Then you realize that you never left it and that your attempt to lift yourself up was a bad dream, a game, a cosmic joke you were playing on yourself. When the game is over and striving comes to an end, you are perfectly still and disinterested. In this state

> a man has no regard for anything, no inclination to be above this or below that, no desire to be over or under; he remains what he is, neither loving nor hating, and desiring neither likeness to this or unlikeness to that. He desires only to be one and the same; for to want to be this or that is to want something; and the disinterested person wants nothing. (Blakney 1: 83)

So, according to Eckhart, as we transcend the dualities of likes and dislikes through disinterest, limitations imposed by differentiation of reality into this and that fall away; desiringness and our identity as a separate entity comes to an end; and all fixations, programmings, and constructs that could separate us from anything disappear. Thereupon our oneness with all things and with the formless essence that is Godhead is revealed. Quoting St. Augustine, Eckhart states, "the heavenly door...into the divine nature... is precisely disinterest," for it allows you to "absorb God." "Therefore," he advises, "discard the form and be joined to the formless essence" (Blakney 1: 89-90).

The Sufis likewise teach that the only way we can find fulfillment is by freeing ourselves from the fixation on finding satisfaction of our desires in the object-world. In his *Parliament of Birds,* an allegorical tale of human progression through seven states of consciousness before realizing oneness with God, Farid ud-din Attar tells us that we must progressively let go of our desires and finally the quest itself before we can come to the realization that we already are that of which we were in search. But so long as our quest remains, it is impossible for us to find it because of the separation caused by the desire and the quest.

To see this and become free of desiringness, however, we must come to a direct experience of the futility of our striving to make ourselves Real and complete, and drop it. Emphasizing this need, Rajneesh says that the path of desiringlessness consists in seeing the futility of all desires, giving them all up, and arriving at a state of complete cessation of all desiring. As this happens, suddenly the very movement to give rise to anything stops. This brings about a complete absence of any striving or any object in consciousness. Thereupon the mind becomes totally silent, empty, and still. At that moment the mind is absolutely free. You are off the Wheel of *Samsara* or conditioned existence, and no new cycle begins. You are transformed into a new level of awareness and being (1: 128-131).

With its emphasis on the complete cessation of all striving by removing its very root, duality, Zen Buddhism attempts to lead the practitioner to a direct experience of the futility of all striving, seeing it as a dead end, and dropping it. Huang Po, for instance, categorically states that since any seeking implies a separation from what is, when in reality there is none, not only is it useless but also impossible to attain Reality by trying to satisfy desire or through any kind of striving. As long as we continue to seek we will never find it. He states, "By their very seeking they lose it, for that is using Buddha to seek for the Buddha and using mind to grasp Mind. Even though they do their utmost for a full eon, they will not be able to attain to it" (Blofeld 1: 29-30).

The reason is that striving assumes a separation from Reality and then attempts to overcome it. Not only is this contradictory, which makes its attainment impossible, but it also creates and maintains a sense of separation, duality, and the human condition. So long as we continue to strive, we remain lost. So Huang Po advises: "Learn only how to avoid seeking for and attaching yourselves to anything." For, "if, at this very moment, you convince yourselves of its unattainability, being certain that nothing at all can ever be attained, you would already be Bodhi-minded" (Blofeld 1: 40, 83).

The same teaching is repeated by Huang Po's disciple, Lin-chi (Rinzai), when he says, "Followers of the Way, the resolute man must know right now that from the outset there is nothing to do. But because your faith is insufficient, from moment to moment you rush about seeking; you throw away your heads and then go looking for them and are yourselves unable to stop" (De Bary 227). This teaching is even more directly set forth in the following abbreviated koan, substance of a conversation between master Nan Chuan and Chao Chou, who was himself to become a legendary Zen master:

> Chao Chou asked Nan Chuan, "What is the Tao?" Nan Chuan answered, "The ordinary mind is Tao." Chao Chou then asked, "How can one approach it?" Nan Chuan replied, "If you want to approach it, you will certainly miss it." (Chang 1: 17)

Thus, for Huang Po, Lin-chi, Nan Chuan, and Zen Buddhism generally, the situation of desire and striving is like that of Yagnadatta, who thought he lost his head and went around looking for it. Since there is no approaching, attaining, or becoming that which we are already, all striving and search keep us locked in separation and bound to our world, making us miss our true identity. The way to free ourselves from this endless cycle of desire and striving is to stop it entirely. When there is complete absence of desiringness, we come to realize that we had never parted from Reality as Such in the first place. So, in the koan, Nan Chuan goes on to tell Chao Chou to make himself "as vast and free as the sky" or realize *Sunyata* and Nirvana by shedding his striving mind.

Nan Chuan's response also expresses the core of Taoism and reveals its influence on Zen. For, as we have seen, central to Taoism is *wu wei*, not-doing, or complete cessation of all striving as the way to realize Tao. That is why the *Tao Te Ching* says that those who are bound by desire cannot see Tao; and those who try to grasp it surely miss it: "Doing spoils it, grabbing misses it" (Blakney 2: 117). Desires disturb the mind and make it restless. And, as there is no reaching Tao, striving has the opposite effect of assuming and maintaining a separation; and because we believe it to be real, we get caught up in the game and our very effort to reach it moves us away from Tao. So we find Chuang Tzu saying that by seeking you will never find happiness or reach Tao. Striving separates you from your goal and makes you settle for substitute gratifications. This requires you to double the effort, as it increases your dissatisfaction and confusion. In the end it destroys you. To show this, Chuang Tzu has Lao-tzu advising Keng's disciple, who came to him in search of Tao, in the following words:

> If you persist in trying
> To attain what is never attained;
> If you persist in making effort
> To obtain what effort cannot get;
> If you persist in reasoning
> About what cannot be understood,
> You will be destroyed
> By the very thing you seek. (Merton 2: 133)

However, when we completely stop striving so that nothing is left that could create otherness, the only thing that remains is Tao. So the *Tao Te Ching* advises:

> Touch ultimate emptiness,
> Hold steady and still. (Blakney 2: 68)

Thus, when we are empty of everything and live in the Void State of pure Being, according to Chuang Tzu, we are liberated:

> No desires, no compulsions,
> No needs, no attractions:
> Then your affairs are under control.
> You are a free man. (Merton 2: 112)

A comparable teaching in Christianity is that you cannot be justified through your own effort or attain the true Self by striving. There is no way that you can become God or the creature can become the Creator. Since all striving is finite, you can never bridge the infinite gap it creates in attempting to reach the Infinite. As there is no reaching God, nothing can go to or realize God except what is God. When everything that is not God is burned up or dissolved, only God remains. So, when you give up all striving, there comes the awakening of the Infinite in you as your Identity.

To be free of desire and arrive at such a state, which is marked by a present-centered consciousness, St. John of the Cross advises us to let go of hope, that "ace up the sleeve," which keeps us bound to our world and from facing the futility of all striving. When we let go of the illusion that striving will bring about the desired fulfillment and reveal life's meaning in the future, the blinder that prevents us from seeing that tomorrow will never come — because it is already here — is removed. Then there comes the real self-transformation.

We see that while desiringlessness stops the Wheel of Life from turning, nonattachment unstraps us and disidentification untraps us from it. Disidentification cuts us loose from our present reality-construct; nonattachment frees us from fixation and immersion in our present programming and habituation; and desiringlessness stops us from maintaining them as it frees us from the illusion that by creating and having more things, experiences, and relationships we will get the satisfaction we want. Without this reinforcement, the entire structure loses its hold on our consciousness and eventually collapses. Thereby we become free.

It is clear, then, that upon attaining desiringlessness, all desires that arise from our separation from Reality and the separate self, the feelings of unreality and incompleteness, and the drive to make ego real and complete by creating and maintaining a world, come to an end. In their absence ego is deactivated. Thereupon we go through a fundamental transformation and arrive at a state in which no one is left to raise the question of how life could go on without desires. In the absence of all desires as our world becomes transformed, we realize that life's meaning and purpose arise from a far deeper source than desire — from a completeness that moves toward an ever more complete manifestation of itself. At this level, there remains no need to fill an absence, make ourselves Real, find an identity, have a goal, or prove anything. Nor does there remain any craving, clamor, panic, compulsion, restlessness, dissatisfaction, or striving. Thus nothing remains to give rise to any conflict, confusion, or problem. Desire simply arises from completeness as a spontaneous manifestation of our own true Being.

Chapter 16
Emptying the Mind – Stopping the World

A third essential step toward Self-realization and liberation is what may be called "emptying the mind and stopping the world." This step is necessary because bondage is created by the mind as it constructs a world and becomes trapped in it. Thus liberation is not possible without emptying the mind of its contents or objects, constructs, programming, thoughts or inner dialogue, and arriving at the Unconditioned State. "Emptying the mind" or deconstruction of consciousness is, then, central to experiential religion.

For an explanation, recall that all that we are, all that we perceive as real, and the very structure of consciousness result from programming; that everything programmed is in the mind; and that whatever is programmed traps awareness and creates bondage. Since the entire human condition is a result of the way consciousness is constructed and maintained, so long as there is a single object on which consciousness can fixate and maintain itself and the dualistic framework, it will remain bound and separated from Reality; and awareness will remain trapped and lost. Unless ordinary consciousness is destructured and transcended, therefore, no liberation from conditioned existence is possible.

It follows that liberation is essentially in and of the mind. So we find one of the central teachings of Hinduism stated by *Maitri Upanishad:* "The mind is indeed the source of bondage and also the source of liberation" (Mascaro 104). That freeing the mind is essential to liberation is emphasized by the *Srimad Bhagavatam* when it says, "There is no salvation or freedom until a man frees himself from his own mind" (Prabhavananda 113).

This liberation consists, then, in deconstructing ordinary consciousness, reality, and self – and breaking free of the control exercised by the world on the individual through mental and emotional fixations. Now as fixations and entrapments occur in the very construction and functioning of consciousness, essential to freeing the mind is stopping consciousness from functioning through a system of programming, models, concepts, and thought. As we saw, as long as consciousness continues to perceive through them, it will continue to be fixated, duality will persist, awareness will remain trapped, and the mind will be unable to become free.

The key to emptying the mind and stopping the world, then, is stopping the operation of the dualistic mode and deconstructing it, however temporarily. As long as the dualistic mode remains operative and dominant, it will keep its control over the mind. Acting like a lid, it will prevent Awareness from breaking through to the conscious sphere. Thus the entire programmed mind, both the conscious level of thought and the subconscious level of the inner dialogue, must be penetrated by awareness, stopped, broken through, and transcended. Using different imagery, David Bohm has stated:

> If consciousness is full of all this content (ripples and movements) which then begins to keep itself going, self-generated...the plenum which consciousness is is not seen or is not able to operate. So the notion is that if consciousness can empty itself of its contents...by ending these ripples in the manifest and the nonmanifest, ending these ripples in the manifest and the germs in the nonmanifest which create them, then we have an emptiness which makes consciousness somehow a vehicle or an instrument for the operation of this totality—of intelligence, compassion and truth. (Weber in Wilber 4: 94)

To stop the functioning of the dualistic mode and to destructure consciousness, the programming by which the mode maintains itself must be stopped from reinforcing it. And the most direct way to do so is to cut off the two essential ways in which consciousness maintains itself: thoughts, the inner dialogue and the deeper currents of the unconscious; and constant scanning of the environment for new and diverse sensory stimuli. To stop the latter, consciousness must take a direct hold of itself and reverse its orientation by shifting attention away from external stimuli and toward itself. And the former is to be accomplished by focusing attention directly on the primary stimulus before anything arises in the mind or the information-processing activity is triggered, thus keeping itself free from entrapment when anything does arise. These two procedures will eventually reverse the orientation of consciousness, disidentify and free it from fixation on the object-pole and from the latter's control over it, and bring about a shift toward its source.

When the mind is not fixated on anything, it is emptied and bound to nothing. As fixations dissolve and consciousness is emptied, it is destructured, duality collapses, and the world ceases to control it. Structurally, since consciousness and the world depend on each other for their maintenance in separation, when one pole collapses, so does the other. When both collapse, the mind is totally emptied. In this void state attention, freed from entrapment, makes a profound inward shift away from contents and turns toward its source or nature. Viewing all phenomena from this void state, it experiences another, most radical shift, transcends all contents, objects, models, concepts, programming, thought and inner dialogue, and directly experiences its identity as pure Awareness, which is identical with Reality as Such.

Liberation consists in this transcendence whereby, freed from all conditioned states, the mind assumes its natural, Unconditioned State of pure Awareness in which it is not fixated on anything and so is limited by or separated from nothing. Correspondingly, freed from the limits imposed by conditions, constructs and frameworks, Reality assumes or is experienced in its Unconditioned State as identical with the mind, since in this state there is nothing to create a separation between mind and reality. Thus emptying the mind is the key to stopping or transcending both consciousness and world.

Because of its centrality to liberation, the sources of experiential religion, particularly those centered in meditative traditions, such as the Hindu yogas, Buddhist meditative traditions, and Taoist yoga, and to a certain extent other traditions, insist on this step in a variety of ways, almost to the exclusion of all else.

For Hinduism, stopping thought and inner dialogue as a key to emptying the mind and freeing awareness, and transcending the duality of consciousness and world constitutes the core of its main yogas. Indeed, so essential is this step that the ancient sage Patanjali defined *yoga* as "stopping mind-waves." The process of emptying the mind and successively transcending various relative or conditioned stages and states is likened, by the *Taittiriya Upanishad*, to peeling off various sheaths, like onion peels, until the Mind or Self stands in its naked purity, void of everything other than itself, for "beyond the sheaths is the Self" (Prabhavananda & Manchester 55). In this way we not only transcend ordinary consciousness but also overcome the world as it ceases to have any controlling influence over us. So the *Srimad Bhagavatam* declares, "He who has conquered his own mind has conquered the universe" (Prabhavananda 138).

Arising from the meditative tradition of Hinduism, from its inception Buddhism has insisted that the direct path to liberation is emptying or freeing the mind of conditioning and construct and thus transcending conditioned existence. This teaching is the core of Buddhism.

According to the Buddha, since *dukkha* arises from the dualistic construction and functioning of consciousness, the direct way to liberation is by stopping and transcending it. This is accomplished by cutting off dualistic thought and inner dialogue on the one hand, and freeing the mind of its fixation on programming, objects, and constructs on the other. He says, "If there is an object, there is a foothold for consciousness. With consciousness growing in this foot-hold, there is a descent of mind and body...With consciousness having no foothold or growth, there is no descent of mind and body. From the stopping of mind and body is the stopping of the six sensory fields...Thus is the stopping of this whole mass of suffering" (Conze et al. 71). Thus, as long as a single object remains in consciousness, the dualistic structure will remain. But, as the *Majjhima-nikaya* explicitly states, when consciousness is unable to fixate on anything and maintain itself, it is unable to maintain the dualistic structure (mind and body). When the latter is stopped and transcended, so is the mind (six sensory fields), which thereby becomes objectless and subjectless, pure void (Conze et al. 64). In this void state, according to *The Lankavatara Sutra*, as nothing remains in consciousness to limit or condition it, the most profound turning about in its deepest seat takes place. Awareness first shifts away from the world and toward its Source, and then, breaking through all frameworks, constructs, contents or objects, and conditioned states, it experiences its identity as that Source and becomes free of *dukkha* (Suzuki 2: 129-141).

Realizing this truth, Zen masters have insisted that liberation is not possible without emptying the mind. As master Tsung Kao observes, "If the mind is not uprooted, no liberation is possible" (Chang 1: 88). With this master Dogen concurs: "As long as one hopes to grasp the truth only through the mind, one will not attain it even in a thousand existences or in aeons of time. Only when one lets go of the mind and ceases to seek an intellectual apprehension of the Truth is liberation possible" (De Bary 373). Emphasizing the need to cut off all fixation on object-world as a way of "uprooting," emptying or transcending the mind, master Takuan states, "since thought, in dualistic consciousness, attaches to its objects," so long as it persists, liberation will be blocked. But "when the mind is free from attachment and free from thought, the ultimate stage is reached in which the mind operates without abiding anywhere." Cutting off thought is therefore essential, for "not fixated anywhere, the mind is everywhere" (De Bary 373, 378). Thus, when the mind is not attached to anything, it is completely empty. It is without any limitation, which is the absolute freedom of the mind to be the omnipresent and ever-present reality of the Unconditioned State.

Recognizing that the most direct way to liberation is to empty the mind by cutting off dualistic thinking, many Zen masters have emphasized it almost to the exclusion of all else. Thus Hui-neng says, "If one instant of thought is cut off, the Dharma Body separates from the physical body, and . . . you will be reborn in another realm" (De Bary 219, 220). This clearly means that when such thought is stopped, the mind is emptied. In this void, Awareness or "Dharma Body" "separates" or breaks free and transcends "physical body" or forms, objects, constructs, and conditioned states, and experiences its true nature as the Unconditioned.

Echoing Hui-neng, Huang Po points out that if you spend all your time learning to stop your thinking process and keep the mind motionless at all times, "concentrating entirely upon the goal of no thought-creation, no duality," ultimately you will pass beyond all duality and arrive at the One Mind besides which nothing exists (Blofeld 1: 63, 79, 90). Similarly, his disciple Lin-chi insists, "The one instant of thought in which you of yourself unfetter your bonds and are emancipated wherever you go – this is becoming one with Avalokiteshvara" (De Bary 229). And master Tsung Kao advises: "If one can abruptly put everything down, stripped of all thoughts and deliberations, suddenly he...realizes that this sentient consciousness is the true, void, marvelous wisdom itself" (Chang 1: 92).

Explaining how cutting off dualistic thinking drives consciousness to its very limit and makes it give itself up altogether, which suddenly opens the doorway to the Unconditioned, master Han Shan states, "Those who drive their minds to the very dead end will find that their thoughts suddenly stop. Instantaneously they behold their self-mind" (Chang 1: 117). Cutting off dualistic thinking is, therefore, as Hui-neng states, the key to liberation: "To discard false views, this is the great causal event...If you awaken to this Dharma, in one instant of thought your mind will open ...[to] Buddha's wisdom...and with this you will see into your own nature, then you succeed in transcending the world" (De Bary 229).

Explaining the *Mahayana-Sraddhotpada-Sastra's* commentary on *The Lankavatara Sutra,* from the Tibetan tradition Lama Govinda says that the mind has two doors. One leads to the realization of its pure essence; the other to discrimination. So long as the latter dominates the conscious level, opening the former is impossible. Since the latter is turned away from the pure essence and turned toward the objective world, in order to open the door to the former, this habit of looking out toward the outside world must be given up by turning away from external stimuli and internal thought, and directing attention toward the Source of consciousness. This practice will empty the mind of all thought and object, bring about a complete turning about in the deepest seat of consciousness, and open the door to a direct experience of Ultimate Reality or *Sunyata* (1: 77-79).

According to Taoism, this emptying the mind of dualistic thinking is necessary because it is the essence of the reversal of the ordinary perceptual and behavioral processes required for a realization of Tao. Thus Chuang Tzu teaches that to become one with Tao you must be absolutely empty of all that is not Tao itself. This emptying is most clearly implied in a text in which Chuang Tzu speaks of "forgetting everything while sitting down." There is a clear reference to meditation in this "sitting down," and to making the mind empty in "forgetting everything." He relates this through a dialogue in which Confucius is cut down to size:

> Another day Yen Hui saw Confucius and said, "I have made some progress."
> "What do you mean?" asked Confucius.
> Yen Hui said, "I forget everything while sitting down."
> Confucius' face turned pale. He said, "What do you mean by sitting down and forgetting everything?"
> "I cast aside my limbs," replied Yen Hui, "discard my intelligence, detach from both body and mind, and become one with Great Universal [Tao]. This is called sitting down and forgetting everything." (Chan 201)

Clearly, Chunag Tzu is stating that by reversing the orientation of consciousness through cutting off sensory stimuli (casting aside limbs) and stopping discursive thought (discarding intelligence), Yen Hui is able to empty his mind and transcend duality (detaching from body and mind), which leads to the experience of oneness with Tao. So he admonishes us to empty our minds and become "united with the Universe" and "personally realize the infinite to the highest degree and travel in the realm of which there is no sign" (Chan 207).

When "there is no sign," or not a trace of any object, construct, programming, thought, or attachment to anything, when the mind is a pure void, empty of anything other than itself, declares Chuang Tzu in an analogy often repeated by Zen (also appearing in the Upanishads), it becomes like a clear mirror, transparent to itself and reflecting all things. For, without the obstruction and distance created by objects, programming, attachment, identification, or construct, being purely itself and attached to nothing, the mind assumes its natural state of self-transparency and becomes the mirror of all things. So Chuang Tzu says, "When the mind of the sage is tranquil, it becomes the mirror of the universe and the reflection of all things" (Chan 208).

In the New Testament Jesus speaks of the need to overcome or transcend the world, while St. Paul reminds Christians of the need for mental transformation: "Adapt yourselves no longer to the pattern of this present world, but let your minds be remade and your whole nature thus transformed" (Rom. 12: 2). Since the world is in your mind, not to adapt yourself to the pattern of this world means to become free of the programming through which the world maintains its control over us. This requires us to cut off all fixations on the object-world and stop dualistic thinking. When the mind is thus emptied, it can be remade and the entire nature transformed from the limited identity of the separate self to the limitlessness and absolute freedom of the Spirit.

The emptying of mind as a necessary condition for union with God is clearly taught by many Christian mystics. Thus the author of *The Cloud of Unknowing* says that the way to God is through "forgetting all creatures that God has made." This forgetting means emptying the mind of its identification and preoccupation with contents or the object-world. As the mind becomes free of fixation on the external world and turns inward, it enters "the cloud of unknowing," which consists in "leaving all discursive thought beneath the cloud of forgetting." Thus cutting off discursive thinking, you are able to arrive at what he calls "pure thought," or the void state in which only bare intention and awareness remain. In this state, as intention and awareness remain wholly focused on God, "he" reveals "himself" to us (Johnston 53-92).

Expressing the same need, Meister Eckhart says that when all attachments and fixations are gone and we disidentify with everything, including our separateness and individuality, our consciousness appears completely void of all knowledge and distinctions (Blakney 1: 229-232). Eckhart calls this void state "ignorance" because it is marked by absence of any activity of ordinary consciousness and absence of any object, concept, or image. That this signifies deconstruction and transcendence of ordinary consciousness is clearly intended when Eckhart states that this ignorance is arrived at "from knowledge," and not "from ignorance" and that it is a state of "transformed knowledge." No movement remains in the mind, where only silence and stillness reigns (Fox, *Breakthrough* 256-257). Then nothing remains in the mind which could cause it to become fixated on or separated from anything. In this state, since only God remains, we realize our oneness with God (Blakney 1: 229-232).

A similar view is expressed by the Sufis in terms of what a text calls "choosing," which consists in "the emptying of the heart of all things other than the search for completion." This empties the mind of all thoughts and allows "the true thoughts" to "flood in" (Shah 2: 240). Like *The Cloud of Unknowing*, this text implies an emptying of the mind of all objects and dualistic thinking by cutting them off at their roots. When the mind becomes void of everything, "true thoughts" flood in, that is, pure Awareness emerges to the conscious level.

Similarly, Shabistari instructs the Sufi to cut off dualistic thinking, transcend the world of separation, and awaken to the world within: "In an instant, rise from time and space. Set the world aside and become a world within yourself" (Shah 3: 232). This statement not only echoes the Zen teaching on sudden enlightenment; like the latter, it also teaches how to experience it. Like

Hui-neng and Lin-chi, Shabistari says that when we cut off one instant of thought, we rise above the space-time boundary of ordinary consciousness and suddenly awaken to the eternal, boundless, and omnipresent reality of our true nature.

A similar view is expressed by Rumi when he says, "You belong to the world of dimension. But you come from nondimension. Close the first 'shop,' open the second" (Shah 2: 144). According to Rumi, we live in a world of dimensions created by programming and mental constructs. These constructs become a barrier to the disclosure of our true nature, which is beyond all dimension, condition, or form. To experience this revelation, we must stop the first and open ourselves to the second. For this opening, we need to remove the dimensions by cutting off thought (close the "shop") and destructuring the mind.

Rumi seems to view the two worlds as Janus-faced or like a swinging door that swings closed on one and open to the other. He says, "You have two 'heads.' The original, which is concealed, the derivative, which is the visible one" (in Ornstein 2: 309). Rumi is implying that only when the visible head, the dualistic consciousness, is stopped from looking at the manifest world, is it possible for the door of the mind to swing open to the original Mind, the unmanifest universe of limitless Awareness and Being. The way to stop the first is to turn it around or reverse its orientation and direct it toward the invisible one. So Rumi writes: "Shut both the eyes of the head, so that you may see with the inner eye" (Shah 2: 147). When both eyes—sensory stimuli and thought—are shut or stopped, the mind becomes empty, and fixation on the world ceases. Then the "inner eye" opens or intuitive insight and direct experience occurs, as attention pivots on itself, sheds all its limitations, conditions, and constructs, and realizes its identity as pure Awareness.

One of the writers who has most frequently expressed the idea of stopping the world is Carlos Castaneda. By stopping the world Castaneda means stopping our description of reality. Since the world as we know it is a description upheld by our internal dialogue, when that is shut off, the description collapses. Without the thinking that maintains it, our idea of what the world is loses its hold on the mind, which thereby undergoes a revolution. So the way to stop the world is to silence the internal dialogue, thus emptying the mind of its contents and constructs.

You may ask, "Why should I want to stop the world?" "Why should I want to change my idea of the world?" Don Juan answers by saying that it is only by stopping the world that you can see things as they are and arrive at the totality of yourself. As long as we remain within the description we learn from birth, we merely look at the world, which appears to be separate from us, and remain trapped in the bubble of perception, bound to our limited reality-construct. Within this narrow mold we go back and forth, our thoughts become listless, life becomes narrow, divided, incomplete. We become restless, frustrated, dissatisfied, bored, at odds with life. Meanwhile our description has complete control over our life by programming us with its desires, values, beliefs, judgments, attitudes, and ways of thinking and living. Stopping the world is stopping this hold of the world over us, so that we can step out of its bondage, out of the Wheel or the cycle of repeatedly going over the same feelings, thoughts, and actions within the narrow limits of our world until we die. Since stopping the world is becoming free of these limitations, it is a way of transcending the world and realizing the totality of ourselves or total awareness. For when the internal dialogue stops, the bubble of perception is deflated and shrunken, and our world is rearranged or realigned. In the empty space opened up in our mind the transpersonal states can dawn, enabling us to attain total awareness. As our center shifts to it, we return home. We are then at home in the universe, at home wherever we are.

The process of deconstructing or emptying the mind and stopping the world is then essentially the mind's journey from the outer to the inner dimensions of consciousness and reality. Unlike the centrifugal drive of ego, which loses itself and Reality by striving to be Real, this is a journey toward directly experiencing the heart and center of Reality by shedding all that is not Real. Such is the meaning of this inward turn.

Chapter 17
Leaving Self Behind

We saw in Part II that as the entire dualistic structure solidifies around ego, it becomes the pillar that holds up not only that foundation but also the superstructure of the human condition. Consequently, as long as ego remains what it is—the Gordian Knot at the core of our feeling of unreality and incompleteness—separation and bondage will remain; and the final barrier to Self-realization will be held firmly in place. It is therefore easy to see why leaving ego behind is an essential aspect of experiential religion. Without transcending ego the human condition and its causes will continue to be maintained, and none of the aspects of liberation will be effectively realized.

So Hinduism declares that if we want to be free of bondage and suffering, we must disidentify with and let go of the ego. The *Ashtavakra Gita* puts the matter succinctly: "When there is no I, there is liberation. When there is I, there is bondage" (Johnson 125). Since the Buddha saw ego as the core around which the causes of *dukkha* concentrate and from which it ultimately issues, he said that in order to gain liberation, we must "uproot false view of self" (Conze et al. 91). Seeing ego as the source of suffering, the *Tao Te Ching* states that in order to be free of suffering, we must let go of it:

> I suffer most because
> Of me and selfishness.
> If I were selfless, then
> What suffering would I bear? (Blakney 2: 65)

According to the sources of experiential religion, as our true Self is utterly beyond ego, so long as the latter remains the center of our consciousness and world, no realization of the former is possible. Thus the *Srimad Bhagavatam* declares, "By reaching the end of one's ego, one realizes the divine Self and attains freedom" (Prabhavananda 49).

Buddhism repeatedly states the necessity of this transcendence. A commentary on Nagarjuna points out the reason when it states, "All defilements have the false theory of individuality for their root, for their origin, for their cause" (Conze et al. 167). So, to be free of this condition and its cause and to realize our true nature, Zen master Seng Ts'an says that all we have to do is to "banish the dualism of self and not-self, is and is-not, for in the transcendent sphere of reality as such there is neither, since there are no separate things" (Burtt 227-230). This need to transcend the ego and duality arises from the fact that, as Yasutani Roshi explains, they are deeply embedded in the unconscious mind. Unless they are uprooted in their source, we cannot realize our true identity (Kapleau 1: 137). That is why master Bassui admonishes, "As long as the illusion of an ego-self does not vanish, man must undergo intense suffering in the three worlds" (Kapleau 1: 165). It is precisely by letting this sense of a separate self, including the higher, archetypal self, "die" (i.e., disidentified with) that we are able to transcend the last barrier of duality and realize our true Self, in which lies liberation. As one text has it:

To save life it must be destroyed.
When utterly destroyed,
one dwells for the first time in peace.
(Sohl & Carr 29)

The New Testament expresses the same view in a pivotal text in which Jesus explicitly declares: "If anyone wishes to be a follower of mine, he must leave self behind, take up his cross and come with me. Whoever tries to save his life will be lost; but if a man will let himself be lost for my sake, he will find his true self" (Matt. 16: 24-25). In this text Jesus not only enunciates the heart of experiential religion — transcending the separate self in order to realize the true Self — but also says how it is to be done.

First, Jesus says that unless we let go of our separate self, we cannot be his followers. We may do all kinds of wonderful things in life — become a Pope or a President — but as long as we do not take the decisive step of crossing the boundary of the exclusive self, we are not his followers.

Second, the reason is that without leaving the self behind, we cannot realize the true Self. Without death there is no rebirth or resurrection. Unless ego dies, or unless we disidentify and let go of it completely, we cannot journey through the transpersonal states and arrive at Reality as Such, which is the true Self. As Jesus says elsewhere, we cannot have two masters or centers of being: ego and the Self. If we wish to realize the latter, we must let go and transcend the former.

Third, we have a choice of directions in life: to transcend ego or try to save it by clinging to it, living within its limits, protecting and enhancing it, and attempting to make it a real and permanent self. Whoever aims at the latter will be lost. All our attempts to find identity, meaning, and the purpose of existence within the limits of the personal and among the things we create will ensure self-loss, bondage, and suffering. No matter what we do, nothing can save ego from death, dissolution, and oblivion. As long as we hold onto it, we will be bound by our conditioning and constructs, and remain separated from the goal of existence.

Moreover, if we keep striving to make ego a separate center, we will stop growing. If we hold onto the present self-structure beyond the point of its maturation, instead of disidentifying with it and allowing ourselves to develop beyond the personal, our life will remain frozen at the ego level. We will become further detached from reality and move away from our true identity. Thus we will become "less than" or false to ourselves. Since in the evolutionary arc life does not stand still but, as the Buddha said, constantly shapes and reshapes itself, the paradox of self-growth is that if we attempt to preserve the self, it will become the very thing we fear: dead to all that is real, vital, and alive. In such a situation, while ego will be lost among the very things it creates in the attempt to save itself and become real, the Self will also be lost. For, while trying to save ego, we will miss our chance to realize the Self.

Fourth, this disidentification with ego is to be undertaken "for my sake," that is, for the sake of realizing the true or Christ-Self. It is not to be done so as to run away from life, to withdraw from the world, or to transfer our responsibilities to someone or something else, bypassing the task of developing a healthy, mature ego. It should be done for the sake of the greater, transpersonal stage of growth and realization of destiny. This presupposes a developmentally complete self as a point of departure.

As a stage in each individual's growth and ultimate transformation, the development of ego is a necessary step that cannot be short-circuited or bypassed. As Jack Engler points out, all stages in our development are such that each stage must be experienced, lived through, and brought to completion, before moving on to the next. Thus, each individual must face the task of forming a stable, cohesive, integrated personality capable of forming satisfying relationships, living a normal life, and dealing with the world on a mature, adult level (1: 29-30).

Any attempt at surrender or transcendence without successfully completing the personal stage of development is fraught with dangers. One such danger, as Jack Engler reminds us, is psychosis, an unstable personality disorder. Another is avoidance of life's responsibilities or the task of forming lasting or satisfying relationships. In narcissistic individuals the danger is transference — to a teacher or an idealized self (Engler 1: 26-31). In others surrender may be an expression of ego's need to worship something believed to be greater than itself. Unless we have an ego in which, to use Norman O. Brown's phrase, "there are no unlived lines," disidentification and letting go may not be complete. The ape character of ego may step in and only pretend to surrender but in actuality remain a holdout. To jump, we need a jumping-off point; and that point for transpersonal stage of development is a developed and integrated self. As Bernadette Roberts says, "To have no-self, there must first *be* a self—a whole self" (1: 174; italics hers). Similarly, Jack Engler observes, *"you have to be somebody before you can be nobody"* (1: 24; italics his).

Fifth, we must take up the cross and follow Christ. And this taking up the cross or walking on his path of transcending the separate self is precisely what constitutes leaving the self behind. It follows that, contrary to what Christians believe, taking up the cross does not mean taking up suffering, but just the opposite—taking up the path of self-transcendence that ends suffering. Since ego is the basis of suffering, as Bernadette Roberts also found (1: 178), when it is transcended, so is suffering. When there is no ego, there is no one to suffer. Thus taking up the cross is a way of leaving self and suffering behind—leaving the entire baggage and burden of existence. The cross does not, therefore, symbolize suffering but the path by which (just as Jesus did through his death and resurrection) one experiences a psychological "death" of the separate self. It is through this death or transcendence of ego that each one experiences rebirth, resurrection, or realization of the true Self. Thus each one can experience the resurrection when the true or Christ-Self emerges or becomes his/her new center and identity. Since this resurrection or realization of new identity is the human destiny, the cross essentially symbolizes the human destiny of crossing, passing beyond, or transcending of the personal and arriving at the transpersonal stage, where lies the realization of the true or Christ-Self.

Christian mystics have thus spoken of leaving self behind as a condition for awakening to oneness with God. The author of *The Cloud of Unknowing* instructs you to "forget yourself" as you embark on the path of contemplative union. For, since "all your knowledge and experience depends upon the knowledge and feeling of yourself," you cannot "forget creatures," that is, disidentify with the mental contents that make up your world, without "forgetting," that is, disidentifying with ego (Johnston 102-103, 136-138). Without this disidentification, then, no emptying of mind and union with God is possible.

Similarly, Meister Eckhart says that you must begin your quest of union by first forgetting yourself. Whatever else you may accomplish, unless you let go of ego, you will find obstacles and become restless as the barrier to union, which is yourself, remains. For, one who empties "himself of his ego, keeping nothing back for himself...such a person has everything, for to have nothing is to have everything" (Fox, *Breakthrough* 166).

In order to experience union, then, you must reduce yourself to nothing. When you completely let go so that no trace of ego remains, then only God remains. In the complete emptiness of your being, which is the fullness of God, God gives birth to his Son. This is the new birth or resurrection, the true or Christ-Self rising to the conscious level as your new center and identity (Blakney 1: 5, 246).

St. John of the Cross expresses the centrality of this letting go most succinctly when he says:

> When the mind dwells upon anything, thou art ceasing to cast thyself upon the All. For, in order to pass from the all to the All, thou hast to deny thyself wholly in all. (Peers 1: 72)

To be one with the whole, we have to let go of our identification with the part that separates us from it: ego. To realize the Unconditioned, we must be completely void of identification with anything conditioned. Nothing must remain. Attachment to even a single thing, as the Buddha and the Zen koan, "Buffalo's Tail," intimate, will separate us from the All. Consequently nothing will have passed through. For anything less than the All is nothing at all. So John says that in order to pass to the All, we must let go of everything that is not the All. Then All and Everything will remain, as Bernadette Roberts realized. She says that when the self is completely gone, even the higher self of the archetypal and subtle states, there remains no relative point on which consciousness can fixate so as to create a separate framework. Then "what is left is what Is, all that Is, and Its identity is unmistakable" (1: 178).

The Sufi teaching which corresponds to, if not reflects, Jesus' teaching on losing our self in order to gain the true Self is contained in the following story: When the world was presented to the souls before their creation, ninety percent chose it. When paradise was next presented to those who were left, ninety percent of them ran toward it. At the sight of hell ninety percent of those who remained ran away in horror. Then the Celestial Voice asked those who were not moved by any of these phenomena, "What is your desire?" They answered in chorus, "All we want is to remain in Your Presence." The Voice said, "Such a desire is fraught with innumerable hardships and perils." They answered, "We will gladly do anything for the sake of being with You, and lose everything in order that we may gain everything" (Shah 2: 68).

To realize oneness with God, according to the Sufis, we must be prepared to lose everything other than God. This everything is what creates separation, which is ego; and ego, if you recall, is nothing at bottom other than a fear of, a resistance to, and a striving to be a center separate from God. In the final count what is lost when everything perishes is this fear, resistance, and striving—everything that is not Real—which keep us from realizing our true identity. So the triple terror becomes the final barrier to transcendence. Only when the fear and resistance to Being and nothingness that render the self nothing die, do we rise as the Being that we really are.

This is also clearly attested to by those Kabbalists who believe transcendence of self to be a necessary step toward union with God. As Baal Shem Tov observed, ego stands in the way because its fear and resistance create a barrier to surrendering separateness. Letting go of ego is therefore necessary to realize oneness with all (Shaya 134).

A recognition of this barrier and how to transcend it is vividly portrayed in the following Sufi story: When asked about how he was guided on the path, Sheikh Shibili said that it was a dog. One day he saw a dog standing by the water's edge, almost dead with thirst. But every time it tried to drink, it was prevented by its reflection in the water. At last, such was its dire need that it cast away fear and leapt into the water, whereupon the "other dog" vanished. Similarly, his own obstacle vanished, when he knew that the barrier was what he took to be his own self. (Shah 2: 168).

This story illustrates how ego becomes a barrier to realizing what we most deeply desire because we take it to be something real. Although ego (the "other dog") is a mere reflection of consciousness, when we believe it to be real and identify with it, a barrier is created between us and the goal of life, here symbolized by the water. Afraid of being nothing and being rendered nothing by Being or dying, ego drives itself as a wedge between us and our goal and emerges in us as the fear of losing our individuality or identity as a separate center on the one hand, and the fear of the unknown or transcendence on the other. As a result, according to the story, we are usually like the dog—consumed by the thirst for the Real, standing at the edge, but unable to leap into it and quench our thirst. This contradiction between fear and desire becomes the obstacle.

Only when it becomes a matter of life and death, when we directly experience the limits of the separate self, its inability to drink or to BE, the futility of the fear and resistance, and only when the desire becomes stronger than the fear, are we finally able to let go and leap into the unknown. Thereupon the barrier, which was only a projection of our fear and therefore an illusion, vanishes; and we are able to realize the Reality from which we had never been parted.

Now, what do we have to do to let go? What is involved in leaving self behind? Does it entail our having no self, destroying our character or personality? Do we have to give up everything we hold dear, give up all our possessions and withdraw from the world? Does it require us to destroy ego and turn into a blob or a vegetable? Wouldn't that make us wishy-washy persons or get us hopelessly lost? What, then, can leaving the self behind entail?

First, it involves letting go of the fear and the resistance to Reality as Such or God. As Bernadette Roberts says, "as long as there is any fear of losing the self, the self remains" (1: 179). Unless we let the fear of and resistance to death, annihilation, and loss of individuality die or cease, as the Sufi story depicted, we cannot take the final step of transcendence.

Second, with the disappearance of fear and resistance, the drive to be real, to find completeness and fulfillment on the basis of being a separate center of being and consciousness, entirely ceases. Since this striving is the core of ego and the source of all our strivings, with its disappearance all other strivings likewise cease. It is this shift that most appears as death, for it is the death or cessation of the sense of oneself as a separate entity.

This is clearly the import of the Buddhist view of two-fold egolessness. Referring to *The Lankavatara Sutra's* view on it, Chogyam Trungpa says that there are two stages of understanding egolessness: First, you see that there is no such thing as a solid, permanent entity or ego. Second, you let go of the concept of egolessness, the abstract watcher of egolessness or of events. Since there is no perceiver and nothing to perceive or be perceived, when you drop all reference points, what disappears with the sense of being a separate self is this abstract watcher, someone who looks at and is conscious of rather than being that which is being conscious of (4: 13-14). In effect, what remains, as Nisargadatta Maharaj also points out, is only perceiving, with nothing to perceive and no one perceiving anything (Balsekar 40). With the cessation of ego, otherness perishes; and there remains nothing to look at and no one to look at anything that is not identical with the seeing itself. The subject-object duality is thereby lost.

This cessation of the sense of oneself as a separate entity is implied in the biblical saying that no one can see God and live. To see God you have to pass through death, which the Hasidic masters believe can happen in this life since, as the Baal Shem Tov remarked, the transcendent can be found everywhere and in everything. And as Leo Shaya says, "to be one with the One and again to be infinite with the infinite, a human being has to be separate from the separate and die to what is mortal, to what is finite" (135). To be separate from the separate is the death of separation, which is ego. As this sense of separation ceases, you pass from the present form of life to the new life of oneness with God. This transcendence of ego and duality, which is a culmination of the spiritual journey, is described by many Kabbalistic masters through various metaphors, such as "annihilation of individual existence," "death of ego," and so on (Idel 63-73).

This view of the transcendence of ego as the death of the separate self-sense is so central to Sufism that Sheikh al-Junaid was moved to define Sufism as dying to oneself and living in God (Arberry 58). This dying to oneself is called *fana,* a term often translated as "annihilation," and has many meanings. Annemarie Schimmel notes three, while Sheikh Javad Nurbakhsh, following Ibn Arabi's classification, observes seven.

One meaning, emphasized by Nurbakhsh, is that *fana* is the cessation of ego as a separate center of being and consciousness (2: 86-114). Agreeing with this interpretation, Sheikh Surawardi says that in this state "the awareness of one's own selfhood is nullified." And Sheikh Ansari observes that "annihilation is the dissolution of everything other than God" (quoted by Nurbakhsh 2:112). By *fana* we pass beyond the boundary created by the separate self. As there remains nothing to separate us from anything, we are able to pass into the boundless being of God. Thereupon only God remains. This is what Ansari means when he says that it is the dissolution of everything other than God.

For others, however, such as Sheikh Hujwiri, *fana* means annihilation of one's "own existence." Similarly, Ezzuddin Kashani speaks of "the annihilation of the essence" (quoted by Nurbakhsh 2: 112). There is, therefore, a difference of viewpoints among Sufis on whether *fana* is annihilation of essence or only of "attributes" or programmed states, that is, whether the transcendence is absolute such that the duality between God and the self disappears and only one center — God — remains; or relative, in which case primary duality remains. Some, such as Nurbakhsh, insist that *fana* does not mean that a person's reality ceases to exist but that the human side of our nature passes away into the divine side (2: 112). On the other hand, the passages quoted above imply absolute transcendence. Furthermore, this difference also depends on whether ego is believed to be real in itself — whether humans have a separate essence. In any case, since the separation is not anything real but is the core unreality which gives rise to others, when we leave ego behind and pass completely into God, nothing real is annihilated or lost. What completely vanishes is duality or the sense of separation. When this illusion dissolves and disappears, what remains is Reality as Such.

Third, with the loss of separation and the shift of center, ego ceases to be the driving energy or center of power to organize, control, run, or terrorize our life according to its desires, designs, and purposes. As Bernadette Roberts states, at the final stage of the journey, ego as the consciousness of a personal energy or organization of a personal being disappears without a trace (1: 170, 173). This loss, which also appears to ego as death, should not be called, strictly speaking, death or annihilation. What appears so from ego's point of view, from a developmental viewpoint, is a transcendence, growth, and expansion, beyond the limited state of the separate self, into the limitless state of the all-inclusive Self. Just as we do not say that adulthood is the death of childhood, so the transcendence of ego does not signify any death but growth of the individual from separation toward unity, from fragmentation toward wholeness and integration, from limitation toward limitlessness, and from incompleteness and imperfection toward completeness and perfection.

Fourth, leaving self behind means, therefore, giving up a limited identity or definition of who we are. As we leave the personal and pass through the transpersonal stages by successively disidentifying and letting go of everything that can limit our development and prevent us from realizing the fullness of who we are, this transcendence of ego becomes a crucial step toward the ultimate stage of our growth and evolution. By disidentifying with an identity that comes to a halt with the emergence and maturation of ego, we are able to reach the transpersonal realms and realize an identity that knows no bounds. As we lose our limited center, we gain a limitless one that includes, and indeed IS, all — a center that is everywhere so that we experience everything as this center and ourselves as centered. Thus it leads to a realization of the true Self. So Ramana Maharshi declares:

> The individual being which identifies its existence with that of the life in the physical body as 'I' is called ego...This ego or individual being is at the root of all that is futile and undesirable in life. Therefore it is to be destroyed by any possible means; then That which ever is alone remains resplendent. This is Liberation or Enlightenment or Self-realization. (Osborne 21)

And, according to *Tao Te Ching*, such a realization brings fulfillment and an end to suffering:

The wise man chooses to be last
And so becomes the first of all;
Denying self, he too is saved.
For does he not fulfillment find
In being an unselfish man? (Blakney 2: 59)

Thus when the limit-barrier of the separate self — both ego and archetypal self — that stands in the gateway to the Unconditioned is dropped, all separation vanishes from our mind. Thereupon we arrive at a state which is no state because there remains no observer to mark it and hence no ego or egolessness, higher, archetypal, or witness self; no world; no dualism or nondualism—just the infinite, open space of pure Being, which is the actual state of all things just as they are. As Ram Dass observes, "By letting go of even the thought 'I', what is left? There is nowhere to stand and no one to stand there. No separation anywhere. Pure awareness. Neither this, nor that. Just clarity and being" (2: 137).

A recognition of this crucial step leads Zen to urge its practitioners to let go of all vestiges of a limited identity, however universalized or cosmicized, and leap into the Abyss of Ultimate Reality. Only through such a death or transcendence can one rise to the fullness of that Reality:

Bravely let go
On the edge of the cliff.
Throw yourself into the Abyss
With decision and courage.
You only revive after death.
Verily, this is the Truth. (Chang 1: 103)

This entire matter is summed up in the beautiful Sufi story, "The Tale of the Sands," which runs as follows: From the far-off mountains, passing through winding countryside, a stream reached the desert. Every time it tried to cross this barrier, it found that its waters were getting absorbed and disappearing in the sand. Although it was convinced that its destiny was to cross this desert, it found no way to accomplish it. Then a hidden voice from the desert whispered that just the wind crosses the desert, so can the stream. The stream objected that all its efforts to cross the desert were turning futile. The wind could fly, it could not. The voice said that in its accustomed way it could not get across. It would either disappear or become a marsh. It must allow itself to be absorbed by the wind and carried over to its destination. This idea was not acceptable to the stream because it had never been absorbed before and it was afraid of losing its individuality. If it allowed its individuality to be lost, how was it to know that it could ever be regained? The sand explained the process of how the wind takes up moisture, carries it over the desert, and then lets it fall as rain, which again becomes a river. As the stream still remained incredulous, the voice said that if it did not accept this path, its habitual way would turn it only into a quagmire. It could certainly not remain a stream. Neither path could keep it a stream forever. Its essential part will either be lost or be transformed. Because it did not know its essence, it was having such fear and doubt. When it heard this, the stream began to remember, dimly, a state in which it had experienced such a change. And so it did as it remembered and then reflected, "Now I have learned my true identity" (Shah 1: 23-24).

This story is so rich in Sufi teachings that I shall have to confine my comments to the essentials relevant to our discussion.

First, it speaks of human destiny, which is to return to the Source, here symbolized by the ocean. At birth we are projected onto the world with the aim of completing the revolution through successively breaking free of limited forms of identity until we return to the Illimitable, Formless Source, which is our essential nature. Since this Reality is present in and as each stage and at all times, the projection and the journey are really its way of being and manifesting itself in the universe as each thing and returning to itself as itself. Thus each human life is an expression of the Unmanifest endowed with the purpose of consciously manifesting it to the world, which is also itself, and so to return to itself.

Second, we cannot, however, realize this aim without crossing the desert, which is the human condition. The desert is the place of testing or temptation. It poses the risk. In spite of the risk, our destiny is not to remain in our present condition or within the limits of our world but to transcend it and realize our essential nature. But because we think our present condition is the natural state and we identify with it, we are unaware of our essential nature.

Third, dimly sensing that our destiny is to transcend the present state and yet having identified with it, we try to find fulfillment within the limits of our world. But in our drive to overcome our condition within itself, we turn life into a quagmire. As we use striving to overcome striving, we become mired in desire, dissatisfaction, frustration, and further striving. By creating more things or changing the external conditions of life, we become further bound and arrive at an impasse.

Fourth, when we listen to it, our inner voice tells us that the only way we can realize the aim of life is to recognize the futility of our efforts, stop such activities, let go of our identities as separate selves, and allow ourselves to be transformed, thus transcending our condition and realizing life's meaning.

Fifth, it is now clear that the fear of losing our individuality and of the Unknown prevents us from taking the path to the realization of our true identity. From fear arise doubt, resistance, and deflection of the aim of the purpose of existence onto our world and settling into the mire of substitute gratifications.

Sixth, as Jesus said, if we cling to the separate self and try to save it, we will be lost. All our attempts to keep it intact will be powerless to prevent it from splintering among a multitude of conflicting desires and becoming lost in the pursuit of their contradictory objects. And our efforts to overcome this condition will detach us further from reality and turn life into a quagmire of confusion, contradiction, paradox, and impasse, which will prevent us from fulfilling our destiny.

Seventh, we can make the crossing, transcend the separate self, and return through remembrance—*dhikr*—and breathing meditation, which allow the Source to rise to the conscious level and establish itself as the new identity and center. In the process of this return, the story emphasizes, as does Zen, the importance of doubt and the need to dispel it. Thereupon the Awareness of the true identity dawns.

As a result of this realization, we experience a mental revolution. As ego stops being a separate center and its striving to control everything ceases, our desires, needs, wants, and interests undergo a fundamental change. No longer driven by the desire to make ourselves Real or complete, secure or permanent, all desires of ego disappear, replaced by those of the Self. The need to have our identity confirmed from outside vanishes. As we disidentify and our attachments dissolve and disappear, our personality floats, without a life of its own, in the new center, the ocean of the Self. The energy of the Self now shines through, transforming the personality into an instrument of its manifestation to the world.

Underscoring the need for this transformation by pointing to a piece of cork bobbing up and down the river, a Zen master tells Janwillem van de Wetering, "This piece of cork is your personality. It must crumble piece by piece until nothing is left." And on another occasion he urges:

> "Let go! Let go!" The Zen master is talking to his disciple. The disciple is always asking. He wants to know. He wants to be. He wants to have. He wants the teacher to give. But the master does not give anything. "So what do I have to let go?" the disciple asks, but the master has walked off and isn't listening. He has to let go of himself. His ideas. Even the insight he thinks he has found. No attainments. Nothing at all. He has to forget his own personality, his own name. (184)

To illustrate this point, van de Wetering tells us a Chinese allegory according to which a monk in search of the Buddha came upon a river:

> As he crossed the river, he saw a corpse coming toward him. He recognized it as his own. There he floats, dead. Nothing remains. Anything he has ever been, ever learned, ever owned, floats past him, still and without life, moved by the slow current of the wide river. It is the first moment of his liberation. (184)

This transcendence of the river of conditioned existence that the death of ego brings about does not mean that the liberated ceases to be an individual. On the contrary, the sources declare that what ceases is the false sense of individuality based on the separate self. Thus the *Srimad Bhagavatam* declares that what is given up is not anything in itself real but "the false idea of individuality" (Prabhavananda 49). Similarly, the Buddha declares that, as quoted earlier, what is uprooted is a "false theory of individuality." What is given up, then, is not our true individuality, which is something real, not separate from anything and to which nothing is opposed, but the false one founded on the belief in separateness and created by the striving to become and remain a separate center of being and consciousness. Giving up this false identification is simply correcting an error, removing a fundamental illusion that stands in the way of our ultimate growth. When it is removed, we stop the game of trying to make the unreal real and realize our true identity, which is universal and individual at the same time. For it is an individuality to which universality is not opposed and a universality that always reveals itself in and as each individual.

This resolves what is merely talked about in Western philosophy but never actually reconciled, namely, the problem of the one and the many. According to experiential religion, this resolution is not possible within the constructions of reality, consciousness, and self in which Western philosophy operates. It is possible only on the transcendent plane of the Supreme Identity, where there is no separation of oneself from anything or anything from anything else, and therefore where the many are no other than the one and the one no other than the many. Here, individuality and universality are experienced as "not-two," that is, not separate or opposed.

This resolution, however, cannot be anything verbal or conceptual, nor can it be a matter of faith. It must be a direct experience that pertains to the ontological domain — the experience itself being identical with the nature of the Reality experienced. As Lama Govinda observes, this unity is brought about through a dissolution of the illusion of separate individuality on the one hand, and on the other, a realization that oneness is precisely the individuality of all things just as they are. "The Buddhist therefore," he continues, "does not try to dissolve his being in the infinity, or to fuse his finite consciousness with the infinite consciousness, but to awaken to his identity as precisely that universality from the point of his individuality." Referring to Edwin Arnold's line, "the dew-drop slips into the shining sea," in "Light of Asia," he goes on to say, "You get close to the Buddhist experience if you reverse Arnold's simile: it is not the dew-drop that slips into the sea, rather, it is the sea that slips into the dew-drop. The universe becomes conscious in the individual in regard to which we can neither speak any more of 'individual' nor of 'universe'" (1: 80-81). Or we may speak equally of both, since both are identical with and manifestations of the One to which there is no "other." Or we may say that, using Swami Vivekananda's analogy, just as there is an identity of water or the ocean and yet a distinct, individual configuration for each wave, so there is identity of the One Reality and yet distinctness and individuality or uniqueness in each form.

In his *Parliament of the Birds* Attar expresses the same nonduality of individuality and universality in the ultimate state of transcendence when he has the thirty birds see in the presence of their king, Simurgh, that

> they were the Simurgh and that the Simurgh were the thirty birds. When they gazed at the Simurgh, they saw that it was truly the Simurgh that was there, and when they turned their eyes toward themselves they saw that they themselves were the Simurgh. In perceiving both at once, themselves and Him, they realized that they and the Simurgh were the same being. (Quoted by Naranjo and Ornstein 35)

Thus when you cross the final barrier of ego and realize your Self, your individuality is not thereby lost. You experience yourself as yourself and at the same time you experience your very being, your individuality, as no other than Reality as Such. As Bernadette Roberts likewise states, "the manifest does not vanish, but like the crust on a loaf of bread, the unmanifest is the manifest, and the manifest the unmanifest. They are two aspects of the One Reality Be-ing itself" (1: 160).

It must be emphasized again that, before leaving the self behind, you need to experience the limits of dualistic constructs and the very dead end of ego: ego as contradiction, paradox, and quandary; its core as fear, resistance, and separation; and the futility of desire and striving to overcome this condition. Only when this state becomes a palpable, living mass that grips you thoroughly on both conscious and unconscious levels, should the transcendence be attempted. Otherwise self-surrender may actually be an attempt to escape the burden of facing life, and this may lead to various kinds of personality disorders. As previously noted, only a fully developed and integrated self can let go completely. When that happens, the limitless life of the Self opens up. The nature of this life or Self is what will be discussed next.

Chapter 18
The True Self

From what I have said so far, it should be clear that the true Self, the realization of which brings liberation, is very different from what we think ourselves to be. In attempting to understand it, we have to leave our familiar world far behind and enter into a world where the usual landmarks disappear. As I have already stated, the Self is not ego, personality, or the separate self. Nor is it the soul. It is not even the archetypal self on the subtle, transpersonal level of consciousness. Nothing in the world can be equated with or resembles it. And since our language was formed to speak about our world, the Self cannot be described or defined in ordinary language. Strictly speaking it cannot be conceptualized or expressed. Communication, however, requires conceptualization and the use of language. For this purpose, the sources of experiential religion have coined a variety of expressions to refer to the Self. In what follows I shall attempt to clarify their meanings.

Atman, the term Hinduism uses to speak of the Self, denotes pure, absolute, unconditioned, undifferentiated Reality and Awareness. The Upanishads state that the Self is "one without a second" and that "all beings are to be seen in the Self, and the Self in all beings" (Prabhavananda and Manchester 27, 51). This statement is more than an expression of belief in one God. Rather, it means that the Self is transpersonal Reality, beyond God conceived as a personal Being. It is Reality as Such. It is not anything other than, opposed to, separate or apart from anything; nor is anything apart from it. Were the Self an object or being beside other beings, or anything in itself separate or apart from anything, no matter how great or infinite, it would still be one being among other beings and so would be limited by that from which it was separated. For this reason, the Self is not an infinite being separate from finite beings. As Ramana Maharshi points out, if the infinite were apart from the finite, it would be limited by that from which it was separated and so would cease to be infinite (Osborne 47). So it cannot be a transcendent other, God or Creator separate from "his" creation; a substance or noumenon underlying the phenomenal world; or anything in another, shadowy, invisible world or heaven. For the same reason, the Self is not an infinite subject, a "he" or "she" apart from finite subjects.

You can see, then, why Hindu scriptures say that the Self alone is and all that is (Prabhavananda 160). It is That other than which nothing exists. Nothing can be real and be other than or apart from the Self. If anything were real and separated from the Self, it would have to be no other than it; otherwise it would be nothing at all. Thus whatever is, is it wholly; founded on and formed in it, wholly its being and manifestation. There is not the slightest shred of separation or differentiation of it from anything or of anything from anything else. This nonduality must not be thought in the sense that there is an entity called "the Self" and there are entities called "things" or "the world," of "the infinite" and "the finite," and somehow there is no separation between the two. Rather, it means that there is no duality or otherness anywhere in reality just as it is — no "between," no "two," no "other," and no "thing." Being precisely what it is, each thing is without any otherness or duality — "not-two"; without any separation, limitation, construction, or condition. Since the Self is not anything in itself, it is a way of talking about the nature, reality, or actual state of all things just as they are beyond their conditioned state. Any otherness is *maya,* illusory.

Second, for much the same reasons, the Self is not a part of anything. Were it otherwise, it would be an object or a part of objects, or it would be one thing or self separate from other things or selves. Thus the Self would be not One, without a second or infinite, but many, separated, limited, finite, as pantheism asserts. The Self would then be other to itself, which is impossible. For this reason the separate self or ego cannot exist or be real.

Just as the Self is not a part of anything, so nothing is a part of it; otherwise, it would not be One without duality. We must not imagine the Self to be a container or a sum of finite beings, or an infinite ocean with finite beings like drops in it. Edwin Arnold's metaphor of dew-drops slipping into the sea is misconceived. Nor is the Self to be conceived as a soul — world soul — in relation to the world or matter as the body, as is usually understood, dualistically. It is true that some Hindu scriptures and traditions hold such a dualistic view by distinguishing between the individual self *(jiva)* and the universal Self *(Atman).* Even some of the Upanishads contain dualistic views. However, their overwhelming and, to some, highest teaching is nondualist. Reflecting this viewpoint, *Kaivalya Upanishad* declares, the Self is "infinite, indivisible" (Prabhavananda and Manchester 115). As the infinite totality, the Self wholly constitutes each thing such that were some parts separated from it or from other parts, parts of it would be other to it and to one another. In that case the Self would be other to itself, which is impossible. And, as Ken Wilber explains:

It isn't that a *part* of the Absolute is present in everything—as in pantheism—for that is to introduce a boundary within the infinite, assigning to each a different piece of the infinite pie. Rather, the *entire* Absolute is completely and wholly present at each point of space and time, for the simple reason that you can't have a different infinite at each point. (5: 297; italics his)

Third, the Self is the identity of all things. Whatever is, is identical with it. Each thing is nothing other than this one Identity, which is Reality as Such. This assertion is not a denial of diversity or a reduction of everything to one thing or an expression of monism. Rather, it is a denial of otherness and an affirmation that while being exactly what it is and only so being, the very being, reality, or nature of each thing consists in its being identical with it, that is, with all. In the infinite multiplicity of the universe, every fiber of every being, from the subatomic atomic particles to the billions of galaxies, is absolutely nothing other than this Supreme Identity. Thus the Upanishads say that, exactly being what it is, each thing is wholly the Self, the Self only and nothing else.

It follows that there are no separate Selves. This is one reason that the Self cannot be equated with the soul. There are not two Selves. Your Self is not other than mine. In fact, it is neither yours nor mine; it belongs to no one. There is only this One "I"—the "I" that is "not-I." So the *Srimad Bhagavatam* says that the Self is the one "I am" of all things (Prabhavananda 259). There can be only this One Identity, otherwise there would again be duality. Since the Self alone is "I", to try to create other "I's" in separation from the Self is, according to Hinduism, *ahankara*. Void of distinctions and limitations, the Self manifests itself in its universal, all-inclusive character in the particularity of each thing as that which is. Summing up this point, Ramana Maharshi says, "Everyone is the Self and, indeed, is infinite. It alone exists and is real. Reality is one. The Self is the one 'I am' of all that is, and perfectly corresponds to the 'I am that I am' of the Bible" (Osborne 16-17, 23, 53). That is why the Upanishads hammer it home: "Tat tvam asi!" You *are* That! You do not *have* it. You *are* it! As you are wholly the Self, in reality nothing is other than you.

Fourth, the Self is the identity of all precisely as it transcends each thing; otherwise it would not be One without duality but would be split up into separate, limited identities as pantheism asserts. As *Kaivalya Upanishad* says, "the Self resides in all forms" (Prabhavananda and Manchester 115). The Self is in all forms and yet precisely as such, it is not itself a form and so is not limited, confined, contained, or conditioned by any form. Being undifferentiated, the Self is beyond all form; and precisely as such it is identical with all forms. In itself it is neither form nor formless, conditioned nor unconditioned, finite nor infinite; otherwise there would again be duality or differentiation.

Because, as the *Gita* states, the Self is not conceptualizable (Miller 33) and is beyond all conditions, no term, especially polarities, can be seized upon and applied literally or dualistically to the Self. Thus it is not absolute as opposed to relative, pure as opposed to impure, being as opposed to non-being. All distinctions, qualifications, or characterizations are void in the Self. As there is no way of stepping out that would not be it also, there is no room in which otherness can germinate. That is why ego's efforts to be a separate center of being and consciousness and to be Real by creating a world and satisfying its desires through adding something extra to what is, is *maya*. The only way you can be yourself, *Be* at all, is by purely being the Self.

You can see why Hindu scriptures speak of the Self as "all-pervasive" since nothing can be outside of or excluded from it. In it there is neither inside nor outside. It is neither individual nor universal; neither personal nor im- or non-personal. Its universality means that it is not an individual object, thing or person but is transpersonal. Its individuality implies that it is no other than each thing. Beyond persons and in persons, it is not in itself anything personal since it is not an individual entity separate from other such entities, however infinite a person is conceived to be. It is neither a subject nor an object. It is beyond such designations; and yet it is sometimes spoken of as "pure Subjectivity," just as it is said to be the "I" of all "I's" and yet the "I not-I." For in itself it is subjectless, objectless, pure, self-luminous Awareness and Reality.

The Self is also, as the *Gita* says, "unborn, undying, never ceasing, never beginning, deathless, birthless, unchanging forever" (Prabhavananda & Isherwood 1: 37). It is uncreated, uncaused, and unchanging because it is impossible for it not to be or to be other to itself. By the same token it is also omnipresent and ever-present or eternal. It cannot come into being or pass away, begin or cease. Being eternal and itself without change, it is identical with all things changing, and indeed *is* change—the reality of all change, the Being of all becoming, without itself coming into being or becoming anything. Remaining as it is in the midst of change, all change is a process of its Be-ing or manifestation.

It follows that, for Hinduism, the Self is not anything other than the Godhead or *Brahman*. It is the central teaching of the Upanishads, stated explicitly, repeatedly, and in various ways that *Atman* is *Brahman*. The Self is God as "he" is in "himself", beyond any condition or qualification, personal or impersonal designation. The only distinction made between *Atman* and *Brahman* is one of reference or in relationship to the relative world. As the *Gita* puts it for all Hindu scriptures, "When we consider *Brahman* as lodged within the individual being, we call him the *Atman*" (Prabhavananda & Isherwood 1: 74). *Atman* is *Brahman* indwelling as the heart or reality of each thing. *Atman* is *Brahman* in "his" Self-manifestation in conditioned existence, as incarnated in human history, in the life history of every human being, and indeed of every being or form. Thus the very nature of manifest reality is incarnational. Every person, every being, even the smallest particle of matter, is an incarnation of *Brahman* or the Self.

In the state of realization three characteristics of the Self figure prominently: *Atman* is Being *(sat)*, Awareness *(chit)*, and Joy or Bliss *(ananda)*. These are not separate qualities tacked on to the Self but constitute its very nature, such that it is pure, Unconditioned Being, All-embracing Awareness, and limitless Joy. Or it is Being as such, Awareness as such, Joy as such. The Self cannot be — and not be joyful, aware, or not-be. Its being is its awareness and joy; its awareness is its being and joy; and its joy is its being and awareness. These three characteristics are analogous to the Christian idea of the Trinity: Father (Being), Son or *Logos* (Awareness), and Holy Spirit (Joy).

It has been said that the Buddha denied the existence of a substantial, permanent self. However, the self the Buddha denied is not the Self described above but the self conceived as a separate entity. This is because he rejected the Samkhya phenomenon-noumenon dualism and because he saw the source of *dukkha* in human beings' desire and striving to make themselves permanent. He remained silent on the question of the existence or non-existence of *Brahman* or Godhead because he regarded belief in it useless to liberation from *dukkha*. He saw, as Freud was to do centuries later, that such a belief, prompted by self-preservation, guarantees a continuation of suffering as it makes ego strive to protect and preserve itself. He saw that liberation consists not in preserving but in transcending ego. This requires going altogether beyond conditioned existence and arriving at the Unconditioned State. Not only did he not deny this Reality as our true nature but emphatically affirmed it from his own experience and called it *Nirvana*.

The Buddha remained with the experience and refused to symbolize or categorize it because the Reality signified by *Nirvana* is completely beyond the grasp of ordinary consciousness and is not conceptualizable at all. So he expressed it in mostly negative terms in order to free our minds from the snare of language and our belief that when we are able to conceptualize something we have got the truth. His strategy leaves ego no foothold to attach to anything and to construct a system of belief, ritual, and worship around it. He regarded such activities as ego's futile attempts to stave off its nothingness and extinction. He saw his task as entirely therapeutic and soteriological: to show humans a way out of such deceptions and bring them to the living spring of that experience that liberates.

From expressions we find in early Buddhist scriptures, it is clear that the true nature revealed in *Nirvana* (the term itself means to extinguish or blow out) is the Unconditioned State of Reality as Such. For it is said to be "unborn, not become, not made, uncompounded" (Burtt 113). Thus it is eternal (unborn) and uncreated (not made), without any beginning or end (not become); infinite and One without any duality (uncompounded); and utterly transcends all cause or condition, being or becoming, limitation or differentiation. It is said to be "no-thing," that is, is not anything in itself – an object, being, or construct – and so is not limited to or by anything. Being in itself Reality without any condition or qualification such that it is beyond everything and yet nothing is beyond or other than it, this state signified by *Nirvana* is called "the Isle of no-beyond." The text goes on to emphasize that were it not the Absolute, Unconditioned State, liberation from conditioned existence would be impossible because nothing conditioned can liberate anyone from conditioned existence (Burtt 114-115).

Another early text calls *Nirvana* a plane or state of reality and awareness. By this it does not mean that it is a separate realm but implies that it is both the ultimate state of Reality and Awareness and the Ground and Reality of all states and planes of existence. For the text goes on to say that *Nirvana* is the utter extinction or transcendence of ego, duality, construction, thought, and object. Not being characterizable, we cannot say that it is or is not. So it is "neither this world nor another" and is "where there is no coming or going or remaining or descending or uprising, for this is itself without any support, without continuance, without mental object" (Conze et al. 94-95). Thus the true nature revealed in *Nirvana* is not in itself anything separate from or merely identified with this world but transcends all condition or differentiation. It has no foundation or support but is itself the Foundation or Ground in which all conditioned beings and states appear. And for that very reason it is without any beginning or end, becoming, permanence or cessation. So it is the identity of each and yet transcends all beings. Having no form or mental object in itself, it cannot be grasped and must be subjectless and objectless, Unconditioned Reality and pure, All-embracing Awareness.

Thus, although the Buddha denied the reality of a permanent, unchanging self, what he said about *Nirvana,* using terms very similar to those used by the Upanishads and the *Gita,* shows that it refers to the same Reality as the *Atman-Brahman* of Hinduism. His negative method of ungluing us from fixation on concepts and constructs and taking them for realities was fully developed by the Madhyamika School of Mahayana Buddhism in its "no-doctrine" stance of *Sunyata*.

So treading the path of *Nirvana* we come upon *Sunyata*, the epistemological clearing-house that opens the mind to the ontological reality of our true nature. As will be discussed more fully in the next chapter, what *Sunyata* (the term itself means "zeroness," "emptiness," or "voidness") declares is that Reality as Such is completely empty of separate or self-subsisting entity, otherness, conditioning or construct; void of anything we can think, grasp, formulate, or express. When every object, construct, programming, concept, thought, limitation, and separation — everything that is other than itself — is removed from the mind, what remains is unconditioned, undifferentiated, boundless Reality, which is revealed to be the true nature of each thing that is.

Whereas through *Sunyata* the Madhyamika School aims to clear from our mind everything other than itself so that it becomes open to a revelation of the reality of its true nature, which is pure Awareness; using the term *Mind*, the Yogachara School focuses on pure Awareness itself, in which the reality or true identity of that nature is revealed. For it holds that in direct experience our true nature is revealed to be nothing other than the self-luminous Mind or pure Awareness besides which nothing exists, and which is therefore identical with Reality as Such.

From the Mahayana scriptures, where *Nirvana* and *Sunyata* are stated to be synonymous, it is clear that they both point to the same thing, namely, that our true nature, identical with the nature of each thing, is the Unconditioned Reality beside, beyond, or other than which nothing exists. The synonyms also indicate the basis for later traditions' — especially Zen's — use of positive terms to express it.

Representing a confluence of Madhyamika *(Sunyata)* and Yogachara *(Mind)*, Zen uses a variety of expressions, sometimes interchangeably, to point to the true Self. Thus, reflecting the Yogachara teaching that Mind or All-embracing Awareness is Reality as Such, Huang Po says, "All the Buddhas and sentient beings are nothing but One Mind, besides which nothing exists. This Mind, which is without beginning, is unborn and indestructible." Identifying it with *Sunyata*, he says that it is "the boundless void" and the Source of all things. Speaking of it as the Unconditioned Buddha-nature he says, "Your Mind is intrinsically the Buddha, the Buddha is intrinsically the Mind, and Mind resembles a void," and this "essential Buddha-nature is a perfect whole, without superfluity or lack. It permeates the six states of existence and yet is everywhere perfectly whole. Thus, every single one of the myriads of phenomena in the universe is the Buddha" (Blofeld 1: 29, 30-31, 67, 84). Huang Po not only uses all three expressions — Mind, *Sunyata,* and Buddha-nature — equivalently to describe our true nature but also says that it is the identity of all that is. Completely void, it transcends all duality and differentiation, conditioning and construct. Yet being eternal, it is wholly present in all conditioned states. Infinite and One without any duality, it is always perfect and whole—that to which nothing can be added, from which nothing can be taken away, and besides which nothing exists, so that it is wholly present in and identical with each thing and yet transcends all.

Other expressions used by Zen have the same meaning. It is sometimes spoken of as "the original nature" or "the original face"—the latter expression having been made famous by Hui-neng in the koan, "What is your original face before your parents were born?" It means, "What is your true nature, or what are you, beyond all the conditioning and constructs that have made you the way you are now?" The implication is that what you truly are, right at this very moment, is no other than Unconditioned Reality prior to or beyond programmings and constructs (parents) that have formed (born) your reality, consciousness and self. Since each thing, just as it is, is nothing other than this uncreated, uncaused Reality, without beginning or end, it is the state in which you are at all times, even in the midst of your present conditioned state.

As mentioned, another expression frequently used by Zen to designate the Self is "Buddha-nature." The reference here is not so much to the historical Buddha, Gautama, as to the Unconditioned Reality of which Gautama, as one who had completely realized it in himself, is the incarnation. Both because of this and because the same nature is revealed in enlightenment as the true nature of each thing and realized by all who reach Buddhahood, this Unconditioned State of our true nature, similar to the Christian concept of the "Logos" incarnating in Jesus, is called "Buddha-nature." As master Daikaku explains, "Our real nature has never been born, never dies, has no form or shape, is permanent and unchanging—this is called fundamental inherent nature. Since this inherent nature is the same as that of all the Buddhas, it is called Buddha-nature" (Cleary 2: 30). To show that it is not limited to human beings but that each thing is no other than it, Suzuki Roshi says, "Everything is Buddha-nature. When there is no Buddha-nature, there is nothing at all. Something apart from Buddha-nature is just a delusion" (48).

Since Buddha-nature transcends duality and characterization, it can be equally affirmed and denied, including the denial of the affirmation and the denial. So a Zen master can give two different answers to the same question on two different occasions, depending on the state of mind of the questioner: Daibai asked Baso: "What is the Buddha?" Baso said, "This mind is Buddha." On another occasion, a monk asked Baso: "What is Buddha?" Baso said, "This mind is not Buddha." Again, since apart from the Buddha-nature nothing exists, a Zen master can point to whatever is immediately at hand as its embodiment and manifestation: A monk asked Tozan when he was weighing some flax: "What is Buddha?" Tozan said: "Three pounds of flax" (Reps 106, 114, 104-105).

Tibetan Buddhism, too, expresses the same truth in terms of both *Sunyata* and Mind as does, for instance, *The Yoga of Knowing the Mind* in words identical to those of Yogachara, Madhyamika and Zen (Evans-Wentz 1: 211-212). However, Tibetan Buddhism especially emphasizes the trinitarian notion of *tri-kaya* or "three bodies," signifying the fullness of the true nature of all things: The *Dharma-kaya* (the Body of Reality) is the Unconditioned, Formless Ground of *Sunyata*, the Void State of Reality as Such. *Nirmana-kaya* (Manifestation-Body) is its embodiment in and as each form, the full realization of which are the historical Buddhas; and representing complete transformation in five-fold wisdom aspect is the *Sambhoga-kaya* (Bliss-Body), the active, dynamic, transforming energy aspect of the formless in form (Trungpa 5: 106-108). These three aspects must not be thought of as separate entities. They are expressions of Reality in its Unconditioned State. Things just as they are, are the three bodies revealing the full nature of Unconditioned Reality, *Sunyata*, the true Self.

Representing the third pole of the Eastern nondualist axis, Taoism essentially agrees with the above view. Expressing it in terms of "Tao," "Voidness," and "Nameless," Taoism says that our true nature is the Way things actually are in their primordial, natural state beyond any conditioning and construct. As with Hinduism and Buddhism, for Taoism this all-pervading reality of our nature is beyond all duality, differentiation, limitation, or opposition. It cannot be an object; nor a subject in opposition to the world. Being the Absolute, there is nothing other than it to which it could be opposed.

Being formless, undifferentiated, and unqualifiable, Tao is beyond God conceived as a separate, individual being, personal or impersonal. It cannot be conceptualized, grasped, or expressed. So Lao-tzu calls Tao "nameless" and says, "Anything that can be named is not Tao" (Blakney 2: 85). Being nameless, it is beyond language, thought, ordinary consciousness, and its ways of knowing. Its formlessness means that it cannot be differentiated from any form; and precisely because of this it is said to be the "mother" or source and reality of all forms and differentiations.

Furthermore, Tao is said to be a void. This voidness is similar to the Buddhist teaching of *Sunyata:* Because Tao is not a thing among, apart from, or a part of other things, all things are possible in it. Being void of otherness and limitation, it is said to be inexhaustible, indivisible, invisible, inaudible, which means Tao is infinite and eternal. To realize this voidness is to experience the stillness of pure Being (Chan 141, 146-147, 156-157). In addition, it is said to depend on nothing and does not change; is everywhere, present in all things; and it can be manifest in our minds when all separation created by programming and constructs is removed (Blakney 2: 56-73).

More explicitly than Lao-tzu, Chuang Tzu taught the unconditioned, undifferentiated, formless, nondual, void-nature of Tao. According to him, Tao is beyond all relativity or duality. You cannot say that it is or that it is not, since both "is" and "is not" present only a partial, limited point of view: "There is nothing that cannot be seen from the standpoint of 'not-I.' And there is nothing that cannot be seen from the standpoint of the 'I' " (Merton 2: 42-43). For relative worlds produce each other by their mutual conditioning, exclusions, or denials. Thus, even "absolute" and "unconditioned," if used most rigorously to the exclusion of all things relative and conditioned, themselves thereby become relative and conditioned. So, in the end opposites are reducible to the same thing, once they are related to the pivot of Tao (Merton 2: 43).

Tao, therefore, transcends all dualities and partial viewpoints. Since all viewpoints are partial, Tao is not a point of view at all but the Transcendent Unity and indivisible wholeness which embraces all points of view by itself being void of all. On it all points of view converge and in its Unity they all dissolve and disappear. Being beyond all conditions, Tao is beyond all relativities and opposites and yet itself is not apart from anything demarcated by such differentiations. It can therefore affirm whatever is real in relative or conditioned things and states without being bound by them.

Lest affirmative terms, such as the Absolute, the true Self, Reality as Such, or even Tao, be taken as definitions — for then they would become relative and create opposites — Chuang Tzu goes on to issue denials by saying that such terms do not indicate anything exclusively real in Tao, since in it there are no distinctions. To get to the truth of the matter, you have to negate the affirmative and affirm the negative so as to remove any attachment to exclusive points of view; and then affirm the denial of both so as to indicate its void-nature:

> The limit of the unlimited is called 'fullness.' The limitlessness of the limited is called 'emptiness.' Tao is the source of both. It is in itself neither fullness nor emptiness. Tao produces both renewal and decay but is neither renewal nor decay. It causes being and non-being, but is neither being nor non-being. Tao assembles and it destroys, but it is neither the Totality nor the Void. (Merton 2: 124)

Because Tao transcends all differentiation, to take it exclusively as either being or non-being is to create a duality and so to lose it. To show this, he tells the following story:

The True Self

> Starlight asked Non-Being: "Master, are You? Or are you not?"
> Since he received no answer whatever, Starlight set himself to watch for Non-Being. He waited to see if Non-Being would put in an appearance.
> He kept his gaze at the deep Void, hoping to catch a glimpse of Non-Being.
> All day long he looked, and he saw nothing. He listened, but he heard nothing. He reached out to grasp, and he grasped nothing.
> Then Starlight exclaimed at last: "This is IT!" "This is the farthest yet! Who can reach it? I can comprehend the absence of being, but who can comprehend the absence of nothing? If now on top of all this, Non-Being IS, who can comprehend it?" (Merton 2: 125)

Thus, as the Void or Non-Being is not a subject, object, being or anything in itself apart from anything, it is impossible for anyone to see, hear, reach, comprehend, or grasp it. Nor is it a non-being, nothingness, or a mere absence of objects or beings. As absolute nothingness, it transcends both. It is the absence of absence, which is the fullness of what IS.

This fullness of Tao is expressed in terms of Oneness without duality such that nothing can be and not be it. Wherever and in whatever it is, it is wholly present. Its indivisibility means that each thing is wholly Tao and nothing but Tao. Its universality signifies that it is present everywhere in everything as the within, the without, and everything in-between (Merton 2: 123). This immanence, omnipresence and all-embracing nature of Tao is brought out in the following dialogue, which resembles the Zen koan about the Buddha being a shit-removing stick:

> Tung-kuo asked Chuang Tzu, "What is called Tao — where is it?"
> "It is everywhere," replied Chuang Tzu.
> Tung-kuo Tzu said, "It will not do unless you are more specific."
> "It is in the ant," said Chuang Tzu.
> "Why go so low down?"
> "It is in the weeds."
> "Why even lower?"
> "It is in a potsherd."
> "Why still lower?"
> "It is in the shit and piss," said Chuang Tzu.
> Tung-kuo gave no response. (Chan 203)

Because their framework is dualistic, the theistic religions ordinarily conceptualize the true Self in relative terms. It does not signify Absolute, Unconditioned Reality but, to use Ken Wilber's stage differentiation (5: 297), a universal, archetypal form of the transpersonal, subtle plane of reality and consciousness. This self remains a relative, individual entity separate from God and the rest of creation. Beyond this archetypal self, however, many masters in Jewish, Christian, and Islamic mystical traditions express another concept of the true Self that is absolute. For they clearly attest to their experience of transcendence of the archetypal self and realization of identity with the Absolute. Since the expression, *true Self,* is a metaphor for the Supreme Identity of the Godhead or the Absolute, in affirming their realization of this Identity, they reveal this true Self to be the Absolute and the true nature of each thing that is. Thus they view the true Self in two different ways.

Espousing a multidimensional view of reality, some Kabbalists express the relative view of the Self as *Ruah* and others as *Neshamah*. Representing the deepest reality in us, this self is universal. According to Lex Hixon, the Hasidic tradition regards it as a divine spark in us (136ff). Some Kabbalists view it as "the transcendent man," *Adam Kadmon,* the divine in human form, God in "his" essence and manifestation; others consider it to be an intermediate reality, *Metatron,* a bridge between God and creation. It is a dimension of awareness in which the union between God and human beings takes place. Beyond the collective unconscious, it is the state of universal consciousness (Shaya 121-128). Halevi says that it is common to all human beings and yet peculiar to each person (53-55).

While the above view is a clear affirmation of the archetypal self, other Kabbalistic masters definitely speak of the true Self in absolutist terms. As Moshe Idel has shown, the various images used imply its absolute nature. One is that of a circle in which the divine constitutes one half, while the human constitutes the other. The two halves are not seen as separate; they constitute one entity. Rabbi Dov Baer calls this reality "Adam," that is, man (Idel 63-65). Another image used to designate this identity is that of pouring a jug of water into a running stream; a third is a drop of water dissolving in the ocean; while a fourth is being swallowed by the divine, whereupon only one substance remains (Idel 67-71). Such images clearly identify the Self with the Godhead or the Formless Infinite *(Ein Sof)*.

Glimpses of this higher Self are to be found in the New Testament. Except for the pivotal text discussed in the last chapter, nowhere else does Jesus explicitly speak of the true Self. It is as if he lifts the curtain on the mystery only to drop it immediately. However, its place is occupied by an expression which was more understandable to his Jewish contemporaries — the Kingdom of God.

Scripture scholars have, of course, given various interpretations to this expression. In the Old Testament, the Kingdom stands for God's rule or effective presence in the world. Among its various associations in the New Testament, the deepest is its symbolizing the goal of human life lived in communion with God and constituting a community of universal love founded on the Unconditioned as the Ground and Source. Thus, standing for what human beings most deeply desire, the Kingdom is nothing other than God as the source, goal, center, and reality of all things. It is the Unconditioned in the conditioned; God incarnate in time, history, human existence, and in and as each form. Our desire for it on the unconscious plane signifies its presence in the deepest region of our mind. Its being within is its immanence, and its freedom from space-time limitations signifies its transcendence. Not being limited to any one place, the Kingdom is everywhere and always here; being present in every moment of time, it is always present in and as now. This view seems to be confirmed by John, Paul, and Christian mystics.

The Fourth Gospel sees the Kingdom as the Incarnate *Logos* in the heart of all things and as the being of each: "When all things began, the Word *[Logos]* already was. The Word dwelt with God, and what God was, the Word was. The Word, then, was with God at the beginning, and through him all things came to be; no single thing was created without him. All that came to be was alive with his life, and that life was the light of men" (Jn. 1: 1-4). Each thing, insofar as it is, is so because of its being the *Logos* incarnate. It is, therefore, the being of every being, form of every form, flesh of every flesh. It is the within and the without of all things. Becoming fully incarnate or manifest in the human form of Jesus the Christ, the *Logos* is revealed to be the Christ-nature in the heart and center of all things. According to John, this Christ-nature, which is the Kingdom, is our true Self. He also speaks of it as eternal life.

While John approaches the true Self in terms of Reality, Paul does so in terms of its nature as Awareness. While he was on the road to Damascus, Paul came to a blinding flash of realization of the Christ-nature as the identity of Christ and his disciples. Subsequently, he came to see that all forms, the whole universe itself, is the Body or the embodiment of the Christ-nature. He saw that this Christ-nature is the Awareness that embraces, pervades, and indeed, is all. He called it "the Spirit" (Col. 5: 10-11; Eph. 1: 10).

According to Lex Hixon, for Paul, this Spirit is the ultimate consciousness in which the transcendent reality of God and all spheres of beings are revealed as a single and perfectly transparent flow of divine radiance. The Spirit is the divine radiance refracted through the Christ-nature forming the core of all creation, the heart of the universe, which is therefore God's heart. It is the infinite divine life become conscious of itself as each form (137ff).

Christian mystics also came to formulate a twofold view of the Self: one relative, the other absolute. The first view, which is similar to that of many Jewish mystics and is accepted by most Christian mystics, conceives the higher Self as an individual entity separate from God. As the highest part of our nature, a realm between God and the manifest order of creation, it is the meeting point between God and the individual. Echoing St. Paul, Julian of Norwich distinguishes between a lower and a higher nature, and says that the highest sphere of the latter is eternally united with God and with Christ. It is something divine. St. Teresa of Avila calls it "the Empyrean Heaven" and says that it is eternally united with God. Similarly, Louis de Blois characterizes it as a divine temple. Only God may enter it; and from it God is said never to depart. Irradiated by divine light and lifted above all created beings, it is permanently attached to God, and is above space and time. And Ruysbroeck characterizes it as a divine spark which is eternally united with God (Spencer 243-245). Bernadette Roberts identifies this archetypal self as the Kingdom of God and says that it is "the still-point within" where union with God takes place (1: 140). Such statements make it clear that this self is not the Absolute but the relative, universal, archetypal, transpersonal form that one experiences in the subtle state of consciousness. It is the self with which union with God takes place.

One of those who espouses the second view is Meister Eckhart. First, he identifies the Kingdom with God when he says, "The Kingdom of God is God himself with all his fullness" (Blakney 1: 129). Then he identifies God with the Absolute or true Self: "The idea of the soul and the idea of God are identical" (Blakney 1: 148). Next, he says that this Self, which constitutes our essence or core, is identical with God's core or essence. He writes, "The core of God is also my core; and the core of my soul, the core of God" (Blakney 1: 126, 129). Thus, our true Self or identity is the Supreme Identity of the Godhead, for God's essence is declared to be the essence, nature or reality of each individual: "What is God's must be mine and what is mine God's. God's is-ness is my is-ness, and neither more nor less" (Blakney 1: 180). There is not the slightest differentiation between the two. For Eckhart, to be a child of God means to be one in substance, essence, and nature. In the ultimate state of realization, then, "without distinction we shall be the same essence and the same substance and nature that he is" (Fox, *Breakthrough* 327).

For Eckhart, in the ultimate state of Reality and Awareness there are no separate identities. There is only one Supreme Identity – the one "I" of "is-ness" manifested as the identity of each form, and therefore as our true identity. The Self is this "I" which is that of God "himself" (in Suzuki 5: 10). There is no differentiation between the true Self and God: "God and the soul are so nearly [related] to each other that there is really no distinction between them." And to show that this Self is the Christ-Self, he says, "Between the only begotten Son and the soul there is no distinction" (Blakney 1: 214, 215). Thus for Eckhart, beyond space-time limitations, our true nature is unconditioned, infinite and eternal: "The word 'man' means something above nature, above time, and raised up above everything that is inclined to time and place and corporeality" (quoted by Spencer 240-241).

Expressing a similar view, Bernadette Roberts intimates that our true identity is wholly beyond the relative plane of the separate self—both the ego and the higher, archetypal self. She calls it "no-self" because she regards all selves to be relative, for beyond the relative states there are no multiple selves or identities. There is only the One Identity that is God. She calls it "pure Subjectivity," "which is not an identity of self and God (no self rises to God), but the identity of God alone who remains when there is no self." But this is not the personal God, whom she calls "God-as-object," who disappears with the loss or transcendence of self. For "when there is no personal self there is also no personal God." In this nonrelative state of pure Subjectivity or God-as-subject, no otherness remains. So nothing could possibly exist that could be an object or constitute a separate identity. Beyond God-as-object, then, is identity with God—the Identity that is God. This identity cannot belong to anyone, nor can it inhere in anything because it is all that exists. All things, consequently you, are wholly it (1: 142-166).

The Sufis, too, as mentioned in the last chapter, have an absolute and a relative view of Self. Representing the latter, some Sufis hold a view, strikingly similar to those of St. Paul and Julian of Norwich, according to which there is in us a lower and a higher self. While the former is pretty much the same as St. Paul's "lower nature," the latter is not only the deepest part of human nature, but is also, to al-Ghazali, as to Ruysbroeck, a ray of divine light and appears to be divine (Spencer 313). To Martin Lings, this Self is the heart, the bridge between God and the individual, and the center of their intuitive union (50-52).

Representing the other view of the Self as Reality as Such is Attar, who says that the very essence of God is within us as the Self. It is the very heart and soul of what we and all things truly are (Spencer 314). As he expressed in the *Parliament of the Birds,* what remains in the state of final realization is the Supreme Identity of the Godhead, to which the individual appears as identical. Similarly, in the expression, "man-God, God-man," Guru Bawa intimates an equivalence of essence between God and human beings. According to him, our ultimate identity is no other than God, who alone is (Hixon 170-173).

Similar to the views of other paths is the Sufi notion that our true nature is that of the Perfected or Completed Man, who is not an individual being, separate from other such beings but, like Buddha-nature and Christ-nature, appears to represent the Unconditioned Reality. Eternal, unconditioned, and divine, it is identified by some Sufis as the *Logos* (an apparent reflection of *The Gospel According to John*). A further dependence on Christianity is shown by the fact that, just as Christ is believed to be Logos incarnate, so Muhammad is regarded as the embodiment of the Perfected Man. At any rate, the goal of Sufi practice is to realize this Self in all its fullness.

From this brief exposition, it is clear that your true identity is not that of the separate self but the Self that remains when the separate self is gone. It is not unique or proper to you, nor does it belong to you exclusively. The paradox is that you are most truly your Self when you are not your separate self. There is nothing other than this Supreme Identity, a complete realization of which is the aim of all existence. Yet it is not attainable nor can it be an object of striving because from no-beginning time, everything has always been it and nothing other than its manifestation. When you let go of your effort to be other than it, you discover that you are it — the Self that is "I not-I," that excludes nothing, is separated from nothing, and so is at one with and indeed IS all things. To it nothing can be added; from it nothing can be taken away; other than it nothing exists.

The chapters that follow will be concerned with an exposition of the various essential aspects of this Self and in what its realization consists.

Chapter 19
Experiencing Oneness

Nature of the Experience

The pivotal point in the journey of Self-realization is reached when, transcending all differentiation, you arrive at the experience of absolute oneness with Reality as Such. This absolute transcendence of otherness, which is the realization of your true identity, is Self-realization. In this chapter I shall explore the nature of this experience, the meaning of absolute oneness, and in what it consists.

First, this experience is not a matter of abstract, conceptual thinking or discursive reasoning. Nor is it an intellectual understanding. It is not a question of feeling or even intuition, as *Mundakya Upanishad* explicitly states. For, in none of them is duality overcome. None cuts through the filtering mechanisms of programming, concept, model, construct, framework, or thought. It must take place prior to the information-processing activity of ordinary consciousness. So none of the ordinary modes of knowing or experience can be identified with it or can bring it about. It cannot take place *through anything*. For as long as that happens, however great or profound the experience, a separation will be created between it and Reality. And so it will not be an experience *of* Reality as Such but of a construct or what is filtered through it. Hence nothing can intervene or mediate between the experience and Reality.

Second, this experience cannot be *of* anything. Strictly speaking, there is no object of this experience. Since nothing can mediate between it and Reality, there is no separation between them. So, Reality cannot be an object of this experience, otherwise the experience will not be that of Reality as Such but of another mental construction. Moreover, since all objects are constructs and create a distance from Reality, in this experience there cannot be any object in the mind. The experience cannot, therefore, be of a nature different from Reality. Thus it must be strictly "ontological." There cannot be even the tremor of a distinction between the two; else it will not be a direct experience of Reality or the Self.

Third, in this experience there cannot be any duality between the subject and the experience; otherwise it will not be absolutely direct and unmediated. The experience, the experiencing subject, and what is experienced must be identical, so that there is no "you" as a separate individual experiencing an object or reality separate from yourself. In this state, therefore, there is nothing to experience and no one to experience anything. The experience itself is Reality as Such in the process of its unfoldment or Be-ing in the individual and in all things as itself.

Fourth, the experience itself being Unconditioned Reality, what you experience in this state is your identity with the Unconditioned. Thus Self-realization is nothing other than your direct and unmediated experience that you are Reality as Such. It follows that the Self can be realized only directly, only as identity, and in no other way. The only way you can experience the Self is by being the Self, which is nothing other than the Self being itself. In theistic language, Self-realization is nothing other than God experiencing or Being and revealing "himself" in you as your very identity and that of all things.

Since this experience is God's Self-manifestation, it is infinite and eternal, always going on, and can never begin or cease. Were it otherwise, God would be other to "himself," which is impossible. It follows that, strictly speaking, this experience cannot begin in you. You can neither come to it nor do anything to attain it. And since you already are the Self, there is no such thing as realizing it. On this the sources of experiential religion are agreed. So extensive documentation is not necessary. Ramana Maharshi expresses it for all when he says:

> There is no reaching the Self. If the Self were to be reached, it would mean that the Self is not here and now but that it has yet to be obtained. What is got afresh will also be lost. So it will be impermanent. What is not permanent is not worth striving for. So I say the Self is not reached. You are the Self; you are already That. (Bercholz 72-73)

Since you are the Self, you are at all times in the state of realization. What is called "realization" consists of removing from your mind the sense of separation created by conditioning and dualistic constructs, and maintained by thought and inner dialogue. So he says again:

> No one is ever away from his Self and therefore everyone is in fact Self-realized; only – and this is the great mystery – people do not know

this and want to realize the Self. Realization consists in getting rid of
the false idea that one is not realized. (Osborne 23)

When you remove the thinking that breeds the illusion of separation, the Reality that ever is shines forth; and you discover that the experience has already and always been there. That discovery or shining forth, which is God's eternal Self-manifestation in time is, strictly speaking, the revelation of the Unconditioned in you as itself. All you can do to bring it about is to let it become fully conscious in you as your Supreme Identity.

Although this direct experience is always one of identity, that is not the aim of every experience of oneness. In line with the two views of the Self held by the sources of experiential religion, there are two kinds of oneness: relative or oneness of relationship, and absolute or oneness of identity. The goal of the former is union; that of the latter is identity.

The first consists of a relationship between two beings or persons who exist independently of each other, who come together to form a union, and who remain separate throughout the relationship. The common ground of the relationship is the union of two individuals who otherwise remain distinct. This requires a dualistic framework and is never direct. It takes place always through various mediums or filtering mechanisms, such as, faith, love, trust, devotion, grace. This position is generally held by dualistic traditions that conceive God as a person or Transcendent Other.

In contrast, as already explained, absolute oneness is based on identity and being, rather than union and relationship. Because it is identity, there are no terms in this oneness; no separate persons who retain their separateness; and no coming together or merging of two separate selves to become one. There is only the one Self that reveals itself as the Identity that *is* each individual and all that is.

It must not be thought, however, that absolute oneness is anything in itself. Nor does it imply some sort of substance, noumenon, or transcendent secret agent invisibly permeating and making all things one. And it certainly does not imply that in absolute oneness everything boils down to one big pot of stew. Since there is nothing in it other than Reality as Such, multiplicity, even relative oneness, is not opposed to it. For it declares that the very nature of each thing is such that it is Unconditioned Reality, which makes each thing absolutely one with all things, and that apart from this nothing whatsoever exists.

Furthermore, this oneness is not a point of view but declares a complete absence in Reality of any point of view, anyone to perceive it, or anything that can be perceived, conceived, categorized, packaged, or in any way circumscribed or put in any kind of mind-frame. It says that when nothing is added or taken away from anything, when anything that can create a separation or duality is removed or transcended, Reality reveals itself directly as absolutely one. The very being of each thing — the only way anything can *be* at all — consists in its being one with all and all with each. Nothing can be and not be absolutely one without any condition or qualification.

It follows that to say that Reality is otherwise than absolutely one is to declare it to be otherwise than it is and so to render it false and contradictory. For this very reason dualism cannot say anything about how Reality is in itself. Any of its attempts to do so becomes contradictory. Since Reality is utterly void of otherness, in declaring otherness to constitute its nature, dualism contradicts it and thereby demonstrates that it cannot say anything truthful about it. It can tell us only how things appear through its masks of models, concepts, theories or frameworks. Since this is not how things are in themselves, whatever it says, to use Korzybski's words, "a thing is, it isn't" (quoted by Wilber 1: 42).

The untenability of dualism is also a consequence of the view of reality that emerges from relativity, quantum, bootstrap, and holonomic theories insofar as they argue against the duality of subject and object, and the exclusion of the former from scientific explanation. Commenting on this development, Fritjof Capra says: "Scientific research involves the observer as a participator and this involves the consciousness of the human observer. Hence, there are no objective properties of nature, independent of the human observer" (quoted by Weber in Wilber 4: 228). According to this view, in the process of observing or measuring a subatomic particle, the observer and the observed form a dynamic, interacting whole, excluding a separation of the observer from the process. Since the properties of the atomic object have to be understood in terms of the object's interaction with the observer, Capra says that the subject-object duality and the exclusion of the former from a purely objective description of nature are no longer valid. So he concludes: "You can no longer separate the mode of perception from the thing which is perceived" (quoted by Weber in Wilber 4: 231).

Werner Heisenberg concurs: "The common division of the world into subject and object, inner world and outer world, body and soul, is no longer adequate and leads into difficulties" (quoted by Wilber 1: 39). Pointing out the reason for the difficulties, Erwin Schroedinger observes: "Subject and object are one. The barrier between them cannot be said to have broken down as a result of recent experience in the physical sciences, for this barrier does not exist" (quoted by Wilber 1: 38). From his holonomic perspective David Bohm likewise says, "If, according to the new physics, everything is enfolded in everything else, then there is no real separation of domains. Mind grows out of matter. And matter contains the essence of mind. These two are really abstractions from the whole: relatively invariant subtotalities created by our thought" (quoted by Weber in Wilber 4: 194).

In going further and stating that all things exist in a state of interpenetration and undivided wholeness, the bootstrap theory takes its stand even more firmly against dualism. For it holds that the universe is an undivided whole in which mutual interrelations of events determine the structure of the entire web. In this web of relations constituting the nature of physical reality on the subatomic level, "particles dynamically compose one another, each involving all the others such that each particle, for instance, consists of all other particles" (Capra in Wilber 4: 114-115).

The reason for the inability of dualism to describe reality as it is is most trenchantly stated by Spencer-Brown when he argues that any of its attempts to do so becomes a falsification of the nature of reality. He says that since dualism involves cutting reality up into

> at least one state which sees, and at least one other state which is seen, in this severed and mutilated condition, whatever it sees is *only partially* itself. We may take it that the world is undoubtedly itself . . . but, in any attempt to see itself as an object, it must equally undoubtedly, act so as to make itself distinct from, and therefore false to, itself. In this condition it will always partially elude itself. (104-105; italics his)

This means, as Bertrand Russell, Ludwig Wittgenstein, and others have recognized, that dualism can never perceive the whole. Therefore, not only can it not say what the whole is, but, even more importantly, any attempt to perceive reality as made up of objects constitutes a falsification of its nature. No objective view can ever present reality as it is. So Spencer-Brown goes on to say that any construction can present only a token or part, and never the whole, of reality, which must necessarily elude its grasp. Thus, all seeing is necessarily partial; and in saying that the world is other than the perceiver or that in reality things are separate, dualism causes one state to declare how the whole of reality is while excluding itself from it, thereby falsifying and rendering its claim illusory.

Moreover, dualism itself does not hold up in the end. As David Bohm has remarked:

> When you trace a particular absolute notion to what appears to be its logical conclusion, you find it to be identical with its opposite, and therefore the whole dualism collapses, as Hegel found. Reason first shows you that opposites pass into each other, then you discover that

one opposite reflects the other, and finally you find that they are identical to each other. (Quoted by Weber in Wilber 4: 206)

If you make dualism itself absolute and keep excluding everything from one of its members, as we saw Chuang Tzu demonstrating – if, for instance, you keep the subject rigorously separate from the world – you find that it finally cancels itself out by making itself unreal, thereby revealing the unity of reality. Thus in affirming dualism, ego tries to declare reality to be other than it is. However, in so doing, it succeeds in declaring itself to be other than reality and reveals reality to be other than dualistic, i.e., nondual or absolutely one. This absolute oneness has three main characteristics.

Three Characteristics of Absolute Oneness

First, mutual inherence: All that is wholly abides in you and you are wholly in all things. This is more than the traditional sense of God indwelling in all things, where indwelling is conceived as something external to the being of an individual. Mutual inherence, on the other hand, is something intrinsic: Being exactly the way you are and only so being, you are wholly in each thing, wholly in the entire universe, wholly in God; and God, the entire universe, and each being are wholly in you. The only teaching comparable to this is the Catholic trinitarian one – only here it is declared to be the nature of all beings.

Second, interpenetration: There are no individual objects separate from one another and existing independently. Rather, the universe is an undivided whole in which things exist in interpenetration, forming a dynamic web of intrinsic relations on all levels of existence, actual and possible. In their actual, unconditioned state, beyond the duality of finite and infinite, things wholly penetrate one another, flowing into one another. Thus you are wholly in every fiber of every being and every fiber of every being in the entire universe is wholly in you. You are coextensive with and pervade all, and precisely as they are, all things at the same time are coextensive with and pervade you.

Third, identity: Things not only wholly penetrate and abide in each other, but your very being or nature is to be identical with all that is; and all things, being precisely what they are and only so being, they are identical with you. This does not change your nature but makes it precisely what it is. This is the true, supreme identity of each thing, besides which nothing exists. Nothing can be and not be identical with all that is. Not the slightest shred of differentiation can be found in Reality as Such.

Insofar as anything is real, it is in this way absolutely one and cannot be otherwise, or else it would cease to be. Absolute Oneness is the nature of Reality as Such, which means that *Reality* and *absolute oneness* are interchangeable terms. These characteristics of absolute oneness are expressed, more or less explicitly, by the sources of experiential religion.

In its various scriptures Hinduism affirms all three characteristics. While explicitly stating only identity, they seem to imply mutual inherence and interpenetration from the standpoint of that identity of the Self. As already discussed in the last chapter, the Upanishads teach that absolute oneness is the actual state of all things. Thus *Chandogya Upanishad* says that *Brahman* or the Self alone is and all that is. It is the reality of all becoming, the form of every form, the inner and the outer reality of each (Prabhavananda & Manchester 64-67). Other Upanishads also speak of the identity of each with all and all with each "in the Self," that is, in their ultimate, Unconditioned State. The "subtle essence," that is, the nature of each being, is the "subtle essence" of all, and conversely. This is not a reduction of all things into one thing—God or the Self—but a declaration that in the Unconditioned State the very being of each thing consists of its being identical with all. It is because all things just as they are, are absolutely One, here-now, that every finite being is identical with everything else and with the infinite, and every moment with eternity.

Furthermore, the Upanishads teach that all things actually exist "in the Self," or the Unconditioned State. It is precisely because of the Unconditioned constituting the nature of all things that they exist in a state of mutual inherence. Thus *Kaivalya* and *Isha Upanishads* speak of seeing "all beings in the Self, and the Self in all beings" (Prabhavananda and Manchester 27, 115). The emphasis on seeing is important here because the Upanishads are saying that when you see all things in their true nature or Unconditioned State, you see that each actually exists in all and all in each. It is only in this state that this characteristic can be experienced.

Finally, the Upanishads imply mutual interpenetration in the all-embracing reality of the Self. Like butter in cream, it is in and permeates all things as their reality or "subtle essence" (Prabhavananda and Manchester 64, 69, 120). While this text does not directly state it, it seems to imply interpenetration and undivided wholeness in the unity of the Self. And both mutual inherence and interpenetration are implied in the following passage from the *Gita:*

His [i.e., the yogi's] heart is with Brahman,
His eyes in all things
See only Brahman
Equally present,

Knows his own Atman
In every creature,
All creation
Within that Atman.
(Prabhavananda and Isherwood 1:67)

Since the Self is all, its being in every creature and all creation in it implies that each exists in all and all in each in mutual inherence and interpenetration.

These teachings are further developed by Advaita Vedanta. Shankara, who was the most important of its spokesmen, articulated them in his writings. Rudolf Otto summarizes Shankara's position in these words:

Many is seen as one (and only thus rightly seen).
Many is seen in the One.
The One is seen in the Many.
The One is seen. (68)

The first statement concerns a direct experience of all things in their absolute Oneness, which reveals each to be identical with all and all with each. They are experienced thus, the second statement says, because they are experienced in the Self, that is, in their Unconditioned State. Together, they declare that when things are seen in their Unconditioned State, each is experienced as identical with all and all with each. Together with the second, the third states that in absolute Oneness all things inhere in and interpenetrate one another. Furthermore, they imply that this involves no reduction of the many into the One, nor is the One Supreme Identity dissolved but affirmed in its true light when directly experienced as all things. Also, the first and the last statement say that when things are thus experienced, their true nature is experienced. Since this is the only state in which anything can ever BE at all, when you experience things in this way you experience them in their true identity.

The Buddhist teaching on the three characteristics is best formulated in three Mahayana schools: Madhyamika, Yogachara, and Hua Yen. With its doctrine of *Sunyata*, the first establishes the identity of all things in their Unconditioned State; in the doctrine of Absolute Mind the second affirms the direct experience of all things in All-embracing Awareness; while the third completes the teaching on identity with its addition of mutual inherence and interpenetration of all things and events.

The Madhyamika teaching of *Sunyata* is best summarized in the *Heart Sutra*. Glancing at the text, the first point you notice is that *Sunyata* is a matter of direct experience or "seeing" — for it is said to have been seen by Bodhisattva

Avalokitesvara "from the wisdom that has gone beyond," that is, from a realization of All-embracing Awareness, which is altogether beyond any conditioned being or state. Therefore, it represents the ultimate revelation of the nature of Reality as Such. What is the nature of this revelation?

The *Sutra* says that it consists in seeing that "form is emptiness and the very emptiness is form; emptiness does not differ from form, nor does form differ from emptiness; whatever is form that is emptiness, whatever is emptiness that is form" (Conze et al. 152). This is the essential teaching. What does it mean?

First, form is emptiness. This means that each form or being, when directly experienced purely as itself, is experienced in its true nature as altogether void of any conditioning or construct, framework or limitation, object or content, thought or filtering mechanism that could create otherness or become the foundation of its own existence in separation from anything else. In this void state beyond duality, the true identity or nature of each thing or form, being exactly what it is and only so being, is experienced as formless, infinite, unconditioned.

Second, emptiness is form. When directly experienced precisely as such, formlessness or the Unconditioned is experienced as void of otherness or separation from anything else and thus none other than the reality or identity of each form or thing just as it is. As the Unconditioned is not in itself separate from anything, its very nature is to be the nature, suchness, or reality of each being. The Infinite is thus revealed to be no other than the finite, formlessness no other than the entire universe of forms. Emptiness directly experienced, then, is experienced as the absolute, formless ground, condition, reality, and identity of all things.

So while the first statement says that each thing is void of differentiation such that the finite is no other than the infinite, the conditioned than the Unconditioned, and each is identical with all; the second removes the possible misunderstanding by saying that voidness is all things just as they are, and all is identical with each. Such being the nature of all things, *Sunyata* reveals the illusory character of our attempts to introduce otherness in reality through conditioning, thought, and constructs. When it clears away from our mind everything that *is not,* so that only *what is* remains, the duality of form and formlessness created by the belief in separate, substantial entities having inherent existence of their own is completely transcended.

Emphasizing nondifferentiation, the *Sutra* continues: "Emptiness does not differ from form nor form differ from emptiness." Yet to show that this identity does not imply a reduction of one to the other, it continues: "Form is form, emptiness is emptiness." Each thing is what it is; and precisely as such, its being is constituted by its identity with all that is because in "true emptiness" all duality, identity and differentiation, immanence and transcendence, real and unreal, absolute and relative, *samsara* and *nirvana*, form and formlessness are so completely transcended that it is neither one nor the other, nor both, nor neither. When there is absolutely nothing to grasp or attach to, when emptiness is itself empty, then you have the final state of true emptiness in which each thing is revealed to be what it truly is — Reality as Such. And there being nothing other than it in all realms of existence, actual or possible, the experience itself is revealed to be this Reality. The final state is just this, just the dew drop dangling from the grass seed glistening in the radiant sun like a rich jewel glowing in the ear of a beautiful girl.

While the Madhyamika teaching on emptiness cuts through all conditioning and constructs so that Reality can reveal itself directly to the mind, Yogachara teaches that, in the state of emptiness, the Mind or Awareness as Such is revealed in direct experience to be the nature of Reality as Such, and consequently is identical with all. It is this identity of Awareness and Reality that makes the experience of absolute Oneness possible.

While other sources adumbrated the view, growing out of the *Avatamsaka Sutra*, it is the Hua Yen School that completes the Buddhist view on absolute oneness, with its full-fledged teaching of identity, interpenetration, and the mutual inherence of all in each and each in all simultaneously in all states and planes of existence. The *Sutra* states:

> This is the abode [i.e., the universe] of all those who make one age enter into all time and all ages enter into one time; who make one space enter into all spaces, and all space into one space, and yet each without destroying its individuality; who make one reality enter into all reality, and all reality into one reality, and yet each without being annihilated; who make one being enter into all beings, and all beings into one being, and yet each retaining its individuality...who make all things enter into one thought-moment; who go to all lands by the raising of one thought; who manifest themselves wherever there are beings. (Quoted by D.T. Suzuki 5: Third Series 120-121)

According to this teaching, at this very moment, each thing, even the smallest particle of matter, while being what it is or retaining its individuality, simultaneously penetrates and inheres in each particle of each thing in this and all other universes of all time, actual and possible; and each thing in all universes of all time, actual and possible, while remaining exactly what it is, completely penetrates and wholly inheres in each particle of each thing, such that these relations constitute their very nature. As Garma Chang (Chung-Yuan) points out, such interpenetration and mutual inherence are possible only because they are founded on the Supreme Identity revealed in *Sunyata* (2: 136-137). One implication of this is that in the eternal present of Awareness, the universe is not seen as having been created billions of years ago. Rather, each and all things in all universes, while remaining exactly as they are, simultaneously originate, interact, interpenetrate, and mutually inhere and include each and all others. Such relationships make each thing have infinite dimensions. And all existence is constituted by such relationships. That is why, right at this very moment, each moment penetrates and is penetrated by, embraces and is embraced by, all moments that ever were or ever shall be. At this very moment, you wholly penetrate and inhere in each being in this and in all universes, past, present and future; and all things of all universes wholly penetrate and inhere in you.

The Hua Yen School fully fleshed out the above teaching of the *Avatamsaka Sutra*. And the Hua Yen teaching is best expressed in epigrammatic form by master Tu Shun in the following words:

First, one is one.
Second, all is one
Third, one is all
Fourth, all is all. (Chang 2: 219)

The first statement says that each thing is what it is. A form is a form. The second says that, while remaining perfectly what they are, in their very identity, all things in all realms of existence include, penetrate, permeate, and are identical with each thing, thus revealing the nature of absolutely Oneness. The third expresses the complementarity of this mutual relationship by saying that each form, while remaining perfectly distinct, includes, penetrates, and is identical with all things in all realms of all universes, actual and possible. The fourth envisions this process as the state of simultaneous identity, interpenetration, and indwelling of each in each, all in each, each in all, and all in all. The very structure of existence is seen to be such that all things, universes, and realms of existence form this state of undivided wholeness through simultaneous mutual interpenetration, inherence, and being and manifestation so that the interconnected web of relations and dimensions they form are infinite. As Tu Shun says:

> The shih [one thing] remains as it is, and yet embraces all. For example, the form of one atom does not expand, and yet it can embrace the infinite universe. This is because all the cosmoses are not separate from the Dharmadhatu [Reality as Such], so they can all appear in one

atom. If one atom is so, all the dharmas [realities] should also be so, since in their harmonious fusing the individual and the universal are neither identical nor different. (Chang 2: 219)

Various Buddhist sources confirm that this undivided wholeness, interpenetration, and mutual indwelling are not only experienced at the advanced state of meditation but also that absolute Oneness is the final stage of these progressive experiences as it forms the core of the experience of enlightenment. Thus, explaining enlightenment in terms of it, Yasutani Roshi says, "It is seeing into your true nature and directly realizing that you and the universe are basically one" (Kapleau 1: 135). Garma Chang (Chung-Yuan) accentuates the unity and diversity in absolute Oneness when he describes enlightenment as "the direct experience of beholding, unfolding, or realizing the Mind-essence in its fullness. In essence it is illuminating yet void, serene yet dynamic, transcending yet immanent, free yet all-embracing" (1: 162). Expressing the same view, a Tantric Buddhist text declares:

> It is the essence of Dharma, to which nothing may be added and from which nothing may be withdrawn. It is free from the two notions of subject and object, free from being and non-being, from characterizing and characteristics; it is pure and immaculate in its own nature. Neither duality nor nonduality, calm and tranquil, it consists in all things, motionless and unflurried; such is Wisdom-means which may be known intuitively. (Conze et al. 241)

Another text, *The Yoga of Knowing the Mind,* states categorically that until duality is transcended and absolute Oneness realized, this knowledge or enlightenment cannot be attained (Evans-Wentz 1:206, 211).

The heart of Taoism, whether it be Taoist yoga or mysticism, is the realization of absolute Oneness with Tao. Even the immortality sought by Taoist yogis is to be viewed in this light, for true immortality can be attained only by realizing this Oneness. As Lu Kuan Yu points out, the aim of Taoist yoga is to realize oneness with things for the purpose of returning to the Source, which is Tao (3:77).

For Taoism, this oneness is clearly of the nondual, absolute kind. As Blofeld points out, since for Lao-tzu Tao is formless, undifferentiated, absolute Reality, beyond all relativity or opposites (3: 152-153), the oneness realized with it must also be absolute.

That this oneness is beyond any duality or relativity is not only implied in what Chuang Tzu says about the nature of Tao and its realization; it is also categorically stated in the following passage:

> The pivot of Tao passes through the center where all affirmations and denials converge. He who grasps the pivot is at the still point from which all movements and opposites can be seen in their right relationship. Hence he sees the limitless possibilities of both "Yes" and "No." Abandoning all thought of imposing a limit or taking sides, he rests in direct intuition. (Merton 2: 42-43)

Clearly Chuang Tzu is saying that the center through which the pivot of Tao passes is absolute Oneness or the Unconditioned State, which is beyond all condition, form, differentiation, relativity, or opposites. One who is established in it can affirm all limited viewpoints because s/he sees them from their transcendent unity or point of convergence in Tao. For the pivot is the precise point at which awareness pivots on itself, reverses its orientation, and sheds all objects or contents, conditioning, constructs, and relative states and becomes silent, still, and void. It is in this state that awareness comes to a direct experience of its identity with Tao. Thus, according to Taoist yoga, when the dualism of self and others has been transcended and the mind is unified and rendered void and formless, it experiences itself to be coextensive with the universe (Blofeld 4: 152, 153, 163). For Taoism, in this direct, ontological experience of absolute Oneness you realize that you are established at the Center, Source, and Suchness of all that is.

Consistent with what we have seen before, theistic sources of experiential religion, such as many Jewish, Christian, and Islamic mystics, advocate both relative and absolute oneness. The dualist traditions generally advocate relative oneness or union with God. However, while acknowledging the dualistic framework, many masters affirm absolute Oneness or identity with the Godhead. This matter is complicated by the fact that, because of orthodox theology or authority or because the experience is couched in the language of love relationship, some of those who do have this experience do not clearly differentiate it, in their explanation, from relative oneness.

The term many Kabbalists use to refer to relative oneness or union is *cleaving,* together with other metaphors discussed in the last chapter (Idel 65-72). That union is relative oneness is clear, for instance, from Leo Shaya's explanation that it takes place in the state of consciousness in which the distinction between knower and the known remains. This union is said to be an "essential" relationship, that is, in it all things are experienced in God and God equally in all things. However, the addition that it is experienced through the mediation of God's "real presence" shows that union is a relative state. It does not take place with the Godhead *(Ein Sof)*, but in "the subtle," mediant state (136-144, 124ff). For many, the union appears to be ecstatic.

Moreover, concurring with the above and quoting the Bible, Halevi says that no human being may see the face of God directly and continue to live. So s/he is granted a vision of a likeness in the manifest universe. The union takes place through this likeness and in a universal state; but it is not the uncreated state of the *Ein Sof* (163, 207).

As Moshe Idel has demonstrated, union is not the final destination of the Jewish mystical path. The step beyond union is identity, which is characterized by the term, among others, *annihilation*. Union precedes annihilation, which is absolute Oneness. For annihilation signifies utter transcendence of the archetypal self, individual existence, duality, or separation. In this state only one substance, the Absolute, *Ein Sof*, remains. It is the state of undifferentiated unity in which no consciousness of oneself as a separate entity remains (Idel 63-72).

According to Lex Hixon, some Hasidic masters express the absolute Oneness in terms of what they call "the Messiah-nature," which is the indwelling or ultimate manifestation of the divine in human form. It constitutes the core of what humans truly are. When an individual realizes it, s/he experiences a real oneness with God as a particular tongue of flame is one with the fire. In this oneness, his/her individuality does not disappear, however. Only the separation and what causes it no longer remain — there remains only the dance of the flames in the fire (135-145).

The New Testament hints at absolute Oneness as the goal of human life. Thus, in the Fourth Gospel Jesus prays that his disciples may have a perfect oneness: "May they be one: as thou, Father, are in me, and I in thee, so also may they be in us...that they may be one as we are one: I in them and thou in me, may they be perfectly one" (Jn. 17: 21-23). First, Jesus is praying that his disciples may have the same kind of oneness among themselves as he has with the Father. Since his oneness with the Father is absolute, if his disciples are to have the same type of oneness, theirs must also be absolute. Second, the locus of the disciples' oneness with God is the Christ-nature, which has to be absolute as is Christ's oneness with God. One who realizes his identity as the Christ-nature, therefore, also realizes absolute Oneness, having the trinitarian characteristics of identity, interpenetration, and indwelling.

Christian mystics, too, speak of their experience in terms of both relative and absolute oneness. The majority of those who espouse the "affirmative way" describe their experience in terms of relative oneness, since union with God is depicted as a relationship of love through grace, rather than a direct experience of identity. Although the union is said to take place in the highest part of the soul, called the spirit, this part is still an individual entity, an archetypal self, separate from God. In stating that these experiences take place through a mediant reality, these mystics again show their affinity with their Jewish counterparts, who affirm relative oneness.

On the other hand, while ordinarily dealing with relative oneness, occasionally their descriptive language clearly imply absolute Oneness. Thus, in one passage, St. Teresa of Avila speaks of experiencing God's being in all things in a way which, she thought, was impossible (Spencer 228). St. John of the Cross describes God's communicating his "supernatural being in such wise that it [the soul appears to be God himself" (Quoted by Spencer 249). And Luis de Leon says that in this oneness God is not just dwelling in you, but you are indeed God (Spencer 229).

Similarly, Jan Van Ruysbroeck testifies that this oneness takes place "without intermediary" and "within God's essential Unity." For, "this active meeting and this loving embrace are in their ground blissful and devoid of particular form, for the fathomless, modeless being of God is so dark and so devoid of particular form that it encompasses within itself all the divine modes and the activity and properties of the Persons in the rich embrace of the essential Unity" (*The Spiritual Espousals* 152). Since, for Ruysbroeck, God's essential Unity is the ultimate Ground beyond all forms, beyond even the very form of God, signified by the distinction of divine persons, and we are said to become "one with it in its essential subsistence" (149) and become the "very resplendence" we receive (147), it must be of the absolute kind: "In this Unity ... the Father is in the Son and the Son in the Father, while all creatures are in them both. This is beyond the distinction of Persons" (*Espousals* 148-249).

The absolute nature of this oneness is also clear from the fact that it is direct and immediate. Beyond any duality or otherness, in this state there remains only the supreme Identity: "To comprehend and understand God as he is in himself, above and beyond all likenesses, is to be God with God, without intermediary or any element of otherness which could constitute an obstacle or impediment" (*Espousals* 146). This experience takes place beyond reason, understanding, beyond all activities of ordinary consciousness, in the very formless reality of God where there is an identity between Awareness and Being. This experience itself is God being Aware of, that is to say, Be-ing "himself," which is "his" very Being. This is what is meant by "to be God with God." And it can take place only when the mind is totally void of form, content, object, and construct. Thus he states, "Here there is a blissful crossing over and a self-transcending immersion into a state of essential bareness, where all the divine names and modes and all the living ideas which are reflected in the mirror of divine truth all pass away into simple divine ineffability, without mode and without reason" (*Espousals* 152).

In general, mystics of what is called the "negative way" especially affirm absolute Oneness. One of the earliest Christian writers to express this view is Pseudo-Dionysius, a fifth-to-sixth century Syrian monk. He expressed this Oneness in the framework of the Neoplatonic view of the procession of all things from God. This procession can be expressed in the form of a triad: immanence in the cause, procession from the cause, and return to the cause, or identity, differentiation, and transcendence of differentiation in the return to or identity with the One. According to this view, whatever proceeds from God remains in "him." All things are therefore in God and not apart from "him." This "remaining," immanence, or identity is especially true of the first and the third member of the triad.

Regarding the first member of the triad—divine identity—Pseudo-Dionysius distinguishes between God and the Godhead. He characterizes the Godhead as "the super-essential being of God" (53) and regards "him" as being "beyond God," conceived as a personal being (64). Like *Brahman,* the Godhead is formless (65), and beyond being. Further, the Godhead is not a being among other beings; nor a part of nor apart from anything; nor is anything a part of "him" (66). Rather, while transcending every being, form, and person, the Godhead constitutes the identity of each thing beyond all differentiation. Thus, the Godhead is said to be "wholly all things," the "totality of everything while yet remaining within himself" (102), and "the essence of being for the things which have being" (98).

As undifferentiated Unity or Identity of all things and yet transcending each, the Godhead is nondual. As such, "he" is the Ground, Cause, Center, and Suchness of all things. The Godhead is undifferentiated from anything and yet "he" is the Source of all differentiation; the Ground on which all things exist; the Center from which all things radiate and to which they all return; and the Suchness or reality which constitutes all forms. All forms are "his" manifestations or revelations (103).

As formless and infinite, the Godhead is said to be (as the *Tao Te Ching* says) nameless and unknowable (54, 108-9). Being beyond ordinary consciousness, the Godhead cannot be perceived, conceived, thought, characterized, or expressed at all (109,135).

As nondual, this absolute Oneness transcends all relativities, oppositions, dualities, or otherness and yet is present in all. Thus the Godhead is said to transcend the dualities of one and many, relative and absolute, form and formlessness, time and eternity, finite and infinite, being and nonbeing, error and truth, affirmation and denial, since "he" is beyond every limitation, condition, construction, qualification, knowledge, and characterization. This is most succinctly expressed in the following passage:

> It has neither shape nor form...It is neither perceived nor is it perceptible...It is not...greatness or smallness, equality or inequality, similarity or dissimilarity. It is not a substance, nor is it eternity or time. It cannot be grasped by the understanding since it is neither knowledge nor truth...It is not wisdom. It is neither one nor oneness, divinity nor goodness. It falls neither within the predicate of nonbeing nor of being...It is beyond assertion and denial...for it is both beyond every assertion, being the perfect and unique cause of all things, and, by virtue of its preeminently simple and absolute nature, free of every limitation, beyond every limitation, it is also beyond every denial. (*The Mystical Theology* 141)

Another representative of the negative way is Eckhart, who fully delineates absolute Oneness. Consider, as for instance, the following passage:

> There all is one, and one all in all. There to her [i.e., the soul] all is one, and one is in all. It [i.e., dualistic construction] carries contradiction in itself. What is contradiction? Love and suffering, white and black, these are contradictions, and as such these cannot remain in essential Being itself. (Quoted by Otto 64)

Here Eckhart affirms, first, that all is One; and this oneness is no other than the essential Being of the Godhead. For the Godhead is said to be beyond being and so beyond God, conceived as a personal Being: "God is a being beyond being and a nothingness beyond being" (Fox, *Breakthrough* 178). Clearly, Eckhart is saying that God is beyond the duality of being and nothingness, beyond separate beings, and Reality beyond mere absence. So he states again, God is "a not-God, not-mind, not-person, not-image—even more, he is a pure, clear One, separate from all twoness" (Fox, *Breakthrough* 180). This is a clear recognition of the absolute Oneness of the Godhead that transcends all duality, all separation or differentiation from anything that is: "Everything within the Godhead is unity, and we cannot speak about it" (Fox, *Breakthrough* 77). Just as *Brahman, Sunyata* or Buddha-nature and Tao are Reality as Such beyond any form, condition, construction, or qualification, so is this Oneness of the Godhead. Like Lao-tzu, and following Pseudo-Dionysius, Eckhart even calls God "nameless" (Fox, *Breakthrough* 178).

Second, all is One also means that it is the "isness," true nature, or very reality—"one substance and one essence and one nature" (Fox, *Breakthrough* 328)—of all things. Because of this Oneness, while being precisely what it is and only so being, each thing is identical with all without the slightest possibility of differentiation. This is similar to "form is emptiness": In this absolute Oneness the nature of the entire universe and each thing just as it is—"the essence of all creatures," as Eckhart put it—is experienced as one.

Third, "one all": The Formless Essence is not anything apart from the very world of forms. So while "all is one" says that each thing is the Unconditioned; like "emptiness is form," "one all" says that the unconditioned, infinite, and eternal is no other than the finite, limited, temporal world without the slightest differentiation between them. For, "Outside God there is absolutely nothing but nothing" (Fox, *Breakthrough* 188). In this oneness, moreover, everything is identical in its distinctness and all-inclusive unity. So he says, "All remain One, which is its own source," and "all creatures are one Being," and "the Father's eternal One, where every blade of grass, and wood and stone are one" (quoted by Otto 87).

Fourth, interpenetration and mutual inherence are implied in "one is in all," "all in all," and "God is all and is one" (Fox, *Breakthrough* 191). Moreover, this is possible because God is the essence of all, and all creation is said to remain within God. And because this Oneness is the One Reality besides which nothing exists, each and every one is in all things, and all things are in each and every one. Everything penetrates and is penetrated by, abides in and is abided in, by everything else. Thus each is in each and all in all.

Fifth, this is "seen" or directly experienced. When the Godhead is experienced just as it is, it is experienced as absolutely identical with, interpenetrating and indwelling in all beings as itself. This seeing must itself be nothing other than the Formless Essence; otherwise it would not be an experience of the Supreme Identity which remains identical with itself in the midst of all distinctions. For, according to Eckhart, this knowledge is direct and unmediated, as it takes place "without image, without mediation, and without likeness. If I am to know God in such an unmediated way, then I must simply become God and God must become me. I would express it more exactly by saying that God must become me and I must become God—so completely that this 'he' and this 'I' share one 'is' and in this 'isness' do one work eternally" (Fox, *Breakthrough* 179-180). So this seeing is itself the Being happening in and as the experience.

Moreover, according to Eckhart, "since there are no distinctions in God," the only way you can experience "him" is as identity—and in no other way. For the minute you introduce the slightest distinction, you lose identity, God, blessedness, satisfaction — everything. He states, "Since we find God in oneness, that oneness must be in him who is to find God...Neither the One, nor being, nor God, nor rest, nor blessedness, nor satisfaction is to be found where distinctions are." That this oneness is absolute, in the experience of which only the Supreme Identity remains, is stated thus: "For a man must himself be One, seeking unity both in himself and in the One, experience it as the One, which means that he must see God and God only" (Blakney 1: 78-81).

Furthermore, Eckhart says that you can experience this identity only when you go beyond every being and form and arrive at the Formless Ground or "isness" that is God "himself": "Only when all that is formed is cast off from the soul, and she sees the Eternal-One alone, then the pure essence of the soul feels naked, unformed essence of the divine Unity — more, still, a beyond-being" (quoted by Otto 78).

Finally, Eckhart's use of the trinitarian formula to describe this absolute Oneness shows that it includes differentiation and that when you realize it, you arrive at the same identity of nature and differentiation of person or individuality between yourself and God as that which exists among the three persons in the one Godhead. More importantly, according to him, the nature of the trinity is itself the actual nature of all forms, all reality. For he says, "In the inmost core of the soul, where God begets his Son, human nature takes root" (Blakney 1: 125). As all creation is said to remain in God, in God there is only unity, and the soul is "all things" (Fox, *Breakthrough* 191); not only does human nature originate in this begetting, but all nature and all forms, the entire manifest universe is created in it.

Thus when you experience your true nature or Self, you experience yourself to be nothing other than the procession of the Son from the Father. Since this is the very nature of existence, the form or being of each thing is nothing other than this eternal procession. So all beings are the process of Being and manifestation, in form, of the Formless Ground. All things are the incarnation of God. And your realization of it is nothing other than letting the Godhead BE and reveal itself in you as itself so that in the end it can make the full circle and return to itself and continue the process of "One to one, one from One, one in One and the One in one, eternally" (Blakney 1: 81).

From her own experience, Bernadette Roberts describes absolute Oneness as the realization of identity beyond union. She says that although Christian writers confuse or do not recognize it because they regard union to be the end of the journey, nevertheless this step beyond union is unmistakable. Union lies on this side of duality, with God-as-object experienced as separate from the self. When you break through the barrier of duality and transcend both self and this God, you arrive at identity with God-as-subject or pure Subjectivity. She says,

"Union before the breakthrough; identity after the breakthrough" (1: 200). This identity is that of the pure Subjectivity which sees itself in all things as itself: "This identity can never be communicated because it is the one existent that is Pure Subjectivity, and can never be objectified. This is the Eye seeing itself, and wherever it looks it sees nothing but itself" (1: 81). Thus when duality is completely transcended, you come upon this Identity which alone remains as the only thing that IS, revealing itself as the Identity of all. The breakthrough to this identity occurred to her in the experience of a smile which revealed to her the identity of the subject, the object, and the experience (1: 81).

Consistent with Jewish and Christian mysticism, the Sufis attest to both relative and absolute oneness. However, the latter is the goal of the Sufi path. Implying absolute Oneness, sheikh Nurbakhsh says, "The Sufi holds that all that exists is God and that there is nothing and no one other than God. While traversing the stations of the Path, he strives to experience this in practice" (2: 91).

Although absolute Oneness is the goal, not all experience or aspire to it. For various reasons, most remain on the relative plane. Thus, like many Christian mystics, regarding absolute Oneness as a gift from God, al-Nuri recoils from it:

> I had supposed that, having passed away
> From self in concentration, I should blaze
> A path to thee; but ah! no creature may
> Draw nigh thee, save on thy appointed ways. (Arberry 55)

In this passage al-Nuri also implies that absolute Oneness is beyond transcendence of the separate self and is not automatic or assured. Nor can it be attained through striving or effort. You must pass through further stages before you can transcend duality altogether and arrive at absolute Oneness. Thus Bayazid Bistami also finds that after passing through the stages of purification and seeing oneness, he is still prevented from it by his consciousness of a separation or duality. Thereupon God tells him that in order to realize oneness, he must be free of "thouness" (Arberry 59). In order to awaken to oneness all he needs is to transcend otherness or separation that still remained on the stage of the higher or archetypal self. He must go completely beyond duality so that no trace of a sense of separation remained in his consciousness. This is the import of the following story by Rumi: When an individual went to the door of the Beloved and knocked, a voice from within inquired who he was. He said, "It was I." The voice told him that there was no room for both. As the door remained shut, he went away. After a year of purification he returned and again knocked.

In response to the same question he answered, "It is Thou." The door opened (Shah 2: 189).

From the beginning, the door to the realization of the Supreme Identity was always open. What shut it was the consciousness of the separation of "I" from "thou" and the insistence of "I" on keeping itself separate, which creates the barrier to entrance through the door. When that is dropped, the duality between "I" and "thou" ceases; the self vanishes; and the door swings open. In this transcendence "I" is experienced as no other than "thou," which is the only identity that remains when duality is completely transcended. As Rumi says of his own experience, "My ego has passed away, He alone remains" (Quoted by Spencer 322). For Rumi, as for Bistami, you can realize God only by going beyond duality and arriving at absolute Oneness, the term for which is *ittihad*. Bistami sets forth his view in the following passage:

> Once He raised me up and set me before Him, and said to me, "O Abu Yazid, truly my creation desires to see thee." I said, "Adorn me in Thy Unity and clothe me in Thy Selfhood, and raise me up to Thy Oneness, so that when Thy creation sees me, they will say, 'We have seen Thee.' And Thou wilt be That, and I shall not be there at all." (Arberry 63)

Thus, at this stage, when all forms are transcended, the Sufi transcends transcendence and arrives, first, at a state where only God remains and s/he sees in all things only God. Then, passing beyond this, s/he arrives at the final realization of the utterly absolute Oneness in which the Godhead, precisely as such, is experienced as identical with all things just as they are. At this stage, as el-Arabi expresses it, the Sufi sees creation as nothing other than an outward projection of the one absolute existence that is God "himself" so that s/he experiences all things as the Absolute.

As Attar points out, at this stage the realization is paradoxical. In the experience of absolute Oneness the Sufi's true identity is affirmed. But this identity is no other than the Absolute Identity of the Godhead manifested in and as himself and as all things. So s/he experiences unity and differentiation, universality and particularity in their very nature. In this absolute Oneness the identity of the particular is affirmed in the experience of universality; and the universal is seen in the particularity of its manifestation as each thing besides which nothing exists.

Now, what are some of the consequences of experiencing this absolute Oneness in your personal life? First, briefly (I shall discuss the consequences at length later), there is a shift of the center of your being and consciousness from the limited, exclusive self to the limitless, all-embracing center that is God or the Self. In their foundation, with this shift, all the separation and bondage, and all the causes and consequences of your present condition, together with the condition itself, come to an end.

Second, when you live from this oneness as the center, all your problems and suffering cease. Since these arise only where there is duality, in its absence they disappear. Fear, for instance, cannot exist without duality. As the Upanishads declare, where there is the other, there is fear. For the very basis of fear is seeing or thinking yourself to be separate from others who want what you want and who, you believe, are in a position to take what you have or who threaten your survival. On the other hand, if you do not see others as separate, the entire basis of fear disappears, since you cannot really be afraid of yourself. If you are, be sure that you have created a duality in yourself. So where there is oneness, there is no possibility of fear. Imagine how our world would change if there were no fear!

The same is true of any conflict or problem: anxiety, tension, stress, anger, aggression, violence, greed, grasping, competitiveness. Name any problem. At its root is a split-mind or duality that breeds it. When it is transcended with the realization of absolute Oneness, all problems are, in principle, dissolved. I say "in principle" because unless the realization is complete and the shift of center and identity is permanent, the consequences of your present programming, constructs, habit patterns and unconscious tendencies, which become the source of programmed thought, feeling, and behavior will not disappear. Nevertheless, it remains true that only through realizing absolute Oneness can you become finally free from all your problems and suffering. It is, therefore, the axis or pivot of liberation.

This experience of absolute Oneness, which is the absolute or final revelation, is at the same time the beginning and the end of the journey of experiential religion – the end of the search and the beginning of the realized life, which is a journey without end, until you finally realize the Unconditioned State and become completely liberated.

Chapter 20
All-Embracing Awareness

It must be clear by now that absolute Oneness is not something you can experience in the ordinary state of consciousness. Since by its very structure and programming ordinary consciousness is cut off from Reality, of which it is nevertheless an expression, you must completely transcend it in order to awaken as Awareness. As only a mind that is Unconditioned can experience that which is Unconditioned, central to this experience is the realization of their identity. This Unconditioned State of pure Awareness is what I call "the All-embracing Awareness."

By this I mean that this Awareness embraces and is identical with all because it is identical with Reality as Such. Hence the expression signifies its ontological character. It constitutes the very nature of Reality as Such, and thus the nature of all that is. For this reason, although it is sometimes spoken of as intuitive or immediate knowledge, strictly speaking, it is not any kind of knowledge with which we are familiar. Whereas ordinary knowledge, even intuition, implies a differentiation among the knower, the knowing, and the known, there is not the slightest shred of differentiation between this Awareness and Reality or anything in any realm of existence. That is why, identifying it with the Self, in the following passage *Mandukya Upanishad* calls it "the Fourth State" and attests to its ontological nature:

> The Fourth, say the wise, is not subjective experience, nor objective experience, nor experience intermediate between these two, nor is it a negative condition which is neither consciousness nor unconsciousness. It is not the knowledge of the senses, nor is it relative knowledge, nor yet inferential knowledge. Beyond the senses, beyond understanding *(prajna)*, beyond all expression is the Fourth. It is pure unitary consciousness, wherein awareness of the world and of multiplicity is completely obliterated. It is ineffable peace. It is the supreme good. It is the One without any duality. It is the Self. (Prabhavananda and Manchester 51)

According to this text, All-embracing Awareness is beyond conscious and unconscious states — in fact, beyond any form of consciousness. As a result, it is beyond any limited form of knowledge, such as perception, discursive thinking, reasoning or inferential knowledge. It is even beyond intuition *(prajna)* or wisdom. It is beyond any relative knowledge, that is, any form that depends on objects, constructs, or frameworks, that works through any information processing, medium, or reducing valve such as models, concepts, programming, interpretation, evaluation, or judgment. You cannot approach it through thinking; and there is no way to grasp or comprehend it.

Furthermore, it is said to be neither a subjective nor an objective state, nor a state of absence, nor a state among other states. Since in itself it is not a state, it cannot be identical to the world of multiplicity; rather, it is the Formless Ground that makes all conditioned states and forms possible. So the text calls it the Fourth State, "the pure, unitary consciousness" and "the One without duality" — the One other than which nothing whatsoever exists. Thus it is identified with the Self, *Brahman,* Reality as Such. Each thing is nothing other than this pure Awareness. Its complete transcendence of the world of multiplicity enables it to be the reality, nature, or identity of each thing just as it is.

So to be All-embracing it must be void of subject-object duality — sometimes described as being subjectless and objectless. Subjectless means that this Awareness is not separate from or tied to a subjectivity distinct from itself. It is not tied to human beings or to human bodies. Nor is it a "faculty" of a knower. Since it has no subject but is itself the Subject, it is not something you can have, which you may exercise some of the time and not at others. There is no limit to it on the subjective side, for there is no one and nothing other than it that could limit it. That is the reason it is sometimes called "pure Subjectivity," which Bernadette Roberts defines as "a way of knowing in which the knower, the known, and the knowing, are identical and inseparable" (1: 144). Since there is nothing other than it, "pure Subjectivity is actually the way by which everything in existence knows itself; lying below or behind all levels and forms of consciousness, it is that which knows itself as all that exists" (1:153).

Subjectless also means that All-embracing Awareness is not a seer or witness to anything. A consciousness which is a witness or looker requires something to look at, whereas there is nothing other than it at which it could look. (The idea of God as a judge is, to say the least, impossible.) Because of this fact, without transcending all forms of seeing and seer or witness-consciousness, no realization of it is possible. As Roberts explains:

Since what Is is all that Is, it has nothing to see outside itself nor within itself and thus, has no such thing as a relative, reflexive, self-conscious mind. Nor is it a mind at all, nor consciousness, for no man knows what it is, only that it Is. Therefore once we have been rid of a reflexive, relative, self-conscious mind, then and only then can we come upon what Is; that which sees and is seen and the act of seeing itself are ONE. (1: 67; emphasis hers)

Void of a subject-pole, this Awareness is also void of an object-pole. It is utterly objectless because there is nothing other than it that could serve as its object. There is no object or world separate from it *of* which it is conscious, on which it could be focused, or toward which it could be oriented in order to maintain itself. Since it does not function through anything and has no content, thought, or inner dialogue, it can never be trapped or lost in anything, fixated or tied to anything, contained or limited, obscured, or obstructed by anything. You cannot put a construction or framework on it. It is not programmable; nor can you reach it through any programming. It cannot be an object of any search or attainment; and there is no way to reach it. Hence it must be absolutely free.

Objectlessness also means that it cannot itself be an object of any knowing. It utterly transcends the ordinary states of knower, knowing, and known. As Ramana Maharshi states, it "is not to be seen or known. It is beyond the threefold relationship of seer, sight, and seen, or knower, knowledge, and known" (Osborne 25). Since nothing is separate from it, whereas seeing requires at least one object separate from the subject of seeing, it is impossible for it to be known or seen, or to know or see anything. For it there is nothing to see and no one to see anything. It is not that the world does not exist or appears unreal to this Awareness, but that whatever is, is not other than it. As Wei Wu Wei states, "How can there be a 'seeing'? Surely the 'seeing' is false: the object is not over there, it is at home 'here.' I am it, it is I. How can I, then, 'see' it? There is no object there: therefore there cannot be any subject here." So he concludes, "there is no one to 'see' and no 'thing' to be 'seen'; the 'seen' is the 'see-er' and the 'see-er' is the 'seen,' and that is a definition of noumenon," which, according to him, is pure Mind or Awareness (2: 28).

Signifying this ontological nature and transcendence of all conditioned states of reality and consciousness, Hinduism identifies All-embracing Awareness with *Atman-Brahman*. *Aitareya Upanishad* says, "The Self, who is pure consciousness, is Brahman" (Prabhavananda and Manchester 62). It is the central teaching of the Upanishads that All-embracing Awareness is the very nature of Ultimate Reality: *Brahman,* Self, or God. As such it is the Supreme

Identity, manifesting itself as wholly the reality and identity of each form, each conditioned reality, in all realms of existence.

The same emphasis on its ontological nature forms the core of Buddhism, for the essence of Buddhism consists in one's being established in All-embracing Awareness as his/her permanent identity and center. This is what the Buddha realized when he attained *Nirvana*. For the Madhyamika School, it is the seeing in which Reality as Such appears *sunya,* completely void of anything other than itself as pure Awareness. When everything that is not *Sunyata* is removed from the mind so that it arrives at its pure nature, it experiences that nature to be All-embracing Awareness, identical with Reality as Such. Alternately, when Reality is completely void of anything other than itself, it is revealed to be pure, All-embracing Awareness. For Madhyamika, therefore, the very nature of Reality, and hence of all things, is nothing but All-embracing Awareness.

Recognizing the centrality of this teaching for Buddhism, the Yogachara School held that without All-embracing Awareness there is no Buddhism, since without it there is no awakening and no Buddhahood. For enlightenment is nothing other than this Awareness suddenly emerging on the conscious level and revealing itself to be the identity or totality of all that is. And Buddhahood consists in completely realizing and living as its embodiment. That is why everything the Buddha taught was geared toward realizing absolute Oneness, in which Awareness ever remains as the only Reality. In this final embodiment of each thing as All-embracing Awareness, you have the marrow of Buddhism and Buddhahood.

So we find one of the Yogachara scriptures, *The Lankavatara Sutra,* declaring that things just as they are, in their totality, are nothing but Mind, besides which nothing exists. Each thing in the manifold universe, even the dualities of mind and body, consciousness and world, insofar as they are real, are Mind only. The *Sutra* says, "Suchness, Emptiness, the limit, Nirvana, the realm of truth, variety of will-bodies — they are nothing but the Mind." Since All-embracing Awareness is the "suchness" or nature of all things, inside and outside, unity and multiplicity, reality in all its variety and differentiation are nothing but its expressions. The *Sutra* goes on to explain, "What appears to be external does not exist in reality; it is indeed Mind that is seen as multiplicity" (Suzuki 2: 241-242). The *Sutra* is not reducing everything to one single thing called "Mind," but declaring that each thing in all universes, states, and planes of reality and consciousness is nothing other than or apart from, external, or opposed to All-embracing Awareness. So it concludes, "apart from the Mind nothing whatsoever exists" (quoted by Chang 2: 173).

Agreeing with this view, the *Surangama Sutra* says that Mind is neither objective nor subjective. It is not an object among other objects; nor is it a thought, idea, or point of view. It is beyond all conditions; and yet all conditioned states that make up the phenomenal world are possible because of it. From it the world of multiplicity evolves, and yet in its absolute emptiness it remains ever identical with itself without any multiplicity or otherness.

Since All-embracing Awareness transcends duality altogether, we cannot make any exclusive affirmative or negative statement about it. It is not a part of or apart from anything. So the *Sutra* says, "It is independent of all forms and ideas, and yet we cannot speak of it as not dependent on them." It is "neither in the world nor of the world, nor is it outside the world." Since it transcends exclusive identification and differentiation, it is "neither to be identified nor not to be identified with the world; it is at once this and not-this." Identical with all precisely as transcending each, it is the one Identity that reveals itself as all things. So "all assertions and negations start from the truth of its absolute identity with all things, and this is no other than the original illuminating Mind-essence." Because it is the Supreme Identity and Ground of each being, the *Sutra* continues, "Each one's mind is co-extensive with the universe . . . all things in the universe are all alike merely the excellently bright and primordial mind of Bodhi; and . . . this mind is universally diffuse and comprehends all things within itself" (Suzuki 1: 66-68).

Another Yogachara text, *The Awakening of Faith,* similarly teaches that all things are nothing but All-embracing Awareness, and, because of that very fact, are infinite and eternal, cannot be changed or destroyed, and are not conceptualizable or describable: "All things from the beginning transcend all forms of verbalization, description, and conceptualization and are, in the final analysis, undifferentiated, free from alteration, and indestructible. They are only of the One Mind; hence the same as suchness" (Hakeda 31-35). Identified as "suchness," that is, the very nature and reality of all things, this Awareness is whatever is; and whatever is, is wholly this Awareness. As the text says again, "Whatever is real, is the one and true Mind, which pervades everywhere" (Hakeda 36).

Because all things are this Awareness, in their true nature they transcend all conditions, constructions, programming, or limitations. Being the reality of all things under all conditions, no condition can oppose, limit, or contain it. So, echoing Nagarjuna, the text goes on to say:

> [In its essential nature All-embracing Awareness is] neither with marks nor without marks; neither not with marks nor not without marks; nor is it both with and without marks simultaneously; it is neither with a single mark nor with different marks; neither not with a single mark nor not with different marks; nor is it both with a single and with different marks simultaneously. (Hakeda 34-35)

Applying Nagarjuna's fourfold negations, in order to show that it transcends all differentiation, the text is here saying that All-embracing Awareness is neither conditioned nor unconditioned, nor both, nor neither. Under whatever condition or viewpoint you may wish to consider anything, nothing can make it other than it, for in their very nature all things are wholly Awareness and its manifestations. As Philip Kapleau Roshi observes, "According to Buddhist psychology, the whole universe is nothing but consciousness, nothing exists outside of Mind" (2: 70). The infinite multiplicity of this manifold universe is nothing but a hymn of Awareness rising to itself.

In this teaching, which is above all a result of direct experience, Yogachara uses the term *Mind* and identifies it with *Sunyata,* Suchness, Nirvana, because in enlightenment Reality as Such is revealed in and as All-embracing Awareness. When the conscious and unconscious operations of the mind are brought to a dead stop and all duality and limit constructs are broken through and transcended, the mind appears in its Unconditioned State. Then its identity is revealed to be the identity of all things, to be Unconditioned Reality or *Sunyata.* Thus Awareness as *Sunyata* experiences all things in their true nature as *Sunyata,* which is its Self-transparency to itself or Self-revelation of Being as Being. It is this revelation, repeatedly experienced by Buddhist sages, that led them to endorse the Yogachara teaching which, together with Madhyamika *Sunyata,* forms the living spring of Buddhism. As the two sides of the Mahayana expression of how things are in their true nature, they are equivalent to the Hindu view that the Self is Unconditioned Reality and All-embracing Awareness. Their confluence is the core of Zen.

With its insistence on enlightenment, Zen is in direct line with Yogachara. The fundamental teaching of Zen is that enlightenment is the direct experience of the nature of Reality as Such, that is, All-embracing Awareness. From the beginning all Zen teachings and practices have been geared toward bringing the practitioner to this direct realization.

This teaching is epitomized, for instance, by Huang Po, who states most explicitly that All-embracing Awareness is Reality as Such. He says, "All the Buddhas and all sentient beings are nothing but the One Mind, besides which nothing exists" (Blofeld 1: 29). Every particle of every being in whatever universe or state of existence it may be, is wholly this Awareness. Nothing can be and not be it; and only it, purely and simply, IS. So Huang Po goes on to say, "There is only the One Mind and not a particle of anything else on which to lay hold, for this Mind is the Buddha" (Blofeld 1: 31). Nothing is beyond, beside or other than it, "for there is nowhere which is outside the Buddha-mind" (Blofeld 1: 37).

After stating the identity, Huang Po applies to All-embracing Awareness the characteristics of Reality as Such. He says that it is uncreated, infinite and eternal; without conditioning, object, or construct; beyond all dualities of existence and non-existence. Formless and undifferentiated, it "transcends all limits" and for that very reason is separated from nothing and identical with all things: "Whatever Mind is, so also are phenomena — both are equally real and partake equally of the Dharma-nature, which hangs in the void" (Blofeld 1: 42, 111). Furthermore, it is said to be "neither subject nor object"; to be "void, omnipresent," and "the source of all forms" without itself having any form and, therefore, is "boundless" (Blofeld 1: 29-44).

Similarly, Shen Hui says that in the natural state it is "tranquil and pure, completely void, unattached, omnipresent, and is identical with the ultimate Reality realized by the Buddhas" (Burtt 235). Even more trenchantly, Bassui says that All-embracing Awareness is the true nature and reality of all forms and precisely as such utterly transcends all forms and conditions. It is identical with Ultimate Reality and *Sunyata*. Using Nagarjuna's fourfold negations, he says further that because of its complete transcendence of duality and differentiation, it cannot be exclusively identified with anything and so can be the very ground, nature and identity of each thing:

> Mind is the True-nature of things, transcending all forms. The True-nature is the Way. The Way is Buddha. Buddha is Mind. Mind is not within or without or in between. It is not being or nothingness or non-being or non-nothingness or Buddha or mind or matter. So it is called the abodeless Mind. (Kapleau 1: 170)

From the special focus of the Hua Yen School, with its teaching of identity, interpenetration, and mutual inherence of all things, states, and planes of consciousness, Yung Ming says, "Inasmuch as all minds enter into this One Mind, the principle of mutual penetration is seen. Inasmuch as this One Mind is all minds, the principle of identity and the principle of simultaneous correspondence is seen" (Chang 2: 157). Similarly, attempting a synthesis of Madhyamika, Yogachara, and Hua Yen teachings, in his book, *Space, Time and Knowledge,* Tarthang Tulku says of All-embracing Awareness, or what he calls "great knowledge": "Great Knowledge shows us that one point is all points," and "everything includes everything, and no separation or disharmonies are found when appearance is seen as the embodiment of Knowledge." This is so because its "'knowing' clarity does not radiate from a center, but is rather in everything the center and everything in it" (282).

A parallel teaching in Taoism is the identification of All-embracing Awareness or Mind with Tao or Reality as Such. As a Taoist adept told Blofeld, "Mind is all! Eliminate thought and the mind is no longer to be differentiated from the formless Tao." When everything other than itself is eliminated from the mind, it becomes a formless void, in which state its true nature is revealed to be limitless and unconditioned, and hence no other than the source and reality of all things, which appear as its manifestations. So Blofeld continues: "Mind is the only reality. All physical objects and processes have their being in mind" (3: 97-99).

Among Christian mystics, Nicholas of Cusa and Meister Eckhart, for instance, clearly affirm that All-embracing Awareness is identical with the uncreated, formless divine nature and the reality of all things. Thus Nicholas says that "Absolute Sight," or All-embracing Awareness, is beyond all limitations, and so it simultaneously embraces each and every mode of seeing (10). Since in God knowing is identical with being, this Absolute Sight is the very essence of God. As the essence of God "pervades all things," so does this Sight, which is "his" essence (41). Furthermore, God is "the Absolute Ground of all formal natures" and embraces "in Himself all nature" (12). It follows that All-embracing Awareness pervades all things. As the Absolute Ground, it is the source and suchness of all forms and natures. Because it transcends all forms, duality and identification, in it "all otherness is unity, and all diversity is identity" (13).

For much the same reasons, Eckhart affirms the identity of All-embracing Awareness with the Godhead. Additionally, he says that God in "his naked awareness" is present to the individual in his "naked essence." And this presence is "without image, without mediation, and without likeness" (Fox, *Breakthrough* 179). Since this presence is direct and unmediated, the same essence is experienced by the individual as his/her own in and as All-embracing Awareness. Not only is this Awareness "above all knowledge," and hence objectless; it is also subjectless, for it is "nothingness beyond being," and is "inexpressible" (Fox, *Breakthrough* 178). And the mind which experiences it as identity transcends the subject-object duality and thought, knowledge, image, and concept, and arrives at the essential state of the Unconditioned. Moreover, he says that this Awareness has no "before" or "after;" that is, it is eternal; and is "uninfluenced by any idea," which means it is objectless, unprogrammable and everpresent—"anew with each Now-moment." And it is the omnipresent reality of God in "his" Self-manifestation as the *Logos*—through all, in all, as all (Blakney 1: 214-215).

Jan Van Ruysbroeck not only calls God the "incomprehensible light," but also says that the contemplative becomes identified with it: "The spirit ceaselessly becomes the very resplendence which it receives" (*The Spiritual Espousals* 147). This identification occurs only when s/he transcends ordinary consciousness, ego, and archetypal self, and arrives at the void state. In this "essential bareness," when All-embracing Awareness emerges, the contemplative becomes identified with it and experiences the essential Awareness whereby God is aware of "himself," for it is nothing other than the absolute Oneness of God beyond all forms: "This hidden resplendence...is so great a resplendence that the loving contemplative neither sees nor feels in the ground of his being, in which he is at rest, anything other than an incomprehensible light. In the simple bareness which envelops all things, he feels and finds himself to be nothing other than the same light with which he sees" (147).

The Sufis also clearly recognize this Awareness as the goal of the path. Likewise, they consider its nature to be ontological and its experience direct and unmediated. Thus Al-Ghazali says that the identity between God and All-embracing Awareness is experienced in "immediate knowledge" or direct experience. And in this experience all things appear as nothing but its expression (49). Thus, All-embracing Awareness is affirmed to be the nature and reality of all things. It transcends all; and yet precisely as such all things are its manifestations.

Besides the ontological, other characteristics of All-embracing Awareness are also noted by the sources of experiential religion. One is that it is "pure Awareness." This purity must not be understood in contrast to some kind of impurity. Rather, purity is the absence of unawareness and otherness, and pertains to its very nature: To be All-embracing Awareness is to be pure because there is nothing other than it in any realm of existence that could make it impure. And since it constitutes the nature of being itself or Reality as Such, in its true nature each thing is wholly this Awareness without the slightest shred of unawareness. Thus nothing could make it impure or could mar, obscure, becloud, or introduce any unawareness in it. So whatever is experienced in this state is experienced as pure Awareness. As Ramana Maharshi says, "Pure consciousness is indivisible, it is without parts. It has no form or shape, no 'within' and 'without.' There is no 'right' or 'left' for it. Pure consciousness, which is the heart, includes all; and nothing is outside or apart from it" (Bercholz 107).

As this purity is a consequence of its being objectless, unconditioned, One without duality, and identical with Reality, it is impossible for All-embracing Awareness to have even a speck of impurity or for there to be anything other than it that could obscure it. You can understand the mistake of Shen-hsiu, therefore, who thought that dust—unawareness, thought, conditioning, or construct—could obscure it, and who therefore admonished others to keep it at all times clean and polished. To correct this error, Hui-neng wrote the following famous stanza:

> The Bodhi tree is originally not a tree,
> The mirror also has no stand.
> Buddha nature is always clean and pure;
> Where is there room for dust? (De Bary 217)

Since nothing is other than it, so that even a particle of dust is also wholly its manifestation, its purity also means that nothing can obstruct or prevent it from being and appearing to itself as itself and as all things. It is not like a tree that comes into being, grows and dies, but is the Formless Ground in which all forms appear and disappear as moments of itself. Nor can it be a mirror separate from a stand but is itself the stand or support, foundation, and mirror on which all phenomena appear as refractions of its self-luminosity and self-transparency.

Thus the Upanishads, Huang Po and other Zen masters, and Chuang Tzu declare that All-embracing Awareness is self-luminous, self-transparent and all-pervading. And, using Hui-neng's own imagery of a bright mirror, his chief disciple, Yung-chia Ta-shih declares:

> The Mind like a mirror is brightly
> illuminating and knows no obstruction,
> It pervades the vast universe
> to its minutest crevices;
> all its contents, multitudinous in form
> are reflected in the Mind,
> Which, shining like a perfect gem,
> has no surface, nor the inside.
> (Suzuki 1: 96)

Yung-chia is saying that the self-transparency of All-embracing Awareness means that all things in their Unconditioned State—without conditioning or construct—are self-transparent. Because nothing is other than it, nothing can obstruct its self-transparency. As all forms issue from it, they are reflections of its radiance. They mirror its self-transparency and are simultaneously reflected back in it. All things are like facets of a perfect gem that is transparent to itself.

In the same vein, master Tsung Kao observes:

> The originally vast, serene and marvelous mind is all-pure and illuminatingly all-inclusive. Nothing can hinder it; it is free as the

firmament . . . clear and bright, unmovable and immutable, neither increasing nor decreasing. In daily activities it illuminates all places and shines out from all things. (Chang 1: 89)

Similarly, master Han Shan declares that All-embracing Awareness "is originally pure, genuine, vast, illuminating, perfect and devoid of objects," precisely because it is nothing other than "the infinite and all-inclusive totality of the universe" (Chang 1: 111, 123-124).

And, neatly summarizing all the characteristics of All-embracing Awareness, from the Tibetan tradition *The Yoga of Knowing the Mind* declares:

In its true state Mind is naked, immaculate; not made of anything, being of the Voidness; clear, vacuous, without duality, transparent; timeless, uncompounded, unimpeded, colorless; not realizable as a separate thing, but as the unity of all things, yet not composed of them; of one state, and transcendent over differentiation. (Evans-Wentz 1: 212)

Thus, declaring that it constitutes the very nature of Reality as Such, this passage states that All-embracing Awareness is objectless and subjectless pure Being, not apart from nor a part of anything, identical with each and yet transcending all, omnipresent and eternal, infinite and unconditioned and for that very reason no other than all things finite, self-luminous, and self-transparent.

Moreover, this self-transparency is due to the fact that it is void of content or object, programming, construct, otherness, and unawareness. There is absolutely nothing to which it could be attached or fixated, or in which it could be trapped or lost, which is what could prevent it from being transparent and revealed to itself as itself. By its very nature, therefore, All-embracing Awareness could not be and be not self-transparent. The reason is that when the mind is absolutely void of anything other than itself, nothing can obscure it, obstruct it, introduce otherness or separation, or orient it toward anything other than itself.

Thus when the mind is purely be-ing, or, so to speak, "mind-ing" itself, void of anything other than itself, it comes to directly experience its nature in the pure state as completely clear and transparent to itself. This is the Self-transparency of the mind in its essential nature as pure Awareness. And since this Awareness is the nature of all things, the essence of all reality is this Self-transparency. To *BE* absolutely, is to be Self-transparent. This

Self-transparency of Awareness is the Self-revelation of Being to itself. As there is nothing other than itself, what this Awareness reveals, when you experience it, is only itself in the process of its Self-manifestation as infinite, all-embracing whole. As all things are merely forms or expressions of this Self-transparency, they are nothing other than pure Awareness Being Aware of, that is to say, Be-ing itself. So the entire universe is nothing other than the Self or God Be-ing Aware of "himself," which means God Be-ing God. All things are only refractions of this self-luminous "I am," which is always in the process of reflecting itself. Such is its dynamic, self-revealing character. Nothing is ever hidden. The universe is a show-off of Awareness, Self, God. Such is the exhibitionistic character of this self-transparency that what it reveals is always itself to itself and as all things.

For the above reason, when you experience it, you experience yourself and all things as transparent. Enlightenment often reveals this self-transparency in which all forms appear as nothing but the Self-projection of All-embracing Awareness. Thus, *Chandogya Upanishad* says that the universe is a projection of *Brahman*. Similarly, describing his own experience of enlightenment, Zen master Han Shan says, "Suddenly I stood still, filled with the realization that I had no body or mind. All I could see was one great illuminating whole — omnipresent, perfect, lucid, and serene. It was like an all-embracing mirror from which the mountains and rivers of the earth were projected as reflections" (Chang 1: 130). Master Hsueh Yen says of his experience, "I actually felt that all phenomena and manifestations...flowed out of [my] own bright, true and marvelous mind" (Chang 1: 147). Similarly, to Eckhart all creation is nothing other than a projection of God's Be-ing and Self-Awareness in and as the process of the *Logos*. And to Guru Bawa the whole universe itself is nothing but a projection and Self-manifestation of Awareness (Hixon 175).

Many of the above texts have spoken of the All-embracing Awareness as being always and everywhere simultaneously whole. Since it is not bound by space, time, or any condition, it is omnipresent and ever-present or eternal. As Ken Wilber explains, being indivisible and indistinct from itself and transcending space and time, it is simultaneously and wholly present at every point of space and at every moment of time. In it there is no linear progression from one thing to another, or successive moments of past, present, and future. Nor is there a duality of "here" and "there," "now" and "then." Rather, "since the infinite is present in its entirety at every point of space, *all* of the infinite is fully present right HERE;" and since "*all* of eternity is wholly and completely present at every point of time," "all of eternity is already present right NOW" (5: 298; italics and emphasis his). In it, then, the entire universe is wholly present simultaneously here and now. In this eternal present of Awareness all universes, actual and possible, are always in the process of being created or projected. In this no-moment, which is all moments, all universes are always in the very first moment of existence without a second, here and now, as its expressions.

When you realize this omnipresent and everpresent Awareness, you become present-centered and experience all things always and only in the here and now. You do not experience the present as you do in the ordinary state, as fleeting moments succeeding one another, hardly discernible to your consciousness. But, as Bernadette Roberts tells us, in All-embracing Awareness you experience it as the infinite and eternal present in which "the mind moves neither backward nor forward but remains fixed and fully concentrated in the present" (1: 157). In this state all moments arise as a succession of nows, like a succession of ripples or waves, in the vast expanse of the ocean of Awareness, stretching out from infinity to infinity.

The reason that some of those who have realized it can see events in the present that are to take place in the future is that in All-embracing Awareness, all things are always simultaneously present as now. This provides a clue to the import of some of the Zen koans, such as the one about "The Flying Geese": One day Pai-chang, who was himself to become a great Zen master, went out with his master, Ma-tsu. A flock of wild geese was seen flying and Ma-tsu asked, "What are they?" "They are wild geese, master," said Pai-chang. "Where are they flying?" "They have flown away, master." At this, Ma-tsu took hold of Pai-chang's nose and gave it a vigorous twist, which made Pai-chang cry out in pain. Ma-tsu then said, "You say they have flown away, but all the time they have been here from the very beginning." Hearing this, Pai-chang broke out in a sweat. He was enlightened (Barrett 92). Transcending the duality of "here" and "there," Pai-chang had awakened to the eternal NOW of All-embracing Awareness in which "here" and "there" are always HERE; and past, present, and future are always NOW. You can experience it only as NOW and always as HERE because reality can be only in the present and because Awareness reveals the ultimate nature of reality. Thus you can experience anything real, anything at all, only in the present.

In contrast to discursive thinking, another characteristic of this Awareness often mentioned is its instantaneity, which is a consequence of its infinity and eternity. Since it is always wholly present at each moment of time, it can manifest itself suddenly only when the rational mode has been stopped, however temporarily, from dominating the conscious sphere. Thus, in "The Flying Geese" koan, when the sudden twist of the nose and the pain cut off Pai-chang's discursive thinking and cleared his mind, All-embracing Awareness suddenly broke into the conscious sphere. The duality of "here" and "there" disappeared, and he awakened to its eternity and omnipresence and experienced them both instantaneously as its expressions. Thus the approach or preparation may be gradual, but enlightenment always appears in full dress suddenly, instantaneously. For this reason it is also always beyond the bounds of reason and cannot be arrived at by discursive or deductive thinking. A leap beyond the dualistic barrier, guarded by reason, is absolutely essential for its realization. Those who are glued to the two-valued logic, particularly its principles of contradiction and excluded middle, will encounter insurmountable obstacles in understanding it. However, its complete transcendence over duality is its absolute freedom to be wholly present always and everywhere; and for that very reason it is beyond any limitation, condition, confinement, or grasp, but is open, direct, boundless, and all-pervading.

We can, then, conclude that the very ground, fabric, and form of all things is All-embracing Awareness; all things are founded on, rooted in, "made" of this Source. As this Awareness, all things are One; as its manifestations, they are many. Being wholly this Awareness, in your uniqueness and individuality you are formless, unconditioned, infinite, all-embracing, all-pervading, boundless, and absolutely free. As Ken Wilber puts it:

> As all-pervading and all-embracing Consciousness, it is both One and Many, Only and All, Source and Suchness, Cause and Condition, such that all things are only a gesture of this One, and all forms a play upon It. As Infinity, it demands wonder; as God, it demands worship; as Truth, it demands wisdom; and as one's true Self, it demands identity. (3: 149-150)

The realization of All-embracing Awareness as your identity is the summit of the journey of experiential religion. By the same token, it is also the ultimate revelation. Although the way to that revelation begins at the level of your experience of separation, entrapment, and loss of awareness, as you begin to be free, the barriers begin to fall away. When the last barrier is overcome, you come to realize that All-embracing Awareness is Reality as Such and that it was already and always there, from the beginningless beginning, ever active, ever Being and revealing itself as all that is. And you realize that you had never departed from it, in all your wanderings — only you did not notice it because your head was turned elsewhere.

This summit of realization is at the same time a homecoming. From the summit an endless path stretches out before you. As you begin to walk on it, things you have accumulated in a lifetime begin to lose their hold and fall away until, completely transformed, even the most ordinary things become complete embodiments of this All-embracing Totality — of all life, all beings, all consciousness. Such a realization is the first moment of your liberation. In what this liberation consists is the subject matter of the next chapter.

Chapter 21
Completeness and Liberation

To be a separate self, to live in a world populated by such selves, to live with a consciousness that sees things only in terms of separation and in a world that remains separate from, in spite of our striving to make it a part of, ourselves is to remain incomplete. Incompleteness is humanity as we know it now and believe it to be. Whence did it arise?

In his book, *Earthwalk,* Philip Slater suggests that the experience of incompleteness is a peculiarly modern disease (62-66). Arthur Deikman explains that we acquire the belief that we are incomplete in childhood, when we are taught that everything, especially the individual, is flawed, imperfect (1: 5). In a somewhat similar vein, Tarthang Tulku observes that our world is largely run on beliefs, the most fundamental of which is that we lack something in our lives that we must fill by our striving (the assumption being that fulfillment is a matter of acquiring something) (2: 227- 228). As if to confirm this view, the Human Potential Movement told us that we have a "potential" that we must "realize" in order to be fulfilled. Is our belief that we are incomplete derived from any of these sources or from the Christian teaching that human beings are fallen, corrupt, and cannot do anything to save themselves?

It should be clear from the preceding chapters, especially from Part II, that the experience of incompleteness is not a disease peculiar to the modern world. Having dismantled the familial and social structures by which traditional man set up barriers against its invasion, however, and having become more fully self-conscious as separate individuals, modern humans have come to experience incompleteness most acutely, as modern art, literature, philosophy, psychology, and sociology abundantly attest.

As I have shown, however, the feeling of incompleteness arises from the very core of the separate self – from the severance from Reality as Such and the creation of primary duality; from fear and resistance to overcoming the separation, and the striving that maintains the separation. This feeling permeates every structure and operation of the self and its world. It is reinforced by the belief, fed from childhood on, that the individual is incomplete, and by an entire culture based on this incompleteness and bent on keeping it intact. Furthermore, the culture projects glittering symbols of completeness that ensure our striving for it, all the while guaranteeing failure. So it does not matter whether the period is ancient or modern. To be an individual separate from others and the world and to be conscious of that fact is to feel incomplete, exiled from reality, condemned forever to strive to become real and complete but never succeeding. In such a predicament how can human beings find completeness or fulfillment?

First, although the *feeling* of incompleteness is real, incompleteness itself is not, based as it is on the fundamental illusion that we are separate from Reality. Because this is a mental creation having no basis in reality, by its very nature it cannot be overcome; and our attempts to do so result in the consequences discussed in Part II. So long as we continue to construct our reality, consciousness, and self on separation and to act on that construct, we will continue to feel incomplete.

Second, once we get caught in the striving for fulfillment, we become afraid that if we ever stop, life will lose its appeal and meaning. Finding that things or relationships do not give us the hoped-for meaning, we stake our life on the striving itself and so keep moving on its programmed grooves. To justify this stance, in a reverse spin toward infantilism, some of us even consciously choose to remain incomplete and "vulnerable."

Third, for reasons given in Part II, the separate self can never be — or be made — complete, primarily because it is not in itself anything real and so cannot be made real or complete by adding anything external to it. Nothing outside ourselves can make us complete. Where there is otherness, there can be no completeness. Nothing that is separate can overcome separation. No object — not even God-as-object or a personal God — no achievement, event, or relationship can make the self complete, not only because any such addition would remain apart from, rather than becoming a part of, it, but also because by their very nature all objects are limited, separate from other objects, and incomplete. Nothing that is in itself incomplete, even an infinite number of them strung up together, can overcome incompleteness. Since all finite and limited objects, and duality itself, are founded on separation from Reality as Such, none can help us overcome the feeling of incompleteness that is the result of that separation in the first place.

Thus we can never be or be *made* complete as long as we remain within dualistic constructs or pursue limited objects and states. So, according to Hinduism, Buddhism, and Taoism we cannot become complete by any striving or attempt to satisfy desires. Nor can we in any way attain, achieve, or become complete, since all such activities assume a lack, which is nonexistent, and then try to overcome it. That is the reason we can never become complete through achievements, acquisitions, relationships, or trying to find identity and meaning. Completeness cannot be anything external, limited, or foreign to our nature, since they can also be lost and therefore cannot give us complete satisfaction. It can come only from a state of being and not from any momentary experience that must perforce remain external to our make-up. So long as we look for it in something other than ourselves, we will never find it. We are *bound* to be disappointed, disillusioned, dissatisfied, and trapped in the cycle of wanting, striving, and remaining incomplete.

Now experiential religion is not saying that things outside ourselves are not important or that we should not seek them. There is absolutely nothing wrong in pursuing wealth, success, achievement, and the myriads of cultural values that form the normal web of life. Nor is experiential religion advocating selfishness or narcissism, the "looking out for number one" rage of our age. In fact, it insists on the very opposite. It holds that unless we destroy the very roots of selfishness, transcend the separate self, become wholly open, and direct our energies toward the care for all life with no thought of any gain for ourselves, we cannot realize completeness. Moreover, experiential religion recognizes that for the development of a healthy personality and positive self-image, it is important to regard oneself as a success rather than a failure. But it emphatically asserts that so long as there remains otherness in our consciousness, no object or relationship will bring us one iota closer to completeness. Since all desires arise from and feed on incompleteness, no attempt to satisfy them will bring completeness or any resolution of the deep-seated problems that make up the fabric of ordinary life.

Fourth, either there is a self that is in itself complete and that is what we truly are or we can never be complete. Only a self complete and perfect in itself can make us complete and perfect. Such a self must be Reality as Such, which is limitless and infinite Subjectivity, without any lack and needing nothing from outside to complete it — that to which nothing can be added, from which nothing can be taken away, and outside which nothing whatsoever exists. And such a self must be our identity, for anything other than identity cannot constitute the core of our being or subjectivity and so will fail to bring completeness. Being limitless and indivisible, it must be simultaneously whole and wholly present, yet precisely because of this, it cannot be something that is once and for all realized and done with. Otherwise it will become something limited and so will not bring completeness.

Fifth, since only the true Self is such, only it and nothing else can constitute our completeness. And since we already are this Self and can never be anything other than it, we and everything else have always and already been complete and perfect. So there is no such thing as attaining perfection. Moreover, this completeness can never be gained or lost because it is infinite and eternal.

According to experiential religion, then, completeness consists in simply, absolutely, unconditionally Being. It is the absolutely pure "isness," suchness, or being of all things at all times and in all realms of existence.

From the above we must not conclude, as have some contemporary movements, that when experiential religion says that just as you are, you are complete and perfect, it means that whatever you are experiencing right now in your present condition is complete and perfect. To apply its statement, which refers to the Unconditioned State of the Self, to the conditioned state of the separate self is to pile up delusion upon delusion. Such a reduction is not only outrageous but extremely dangerous. Not only does it smack of the Leibnizian, Pollyanna view that this is the best of all possible worlds and there are no problems in it, but far more damaging, it also sanctions horror and suffering, hunger and starvation, poverty and injustice, the cruelties and atrocities people have experienced or are now experiencing or that some are inflicting on others. It not only justifies those who inflict such things on others but also absolves those who have the responsibility to prevent them. Such an interpretation of the position of experiential religion is a product of the contemporary solipsistic self-absorption that collapses ethics into sociology, or sanctions whatever goes on in society under the false pretense that one must not criticize others.

The distinction, at the heart of experiential religion, between the conditioned state of the separate self, which we ordinarily experience and from which springs our feeling of incompleteness, and the Unconditioned State of our true nature, which is complete and perfect and which is what we nevertheless actually and at all times are, must never be collapsed. Otherwise we may lose our humanity and let the world plunge into delusion, unawareness, chaos, greed, possession-aggression, and the most unspeakable evils imaginable.

Instead of putting on blinders and overlooking the horrors some humans inflict on others, we must awaken to completeness. We will then see things exactly as they are — see the human condition as it actually is, perceive the imperfect world we have created, and the completeness and perfection that nevertheless constitutes our very nature or Self.

Sixth, there is no cure for incompleteness except by directly experiencing and completely realizing the Self. To awaken to this completeness, we must cut through the former and directly experience the latter as our identity. Thus completeness consists in being established in the Self or Reality as Such as our permanent identity and fully manifesting it in and as our very life.

When we realize this completeness, we attain the purpose of our existence and come to see that the entire aim of all existence is to Be and manifest the Self, God, or Reality as Such. To let God or Reality as Such Be completely itself in all things so that it is all and in all as itself is the final step of the journey of experiential religion.

Seventh, this realization requires a shift of plane and of center: a permanent shift of attention and orientation of consciousness from the finite plane of conflicting and insatiable desires to the infinite plane of Unconditioned Reality, which is the fulfillment of all desires. It requires a permanent shift of identity and center of being and consciousness from the limited identity of the separate self to the limitless identity of the all-embracing, infinite Self.

There is a difference between the initial experience of completeness and its complete realization. As the final stage of the Way, realization occurs when your identity and center shift completely to the Unconditioned State and you are fully and permanently established in it. There no longer remains a consciousness of a separate center or a different organization of life. With ego no longer a separate center, All-embracing Awareness becomes the only, permanent, and completely natural state in which you normally and continuously live and from which you think and act. In this vast and limitless center, you float like an island in the ocean. Having no consciousness, life, or activity to call your own, the life that remains is that of the Unconditioned. It radiates and acts through you, assuming, transforming, and integrating your personality to itself, so that the very distinction between the conditioned and the Unconditioned disappears. Thus the Unconditioned becomes the conditioned; the formless the formed; All-embracing Awareness the ordinary mind; and yourself and all existence are fully revealed to be the Unconditioned, Being and manifesting itself in you and in all things as all that IS.

In the journey of Self-realization, completeness is, then, a return movement from the summit to the ordinary states, which are themselves fully revealed as the summit. This is liberation—the realization of the absolute freedom of the Unconditioned in the midst of conditioned existence. As the *Srimad Bhagavatam* points out, there are two approaches to this liberation: immediate and gradual. The first directly proceeds toward realizing identity with *Brahman*, from where the yogi transforms and integrates his/her body, mind, and personality into this new identity and center. The second moves toward the same goal by working to free the yogi from identification, attachments, and desires (Prabhavananda 28-29).

According to the sources of experiential religion, both approaches are necessary. For they constitute a dialectical process in which the second enables the mind to become centered, concentrated, and one-pointed more quickly, while the direct approach cuts through mental constructs to get to Reality and Awareness.

The Sources on Completeness and Liberation

The various traditions of experiential religion see the journey to completeness and liberation as a passage from the personal through the transpersonal stages, until you transcend duality, and first experience, then fully realize, and finally become permanently established in the Unconditioned as your natural state. Each tradition has charted a fairly complete map of this terrain, although not all traditions have the same idea of completeness and liberation. Some, especially in the dualistic traditions, believe that liberation is not possible and that relative oneness is the end of the path in this life. Others, even in these same traditions, not only see its possibility in this life but acknowledge that full liberation can be gained only in this life because it is the realization of what we truly are "from no-beginning time."

Hinduism

From what has been said before, it should be clear that, for Hinduism, completeness and liberation consist in being fully established in the Self or Brahman as your true identity and All-embracing Awareness as your natural state. And, since you *are* the Self, you already are complete and liberated; but since in your present condition you do not experience it, Hinduism has developed various paths, called "yogas," to come to this realization.

According to these yogas, the goals, methods, and steps toward this realization are diverse. Thus, for *Yoga Sutras,* and to a certain extent for other yogas, the journey is an ascent from the unconscious to the conscious and through the transpersonal states, until you arrive at the transconscious state of the Self. However, all the paths do not agree on the nature of the Self. According to the nondualist schools, what the dualists mean by the Self is not the Ultimate Reality because they not identify the Self with *Brahman.* In this perspective, only the nondualist Vedantists offer the most fully developed view of completeness.

Again, while all the yogas and philosophical schools speak of liberation as the goal, they do not agree on what this liberation is. In his *Yoga Sutras,* Patanjali offers Self-realization as the goal of the path. But neither his concept of the Self nor his final stage of the path is the same as those envisioned by nondualist *Vedanta.* Patanjali's Self *(Purusha)* is not the Self *(Atman)* of the nondualist Upanishads. Although Patanjali conceives *Purusha* as the Absolute, his concept differs from the nondualist Vedantist concept of *Atman,* which is identified with the formless, unconditioned, undifferentiated, Ultimate Reality—*Brahman.*

The same difference is to be seen in regard to the final step of the journey. The Self-realization Patanjali offers is a form of absolute transcendence in which only the Self remains in Awareness. If you consider the final step to be absolute Oneness, in which the Absolute is no other than the relative, the infinite no other than the finite, the formless no other than the entire world of forms, then this realization cannot be regarded as the final step of the journey. This is also true of the qualified nondualism of Ramanuja and *Bhakti* and other yogas that advocate union, and not identity, with God. On the other hand, in presenting identity with *Brahman* as the goal, nondualist *Vedanta* clearly envisions the goal of completeness in terms of the final step of the path.

A similar difference appears in terms of stages of the path. While Patanjali sees the final stage of the path in terms of *asamprajanata (nirvikalpa)* and *dharmamegha (dharma*-cloud) *samadhis,* nondualist *Vedanta* sees it in terms of a stage beyond—*sahaja samadhi*. According to this view, completeness is reached when you are permanently established in the Self as your identity and center, from which you continuously and effortlessly live and act. This completely natural, Unconditioned State of effortless being is called *"Sahaja Samadhi."* As Ramana Maharshi explains, "Remaining in the primal, pure, natural state without effort is *sahaja nirvikalpa samadhi*...In *sahaja* one sees only the Self and sees the world as a form assumed by the Self" (Osborne 184).

On the other hand, in spite of its use of very different methods and approach, *Tantra* sees identity with *Brahman* as the essence of completeness and liberation. Taking the evolutionary approach and starting by first descending to the unconscious, *Tantric Yoga* describes the trajectory of the path as an ascent of consciousness by going through successive and ever-expanding stages until it reaches the same goal. As Eliade observes, "the yogi works on all levels of consciousness and the unconscious to open a way to the transconscious state" (99). As consciousness evolves from its lower, narrower, and more restricted form to the higher, transpersonal stages, it expands by encompassing and integrating on the higher level the reality of the lower. In this process, you experience within yourself an ever-increasing integration of the polarity of forces, energies, and states. Correspondingly, the feeling of incompleteness decreases until it is finally transcended in the direct experience of your identity as the Self.

Completeness is reached when awareness passes completely beyond duality and emerges on the transconscious plane of its Identity with Reality as Such, which is at the same time the transcendent unity and final integration of all planes and states of reality and consciousness. As Ken Wilber explains, at each emergent state consciousness expands by integrating the prior state until it reaches the state of final transcendence as Consciousness as Such. This state is reached when, "passing through *nirvikalpa samadhi,* Consciousness totally awakens as its Original Condition and Suchness *(tathata),* which is, at the same time, the condition and suchness of all that is." This is the final transcendence of separation wherein Consciousness is revealed to be the Ultimate Reality and complete identity of all things: "This is the final differentiation of Consciousness from all forms in Consciousness, whereupon Consciousness as Such is released in Perfect Transcendence, which is not a transcendence from the world but a final transcendence as the World" (5: 99).

In this final integration, then, there is a recovery of the absolute Oneness of the original state and a return to the beginning and Source in which, observes Eliade, "Consciousness as such recovers its ontological completeness," its identity with Reality as Such, and "the yogi is all being in all its completeness." In this state his/her identity is the identity of all; and the identity of all his/her identity. Altogether beyond duality, s/he is established in the undifferentiated completeness of the Unconditioned, which is at the same time a unity of differentiation of things into finite and infinite, conditioned and unconditioned. Being the Self, s/he is the universe; being pure Subjectivity, there is no object other than him/her; being Reality as Such, there is nothing that s/he is not. In time s/he is in eternity, and in eternity s/he is manifested as time (83, 94-100).

Hindu scriptures make it abundantly clear, through repeated assertions, that the yogi becomes liberated only upon being permanently established in this state and fully realizing it as his/her identity. This teaching is the core of the *Vedanta.* Shankara, for instance, insists that liberation can be attained only by realizing the Self or identity with *Brahman,* and in no other way (Johnson 130-134). Similarly, Ramana Maharshi says, as already quoted, liberation consists in realizing and continuously and effortlessly living in the primal, pure state of All-embracing Awareness (Osborne 193).

Buddhism

More fully than any other path, Buddhism has delineated both the experience of completeness and the stages leading to its complete realization. According to the early Buddhist tradition, as mapped out in the *Visuddhimagga,* there are four successive stages leading to the realization of *Nirvana,* which is the state of liberation. As the literal meaning of the term indicates, *Nirvana* is the utter extinction or complete transcendence of ego, duality, construction, programming, and conditioned states, brought about by a complete realization of the Unconditioned as your natural state. Thus it signifies, as the Buddha states, the final state of realization that burns *dukkha* down to its roots, "like a palm-tree stump." This utter extinction of the causes, condition, consequences, and unconscious tendencies of *dukkha* leaves nothing in consciousness that can give rise to further suffering (Conze et al. 95).

Although the road to *Nirvana* begins with the practice of the Eightfold Path and, more specifically, with concentrative and insight meditation, the four stages that directly lead to it begin with the first or basic moment of enlightenment. When awareness passes beyond thought, object, construction, and framework, it arrives at the pure state of itself in which only silence, stillness, and the pure Awareness that is Reality as Such reigns.

The fundamental shift that ushers in this moment of transcendence is called "cessation of experience" because "the link between event and awareness is permanently severed" (Brown 261-262). Awareness completely disidentifies with and disattaches itself from all contents and objects of consciousness, and thereby radically breaks free and transcends all programming, constructs, and frameworks, and ceases to function through any model, concept, thought, or filtering mechanism of any kind. There is then no movement in the mind. It is completely empty, *sunya,* absolutely free and in the realm of *Nirvana* or the Unconditioned. This happens when there is another and irreversible shift in Awareness, called "Entering the Stream," which is the first of the four stages of *Nirvana* (Brown & Engler 205). At this stage Awareness transcends all constructs, enters the stream of the Unconditioned, and becomes "permanently free from psychological structures ... so that no new *karma* can be generated" (Brown 265-266, 270).

As for the effects of past *karma* — its programmings, unconscious tendencies, habit patterns — as you enter the stream it begins to dissolve or wash away certain mental fixations and addictive programmings, such as greed, grasping, possessiveness, the desire for gain, aggression, resentment, the desire to harm or manipulate others. You no longer engage in lying, stealing, or sexual misconduct (Goleman 33).

As you enter the second stage, called "Once Returner," observable events reappear. But because Awareness has become permanently freed from or disidentified with them, they in no way limit, bind, program, or control it. So there is no falling back into conditioned existence. On the contrary, there is further dissolution of the effects of the previous *karma:* additional and different mental and emotional states permanently disappear. You stop discriminating between people and things, and become fully open to accepting things just as they are (Goleman 33-34).

The causes of *dukkha* burn down to their very roots at the third, "Non-returner" stage: Desire and attachment, together with craving, greed, grasping, striving, and the compulsive character of ordinary life burn off and entirely disappear, never to rise again. All previous motives for action — desire for gain, success, achievement, self-worth, goals, fear of loss — drop off. Discrimination between yourself and others ceases. Dualities are completely transcended in the unity of All-embracing Awareness. Established beyond desire and attachment, feelings assume their natural wholeness; and life regains its natural fluidity and openness (Goleman 34). This stage is similar to the ninth of the Ten Ox-herding Stages of Zen Buddhism.

At the final stage, in which *Nirvana* is fully realized, consciousness is permanently transformed as your identity and center of being permanently shift to the Unconditioned. The very causes, reality, and consequences of *dukkha* thereby entirely cease. As no separation of yourself from anything or anything from anything else remains, all conditioning and *karma* cease. Established in the Unconditioned as your identity and center, with the personality permanently transformed, your natural qualities become a full embodiment of the Unconditioned. Nothing remains in you that could provide a foothold for *karma*, conditioned existence, separateness, ego, or suffering to germinate again (Goleman 34-35). Having gone beyond all beyond and emerged as the No-beyond, you have become a fully awakened sage, a *Tathagata*, one who is undefinable and immeasurable, so that it cannot be said that you are or are not, both are and are not, or neither (Conze et al. 106). You are now a Buddha, a liberated and luminous being whose actions are effortless, natural, and spontaneous — to do what is necessary to maintain life and care for all beings. There remains only just Being and manifesting what IS, flowing out as the crystal clear water of eternal life.

In contrast to this Theravada view, which emphasizes the transcendence of the liberated state, it is the great merit of Mahayana to insist that it is fully immanent, fully incarnational, totally undifferentiated from conditioned existence, from anything whatsoever. Show the slightest tendency to separate *Nirvana* and *Samsara*, or anything from anything else, and you do not have liberation or anything at all. "Unconditioned" means void of *any* condition, absolute transcendence of any differentiation of the Unconditioned from anything that is. This is the ultimate differentiation — differentiation from differentiation itself — in the Supreme Identity of Reality as Such. *Nirvana* is complete realization of Reality as Such, and signifies that whatever is, is in this free state such that anything other than it would not be real but illusory. That is the reason Mahayana insists that *Nirvana* or the Unconditioned and *Samsara* or conditioned existence are "not-two." As *The Lankavatara Sutra* explains, "What is meant by non-duality? It means...as Nirvana and Samsara are, all things are not-two. There is no Nirvana except where is Samsara; there is no Samsara except where is Nirvana" (Suzuki 2: 67).

The Mahayana path leading to *Nirvana* properly begins with the experience of enlightenment in which it dawns on you that completeness is what you are already. Since you are it, you cannot attain, become, gain, lose or be a hairbreadth away from it. To realize this, all you need is to open your eyes and discard the delusive thinking that you lack something. Then you awaken to completeness, which lies in the Unconditioned State of your true nature. This message is driven home again and again by Mahayana Buddhism, especially by Zen.

It is a constant teaching of Zen masters from early on that our true nature, identical with all things, is complete and perfect. The Third Patriarch expresses it as follows:

One in all,
All in One —
If only this is realized,
No more worry about
your not being perfect! (Suzuki 1: 82)

According to Tseng-tsan, then, this perfection consists in directly experiencing absolute Oneness and fully realizing that the Absolute is all that is, and each thing that is is the Absolute. Similarly, for Hui-neng's disciple, Yung-chia Ta-shih, the true nature of each thing is complete and perfect because it is Reality as Such that pervades, penetrates, encompasses, and constitutes the reality and identity of all things, which are its reflections:

One Nature, perfect and pervading
circulates in all natures;
One Reality, all comprehensive,
contains within itself all realities;
The one moon reflects itself
wherever there is a sheet of water,
And all the moons in the waters,
are embraced within the one moon.
(Suzuki 1:97)

As usual, Huang Po expresses the idea most lucidly thus:

The essential Buddha-nature is a perfect whole, without superfluities or lack. It permeates the infinite realms of existence, and yet remains everywhere completely whole. Thus, every single one of the myriads of phenomena in the universe is the absolute. (Blofeld 1: 84)

According to Huang Po, the Buddha-nature or Reality as such is complete and perfect because it is the totality of all that is. Nothing can be added to or taken away from it that would not be it also. Being infinite and indivisible, it is wholly present in and as each thing in all realms of existence. Thus each being in all universes, states, and planes of existence is Ultimate Reality.

Since the Buddha-nature is wholly your true nature, when you fully realize it as your identity, you arrive at this completeness and see that from no-beginning time nothing whatsoever has been lacking in you: "When you have within yourself a deep insight into this you immediately realize that all that you need is there in perfection, and in abundance, and nothing is at all wanting in you" (Blofeld 1: 37).

Similarly, Huang Po's disciple Lin-chi who, upon his own realization exclaimed that he saw "infinite perfection in a single strand of hair," says that there is nothing to attain or to lose because at all times there is no other thing than this Buddha-nature. Because you are already it, you cannot attain it. So, to be complete, all you need to do is to wake up from such delusive thinking that you lack something and see that from eternity you and everything else have always been complete and perfect (De Bary 226-227).

Contemporary Zen masters and experiences of enlightenment bear out this teaching. Thus, Taizan Maezumi Roshi says that things in their fundamental nature are originally perfect, all-pervading and complete. This state is "always, wherever you go, wherever you are, it's right here, and right now, complete, free, and all-pervading" (1: 19, 21). According to Kapleau Roshi, we are intrinsically whole and complete, for our true identity is the "all-embracing, nothing-lacking Buddha-nature" (2: 178). The experience of enlightenment, therefore, reveals "the fact that we are intrinsically, originally the Way itself, which is free and complete" (Maezumi 1: 23). Concurring with this, Yasutani Roshi says that enlightenment brings a "sudden realization that all sentient beings are originally Buddhas and all existence is perfect from the beginning, and absolute" (in Maezumi 1: 70). Speaking of this Realization, Yamada Roshi explains, "After attaining complete enlightenment, making yourself completely free, you realize that, from the beginning, there was no division between the air and the water, the sky and the ocean" (in Maezumi 1: 11).

Kapleau Roshi reports a number of cases in which people describe their experience of enlightenment in terms of completeness: One person speaks of it as the experience in which all beings are revealed to be "complete and perfect, totally free." To another, there appeared to be no inside or outside, "just a wholeness and completeness." Still another says of his experience that it revealed "the perfection and interpenetration of everything in the universe" (2: 145, 149, 166).

The last expression introduces the *Avatamsaka*-Hua Yen view of completeness in terms of identity, interpenetration, and mutual inherence. According to it, to be complete you must penetrate, wholly inhere in, and realize your identity with each thing, right at this moment, in all universes of all time in their distinctness and totality; and each particle of each thing in all universes, actual and possible, must penetrate, wholly inhere in, and be identified with you. As described in the *Avatamsaka Sutra*, in this vision, the universe appears as a magnificently decorated tower, symbolizing its infinite dimensions. The vision is described to the young pilgrim Sudhana by the Bodhisattva Maitreya, in the following words:

> Within this Tower, spacious and exquisitely ornamented, there are also hundreds of thousands of innumerable towers, each one of which is exquisitely ornamented as the main Tower itself and as spacious as the sky. And all these towers beyond calculation in number stand not at all in one another's way; each preserves its individual existence in perfect harmony with all the rest; there is nothing here that bars one tower from being fused with others individually and collectively; there is a state of perfect intermingling and yet of perfect orderliness. Sudhana the young pilgrim sees himself in all the towers as well as in each single tower, where all is contained in one and each contains all. (Suzuki 5: Third Series 133)

Such a view of completeness implies that at this very moment and in your individual being you are infinite, eternal, unconditioned, and wholly all reality and awareness, actual and possible; and the nature and identity of each thing in all universes is constituted by precisely being in this state, with each existing in relationship to each and to the whole. So the *Sutra* continues: "In one particle of dust is seen the entire ocean of lands, beings, ages, numbering as many as all the particles of dust that are in existence, and this fusion takes place with no obstruction whatever" (Suzuki 5: Third Series 131).

Explaining the Tibetan view of completeness in terms of the "three bodies" *(tri-kaya)*, which express the perfection of the Buddha-nature, Lama Govinda says that as infinity is the keynote of Mahayana Buddhism expressed in the infinity of all-embracing wholeness *(Dharma-kaya)*, in the infinity of potentiality in the various interconnected states and planes in all universes of all time *(Sambhoga-kaya)*, and in the infinity of manifesting activity on the ordinary space-time level *(Nirmana-kaya)*, so completeness consists in nothing less than their full realization within ourselves. Ordinarily there is a polarity between individuality and universality. However, since our true nature is the totality of the universe, the complete human being is the one who unites within him/herself both the individual and the universal, the uniqueness of the moment with the eternity of all-embracing wholeness, which is possible only in All-embracing Awareness, in which each thing is experienced in its very individuality and distinctness as the totality of all that is (2: 239, 39, 100).

According to Lama Govinda, this completeness can be realized only when we leap over the chasm of ego that separates us from the completeness and universality of our true nature. As this leap is the direct experience of infinity and all-embracing oneness with all that is, completeness is realized when this experience becomes at the same time a realization of inner unity and solidarity with all life and consciousness. This comes about, not through any fusion or dissolution of finite consciousness into the infinite, but in the full realization of the infinite in the finite. This occurs in both its identity and distinctness such that the realization simultaneously embodies the characteristics of universality and all-embracing totality in the individual existence. Thus completeness lies, not in the dualistic differentiation of unity and plurality, of "I" and "not-I," but in their transcendent unity as "I not-I" (1: 75-82, 215). In adding that such a completeness requires a complete transformation of personality, Lama Govinda hints at the stages each one has to pass through in order to realize this completeness.

According to Zen Buddhism, to be truly complete and liberated you must completely realize, fully embody, and wholly manifest in your life the true nature revealed in enlightenment. Since the initial experience of enlightenment is a momentary affair, unless it is prolonged, deepened, and made permanent, All-embracing Awareness will not become the continuous center of your life and the living spring of your consciousness, thought and action. To live from completeness, to *Be* complete and liberated, therefore, you have to completely realize the Buddha-nature as your permanent identity and fully embody it in your daily life so that your every moment, every action, every gesture becomes its manifestation. Such is the incarnational state realized by the Buddha, expressed in his statement, "He who sees Dharma sees me; he who sees me sees Dharma" (Conze et al. 103). It is similarly revealed in Christ's statements, "He who sees me, sees the Father also," for "I and the Father are one" (Jn. 14: 10-11).

To arrive at this realization, according to Zen, you have to pass through various stages. Tozan distinguishes five stages, called "Five Ranks," while "The Ox-herding Pictures" differentiate ten stages. According to Katsuki Sekida, while the latter moves from the initial stages to enlightenment to Buddhahood, the former is concerned with the post-enlightenment stages leading to Buddhahood and liberation (237). So they are complementary.

The journey begins with "Searching for the Ox." Since the Ox symbolizes the Unconditioned State of the Buddha-nature, the first stage signifies striving for enlightenment through various meditative practices. Here you struggle to concentrate the mind and bring it to one-pointedness and *samadhi*. The second stage, "Finding the Tracks," represents understanding its nature by studying the scriptures and the teachings of the masters, as well as experiencing *samadhi* and insight at more advanced stages of meditation, corresponding to psychic and subtle states. The third stage, called "First Glimpse of the Ox," represents the first experience of enlightenment, when Awareness transcends all conditioned states and experiences its identity as the Unconditioned.

Since after the initial experience, you return to the ordinary world of duality, complete transcendence and permanent realization of completeness begins after enlightenment, with the fourth stage, called "Catching the Ox." At this stage, you begin the process of transformation by working to free yourself from the effects of *karma*—mental and emotional fixations, positive and negative programmings, habit patterns, desires, attachments, unconscious drives, and tendencies.

At the fifth stage, "Taming the Ox," the gap between the Unconditioned and the conditioned state governed by programming narrows. A balance begins to appear in your life. You no longer need to struggle to keep your attention centered in All-embracing Awareness in the midst of daily activities. Although programmed states and habitual patterns still exist, as All-embracing Awareness begins to penetrate and transform them, they no longer have sole control over your life or dictate your behavior.

The sixth stage, "Riding the Ox Home," marks the end of the struggle and the beginning of a life in which All-embracing Awareness flows through and into the ordinary state and transforms the personality. There is no more struggle to keep the attention centered in All-embracing Awareness, which now becomes the living spring of your thought, feeling, and behavior. Hakuin says that at this stage the enlightened Mind "shines through" and dissolves negative and positive programmings, habits of body and mind, desires, attachments, and automatic responses so that "actions and understanding correspond, principles and facts merge completely, body and mind are not-two, essence and appearance do not obstruct each other" (Cleary 2: 135).

At the seventh stage, "Ox Forgotten, Self Alone," the sense of separation between yourself and the Unconditioned disappears. This is transcendence of the separate self or passing into the Unconditioned, whereupon no consciousness of yourself as being other than it remains. Only a subtle consciousness of All-embracing Awareness as set apart from the ordinary state still lingers.

At the eighth stage, called "Both Ox and Self Forgotten," however, even the duality present in the seventh is transcended in a permanent shift of being and awareness to the All-embracing Totality of the Unconditioned. There remains only this Supreme Identity of the Formless Ground, which is perceived everywhere and in everything as that which alone IS. This is the stage of "form is emptiness" spoken of by the *Heart Sutra*. There remains now only this Awakened State of Boundless Being. At this stage, Ken Wilber explains,

> all manifest forms are so radically transcended that they no longer need even appear or arise in Consciousness. This is total and utter transcendence and release into Formless Consciousness, Boundless Radiance. There is here no self, no God, no final-God, no subjects, and nothingness, apart from or other than Consciousness as Such. (5: 97)

At the ninth stage, called "Returning to the Source," like a river emptying into the ocean and reappearing as it truly is, after having returned to and realized the Unconditioned as the identity, Source and Suchness of all that is, you reappear precisely as you are — a sage. The sage IS now the Source, and the Source IS the sage. Everything is experienced just as it is, as the Unconditioned. This is the state of absolute naturalness in which the Unconditioned is revealed to be everything just the way it is. Everything now appears as a spontaneous expression of effortless Being as is clear from the following Zenrin poem:

> Sitting quietly, doing nothing,
> Spring comes, and the grass grows by itself. (Sohl and Carr 56)

Fully established in the Unconditioned State as your identity and center, you now lives effortlessly and spontaneously in the All-embracing Awareness as your permanent abiding place.

The tenth stage, called "Entering the Marketplace with Helping Hands," represents the absolute transcendence of duality wherein the Unconditioned precisely as such returns to and fully reveals itself to be the Supreme Identity of each thing; and each thing precisely as such to be THAT other than which nothing exists. All distinctions, even the subtle attachment to the state of effortless Being, characteristic of the ninth stage, has now disappeared. So there is no need to remain at the Source, which is revealed to be everywhere and all that is. The duality between Formlessness and form, Infinite and finite, Unconditioned and conditioned is now completely transcended as the Unconditioned is revealed to be no other than the conditioned, the Infinite the finite, and Formlessness as no other than entire world of forms. This is the "emptiness is form" of the *Heart Sutra*.

Everything now appears as the complete embodiment and full revelation of the Absolute. Similar to *sahaja samadhi* of Hinduism, in this state the Unconditioned has fully become your natural or ordinary state, which Harada Roshi calls "a condition of absolute naturalness" in which "the mutual interpenetration of the world of discrimination and the world of equality is so thorough that one is aware of neither" (Kapleau 1: 283). Seung Sahn Roshi describes it as "the 360 degree turn of Zen," which is the state of complete nonattachment; and Saraha as "complete and perfect enlightenment" (Conze et al 238). All vestiges of a distinction between and attachment to enlightenment and nonenlightenment having completely disappeared, you permanently abide in All-embracing Awareness and experience everything as its manifestation. Recognizing this, master Daikaku says, "Things are everything; transformation is complete liberation. Transforming things means that your mind is immutable in the midst of all things, turning back to fundamental nature" (Cleary 2: 34).

Thus fully established as the Source and Center, you enter the world of ordinary activity with the open heart of compassion. You have gone completely beyond all beyond, transcended transcendence, and arrived at the No-beyond of the here and now, where there is no going and no return—only Being and manifestation. So, after having returned to the Source and realizing it as your Supreme Identity, you return empty-handed to work for the liberation of all, knowing that the Center is everywhere and the Source this very ordinary world.

Since each thing just as it is wholly embodies and fully manifests the Unconditioned, each thing is its incarnation. This is the import of many Zen koans, such as the following:

> A monk asked Ummon: "What is the Buddha?" Ummon answered: "A shit-removing stick."
> A monk asked Tozan, "What is Buddha?" Tozan said, "Three pounds of flax."
> A monk asked Chao-Chou: "What is the meaning of the First Patriarch's coming to China?" Chao-Chou answered: "The cypress tree in the garden." (Reps 104-105, 119-120, 96)

As the very being of each thing in the universe consists in its completely being and fully revealing the limitless totality of Buddha-nature, a shit-removing stick, or toilet paper, as Eido Shimano Roshi renders it, three pounds of flax or the cypress tree in the garden is no other than it. There is not the slightest differentiation between any ordinary activity, such as removing shit with a stick or toilet paper or weighing three pounds of flax (which is what Tozan was probably doing when he was asked the question) and the Unconditioned. Everything is nothing other than its full embodiment and revelation: the cypress tree in the garden and the birch leaves dancing in the wind like thousands of pinwheels leading the parade of the universe are all its incarnation. Nothing is ever hidden. Everything just the way it is is wholly the Unconditioned. Completeness and liberation are always and already here and now because such is the actual state in which all things at all times abide.

In the ultimate sense, then, liberation is the consequence of the complete transcendence of duality, the realization of completeness, and the full embodiment of the Unconditioned in this very life. Although nothing more is left to do but only to BE fully and manifest the Buddha-nature by Be-ing (Hixon 85-87, 105-107), still, as the Tibetan tradition emphasizes, in the world of forms there is much to be done. But the doing is a manifestation of the Being. Since the sage is a totally free being and at one with the energies of all life, s/he is free to work with everything. So, as Trungpa observes, the energies of ego, its passions and desires, are now transformed into love and compassion, in which the sage undertakes the care for all beings and acts to lead all to the realization of Buddhahood (2: 220-229).

Taoism

All religions are essentially a search for completeness and liberation. They are ways to overcome the feeling of unreality and incompleteness and to find a release from bondage to a world of our own making in which we get trapped, going round and round in repetitive cycles of thought, feeling, and behavior within self-imposed limitations. Taoism is no exception. In fact, the nondualist axes of Vedanta Hinduism, Buddhism, and Taoism share a common perspective. For its part, Taoism holds that each thing in its natural, primordial state completely embodies and wholly manifests the Unconditioned, Tao, apart from which nothing exists. As Chuang Tzu states, "There is nowhere where it is not to be found." As Tao, that is, in the natural, Primordial State, then, each thing is complete. So he states, quoting the *Record*, "When one is identified with the One, all things will be complete with him." Since the One is the Tao, he says again, "To be in accord with Tao means completeness. And not to yield to material things is called perfection" (Chan 205).

According to Chuang Tzu, since Tao is complete in all and wholly all things (Merton 2: 123), completeness and liberation consist in being Tao so totally that nothing remains in us except this Primordial State, and no subjective viewpoints, attachments, programmings, fixations, or anything that could determine, limit, or bind us remains in our life. To be fully established in this axis of Tao, which is the transcendent unity of all partial and limited states, is to be "one with the beginning," to "return to the Source," and become "united with the Universe" or become the universe itself (Chan 207). So he admonishes: "Leap into the boundless and make it your home" (Watson 44).

As mapped out by Taoist Yoga, the way to this return begins with uniting the polar forces within yourself and with those in the universe. When you attain this unity, you arrive at universal or cosmic consciousness and evolve into a New Being, ready to transcend duality altogether and realize your complete identity and release in Tao, which frees you from bondage to limited states of conditioned existence. The scope of this completeness and release was expressed to Blofeld by a twentieth-century Taoist master, Tseng Lao-weng. The following words strike close to the view of Hua Yen School of Buddhism:

> Since the Tao is All and nothing lies outside it, since its multiplicity and unity are identical, when a finite being sheds the illusion of separate existence, it is not lost in the Tao like a dew-drop merging with the sea; by casting off his imaginary limitations, he becomes immeasurable. No longer bound to the worldly categories, 'part' and 'whole,' he discovers that he is co-extensive with the Tao. Plunge the finite into the infinite and, though only one remains, the finite, far from being diminished, takes on the stature of the infinite... The mind of the one who Returns to the Source thereby becomes the Source. Your mind, for example, is destined to become the universe itself. (3: 209-210)

Kabbalah

In Judaism, too, the quest for completeness and liberation is present at the heart of the religious journey. History is seen in *Genesis* as fundamentally a quest to regain the original state of oneness from which humans were cast off and set adrift as a result of the Fall. All human attempts to find meaning and direction by spinning a world out of desires are seen in *Genesis* as attempts in the forward dimensions of time to recover what was lost. Civilization itself appears as a tale of human strivings for liberation and return to origins by forging networks of links. However, these attempts at self-sufficiency in separation from God are seen as failures. But while the Bible puts out hope for the return, the Kabbalah shows the way to it through union with God.

To make this return, the Kabbalah holds that we have to forge a path that unifies multidimensional reality into a whole. Similar to the Tantric axis—Hindu, Buddhist, and Taoist—this view maintains that the universe is a unity of opposite forces, the dimensions of which are intimately interwoven, forming an interconnected, interpenetrating, and undivided whole. Completeness consists in bringing these forces into harmony and integration, both in their individuality within yourself and in their universality with the whole and, ultimately, realizing your oneness with the Infinite *(Ein Sof)*. The path to it is the Tree of Life.

Like a grand *mandala,* the Tree represents multidimensional and hierarchical levels of reality and one's links to it. Its ten stages represent ten forms or levels of energies (somewhat like the "String Theory" in physics) emanating from the Formless Infinite. Interpenetrating on every level, within these ten forms all things simultaneously form four different worlds: the world of divine attributes, patterns of creation, configuration of energies, and matter in motion. Each interpenetrates the others and the ten forms, and forms a multidimensional web of reality. Following the principle, "as above, so below," these worlds and forms exist and flow through each individual. To become complete, you have to awaken these forms of energies within yourself, allow them to flow through the four worlds, and achieve an ever higher unity of being and expansion of consciousness. At the final stage there is a "return to the Source"—union with God (Hoffman 41-62).

According to the Kabbalah, there is no completeness or liberation without this return. According to Moshe Idel, this return is to be made in three stages: (i) nonattachment to object-world, (ii) union with God, and (iii) "annihilation of individual existence," or transcendence of separate self and realization of identity with the Godhead (69). Idel says that major Kabbalistic schools saw completeness—the state of the *devekut*—"as a reintegration of the human into the primordial unity, whose other half is the Divine" (63). This reintegration is completing the circle by the lower half—the human—through ascending to the higher along the Sefirotic Tree. This ascent brings about a total transformation in which you transcend duality and realize the ultimate Unity. The identity that remains in this return does not consist in the merging of two selves in which you retain your sense of yourself as a separate individual; what remains is the one Identity of the *Ein Sof*. The key to this ascent or assimilation is "cleaving" or union. As you cleave to the *Ein Sof,* the Divine radiance shines through you, transforming, assuming, and integrating you into itself, until only the one radiance, one substance, one being remains—that of the Godhead (Idel 64-71).

Christian Mysticism

"Be perfect as your heavenly Father is perfect," Jesus told his disciples. According to him, this perfection or completeness consists in being one with the Father, arrived at through realizing the fullness of the Christ-nature in oneself. Expressed by the Synoptic Gospels in terms of the Kingdom and by John as absolute Oneness—the same absolute Oneness which Jesus has with the Father—the perfection of each thing consists in realizing the fullness of the Christ-nature through identity, interpenetration, and indwelling with God and with all things just as they are.

The Letter to the Colossians, states, "It is in Christ that the complete being of the Godhead dwells embodied, and in him you have been brought to completion" (2:9). Since completeness, which is the Godhead, is fully embodied in the Christ-nature, by becoming its complete embodiment in the same way as Jesus, you can realize it in yourself. This requires a complete irradiation and transformation of your being and consciousness by God so that the ego as a separate center disappears and your identity entirely shifts to the Christ-nature from which you thereafter live and act. As Paul says of his own realization, "I live now, not as I, but as Christ living in me." In this realization Paul's identity as a separate self has disappeared and is replaced by the "I not-I."

To this same end Paul urged the Romans to have their minds "remade" or transformed into Christ-consciousness. Elsewhere he speaks of this transformation as "putting on Christ," which consists in the transcendence of ego and the emergence of the Christ-nature or the Spirit as the new identity and center. Just as Jesus realized the fullness of the Christ-nature through his death and resurrection, so you must also completely transcend the separate self, even the higher kind, and become permanently established in the Christ-nature as the new identity and center of your being and consciousness. This is, for Paul, becoming the "New Man" or the "New Creation." In this concept of completeness we see again the incarnational principle at work: Completeness consists in embodying or incarnating God or the Christ-nature so completely that it is the only thing that remains as your total being.

Beyond the individual, Paul envisions this completeness and liberation to include the totality of all that is. For, becoming the New Creation means bringing to completion all creation within yourself. Paul sees all creations, all forms, the entire universe itself, as the incarnation of the Formless Reality of the Christ-nature awaiting their awakening and completion. And he views each individual to be identical with all things in their undivided wholeness, which is the Body of Christ. So by realizing it completely in yourself, you bring the whole universe to completion. This consists in "holding" or wholly embodying in the unity of your realized Christ-nature the whole universe and each thing through identity, interpenetration, and indwelling. Incarnation is then complete. Everything is complete. And everything becomes the universal dance of All-encompassing Reality and Awareness. Then God is all in all and as all. As such God is all that remains, which is All there IS.

Christian mystics have delineated various stages of the path that, taken together, fairly correspond to the four stages of the journey — purification, illumination, union, and identity — acknowledged by other traditions. Of course, there are variations in this stage-differentiation. Ordinarily the fourth stage is not included. St. Teresa of Avila, for instance, sees the path in terms of the first three, which she describes in six stages, using the metaphor of "interior castle." And some traditions add other stages. According to John Chirban, the Eastern Orthodox Church differentiates five stages: (i) image, which refers to the natural state of the person; (ii) conversion, which consists in one's decision to commit oneself to the spiritual path; (iii) purification; (iv) illumination or insight; and (v) union.

Those Christian mystics who view union with God as the final step of the journey view completion in terms of a permanent state of union with God. Some masters in the Eastern Church, such as St. Isaac the Syrian, call union the state of perfection. Others speak of it as "transforming union" or "deification." In the Western Church, the equivalent expression more often used is "mystical marriage." It represents an inseparable union in which the mystic lives in a continuous consciousness of divine presence. In this state s/he undergoes a transformation of personality, desires, and emotions or "passions." God gradually irradiates, transforms, and assumes his/her entire personality to "himself." Thus God-consciousness becomes the permanent center from which s/he lives and acts (Spencer 228-256).

Other Christian mystics, in both the Eastern and the Western Church, see completeness in terms of complete transcendence of duality and identity with the Godhead. Thus, according to John Chirban, Pseudo-Dionysius and St. Gregory Palamas seem to envision it a formless state beyond concepts (Chirban 307-313). However, Gregory does not say that deification is identification with the formless essence of God. He makes a distinction between divine uncreated essence and uncreated energies. According to him, deification is the transformation brought about by these energies in the state of union (*The Triads* 71-111). Similarly, Maximos the Confessor seems to have identity in mind when he says that the Divine Light transforms and deifies the individual as the mind is "ravished by the divine boundless Light, and loses all sense of itself or of any other creature, and is aware of Him alone" (Spencer 225). This deification "perfects human nature, until it makes it appear in unity and identity" (Spencer 229). But his addition of "by grace" seems to throw the matter back to the realm of union, rather than clearly signifying identity.

On the other hand, Pseudo-Dionysius clearly sees the final stage of the journey as return to or identity with the Godhead. In his *The Mystica Theology*, Pseudo-Dionysius sketches the ultimate purpose of life as transcendence of limitation through differentiation from differentiation and realization of oneness of the Supreme Identity. As procession is a descending order that requires affirmation, this return is an ascending order that requires negation or disidentification, deconstruction, and transcendence of all constructed consciousness, reality, and self. For it requires you "to leave behind everything perceived and understood, everything perceptible and understandable, all that is not and all that is, and, with your understanding laid aside, to strive upward as much as you can toward union with him who is beyond all being and knowledge." In order to realize this you are further instructed to absolutely abandon "yourself and everything" (135). Since the Godhead is beyond anything that can be perceived, conceived, understood, or intuited, the ascent cannot be made through any mediated knowledge. The Godhead cannot be known through anything, for "there is not a trace for anyone who would reach through into the hidden depths of this infinity" (50). This implies that the Godhead can be experienced only directly, only as identity or not at all.

This ascent begins, he tells us, with the deconstruction of outer forms of consciousness and reality—the perceptual and linguistic construction. This is followed by deconstruction of the inner, conceptual layer of the intellect—"beyond all vision and knowledge," and its concomitant images and ideas. Going beyond even understanding or intuition and wisdom, the contemplative enters the void state—the "Darkness of Unknowing," in which the mind turns "completely silent" (138-141). Here the ordinary consciousness, reality, and self are deconstructed, and the contemplative is beyond the subject-object duality, for s/he said to be "neither oneself nor someone else" (137). Out of this void state comes the experience of identity when there occurs a mental revolution—similar to the one spoken of by *The Lankavatara Sutra* ("a turning about in the deepest seat of consciousness")—when "the mind turns away from all things, even itself, and when it is made one with the divine rays" (109). That this is the experience of identity is implied when he says that it is "union far beyond mind" (109). This is made more explicit in the following passage:

> Here, renouncing all that the mind may conceive, wrapped entirely in the intangible and the invisible, he belongs completely to him who is beyond everything. Here, being neither oneself nor something else, one

is supremely united by a completely unknowing inactivity of all knowledge, and knows beyond the mind by knowing nothing. (137)

Clearly, Pseudo-Dionysius is speaking about a state beyond duality where the mind is completely void and silent and no consciousness of one's separation from anything remains. So nothing remains in the mind to create any differentiation or distance between the Godhead and the contemplative. Thus it is the unmediated All-embracing Awareness in which only identity remains. This oneness must, therefore, be that of identity or return to the absolute Ground, Cause, Center, and Suchness.

Two mystics in the Western Church who clearly affirm identity as the state of completeness and the end of the path are Meister Eckhart and Bernadette Roberts. To arrive at this final transcendence, according to Eckhart, you have to pass through five stages. The first is following ethical precepts and undertaking various preparatory practices. At the second stage, consciousness shifts its orientation from the outside world and turns inward toward God. At the third stage, it begins to be destructured as conditioning and outward limitations or constructions begin to drop away. Consciousness begins to be rooted and centered in God at the fourth stage, while at the fifth stage you are fully at one with God. This fifth stage is what Eckhart calls "breakthough" in which you experience the identity beyond union. For, he says, "in this breakthrough I discover that I and God are one" (Fox, *Breakthrough* 218). Finally, transformed by God's eternal nature, you become formless and unconditioned. This happens when God's essence or "isness" becomes your "isness" and you fully embody it in your life. You are then completed and liberated. This is "eternal rest and bliss...for the final goal of the inner persons and new persons is eternal life" (Fox, *Breakthrough* 512-513).

Bernadette Roberts not only clearly differentiates identity from union, she also provides details on the steps leading from union to identity. She distinguishes six phases. First is the dark night of the soul, wherein the outer form of reality and consciousness is deconstructed and the self is experienced in all its nakedness and existential impasse. Second, as the contents of consciousness are pushed from the center to the periphery, a new, transformed and integrated, higher or universal self emerges and becomes the subject-pole, while God assumes the object-pole. The third phase, which is the highest point of the unitive life, is marked by full union, traditionally called transforming union or mystical marriage. The next three phases are not so much new stages as a process of transformation that ends in a final transcendence even of the higher self (2: 9-214). At this stage both the self and the personal God are transcended. As all objects disappear from consciousness, the subject-object duality is transcended, and you come upon the pure void. When you pass beyond this, you finally transcend duality; and union gives way to a state in which God alone remains as pure Subjectivity or Identity of all that IS (1: 149-152).

This final state is very different from the traditional Christian idea of salvation. It is not the separate self that is being saved or liberated because without transcending it, there is no liberation. Moreover, this liberation does not begin in the afterlife. It has no beginning or end; it is always going on and is always in the here-now. The afterlife may remove the veil of empirical construction, but what is revealed is the ever-present reality of All-embracing Awareness, which is also revealed here-now when the present construction is transcended. Since the liberated is already in this state, s/he has already passed beyond death and risen to eternal life. Liberation is nothing other than living this eternal, resurrected life in the here-now.

Sufism

As mentioned before, for the Sufis completeness consists in becoming the Completed Man. In tantric fashion some Sufis conceive of this Completed Man in terms of a complete integration of various states of consciousness in the final unity of All-embracing Awareness.

To arrive at this final state, the Sufi passes through various progressive stages which fairly correspond to the various meanings of *fana*. Of these, the first two involve purification or dissolving negative programmings, fixations, and habits. At the third stage, "annihilation from created attributes," the destructuring of ordinary consciousness proceeds into the symbolic layer and model construction. The Sufi transcends various objects and contents of consciousness and subjective identification with various programmings and constructs, and experiences relative oneness.

At the fourth stage, called "annihilation from essence" (taken together with the fifth), you transcend the separate self and see only Oneness everywhere. Since only God now remains as the object of consciousness, in all things you see God only, experienced as either "He" or "I," depending on whether God or the Self is the object of contemplation. If you contemplate your "subtle" essence or the Self, you may express your realization in such ecstatic utterances as did, for instance, Bayazid Bistami, who exclaimed, "Glory be to me! How great is my majesty." Similarly, Al-Hallaj exclaimed, "I am God." Moreover, believing that human beings are the incarnation of God, he stated, as did Christ in the Fourth Gospel, that anyone who touched him touched God also, for God and he were one (Nicholson 59).

At the sixth stage, which is "annihilation from other than God through God," you pass beyond the higher self and the polarities that still exist in the universal state. Since you contemplate no separate entities, you can either deny that you are anything or affirm that you are all things, for you have arrived at the state of unity beyond all opposites.

At the final stage of *fana*, called "annihilation of annihilation," you pass completely into God, who alone remains as the only Identity there is. Similar to the *nirvikalpa samadhi* of Hinduism, "form is emptiness" of the *Heart Sutra*, and the eighth of the ten Zen Ox-herding Stages, all forms are now so completely transcended that you arrive at the utterly absolute oneness of the Godhead. There is here no self, no God, no subject, no object, nothing apart from the Formless Ground into which you have passed, as Nurbakhsh observes, like a drop of water into the Ocean of Infinity (2: 99). In this state, you see, as Attar put it, all things as identical with God, who is perceived as the All and only thing there is (Hixon 173).

Passing beyond *fana*, you arrive at *baqa*, "subsistence in God," and awaken in the world of forms. This is similar to *sahaja samadhi*, "emptiness is form," the ninth and tenth Zen Ox-herding Stages, returning to and becoming the Source according to Taoism, and the incarnational state envisioned by Christianity. At this stage you experience all things as nothing other than God in the process of being and manifesting "himself." Each thing as such becomes a manifestation of the One Identity besides which nothing exists. When this Awareness becomes your permanent identity and center, you become established in the Supreme Identity and its embodiment. You are now a completed and liberated human being.

Having studied under the Sufis, Gurdjieff adopted a similar view. He held that there were seven states of consciousness that constituted seven orders or states of man. The Completed Man is the one who has realized the Supreme or Permanent Identity and Center at the seventh stage and has integrated all the characteristics of the lower six stages within him/herself. S/he has then realized the completeness of the permanent "I" – a Self that is universal and individual at the same time (Riordan in Tart 2: 307-310).

When the Completed Man is established in the Supreme Identity, his/her personality is not thereby lost. The Unconditioned so totally penetrates and transforms it that s/he becomes a revelation of God on earth. As Nurbakhsh states, "The Perfected One is an individual who has become freed from the dictates of the 'commanding self' [i.e., ego]. Both inwardly and outwardly, such a being is the manifestation of the Divine Attributes. Having become one with the Absolute, he is freed from the relativity of 'I' and 'we.' He is a mirror which perfectly reflects God. When one looks upon him, one sees nothing but Truth"

(1: 13). Once again we see that completeness and liberation constitute the incarnational state. For one who realizes it fully embodies in him/herself the All-embracing Awareness so thoroughly that what remains as the final state is the "I not-I," Reality as Such as the Identity, God in all and as All.

Various consequences follow upon a full realization of this state. First, as Hindu scriptures point out, there is freedom from bondage to conditioning, objects of desire, and the mind's fixation on and control by the world. As the hold of the world on the mind ceases, you stop being preoccupied with fulfilling its expectations or acting according to its dictates and demands. The world simply stops defining, conditioning, controlling, or determining you.

Second, "bondage to *karma* ceases." You become free of the Wheel of Life or the cycle of repetitive, habitual, automatic, mechanical ways of thought, feeling, and behavior. As the mind stops running along old tracks, you become free of automatic responses and habit-patterns. Ordinarily, as these solidify to form character or personality and set the Wheel in motion, with their dissolution, the Wheel stops and you are set free from their bondage. Your new behavior does not arise from programmed reactions nor does it give rise to further programming. Free from habituation, in the midst of conditions your mind is able to operate freely and directly without any medium or filter. According to the *Bhagavatam,* this is being in the world, free of the world (Prabhavananda 96).

Third, living continuously in All-embracing Awareness, you are aware moment to moment. As your mind remains fully focused in the here-now, you experience each moment as new, as ever the first without a second, fresh as the first moment of creation. Suffused with Awareness, each moment becomes, in Yukio Mishima's phrase, "a re-creation of existence instant by instant" (40). Within the eternal ocean of All-embracing Awareness acting as a backdrop, each moment arises, like successive waves, as a succession of nows, from nowhere and going nowhere, experienced as the ever-new and ever-present dance of Awareness. Thus your mind always remains present-centered, rather than doing the usual shuttling back and forth between the past and the future. And you always respond to things directly from the fullness of this ever-present Awareness.

Fourth, you experience freedom from ego. The *Ashtavakra Gita* even defines liberation in terms of the transcendence of ego (Johnson 125); and Ramana Maharshi says that in the final stage of liberation, ego is completely dissolved without a trace (Osborne 119). With the complete transcendence of ego and duality, there remains nothing to organize or run your life on a separate basis.

Fifth, since ego ceases to be a separate center, the very roots of desires that have ego, and its feelings of emptiness and incompleteness as their basis, dissolve, bringing desiringness or craving to an end. You no longer want to possess something so as to become real, to find identity or meaning. The desire for gain or the fear of loss as a motive for action entirely vanishes, along with striving, greed, and competitiveness. All motives, purposes, and goals of the separate self also disappear. Instead, desires spring from the Self and become its pure and spontaneous expression. You simply desire from the fullness of what you are. Since your desires now well up from the Unconditioned State, you desire what God desires, which is nothing other than "his" Self-manifestation as the world.

This state brings clarity and transparency to your life. No confusion or uncertainty remains. Since all programmings have dissolved, negative ones, such as fear, anxiety, stress, frustration, and anger disappear, together with their roots in the unconscious. Freed from restrictions due to programming, your natural qualities, such as love and compassion, assume their natural, undifferentiated state, capable of being extended equally to all without any reservation. The entire affective life, based on dualities, such as likes and dislikes, drops off. As Bernadette Roberts says, with the disappearance of the self, the entire affective system rooted in the feeling of personal being also disappears (1: 170-184). This is what the *Bhagavatam* and the *Gita* call "attaining the eye of equality and going beyond the pairs of opposites," "attaining peace and tranquility." And the latter adds that the sage who attains this state neither loves nor hates. Free of such dualities, your life becomes fluid, spontaneous, and tranquil.

Sixth, you experience complete nonattachment. As the *Bhagavatam* says of the liberated, "Though he lives in the world, he remains perfectly unattached" (Prabhavananda 305). Since in this state you experience nothing to be other than yourself, there remains no possibility of your attaching to anything or anyone. As attachment creates separation, complete nonattachment is its absolute transcendence, brought about by identification with Reality as Such. This makes life absolutely free and open, without any boundary, limitation, or exclusion. Since not to be fixated anywhere or on anything is to be everywhere and everything, the liberated is infinite and eternal while being in a particular place and time. You experience each moment as complete in itself, needing nothing from outside to make it exciting, worthwhile, or meaningful.

Seventh, suffering entirely ceases. As the *Bhagavatam* puts it simply, liberation means a complete cessation of suffering and miseries — not their denial or repression, not wishing them away or ignoring or pretending that they do not exist, not stoically accepting them, but their complete cessation (Prabhavananda 79-80). When a tree is uprooted, its branches wither. With the cessation of separation from Reality, bondage, ego, attachment, and desiringness, there remains nothing to cause suffering and no one to suffer.

Thus, not only is Eliade's view that liberation or *moksha* is a denial of human suffering (34) entirely mistaken; but several other views regarding liberation are mistaken as well. One misconception is that this state is a withdrawal from the world and that it would render life void of any purpose or meaning. If such a view still lingers in your mind, you have not understood what I have said so far.

Where there is no separation from anyone or anything, no withdrawal is possible. As the liberated does not experience any separation from anything but experiences everything as complete, none of the reasons for withdrawal — disappointment, disillusionment, inability to relate or cope, the feeling of being a failure, fear, anxiety, alienation — is present. So nothing could motivate him/her to withdraw. What appears as withdrawal from the ordinary point of view — since s/he does not engage in the usual activities that occupy most people — is, in reality, a result of a complete absence of striving for substitute gratifications in the advent of the Reality which is the goal of human existence. It is not that s/he feels a need to withdraw, for instance, from the business world but, in the absence of the usual motives which drive people to it, should s/he still choose to engage in it, such a decision would be an expression of his/her care for the well-being of others: a life-saving activity.

Eighth, you have no purpose or goal. It is true that in the absence of ordinary goals external to the action, the liberated life can have no purpose or goal other than itself. But such a life leaves no room for not acting. Since s/he does not require an external goad pushing him/her to act, to him/her everything is of intrinsic worth and every action arises spontaneously and effortlessly from within as a manifestation of completeness. In such a situation, action becomes a revelation of the Identity already realized, rather than a way of acquiring one.

Moreover, the Being of the liberated seeks Be-ing or manifestation because that is the nature of Reality. The Self is ever active to manifest itself. It has not the slightest inclination to withdraw, hide, or stop acting, because that is impossible. Since everything in the world of forms is a manifestation of the Formless Reality, nothing is ever hidden. Reality is a state of pure activity, which is its dynamic character. Its self-creative character is to push itself out, expressing itself in infinite forms, as if the Divine Artist were making copies of "himself." Everything is frame upon frame of God; everything is a snapshot of God, like a camera clicking away. Singularly exhibitionistic! Alternately, you could say that action itself is the Self Be-ing itself, which is its Self-revelation. Action in essence is Being Be-ing itself, which is pure Being. So pure action (*Actus Purus* of Aquinas) is pure, Unconditioned Being. Action that is the manifestation of Being is the only real action possible. Since Reality as Such is always by nature dynamic and active, in the process of revealing itself, having realized your identity with it, you cannot possibly stop acting or withdraw. Rather, action arises as the within manifesting itself as the without. What remains for you at this final stage, therefore, is to BE and manifest yourself by Be-ing, acting or unfolding, thus joining in the symphony of all forms constituting the universe. At this stage, therefore, there is truly nothing to live for — but for the first time you begin to live the fullness of life — completeness growing ever more complete as you move from infinity to infinity in the everlasting but ever-new dance of life!

From the point of view of experiential religion, liberation represents the fully developed state of humankind. Only one who has realized it is a fully evolved, completely free human being. Without this realization any claim to being free is illusory. This does not mean that the struggle for economic, political, and social freedom are unimportant. Rather, what I am saying is that without the absolute freedom of the Unconditioned, these others in the end enslave us. What experiential religion offers humankind is this absolute, complete freedom — which can be the only real basis for the others — living the freedom of the Unconditioned while being in the world and engaged in the affairs of daily life. How each person can realize this freedom is the subject matter of Part V.

Chapter 22
Love and Compassion

The journey of experiential religion cannot be complete, no matter what you realize, if it is done for yourself alone, since that involves splitting yourself off from others, creating duality and rendering the claim to realization false to itself. Being a state of unity and differentiation at the same time, in order to be complete, liberation must be open to the reality of others, although, strictly speaking, from the point of view of the realized, there are no others. This openness is a natural result of liberation. For a life completely free of self-concern becomes open to universal concern, which is the soil from which love and compassion spontaneously spring. They are the dynamic elements of the liberated personality.

Rooted in absolute Oneness, love and compassion grow to maturity through the other stages and are released at liberation. At this stage, since there is no consciousness of yourself as a separate entity around whose needs your life is organized, the love that arises is selfless and directed, in John S. Dunne's apt phrase, to "the care for all beings" (67). Out of an awareness of the world's needs arise love and desiringless desire to serve others. Desiring nothing for yourself and expecting nothing in return because there is no self to desire and no hope for any gain, your action becomes, as the *Gita* teaches, *Karma Yoga* — giving yourself solely out of love because of others' needs without thinking what you will gain out of it or how it will come out in the end (Prabhavananda & Isherwood 1: 61).

You cannot be prompted to act selflessly, I have said, without realizing oneness and completeness. For without a complete transcendence of ego and a permanent shift of identity to the Unconditioned State, some self-seeking motive will always remain; and this will prevent selfless love and compassion from arising. As Garma Chang (Chung-Yuan) has observed apropos Zen Buddhism, ultimate and unconditional love can be attained only through a complete realization of *Sunyata*, as the highest compassion follows a realization of the highest wisdom. In the ultimate sense, compassion arises naturally and spontaneously, brought about through a deep realization of *Sunyata* and a complete identification with totality (1: 197-198). This is essential and contrasts with the social, political, economic, and other struggles for liberation I have mentioned before.

Contrary to what John Dunne says, without first destroying the roots of suffering in yourself it is not possible to become free of your suffering by passing over into other lives (55ff). Unless you are established in a state from which you can see things exactly as they are, you will not know the kind of help others really need or whether what you are doing is helping others. You cannot see into the needs of others without realizing oneness with them and without being free of your own needs. Moreover, when you do not know what will really help, your action may serve to bring more misery into their lives.

Furthermore, without liberation, the ego will always be preoccupied with satisfying or projecting its desires, needs, ideas, or compulsions on others, including the compulsion to save them, which is doing what will ultimately save itself. As D.H. Lawrence put it in *The Man Who Died*, this is the "mania of cities and towns" (184) – the compulsion under which humankind operates. So, passing over into other lives will not necessarily make your suffering disappear. The Buddha neither taught nor practiced anything of the sort. He got rid of his own suffering first. It was then that compassion arose in him; and that happened only after he overcame the final temptation of staying with his own realization and not going out into the world to work for the liberation of others. Similarly, compassion arose in Jesus after his own realization.

Thus, without attaining liberation, you cannot transform ego's former drives into pure, egoless energy working for the good of others. On the other hand, without compassion liberation is not complete, as vestiges of duality, attachment, desire, and ego will still remain and keep you absorbed in your own attainment without its flowing into the liberation of others. As Saraha well put it:

> He who clings to the Void
> And neglects compassion
> Does not reach the highest stage,
> But he who practices only compassion
> Does not gain release from the toils of existence.
> He, however, who is strong in the practice of both,
> Remains neither in Samsara nor in Nirvana.
> (Conze et al. 239)

When there is no self around which to organize life and to propel yourself to create a world out of desire and attachment, the love that arises is selfless.

With no duality between yourself and this love and nothing to direct it toward yourself in opposition to others, your whole being is revealed to be Unconditional Loving, which manifests itself without any limitation or differentiation. This is what the New Testament means when it says that God is love and that we should love as God loves. Unless you realize the Unconditioned State, signified by the word *God,* in which love and being are identical, your love cannot be unconditional, for such love can arise only from Unconditional Being and as its revelation. When you realize this absolute love, in relationship to the relative world, it becomes your dynamic energy. This energy reveals your being in action, pouring itself out as the "care for all beings" and relating to everyone and everything without discriminating one person or thing from another.

Compassion, then, is dynamic love—love in action. It presupposes both absolute Oneness and the wisdom of differentiation in which you see other human beings just as they are in their suffering. Through Oneness you become identified with others and are at one with them in their suffering. But the wisdom of differentiation prevents you from suffering. For the Self in and with which you experience Oneness is not your ego or that of others, which cause suffering; and having transcended your separate self, there remains nothing in you or in this Oneness that could make or keep you suffering. Compassion, therefore, enables you to be identified with others, to see their condition exactly as it is without getting caught up in it, and to work for their liberation.

It should be noted here that compassion is not the same as mercy. The latter is based on duality and an inferiority of one party, which is indebted, or has done something offensive, to the other, superior one. As a result, mercy has an element of subservience and fear. Moreover, it is external to the one who shows it, and does not involve either party to any depth. Such is the case, for instance, with the Christian idea of mercy as applied to the relationship between God and humankind. The entire transaction is conducted like a business deal. An external, far superior Being is asked to remove some offense (sin), which is external to both it and the individual, as it involves transgression of a rule, law, or order believed to have been set up by this Almighty King. The individual asks the King-Judge to pardon the transgression so that s/he can go on, in an easy conscience, with business as usual. S/he wants life to continue as smoothly and undisturbed as before, without God invading his/her life and threatening the equilibrium s/he has worked so hard to achieve and maintain. So s/he begs for leniency or mercy. This is a Judge-perpetrator transaction, with conscience acting as accuser-policeman. Once s/he has been, or believes s/he has been, shown mercy, or has pleaded his/her case before the Judge, the accuser-policeman is appeased and lets him/her off the hook. S/he is, or believes that s/he is, set free. This is thought to justify his/her mode of life. Because the entire transaction is external, it brings no real change in him/her. Life continues to be the way it was.

Not so with compassion. Without having to desire anything for yourself, it makes, in Chogyam Trungpa's words "tremendous demands." It calls for giving up your fantasy games; giving up your secure little world; your habitual ways, repetitive programmed behavior; your fixations, attachments, and desires. It asks you to open up and surrender yourself and thus become free of suffering. Since ego wants to protect itself, its world, and its way of life, the self-surrender that compassion demands strikes terror in its heart. As Trungpa says, "True compassion is ruthless from ego's point of view, because it does not consider ego's drive to maintain itself" (2: 210). Since it wants to maintain itself and its world the way it is, ego becomes terrified at the prospect of losing itself and everything it has. It feels threatened by the surrender that compassion deems necessary for self-growth and freedom from suffering. So it fears and resists it.

Compassion may even appear cruel from ego's point of view. Thus the demands that Zen and other enlightened masters have made on their disciples — Ma-tsu vigorously twisting Pai-chang's nose or kicking another in the chest to bring him to realization; Marpa driving Milarepa to the point of suicide before beginning formal instruction — may appear cruel. But, setting aside cultural and personality differences, such demands do not necessarily mean that the masters are cruel or on a power trip. Rather, their strategies are directed toward helping students to let go of ego and dualistic thinking and make the final leap into the Unconditioned. That is why, as Tarthang Tulku observes, in itself compassion involves no demand or expectation (1:41). It is like the sun shining on all at all times. But, as Jesus says, those who prefer darkness and do not want their actual situation exposed hide from it. The ego wants to hide from compassion because it does not want its illusions, especially its greatest illusion — itself — exposed. Arising from wisdom, compassion reveals to the individual his/her situation exactly as it is and brings him/her to face him/herself, which is not to the liking of one given to avoidance and deceptive games.

As Trungpa observes, in contrast to the deceptive games ego plays, compassion is a completely naked, open, and welcoming attitude. It requires a brutal honesty toward oneself and others and a total self-giving toward others. In compassion the liberated one responds directly and spontaneously to the needs of the situation without blaming or condemning others or defending or justifying oneself. This point is illustrated by the following story:

> A beautiful Japanese girl, whose parents owned a food store near where Zen master Hakuin lived, was discovered by her parents to be pregnant. Her parents were angry at her, but she would not tell them

who got her pregnant. After much harassment at last she named Hakuin. In great anger the parents went to the master and accused him. "Is that so?" was all he would say. After the child was born, it was brought to Hakuin. By this time he had lost his reputation, but he was not concerned. He took very good care of the child. A year later the girl-mother could stand it no longer. She told her parents the truth— the real father was a young man who worked in the fish market. Her parents again went to Hakuin, apologized to him, asked his forgiveness and wanted the child back. In returning the child, all he said was, "Is that so?" (Reps 7-8)

Here is an example of liberation and compassion at work. Instead of defending himself for being falsely accused, condemning the girl, or refusing to take care of the child, Hakuin simply responded directly to the need of the situation, which was care for the child. Because there was no ego to advance its own gain or to set conditions for its exercise, compassion involved the whole individual, who was able to be completely open to all and all-embracing.

The unconditional openness of compassion enables you to be aware of what is going on and to respond to the realities of the present. As there are no screens between you and a particular situation, compassion gives you what Trungpa calls a "panoramic view," which allows you to see the total situation clearly and completely and to act spontaneously according to the real needs of people without their being able to take advantage of, manipulate, control, or walk over you. Literally, it is the situation that calls you to act. The universe is erupting, manifesting itself, and, being one with it, you erupt into action. There is no compulsion to act or desire not to act; nor are you conditioned to react in a certain programmed way or from the controlling effects of the situation. Rather, the action is the free flow of the universe manifesting itself through you. In this there is nothing to limit compassion or cause discrimination. So no games, self-deception, defense, role playing, expectation, or holding yourself back is operative here. Unconditional compassion makes you directly and totally open to others, which allows open communication to take place.

Thus, upon attaining liberation, you do not abandon the river of life. As it brings complete oneness with and openness to all life, liberation makes you turn around, so to speak, and compassion moves you to open up and give yourself completely and joyfully for the liberation of all life. This is the Bodhisattva ideal expressed in the vow: "All beings, however limitless, I vow to save. I take upon myself the burden of all suffering...At all costs I must bear the burden of all beings...All beings I must set free" (Conze et al. 131).

In spite of the vow, there is a "paradox" in regard to liberation and compassion that needs to be addressed here. It is this: Having realized Oneness, you tend to see everything as one. Since the universe is not separate from you, upon attaining liberation you see that the whole universe has been liberated in and as you. From this there is a tendency to conclude that, since others are not separate from you, you need not work for their liberation. This is a temptation to which many so-called realized individuals, particularly in the East, succumb. But a further conclusion may be drawn: Since the source of all suffering is internal, you do not have to do anything on the external, social level to alleviate such suffering as hunger, poverty, disease, racism, injustice, inequality, etc. The next step you may be tempted to take is that you do not have to do anything. You can withdraw from the world and live in blissful isolation while suffering goes on unabated. Eastern religions are especially vulnerable to this temptation. Even Mahayanists, while they take the Bodhisattva vow to liberate all beings from suffering and talk endlessly about compassion, do nothing to alleviate suffering on the social, economic, political, or ethical level, and little on the internal level on a wide scale. Even Westerners who have embraced Eastern ways behave in this way. How are we to explain this phenomenon?

It must be emphasized that this "paradox" is not a necessary consequence of absolute Oneness or liberation as such. Instead of excluding differentiation, liberation includes it. While in this state you experience all things as One, you also experience each thing exactly as it is. If human beings suffer, you see them as suffering. Oneness is not blind but makes you see suffering and its causes directly, from the inside. Otherwise there would be a failure of discriminating wisdom here. It follows that, the world being One, the enlightened individual ought to be able to see that s/he would be contributing to the perpetuation of misery and suffering if s/he did not do anything to alleviate them. Besides, s/he ought to be able to see that one person's realization does not redound to another. When s/he became enlightened, others thereby did not. When a Zen master eats, another man's belly does not thereby become full; otherwise by pampering the master like a queen bee, we could remove from the world not only hunger but other ills as well. Moreover, s/he ought to be able to see that, although to one who is established in Oneness duality is illusory, in the mind of the unrealized it is very real and creates its own reality, from which suffering springs. Something must be done, therefore, to enable the latter not only to see his/her condition and change his/her mind, but also to change the external conditions that reinforce and perpetuate suffering.

The "paradox" is not, then, a consequence of absolute Oneness or liberation, or even of the Eastern religions themselves. Rather, its roots lie in the Eastern cultures. As I have said before, being inward-directed and cosmos-centered, the East does not see the individual as separate from but as a part of the whole. Thus it does not see the individual but the group as the highest value. Moreover, while the inward direction has led it to develop a powerful technology for self-transformation, it has prevented it from developing a strong sense of individuality, uniqueness, and separation of the individual from the group. These factors have prevented the East from seeing the need to transform the environment for human needs, desires, and purposes. Consequently, it has failed to develop a technology to transform the external world. Emerging in this context, Eastern religions simply accepted this attitude without questioning it and gave it a religious sanction. So they proceeded to develop the inner world and a profound psychology, to explore the highest realms of consciousness, and to map out paths of personal transformation without engaging in a corresponding transformation of society and environment. As a result, their world has remained basically unchanged. Millions who have not experienced the inner transformation have been living miserable, poverty-stricken, disease-ridden lives, engulfed and overwhelmed by their condition and dragged on by unawareness, delusion, inertia, and stupor. Real compassion consists in seeing through this quagmire and being moved to do something about it, not just talking about compassion.

The opposite is the case with Christianity and Western religions in general. While the East developed an active attitude toward self-transformation, its attitude toward the world and toward alleviating the miseries of its teeming millions whose lives are no higher than what the Kabbalah calls the "vegetable level of existence," became passive. Christianity took on the opposite development, spurred on by the twin forces of Western culture and the Bible. Guided by the belief that salvation consists in God's action on human beings accomplished once and for all in the death and resurrection of Christ and that the individual can do nothing to save him/herself, it developed a passive attitude toward self-transformation. On the other hand, imbued with the biblical attitude expressed in Genesis and the dominant Western culture's emphasis on the individual as the highest value and with its active standpoint toward the world, Christianity developed an ethic of action, a dynamic attitude of transforming the environment and alleviating human miseries. It relegated transformation of the inner world to mystics and monastics. As a result, it developed great ethical systems, social concerns, and compassion in terms of removing human suffering by improving the human condition. St. Paul's dictum that what really matters is faith active in love became the final stance. While the East talked about compassion, the West practiced it. However, without the inner transformation, the attempt to eradicate social, economic, political, or even psychological ills is like trying to save a tree, when its roots are being eaten away, by pouring water on it.

The result of all this, East-West, is that religion has become immured in illusions and half-truths. Because of fatal flaws on each side, in spite of endless talk about saving the world, not only has it not changed or been saved, each type of religion has contributed to the inner and outer human degradation and destruction. The Western drive to transform the outer at the expense of the inner world has led to misery and suffering in the latter domain which, since it is projected to the outer realm, has resulted in destructiveness on both planes. The opposite development in the East has brought about and perpetuated suffering and misery in the outer which, since it is introjected, has contributed to the inner poverty and suffering of millions who have not attained the inner transformation, thus resulting in human suffering and degradation on both planes. As a result, no fundamental, structural change has occurred; only a perpetuation of human misery. New cultural inventions only shift human problems onto different planes and deflect suffering by providing new avenues of diversion to keep people busy and temporarily forget their suffering.

Getting humanity off this Wheel of Life is the real Bodhisattva compassion. What is necessary for the world as a whole are paths of complete inner and outer transformation. Half answers will not do. We need one whole answer which will bring completeness and liberation to humankind as a whole. Since, East-West, each has only half an answer, what is necessary for a complete answer is to unite the two halves into one whole project for the total transformation and liberation of humankind as a whole. In this, the East can teach the West the inner, while the West teaches the East the outer transformation. Without such a project, the transformation and liberation of the whole human person and the entire species on a planetary scale cannot or will not take place.

This union can come only from the West. Because of its passive attitude and lack of cultural dynamism and drive for outer transformation, in spite of having a global perspective, the East will not move toward a global transformation. Once the West takes on the Eastern inner and cosmocentric perspective, as inner transformation flows out of absolute Oneness and liberation, with its active and dynamic stance toward the world, it will be able to integrate the inner and the outer into a complete path of global human transformation and evolution. Only then will human suffering cease entirely and completeness and liberation on a planetary scale be realized. Then the Bodhi Tree will abound with flowers and heaven and earth will become One.

Part IV

One Who Shows the Way

> If you wish to know the road up the mountain,
> You must ask the man who goes back and forth on it.
> -The Zenrin

Chapter 23
The Way of the Founders

The way of liberation has made it amply clear that religion is born of the womb of experience. The experience of life asks the question, to which religion provides an answer. Now the experience that poses the question is not the one that provides the answer. While the question arises from the limited world of everyday living, the answer comes from the Illimitable, where questions resolve in the illuminating silence that reveals to you your destination. Because the ordinary world *is* the question, it has no dimension from which it can answer itself. For the limits of this world create the lack and prompt the question, drive you to find an answer, and yet prevent you from seeing it. A metacontext or transcendent dimension is, therefore, needed to see the answer that can resolve the question by transforming the ordinary world. While this seeing is the key, the pressures of daily life usually do not enable people to see their world as the fundamental question which their very living itself poses, let alone to see the transcendent source of the answer. This means that not every experience rises in everyone's mind in the form of the question; otherwise everyone would enter into the path of realization. Before exploring the realms of the question or answer, in this chapter I shall first discuss the sort of experience that rises to the conscious level in the form of the question.

It may be said that there are three styles of ordinary life. The first enfolds those who feel the pain but succumb to their situation by sinking into unawareness. They feel that they have nothing to live for, and that life is worthless and void of meaning. Or they see the futility of trying to find an answer, since the same oblivion awaits both those who find the answer and those who do not or see no need to. As Qoheleth has stated, both the wise and the fool meet the same dissolution at death, since the present form of consciousness cannot survive. So the first group may consign life to a slow, painful process of death by compulsive, excessive or self-destructive behavior, or resort to various strategies of escape. Needless to say, although this type of experience is part of the question, being on the elemental level of survival or living in a closed world, it does not become a conscious questioning of existence.

The second style embraces the vast majority of those who, while they feel the pain, are afraid to face it. As a result, life becomes a way of escaping the pain and the question by engaging in various pursuits, ranging from the pleasure-oriented consciousness given to diversion, entertainment, and the endless search for different experiences and excitements; to the power-oriented consciousness dominated by drives for power, success, status, achievement, control, manipulation of others, and so on.

The path of pleasure does not become a conscious questioning; it is a way of avoiding it. On this point Blake was very much mistaken when he said that the road of excess leads to the palace of wisdom. Unless one consciously undertakes to test its limits so as to discover the truth, as was the case with the Buddha, the path of excess can only dull the sensibility to indifference, stupor, self-indulgence, or narcissism. Or it can set you in a rage against yourself and the world—driving you restlessly from one experience to another, or making you constantly avoid facing yourself and your situation.

On the other hand, the path of power leads to the same avoidance or to immersion in the drive for power, control, and self-importance, or to attainment of the objects of desire and striving, which creates the illusion that the answer will be found in them. Since for both pleasure- and power-dominated consciousness the experience remains on the narrow, shallow, and individual level of the separate self, neither allows the experience to turn into a conscious questioning of existence as a whole.

In the third type, the experience does not remain ego-bound but the initial, inchoate question sinks deep into the universal unconscious level. This allows the experience to embrace the entire human condition and rise in the form of a conscious questioning of the very foundation of conditioned existence. As the individual experience becomes universal, in questioning your own existence, all existence stands questioned. In such an experience you see through the very limits not just of your own life but of all human life. As your experience encompasses that of humankind, your pain becomes the pain all human beings suffer in their life situations. It is as if in your situation all human situations become focused, and in your questioning they all find their expression.

Thus your experience *becomes* the human condition itself and reveals to you its nature as being insufficient unto itself. Such is the type of experience that turns human existence into a questioning of its very nature, source, and foundation. Unless the question thus becomes all-embracing, the answer cannot be liberating and so cannot form the core of experiential religion. As answers to such questions arise from a direct experience of the transcendent dimension, they are, strictly speaking, revelatory. And some of those who first experienced them became founders of religion. Their followers, who experience the same, become masters of the Way; and they in turn help others to come to the same experience.

Since such questioning of existence and such life-transforming answers form the core of experiential religion, we cannot hope to understand it except in the context of the life that gave it birth and in the lives of those who are its living embodiment, or who experiment with its truth in the concreteness of their lives and arrive at the same realization as the primal ones. Without this concreteness religion remains empty, like musical scores on a sheet of paper. To understand experiential religion fully, we need to enter into the lives of those in whom it was the primal force. We need to explore the psychic and experiential ground from which the question originated and the moment in which the answer broke through into time, revealing the primal truth of religion and the meaning of all life and existence. As such, a revelation is not something separate from their lives; the lives themselves become revelatory, and to understand it fully we need to enter into those primal experiences and study the revelation in its original inspiration.

Although this step is necessary, it is not by itself sufficient. We need to explore the context of the communication of the revelation and the dynamics of the relationship in which it took place. Since this can be done only in the living context, we need to study the master-disciple relationship. It is useless to try to gain this understanding from theologies, rituals or worship, the official ministers of religion, or even from scriptures alone. No one except those who are its embodiment can put us directly in touch with the living truths of the primal revelation. Since such a contact is not available in churches, synagogues, temples, or mosques but can be found only in the personal context of the teacher-student relationship, we need to explore it if we want to understand experiential religion fully.

These reflections set a threefold task for this Part. I shall first discuss the sources of experiential religion in the primal revelatory experiences of some founders of religions. Second, since most people need an experienced guide to help them make their way through the jumble of choices and the stages of the path, I shall examine the qualities of such a guide, his/her functions in relation to an aspirant, the qualities of an authentic teacher, the criteria for choosing one, and how you can find such a teacher. Third, I shall explore what an aspirant requires in relationship to the teacher, so that the revelation that occurred in the teacher's life, and indeed in that of the founder, may also take place in his/her own.

Primal Revelation

A religion comes into being when an individual life opens to the truth of all beings, which reveals to it the meaning of all reality and the purpose of existence. What is it that brings about such an initial breakthrough and changes forever this life and those who come into contact with it?

Although each primal revelatory experience is unique, still a definite pattern is discernible in the lives of those who first came to realize the truth and opened the way for others. We find that, prior to the experience of illumination, there is intense concentration on the question that so thoroughly occupies the individual that it saturates his consciousness on all levels. He becomes the question itself. The question sinks into the unconscious, both in its individual and universal, collective form, and encompasses the entire human condition, which thereby assumes the form of the question. At this stage, existence itself is seen as the question, as the problem which cannot be resolved within the structures of existence. When the question goes beyond even the collective unconscious and breaks into the transconscious realm, it becomes suddenly transformed into the answer. Such is the case with the founders of some religions.

The life of the Buddha is, perhaps, the clearest example of this pattern. The story of Buddha's enlightenment is well known, so I need not reiterate it here. My concern is simply to inquire into what led the Buddha to his search, what the issue was, and how he arrived at the resolution.

Although the question rose to the conscious level from seeing a few incidences that are common occurrences, it soon took possession of both the conscious and the unconscious spheres of the Buddha's mind. He came to realize that the individual instances were not isolated or confined to some lives or aspects of life but were symptoms of a condition that is endemic to, permeates, and defines all conditioned existence. Individual cases thus revealed a law-like state: the law of conditioned existence. From top to bottom human existence was seen as a problem to itself, as *the* central problem — the problem of being conditioned — which existence itself is unable to resolve and which makes it insufficient unto itself.

Once the problem took possession of him, the Buddha found it impossible to go on living in his accustomed way, since it failed to provide a resolution. Out of this experience arose the central question: In the face of *dukkha,* how can life be meaningfully lived? He found that *dukkha* itself is not the meaning; rather, it is the problem. Under its sway human beings are like dumb animals, mechanically plodding along and suffering from life's vicissitudes, striving to disentangle themselves but becoming more entangled in the attempt. So meaning is not to be found in suffering but in liberation from it. Since the life he had hitherto been living was under the sway of suffering, it did not, nor could it ever, provide the answer. So he had to leave home and his way of life in search of the solution.

The Buddha's action illustrates one of the essential features of experiential religion, namely that, if you desire liberation, you must be prepared to let go of any way of life that will not lead you to it. Before letting go, however, you should experience it fully and see it through to the end; otherwise it may hold you back. The Buddha renounced the ways of sensuality, possessions, achievement, success, and power not because these were evil but because he found such ordinary goals, which span the entire human condition, to be themselves part of *dukkha* and hence incapable of delivering anyone from it. Such insights into the ordinary aims of life themselves did not bring him liberation, but he knew that it was not to be found in them. He had to search for it elsewhere.

Leaving home, the Buddha sought out two of the foremost teachers in the vicinity—Alara Kalama of Vaisali and Uddaka Ramaputra of Magadha. From them he learned meditation and various ascetic practices.

Always learning from direct experience, the Buddha tried the way of asceticism. Again trying a path to its very end, for six years he engaged in ascetic practices so thoroughly that, at one time, when he touched the skin of his belly, so we are told, he could feel his backbone. But "tormenting his body through such austerities availed nothing" (De Bary 68). Thus, neither depriving the mind and indulging the body, which is the way of luxury and other ordinary ways, nor depriving the body and indulging the mind—the way of asceticism—by itself brings illumination. Both are part of the problem they attempt to cure. The first makes the mind dull, shallow, muddled, distracted, listless, easily bored, indifferent, restless, and always hungry for more. The second renders it narrow, fixated, suspicious, critical, fearful, negative or insensitive, and unaware. The first represses the mind, while the second represses the body and attempts to repress desire by depriving ego of its objects, although desire continues unabated, and may even increase, due to the privation. That is why asceticism or self-denial fails.

Thus both ways can become forms of escape, indulgence, or self-deception, if by engaging in them you think you will gain liberation. Such pursuits may give you a feeling that you are on the road to realizing the aim of your life. You may swell with pride or with a feeling of superiority over those who are not similarly disposed, when in fact you have veered off course. There is no liberation so long as either the body or the mind is repressed. Repression can only cause a split and a consequent conflict, leading to further repression on the one hand; and a desperate, rigid clinging to the unrepressed side on the other. It is not, then, surprising that asceticism brought the Buddha no liberation. He realized that, as one text puts it, "this is no way to achieve passionlessness, enlightenment, liberation" (De Bary 68). As neither the pursuit of the satisfaction of desires nor their denial or repression led to liberation, he abandoned the way of asceticism, took food, got his strength back, and then resumed his quest.

Abandoning both ways (always coming to his conclusion through experimentation), the Buddha discovered the Middle Path. This is not an Aristotelian or a Confucian mean or a path of moderation between excess and deficiency. Moderation makes solid citizens out of people; it makes them stolid, repressed, or dissatisfied, seething or compelled to vent their repressed feelings in various escapist or destructive ways. It cannot lead to the extinction of *dukkha* by freeing people from their cause, which is what the Middle Path is said to do. It must be a path that transcends both by steering a middle course between repression and indulgence; between the dualities of attachment or grasping and withdrawal, desire and avoidance, pleasure and pain; and between eternalism or substantialism and nihilism or materialism. It is the nondual path that transcends all ontological and psychological dualities and the reactive mind in the realization of complete identity with Reality as Such – the realization of what Chogyam Trungpa calls "the complete state of 'being as you are'" (2: 20). That is the reason it is called "the direct path" as it brings insight, which leads to the direct experience of the Unconditioned and liberation (Burtt 29-30).

To discover this Path, the Buddha had to go beyond the limits of the ordinary ways of life. He found that the hold this world has over people is due to their conditioning, which exists only in their own minds, but which comes to be solidified around the concept of a permanent self. He discovered that this self is not in itself anything real. Its sense of reality is due entirely to the identification people make with their conditioning and various states of body and mind discussed in Part II. He realized that neither he nor anyone else could be liberated from *dukkha* unless s/he went beyond the entire world formed by conditioning and held up by identification, attachment, and desire.

Sitting in meditation, he resolved not to move until he found the way beyond. After he had successively passed through the stages of *samadhi*, he began to gain a series of insight which culminated in liberation. In the first watch of the night of enlightenment, we are told, he *saw* his "former births": stages of programming that formed not only his own past but also the entire human past, locked in the collective unconscious of humanity. In the mirror-like *samadhi* that made his mind empty and calm as the tranquil water of a limpid lake on the surface of which things are clearly reflected, in the second watch, he saw the law of *karma* that governs human behavior. He found no separate, substantial entity in this "world of becoming."

The third watch brought insight into "conditioned coarising," which constitutes the nature of conditioned existence. He *saw* the impermanence of all things—their nature as ever-changing process in which all things are interdependent, interconnected, and held together by mutually linked twelve chains of causation, making the universe an interpenetrating and undivided whole. He *saw* that, beginning with unawareness, conditioned existence inevitably produces *dukkha* and that with the cessation of unawareness not only the links of the twelve chains but also the chain of *karma* are broken, leading to the end of *dukkha*. As he passed through progressively deepening stages of insight, he transcended the separate self and the spatio-temporal framework of ordinary consciousness and came to see the simultaneous arising and passing away of all things and events in the universe.

In the fourth watch, upon the direct seeing of the nature of conditioned existence and upon its deconstruction and transcendence, Gautama's mind took the most radical turn and became completely freed from the law of *karma*, conditioned existence, reality-construct, the twelve chains of causation that give rise to them, and the programmed states, especially the three poisons of desire or greed, avoidance or aggression, and delusion or unawareness. Upon this realization *dukkha* ceased entirely. This did not happen, however, until he passed through the four progressively deepening stages of awakening, which are essentially the stages of enlightenment and *Nirvana* discussed in Part III.

This realization of Nirvana completely stopped anything from determining, limiting, or conditioning him in any way, leaving his present and future entirely open and unconditioned. Thus Gautama arose from his meditation as Buddha—a fully awakened and liberated being. Having attained the absolute freedom of the Unconditioned, he was free to live, free to breathe, free to BE—Being as Such. He declared, "I am freed; and I comprehend: Destroyed is birth, brought to a close is Brahma-faring [i.e., doing good and avoiding evil], done is what was to be done, there is no more of being such and such" (quoted by Drummond 39).

Thus Gautama became the *Tathagata*, the one who has gone completely beyond duality and arrived at the no-beyond of Suchness or the Supreme Identity of Reality as Such. In this utter transcendence that is at the same time his identity with all things, he was now able to fully live in the world without being conditioned or determined by it: "Having overcome the world I abide unsoiled by the world" (Conze et al. 105). Thus he became the full embodiment of the Unconditioned, of the truth of all beings, as well as the truth of all his teachings: "He who sees Dharma sees me; he who sees me sees Dharma" (Conze et al. 103).

Here we have an example of a life in which an individual quest opened up to become a questioning of all existence. This questioning already gave the Buddha a measure of transcendence so that the answer could not have come from the fragmentary events of ordinary life. Only when all human experience became concentrated in his own experience and emerged in his consciousness in the form of the question that embraced not only his entire being but those of all others as well, did the revelation that comprehended all occur. In the measure of the question lies the depth and breadth of the answer. As Zen Buddhism says, "small doubt, small enlightenment; great doubt, great enlightenment." When the question embraces the entire conditioned existence, the answer that reveals the truth likewise comprehends the meaning and purpose of all existence. Thus in the opening of one life, the Reality of all life and existence was laid bare.

A similar pattern can be discerned in the revelatory experience of Moses. If we examine the *Exodus* text, we find that there is first a concentration on a problem, which emerges in the form of a question that fully occupies Moses' mind. Although we are not told so explicitly, for Moses the problem of the liberation of the oppressed seems to arise on the conscious level with his killing of an Egyptian who was beating up a Hebrew. It gathers force in his flight to Median and absorbs him during his stay there. It then finds its resolution in his vision of God on Mt. Sinai.

Perhaps Moses frequented the spot seeking illumination on the problem that had increasingly come to occupy his mind. He might even have frequently prayed there, seeking guidance on what he should do to free the Hebrews from their bondage. Then one day his mind suddenly opened to the Truth and the answer came. The revelation in the form of a vision of God, who was revealed as "I am that I am," became the source of the liberation that was to follow.

The difference between the revelation that occurred to Moses and that which the Buddha experienced has to do with the way the question was posed and what it embraced. While, for the Buddha, the question encompassed nothing less than the truth of all conditioned existence and how humankind can find release from it, for Moses it was confined to the liberation of a group from political servitude. In this case, since the question did not involve the meaning of all existence but the liberation of a group from oppression, the answer revealed likewise did not consist of a direct revelation of the Being but of its active involvement in conditioned existence. This gave the peculiar character to the revelation granted to Moses, which was concerned with action, not with being.

As action requires a separation of the one who acts from that on which s/he acts, so the Unconditioned was not revealed as the Identity of all, but as the

Supreme Other transcendent to all. Moses did not have a direct experience of the Unconditioned as his identity, but a vision of it as the Transcendent Other. God's identity was withheld because Moses did not experience it. This is the significance of "Yahweh" – "I am that I am." God withholds "his" name to Moses because in the subtle state you do not directly experience the reality of God but God in and through a form, such as a vision or an audition, through which communication takes place. That is the reason God appears as Transcendent Other, since the nature or reality of God is other than the form in which the communication occurs. As is typical of the Bible, which projects outside what happens in the mind, what is described in the form of fire, light, and sound – "the burning bush" – is the experience of insight which came to Moses when the problem of Jewish liberation gripped his mind and became an all-consuming, burning question. This purified and brought his mind to a state beyond ordinary consciousness and the events of history, so that the subtle level of revelation could take place. With it came the resolution of the question, the disclosure of Moses' mission, and the significance of the events to follow.

When we turn to Jesus, we encounter a situation in which the answer emerges as a revelation which at the same time discloses his task in life. We do not know what form the question took in Jesus' mind, but from his answer to John the Baptizer and his baptismal experience it appears that it concerned his ultimate identity and the purpose it required him to fulfill. Up to the time of baptism his life had been a preparation for that great opening which climaxed with the revelation during his sojourn in the Negev desert.

When the preparation was complete, the question had matured, and the opening was imminent, he felt impelled by his Self, still in the unconscious state at that time – "led by the Spirit" as the New Testament puts it – to be baptized by John. He felt that that was what God required of him as the way to the revelation. After the baptism, as he came up out of the water, "at that moment heaven opened; he saw the Spirit of God descending like a dove to alight upon him; and a voice from heaven was heard saying, 'This is my son, my Beloved, on whom my favor rests' " (Matt. 3: 16-17). Again, to underscore its reality, the experience is projected outside the mind in the form of an objective event. The description of the experience indicates that it consisted of a sudden opening of Jesus' mind to the Unconditioned – which is the meaning of "heaven opening." However, the presence of sight and sound indicates that the experience was similar to those of Moses and other prophets – on the subtle level of consciousness. The voice hinted at his true identity and mission but did not reveal it in a direct, ontological experience. This is also indicated by the first part of each of his later temptations – "If you are the Son of God . . ." – indicating doubt about his true identity. To seek full illumination on his identity and his mission in life, he was driven, or "led by the Spirit," to the wilderness.

We are not told what Jesus did in the desert, except that he fasted and was tempted by the devil, his darker side. Perhaps he spent the period in intense meditation. As it also happened in the case of the Buddha, the temptations arose prior to enlightenment and represents Jesus' struggle with his dark side on the level of primal polarity—with Jesus representing wisdom; and the dark side or the devil, the energy aspect of the primal polarity. The struggle took the form of a doubt about his true identity and mission and concerned his use of awakened miraculous or paranormal powers, which usually become evident at this stage. The issue was whether he should use these powers to proclaim the goals that ordinarily preoccupies the ego—material gain, magical solution to problems, and power and worship of false values—to be the purpose of existence. The demonic character of these goals consists in the fact that they are deceptive and illusory. They cannot lead human beings to liberation but can only enslave and deflect them from the true path. Jesus' triumph over the temptations signifies, on the one hand, his rejection of the path of desire and, on the other, indicates his teaching that you must likewise overcome them if you desire the liberation or perfection that is the "heavenly Father."

We can only assume that with his overcoming the last temptation, Jesus transcended the primal polarity and experienced the revelation of his identity as the Son of God and of his mission in life. Now there was no more doubt. Coming out of the desert, Jesus began to proclaim, "Repent; for the Kingdom of God is within you" (Matt. 4: 17).

In the case of Muhammad, we know that he periodically withdrew into a cave outside Mecca where he spent long periods in prayer or meditation. It was there that he finally experienced illumination. Here again we see a prior period of concentration on a question involving the reality of God, the purpose of human life, and the purpose of his own life. Before the question resolved into the answer, it gripped his whole being. As Fazlur Rahman observes, "Before his call, the Prophet's mind was tormented by problems concerning the situation and destiny of man; this drove him into periodic retirement and contemplation. From the throes of this agonizing search, revelation emerged and to this the Quran points" (8).

The experience of revelation itself occurred to Muhammad in a state of consciousness beyond the ordinary one and the events of daily life. This is clear from the Quran, which says that the vision took place "on the uppermost horizon" and then drew closer to him. Furthermore, it says that in the vision of the night journey to Jerusalem, Muhammad drew near to the throne of God, just as Isaiah had done in his inaugural vision. So it is clear that at the farthest horizon, beyond ordinary consciousness, beyond discursive thought and everyday concerns, Muhammad experienced the revelation which opened up for him new perspectives on God and life, and a new mission.

This brief account of the experiences of four founders gives us some understanding of the nature of revelation, how it took place in their lives, and how it can and must occur in the life of every human being who aspires to undertake the journey of experiential religion. Without such a revelation, which forms its core, there is neither experiential religion nor revelation of the meaning of existence. However, since there are differences in the experiences of the founders, as the above discussion makes it clear, it is necessary to take a closer look at what constitutes revelation.

Although I have used the term *revelation* to describe the experiences of the Buddha, Moses, Jesus, and Muhammad, the usual practice has been to distinguish revealed religions from nonrevealed ones and to place Judaism, Christianity, and Islam in the former and all other religions in the latter category. Behind this differentiation is the dualistic world view that separates the supernatural, where God dwells, from the natural order. There is also the belief that revelation consists in the disclosure of a divine truth, the communication of God's will, or divine intervention of some kind from the supernatural realm to the natural order. Hence these religions, especially Christianity, believe that revelation takes place in history. Since revelation is said to come from the supernatural realm, any religion that does not teach this is not considered a revealed religion.

Moreover, according to this view, since revelation depends entirely upon God's initiative, it is not something an individual can seek, nor can it take place in his/her life. Rather, it is thought to be the affair of a community and to take place in historical events. Moreover, since it is believed to come from the supernatural to the natural realm, it is not considered a part of one's true nature or an ever-present reality. Rather, it is always associated with a past event, usually in the life of the founder or a divinely appointed messenger or prophet. Since adherents to these religions do not believe that revelation can happen in their own lives, they take it on faith, rather than seeking to experience directly the initially revealed truth and verifying it in their own lives. How are we to understand this situation?

To understand the nature of revelation more accurately and to be consistent with what has been said in this and previous chapters, it is necessary to distinguish two kinds of revelation: relative and absolute or final.

Relative revelation takes place through a medium — through visions, auditory experiences, inspiration, and other paranormal occurrences. In this revelation, God is not experienced directly, as "he" is in "himself," but in an archetypal form commensurate with the subtle level of consciousness. What God communicates is not "his" being but "his" will for the individual or the community. Consequently, relative revelation is task- or action-oriented. Since duality between the experiencer and God is its hallmark, it is clear that this revelation usually takes place in the subtle state in which God remains an object — the Transcendent Other. Hence this revelation is not the experience of Ultimate Reality but its effects or manifestations, like the sound a supersonic jet leaves behind.

In contrast, absolute or final revelation consists in the direct disclosure of the Unconditioned. Here God is experienced not through any form or medium but directly, just as "he" is in "himself," the Formless Ground who is not other than the world of forms. Not being through anything, this revelation is always a disclosure of God as the Supreme Identity, not only of the experiencer but of all things as well. It is final revelation because what is disclosed is the Ultimate Reality beyond which there literally is nothing. So it is the "ontological revelation" — a revelation of the nature, "isness," or suchness of God or Reality as Such beyond any condition or qualification, and beyond the subtle, in the causal or ultimate state of Awareness. As this Awareness is itself ontological, it is revealed to be the content of the revelation.

Thus, in its ultimate form revelation is not the disclosure of the will or action of a Transcendent Being from a realm beyond this world but the disclosure of the nature of this world, of all things just as they are, as no other than the Ultimate; and a disclosure of the purpose of life to be no other than Being and manifesting it. It is indeed the revelation of the Transcendent Other. But this Other is revealed to be no other than all that is.

Several consequences follow from this reflection on the nature of revelation. One is that this view turns the traditional idea of revelation on its head. The traditional view of final revelation turns out to be relative, while religions that are not believed to be revealed turn out to embody final revelation. And what goes unnoticed by the traditional view, namely, the highest realization of the mystics, East-West — that beyond God thought as a Personal Being is the Godhead, the transpersonal Reality, who is the Supreme Identity of all that is, and who can be experienced only directly and only as identity — turns out to be the final form of revelation.

Second, as the final revelation is not the intervention of a Beyond in human history, but the opening of the individual's mind to a direct experience of it as his/her identity, it is not associated with or limited to some historically privileged moment, event, or individual. You need not look for, nor can you find, it in another life, time, or in any past event. Final revelation cannot be anything in the past. Since reality is always and only in the present, this revelation is the disclosure of the ever-present Reality of our true nature. So it can occur only in the present, anywhere, at any time, and in everyone's life. Consequently, it can occur in your own life when you break free of the conditionings and constructs that ordinarily close off the possibility of this disclosure.

Third, although both types of revelation involve the Beyond, since relative revelation considers the Beyond to be a separate realm from which it acts in human affairs, it remains something external and hence alien to human beings, requiring them to hold onto a belief in a past event that has little bearing on the present. This is not the case with final revelation because it brings people to a direct experience of what they truly are, centers their consciousness in the present, and puts them in direct touch with all things. Thus it removes from them everything in which alienation could possibly take root. Moreover, being a disclosure of their true nature and identity, what is revealed cannot be anything separate from or alien to them, but their true identity which finally liberates them from the pursuit of an identity that causes alienation and separation from what is. When experienced, it becomes a saving event as it restores them to the original state of Oneness beyond the creation of otherness. So, instead of alienating you from your time or world, final revelation removes alienation and heralds your homecoming. You are then at home everywhere in the universe, wherever you are.

Fourth, people's attitude toward relative revelation is passive and magical because it is believed to take place solely on God's initiative, while the attitude toward final revelation is active and dynamic, since you can actively open yourself for its occurrence. While the former tethers people to a system of belief, worship, ethical precepts, religious organizations, and rules; the latter is concerned primarily with a direct experience of the living Reality and personal realization of the purpose of existence in the here and now.

Fifth, strictly speaking, revelation does not take place in history. Rather, it is always transhistorical and occurs in transpersonal states, far beyond the empirical. This is true also of relative revelation. There is no revelation in history because it cannot take place in a state of sleep. If history is what human beings do after they thrust God out of their realm, it can only be a concealment of God. Representing futile human striving to be the foundation of their own existence in separation from God and yet an attempt to overcome that separation, history is a problem unto itself which it cannot resolve. It enfolds on itself and turns itself into a "no exit" situation. What is closed to it cannot be the ground for God's revelation. Thus history is itself the question from which the answer cannot issue. The answer to the question which the very being of history—its insufficiency unto itself—poses can come from beyond history and on a road that issues from a transhistorical and a temporal plane. And, as a question, it can be posed by someone who is at least half awake, which is already a transcendence of history. Only when an individual mind is able to go beyond space, time, and the reality-construct within which history operates can it experience the revelation of its meaning and that of all conditioned existence.

If, then, revelation takes place, not in historical events but in the mind's transcending history and in opening to the Unconditioned, how can it come about in the life of each individual? There are essentially two ways that this can happen: through active search and deliberate opening of the mind to the Unconditioned, and spontaneously.

Spontaneous revelation can occur at those junctures, passages, and stages of life in which one is especially apt to be aware or have intimations of higher dimensions of reality and the occasion is present to step out of time and the ordinary functioning of consciousness and come face to face with the questions of what we truly are and the meaning of life. At such junctures, if one remains open to receiving the answer through witnessing or experiencing some event that suddenly stops the internal chatter of the mind or quiets it down sufficiently, one may be suddenly transported beyond the world of fragmentation, separation, and limitation, and experience a unity with all and thus become open to the Unconditioned.

A recognition of such a possibility has led religions to ritualize and celebrate passages of life in which the individual evolved from one psychological stage to the next. At such critical junctures the old identity dissolves. It loses its hold on the consciousness of the individual. As the new stage emerges, s/he has the task of forging a new identity. Since the new structure has not yet been established, it is not yet able to exercise total control on his/her consciousness. This provides him/her the occasion for raising questions about the new possibilities, for discerning different, perhaps altogether new, ways of being, and for coming in contact with the transcendent dimensions of reality.

Although we are already that which we nevertheless seek to realize, identification with our condition and the assumption that anything outside it is unreal ordinarily prevent us from experiencing spontaneous revelation. But when such obstacles are removed from our minds, the true nature of all things discloses itself. Then we stand revealed to ourselves. For the revelation to break through the walls of our triple constructs, all that is necessary is to loosen their hold. This can be triggered by any event that has the quality of stillness, wonder, or awe which silences the mental chatter and shakes the mind out of its ordinary preoccupations.

Although such openings can occur at crucial junctures, passages, or stages of every life, many reasons ordinarily prevent people from being consciously present to them. Such a presence requires that we remain in touch with the flow of life within and around ourselves, listen to its rhythms and currents, and live as close to its source as possible and in openness to what is. And when we discern the openings, we need to seize the moment and decide to enter it, thus becoming part of the Open Way.

Living for the most part in unawareness, however, we do not even know that there are such openings, let alone decide to enter them; and if told, we do not believe that they are possible or that they could occur in our lives. Wanting revelation and yet afraid that it will disrupt our lives or bring changes that are threatening or not to our liking, we close ourselves off to its limitations and go along our accustomed ways, dragged along by inertia, habits, and automatic responses. Thus, everything in our lives works to close off awareness and divert attention away from the openings. Unawareness and confusion work to make us fail to notice them.

Thus, for the most part, it is nearly impossible for us to see, or to live openly, so that we can see, the openings. And even if we do, we regard them as something accidental, unreal, foreign, or unnatural; we think that it is neurotic or abnormal to want them; or that they are threatening or difficult to follow. Afraid of the disturbance or the demand that revelation may make on us, we recoil from it and slink back to the safe, secure world of regular, routine life. Fear prevents us from venturing outside the parameters of programmed life, even if we do not find it very satisfying. Moreover, the pull of attachments, drives or desires, and outside pressures are too great for most of us to cut loose. Even if we try to live openly, various beliefs about revelation bar us from seeing the openings.

Furthermore, since these openings may happen at any juncture of life, it is difficult to detect them. There is no guarantee when they will occur; nor are there any techniques or special ways, short of the deliberate path, of making them happen. As a result, at best such experiences remain accidental, unthematic and momentary, bringing no shift of center or change in the orientation of consciousness. Thus, except for a few, such Jesus, Ramana Maharshi and others, the path of spontaneous revelation remains closed to ordinary lives. For these reasons, with the cultural context and personal lifestyles in our contemporary world ruling out spontaneous revelation, the only real option available to us today is the way of conscious opening. As Jung remarked, "The spiritual adventure of our time is the exposure of human consciousness to the undefined and indefinable" (Quoted by Dunne 112). This requires the path of deliberate opening, which is meditation.

The way of active opening has been kept alive in the living traditions of experiential religion and transmitted from generation to generation in the master-disciple relationship that has become its authentic setting. This is the only viable context for transmitting revelation available to us today. We need to examine its usefulness and applicability to our time.

Once you decide to enter into this way of revelation, you are likely to be besieged by a host of questions. In the next two chapters of this Part, I shall raise and attempt to answer these salient and pressing questions.

Chapter 24
The Way of the Masters

Choosing a Path

Once you decide to pursue the revelation of the Unconditioned in your life, before choosing an enlightened teacher who can show you the way, the most important decision you will face is choosing a path. Of course, before arriving at that decision, you will have to overcome some serious obstacles, one of which has to do with the question of motivation: why should you choose a path at all? I shall discuss this question in greater detail later. However, the reasons for choosing a path should by now be obvious: the experience of the insufficiency of existence as you find it; the desire to be real and complete, and to be free of your present confusion; the promise of completeness and freedom which a path offers; and the realization that there is no other way in which you can realize your destiny and live fully as a human being. If you are convinced of these reasons and feel the urgency to choose now rather than put it off to some indefinite future, you are ready for the journey of awakening.

Here in the West, the question "Which path I should take?" would have once been easy to answer because the options were few. No longer. With the influx of spiritual teachers from the East representing various paths and the mushrooming of various therapies, growth centers, awareness-training groups, weekend seminars, and "New Age" groups, you now have a veritable supermarket of options. This has made the situation bewildering, and the problem of choosing a path at once easy and difficult. In such a situation it is especially advisable to examine the nature of a path; what it aims or claims to do; the methods it employs; the credentials of the teacher and his/her way of teaching; and your motivation for wanting to choose a particular path.

The reason that you should examine the nature of a path before choosing it is that all paths do not offer the same thing. They all do not, nor can they (sometimes hard-sell to the contrary) offer you enlightenment, revelation, or liberation. Because of this, you need to carefully examine their use of language. While they may use the same terms, their meanings change from path to path. Thus, EST claimed to offer you enlightenment, but such "enlightenment" meant no more than coming to an experiential recognition that you are programmed and that you are not your programming.

Before embarking on a path, you need to find out what kind it is: Is it a week-end quick fix, a packaged deal, or a piece-meal amalgam of techniques put together by a self-appointed expert? Or is it an authentic spiritual path that does not attempt to make things easy for you by setting aside the painful task of facing yourself and telling you that, as you are, you are perfect? Real growth, which requires you to break free of programming, ingrained habitual ways, and automatic behavior, is slow and difficult. No authentic spiritual path will tell you otherwise.

As Sheikh Mohamed Daud told Raphael Lefort, "Remember that the path will be hard, and if you falter only you can save yourself. Expect no miracles, but know that at the end lies deep, permanent consciousness" (133-134). Any path that tells you otherwise is only fooling you. So do not look for an easy way out. There is none. Weekend seminars and packaged "training programs" can at most begin the process; they cannot take you to your destination. Sometimes they can stir up more things in you than you can handle by yourself; and they provide no extended help to resolve them. Since the ego loves an easy way out, quick fixes and packaged deals are real temptations you need to watch out for.

In this connection, you need to examine a path to see whether it offers self-transformation or self-indulgence through such fare as seminars and training workshops on how you can have better sex, more enjoyment, earn more, better manage your life, have different and more exciting experiences. Such preoccupations go only as far as the sensation and power stages of consciousness but are incapable of freeing you from a life organized and centered around ego. They only reinforce and maintain it, and so perpetuate your bondage (Ornstein 3: 23, 73, 128-129).

Rather, what you need is a path that, as a first step, will help you face yourself, see your situation exactly as it is right now, and accept it without any selective attention, interpretation, evaluation, judgment, condemnation, excuse, or blame. It should help you face and directly experience the causes of your condition; provide you with a method that will help you to break free of your fixations, attachments, self-defeating behavior, self-absorption, and unawareness of your condition; and enable you to transcend ego so as to realize your destiny. In other words, it should contain the essential steps of Parts I-III and V. A genuine path will inform you of the difficulties you face. It may even discourage you at first in order to test the seriousness of your intention and help you to let go of your expectations. Yet, at the same time, it will reassure you of your ability to reach the goal.

Lastly, you should examine the goal of the path: Does it offer genuine enlightenment? Furthermore, you should closely examine the methods it employs. Do they match the goal? Are the methods designed to massage and soothe the ego or to awaken and expand consciousness?

Once you have eliminated from consideration the paths that do not aim at revelation or liberation, the question of which path to choose becomes a subtler matter. Which one should you follow? Should you try out several at first before settling on one?

It is not easy to suggest, as a general rule, which path is the right one for a given person. Although any genuine path of liberation will enable each person to reach his/her destination if followed to the very end, they are not all equally suitable for everyone. In this respect there is very good sense in Hinduism's recommendation that each person should follow the path that is best suited to his/her aptitude, personality, inclination, or natural endowment.

However, it may be difficult to discover your natural bent, since it is always covered over, constricted, and distorted by massive conditioning. For instance, thinking that you are an intellectual, whereas deep down you may be really an affective type, you may believe that you are inclined to a path of knowledge and try very hard to follow it. But because of an inner resistance, which may not be clear to you at first, you may fail to make any progress and so may be inclined to give up the search altogether. On the other hand, experiencing initial difficulties on a path, you may come to think that it is not suitable for you, but once you overcome them, you may make rapid progress. A personality trait may draw one to the simplicity, starkness, and directness of Zen. Another may be drawn to Tibetan Buddhism because of its rites, symbols, deities, colors, and visualizations. A psychologist may be drawn to insight meditation; while the ecstatic approach of the Sufis may draw another. However, once the initial attraction wears off, these people may encounter difficulties at a deeper or more advanced level. Moreover, as each path comes to the aspirant embodied in the teacher, there has to be a harmony not only between the personality of the aspirant and the path, but also with the path as embodied in the teacher. Still, taking these things into consideration, it may be said that when the personality and the spiritual problem of the aspirant match the path (as it approaches, articulates, and sets out to resolve the problem) — they tend to be right for each other. So, as Ram Dass suggests, at the outset you should choose a method that harmonizes with what you are already good at, one that interests you, creates no inner resistance, one to which you are open and which you can wholeheartedly embrace (1:43).

Before settling on one, try several paths that appeal to you. Here the question of motive again becomes important. I shall discuss this shortly. For the present, it may be said in general that, before settling on one, it is good to have not only theoretical knowledge of several paths and their methods but experiential knowledge as well.

As you start experimenting with several types, according to Ram Dass, you should pick a method that feels right and practice it for several weeks or months. In addition, associate with the people who practice it and observe what kind of effect it has on them. Do you notice any change, or is there no difference between their behavior and those that you encounter in ordinary people? Are they more peaceful, calm, energetic, vibrant, joyful? Or are they restless, critical, complaining, finding faults in others, judgmental, absorbed in themselves, or indifferent to others? Do they have an arrogant attitude? Finally, examine the teachings, teaching style, and personality of the teacher — as well as the way s/he relates to his/her followers (Ram Dass 1: 43).

While you practice a particular method for a period of time ask yourself: Am I really able to get into it, or are there inner resistances? Does this method relax me or make me tense? It may happen that a meditation method makes you agitated at first, but that may mean that it is actually working for you, since one of the initial functions of meditation is to bring all your tensions to the surface; make you aware of and experience them; and then help you release and become free of them. So this effect should not be the sole criterion for dropping it. What you should look for is whether, after a period of what appears to be an increase, the tension is being released and you are becoming calmer.

Furthermore, you may ask yourself whether your mind is able to stay on the meditation. Inability to keep the attention focused is not a good reason for dropping it, since your mind will keep wandering, no matter which method of meditation you choose to practice, until it becomes one-pointed.

In the spiritual supermarket, as you go from one path to another, one thing you need to watch out for is the danger of what may be called "the lateral pursuit of meaning" — going from one path to another on the same level, rather than seriously committing yourself to one. This may be a symptom of avoiding commitment, fear of getting too involved, of facing yourself, of uncovering things that are unpleasant — that may get out of control or require change and letting go. Unless you finally settle on a path and decide to follow it to the very end, you may be stuck forever running around the base of the mountain without ever attempting to reach the summit. Although you should experiment with several paths, you will need to stay with one in order to make your way to the summit. Ultimately, the right path is the one that will lead you surely and quickly to your destination — one on which you can make real progress. But there is no way of knowing that in advance. Progress will depend on your motivation or intention, the effort you put into your practice, and the earnestness with which you throw your whole self into it.

One of the important considerations in choosing a path is that it should not cut you off from the world and require you to adopt a lifestyle and practice suitable to the past but not to the present. On the contrary, it should help you live fully in the world, and not make you withdraw to a monastery—either because you hate, fear, despise, or dislike the world, or because you are unable to cope or function in it. Furthermore, you should be able to continue your practice in the midst of your daily activities, for being able to live in the world is always the ultimate test of whatever you attain. You may, of course, have to go and live for a time in a special setting for the sake of training, in order to intensify your practice, and until you experience a breakthrough. But such a step should be temporary and not for life unless, of course, you want to become a monk or nun. A path should not alienate but should fully incarnate you in your time, so that you can work for its transformation.

This point is emphasized by the Sufis. As Sheikh Daggash Rustam told Lefort, any path of knowledge that requires you to lead a solitary life is unsuitable for today. A path must keep pace with the requirements of the present day. The desire to abandon the world is useless. Of course, you may need to go to a center for the purpose of training, but that is only to develop the skills you need to harness the forces to serve you (104-105). Similarly, according to Lefort, Sheikh Dil Bar Khan Hululi told Gurdjieff, "Do you wish that I should teach you something that you can no longer apply? Or would you choose a developmental path that is organically in tune with a developing cosmos in which man must find a realization of himself?" (133)

Similarly, Ramana Maharshi taught that since the world is only in the mind, whether you live a family life or renounce it and go to a forest, the mental obstacles will be with you wherever you are. In this sense, all modes of life are on an equal footing. Since the obstacles are only in the mind, you must overcome them whether you are in the world or in a solitary place. Since the core obstacles are the programmed mind and the separate self, the essence of a path is neither withdrawal nor engagement but breaking free of mental programming, disidentification with ego, and identification with the Self. And this can be undertaken in any lifestyle (Osborne 78-84). The point of using everything, including sexuality, to bring about self-transformation and transcendence is especially emphasized by Tantrism—Hindu, Buddhist, and, to a certain extent, Taoist.

It should be pointed out, contrary to Ornstein, that a path should not be judged useless for the contemporary world just because it was developed in the past. Rather, what you should look for is whether it can lead you to complete enlightenment and liberation; the practice can be maintained right in the midst of daily activities; it does not require you to withdraw but enables you to live fully in the world; and it frees you from self-concern so that you can work for the transformation of others and the world.

Do Juan instructed Castaneda to choose "a path with a heart." My own suggestion is that you should choose a complete path—one that leads to completeness, to realizing the Truth not only for yourself but also to help others do the same. No path is complete if it does not lead to liberation, compassion, and service, for the elimination of suffering in the encompassing sense of *dukkha*—spiritual, psychological, social, material—leading to complete transformation of self and world.

Ultimately, to find the right path, your best guide is your intuition or the promptings of the Self, which is the inner teacher. But because of your present condition, neither may be available or clear to you at first. In order to be in touch with either, you will have to be open to the stillness within. Then intuition will emerge, one path will begin to feel right, and your choice will be clear.

The Motive for Choosing a Path

One of the critical factors in choosing a path and a teacher is being clear about your motive, about what you want, and why you want to follow a path. Do you seek it because you are unable to face the problems of life, and so want to transfer this responsibility to a teacher? Or do you desire to follow it in search of new and more exotic experiences, like the craze for the latest fashions? Do you want to move in the consciousness circuit because it is the "in thing" to do or because you feel special, get a high in such circles, and want to stay in that high all the time? Is the motive sex? Or do you wish to surrender yourself so that you can satisfy your need to surrender or worship someone or thing?

All such motives are self-deceptions. The first is the security trap: the wish to transfer one's dependency to a path or a teacher. As discussed before, Jack Engler points out that two types of people seem to be especially drawn to meditation: those in late adolescence and in mid-life crisis. People with borderline personality organization are especially drawn to the Buddhist teaching of "not-self" *(anatta);* and narcissistic personalities seek transference to a teacher or to an idealized enlightenment self (1: 29-34). Many, of course, seek a teaching or a teacher to unburden themselves. These are the people who have been dissatisfied in life and wish to empty their burdens onto a guru. Unable to cope, some seek gurus, just as they had sought drugs, sex, or anything else, to transfer their dependency. Individuals in their late adolescence or early adulthood who have been deeply hurt in childhood and disappointed with their parents, or who are confused and anxious, bewildered by the variety of choices and ambiguities of life and who lack a cohesive sense of self or suffer from identity diffusion, are ready for a handy escape to childhood dependency. They may want to throw the burden of choice and the responsibility of developing an integrated, mature self to anyone or thing which promises to take them away. Such people seek a teacher to whom they can cling in order to anchor themselves and find orientation and direction in their lives.

Based on emotional needs, such dependencies are uncritical and prevent them from growing and developing a self capable of relating to others and the world on an adult level. These people desire not so much to free themselves of the need to attach to someone who will take care of them as to continue their dependency. Since one of the greatest obstacles to self-growth, maturity, and complete freedom is clinging to what Freud called "infantile dependency" and wanting others to take care of you, such motives are unsuitable for choosing a path. So you must discard any such motive and avoid any path that promises to take away the burden of decision and responsibility and the task of developing a mature self.

A variation of the dependency motive is the desire to worship someone or thing greater than yourself. This is a characteristic not only of those who lack a developed self and suffer from identity diffusion but also in a somewhat attenuated form of the separate self that senses its nothingness and powerlessness. In order to become real and powerful, and to protect and secure itself, it seeks to worship someone or something that appears real or powerful: technology, business, profit, progress, a thousand other "sacred cows" to which it bows down unquestioningly, and of course, God. This is a consequence of the desire for vicarious redemption—the substance of so many of our prayers. Ego is forever asking, "Give me! Give me!!" It is always adept at taking but seldom thinks of giving of itself, giving up the desire to get something, giving without the thought of taking, which is necessary to embark or make progress on a path of awakening.

One of the common motives for seeking a teacher is to want him/her to make all your problems disappear magically, to give you instant enlightenment—one Arica program was billed "Three Days to Kensho!"—or to bring about miraculous changes without any change in yourself or without any need to work on yourself to bring it about. In a push-button age in which we all want instant answers, painless, miraculous cure-alls, this is another attraction served up by and for ego to keep itself busy so as not to have to face itself.

Christ's second temptation has become the temptation of our age. Ego wants to *feel* good rather than *be* good. Many paths offer an instant feeling of goodness or gratification, rather than a permanent state of goodness. While we can instantly destroy ourselves, self-transcendence is a slow, cumulative, painful task that ego does not want to undertake, since it signals the end of its reign. As is well known, childhood is the stage when we demand instant gratification derived, perhaps, from a feeling of omnipotence, which is illusory. Both the demand and a path geared toward supplying it are expressions of childhood self-absorption, attempts to satisfy ego's wish for self-indulgence. Such deceptions of ego are not proper motives for choosing a path or a teacher. Anyone with such motives is bound to be disappointed as s/he discovers that a path of liberation or a genuine teacher not only does not satisfy them but, on the contrary, demands that s/he give them up and, instead, work on him/herself to bring about a real self-transformation.

Since the meditative paths are concerned with helping you to step out of the boundary of ego, they aim primarily at transpersonal stages of growth. As this presupposes a fully developed and integrated ego, these paths are for people who can normally function in the ordinary world and who wish to go beyond it for greater growth. Consequently, those who need psychological help or who have difficulty coping and need to strengthen ego or develop a stable and cohesive sense of identity and positive self-worth could suffer harm by taking up meditation as it will bring up aspects of themselves with which they may be unable to cope. Such people should not turn to meditation but should get professional help first. Of course, meditation does disentangle emotional problems, dissolve negative programmings, and purify, strengthen, and integrate the personality. But since in meditation you do this on your own, unless you feel strong enough to stand on your own two feet (with, of course, help from the teacher), you should seek professional help first before turning to meditation.

Another inappropriate motive is the sensation trap: going from one path to another, sampling teachings like a bee, buzzing from flower to flower; getting new or different or more exotic experiences in order to satisfy a state of consciousness stuck on the sensation level. Or like a tourist, s/he may seek these experiences as a collector, adding to his/her store of accumulated experiences or seeking a confirmation of his/her world. Chogyam Trungpa calls this "spiritual materialism." Such a person is not serious about choosing a path. S/he may rationalize his/her behavior by saying that s/he is pursuing enrichment, which is contrary to sticking to one path.

In fact, such motives constitute a form of greed and craving for experiences, as Ornstein puts it, as the latest stage in one's continual self-preoccupation and self-indulgence, search for new stimulation, or quest for the fashionable (3:115). They further manifest an avoidance of commitment or unwillingness to enter a path or to submit to its rigors; a refusal to stop playing games and to accept the hard task of facing oneself; a reluctance to give up one's present way of life and change; a fear of letting go of the separate self and its world; or, finally, a fear of transcendence or of being God. Thus, Idries Shah tells the story of a Westerner in a Sufi circle in India who had spent three and a half years studying various religions and travelling to various countries, interviewing religious teachers and collecting their teachings. He had been dissatisfied wherever he went because the teachings did not go deep enough; and the teachers were stuck in various practices which left him cold. As the conversation with the Sufi teacher progressed, it became clear that he was reluctant to choose a path because he could accept only those things that conformed to his ideas or preconceptions. He did not really want to commit himself to any path because that would mean giving up all his ideas and emptying himself. So, when his ideas and the actual teachings were found incompatible, he gave up the latter (3: 347-353). To confirm its world and assure its existence, as Trungpa explains, ego may strive to acquire and apply the teachings of spirituality for its own benefits. Whenever there is a discrepancy between its views and the teachings, it interprets the latter in such a way as to smooth over the difficulties and keep its ideas intact. Wanting to have a higher, more transcendental version of knowledge or religion, it eventually builds up a collection of spiritual paths and keeps itself occupied, rather than discovering the truth, which may threaten these enterprises and require their surrender. On the contrary, the aim of spiritual practice, says Trungpa, is "to step out of self-preoccupation, out of the bureaucracy of ego" (2: 13-15).

Since on the sensation level of consciousness we usually seek new and interesting experiences to keep ourselves from facing our inner emptiness and the purpose of existence, we constantly run away from ourselves, from boredom gnawing at the heels, from difficulties, dissatisfaction, and restlessness. As soon as the newness of an experience wears off, we move onto the next. This keeps the rush going so that the deeper question cannot break into the surface of consciousness. This "sensation addiction," as Ken Keyes calls it, cannot be a proper motive for choosing a path, for it will inevitably lead to disappointment and eventual abandonment of the search when the novelty wears off.

There are, of course, other deceptions of ego stemming from the six states of existence discussed in Part I: wanting to feel good, pious, religious; to feel important and superior to others; to be someone influential and to exercise power over others; to acquire paranormal powers; to become a teacher and have a following; and wanting something to conform to our tastes. Such motives can lead only to traps, wrong turns, or dead ends. They cannot take us very far on the path of awakening. Confusion will be followed by disillusionment until a feeling of despair or being overwhelmed sets in. And being discouraged, we will finally give up.

Thus it is extremely important that you have the right motive from the very beginning, for without it you will not choose the path that is right for you nor make progress on the one you choose. The right motive requires that you come to understand and give up the deceptions, defenses, roles, and games behind which you ordinarily hide. Unless you are willing to do that, you will not get very far on a path. For all authentic paths are designed to stop ego dead in its tracks.

Although a desire for enlightenment or liberation is the highest motive, that is not always necessary to embark on a path. Curiosity, a desire to personally experience what a path feels like, a desire to become free of negative programming and stress, an openness to learning, are all good motives to begin practice. As you begin to get results or feel good about the practice and want to continue on the path, such initial motives will be replaced by a more serious one. When the realization dawns that there is no other way to live fully as a human being, the path will become a life-goal. Without a life-commitment, the path you choose, no matter how authentically verified it may be for liberation, will not lead you to that final destination. But once it becomes a life-goal, you will have taken one of the most decisive steps toward that realization.

Choosing a Teacher

Once you have chosen a path that feels right for you, and you are guided by a right motive, you need to find a teacher who will show you the way and guide you toward your destination. But, you may ask: Why do I need an enlightened teacher? Can I not make the journey on my own?

Absolutely speaking, a guru or teacher is not necessary. You *can* come to liberation on your own, spontaneously, as it happened to Jesus, Ramana Maharshi and others, or through the practice of meditation as it occurred to the Buddha and the great sages and masters of various traditions. As Seung Sahn Roshi observes, "If your mind is clear, a Zen master is not necessary. If you are thinking, it is necessary" (Mitchell 22-23). For most people, however, who are at the thinking stage, a teacher is necessary. If you want a Ph.D., you can study and acquire the knowledge on your own. Even so, you need some Ph.D.'s to examine you in order to determine whether you have indeed acquired the knowledge you claim you have. Most people, however, need to study with teachers in a university setting to get the degree. Similarly, even if you become enlightened on your own, you need an enlightened teacher to test the authenticity of your attainment. The possibility of being misled here is truly great. So most people need a guru to instruct them, since they cannot arrive at the realization on their own.

This need is both inner and outer. The sheer weight of the ways of society—its values, beliefs, goals, preoccupations, the entire pull of the social construction of reality, which is so different from those of a path—and other people's attitudes toward the path are such that, unless there is an enlightened guide, you are not likely to continue on it for long. They will place obstacles, cast doubts on your mind, or isolate you so that you will feel lonely, abandoned, and discouraged, begin to question your choice, and finally abandon the practice.

The inner need is even greater. Most people do not know from direct experience how they actually are or what makes them continue to be the way they are. How, then, can they be aware of a path of which they have no experiential knowledge and in which theoretical knowledge is no substitute? Since people are not usually familiar with their mental terrain, they are apt to get lost, as a Hindu scripture expresses it, in the forest of their desires and remain forever chasing after their objects. As Kapleau Roshi observes, unaware of how we have been programmed and the controlling influence of programming over our lives, all of us carry these burdens and are constantly being trapped by them and the ideas, preconceptions, judgments, self-deceptions, and constructs that issue from them (1: 50). That is why, as Raphael Lefort says of the Sufi view, "Cardinal among the tenets of the Sufis is that ordinary man cannot himself recognize and take advantage of the shaping influence he needs. He must, perforce, follow a teacher who knows where these influences can be found and how and to what measure they are to be used" (75). Unless there is a teacher who has worked through his/her own mind and made a clear pathway through to the boundless open space, who knows our mental terrain, the jungle of our confusion, and is ready to help us, we are apt to get lost in the tangle of our emotions and attachments if we venture out on our own. Moreover, directions and signposts on the paths are not always clear, especially to one who has not been initiated. Thus we need an experienced guide who will take us through the stages, help us identify our condition, its causes and how we maintain them, and then help us disidentify and become free.

Moreover, the sheer weight of conditioning is too great an obstacle for most people to overcome. As the theory of *karma* implies, unless internal effort and external pressure are exerted, people tend to act according to their programmings. Most people are habit-ridden and do not want to make the kind of effort fundamental change requires. They would rather plod along their accustomed ways, buoyed by the illusory hope that somehow tomorrow or the next experience will be different and bring the desired change or fulfillment. And since all programming is programmed to maintain itself, unless the effort is made, no structural change will occur, since the present structure cannot change itself. Thus people need external prodding and reassurance to make the necessary effort to arouse themselves from their slumber and to break the chain of programming that has kept them bound since birth.

Even when they have some awareness about their condition and its causes, people cling to it either for fear that life will be unlivable or that they will lose their individuality. Or dismissing their perception or insight, they may sink back further into their condition, instead of attempting to break free, declaring their perception unreal and their condition the only reality (so great is their fear of the truth and their attachment to what they have). Even those brave ones who face their situation courageously and try to rise above it by seeking to realize the truth on their own, get lost in the jungle of their mental creations, emotional fixations, and confusion. As progress on the path is usually slow, after the initial enthusiasm has worn off, sometimes one feels that one has made no progress at all or that one is going backwards. Even when one gets initiated into a path, left to oneself, one may eventually feel discouraged and tend to give up. Save for a few exceptional individuals, therefore, unless there is someone to prod and guide them, people will not embark on the journey of Self-realization.

Furthermore, the need also arises from the fact that people are not ordinarily aware of the illusions, delusions, and deceptions of ego, which is always clever at aping, especially if its equilibrium has been threatened. The ego would rather collect teachings than enter a path, believing that thereby it is becoming spiritual. It would rather go its own way than accept a path and submit to a teacher, thinking that by so doing it will retain its individuality, maturity, and independence, when in fact such a stance indicates its fear of stripping its defenses, roles, and games. Thus we cannot really take up a path until we are willing to accept ourselves as we are and unmask ego. Since this process is painful and distasteful, we would hardly do it on our own. We need someone who sees and accepts us as we really are and can help us do the same and cut through defenses, habits, attachments, and fixations. Expressing his own experience, a Sufi admits: "My teacher liberated me from the captivity in which I thought I was free, when in fact I was actually revolving within a pattern" (Shah 3: 390).

Moreover, a consideration of the path itself makes the need plain. As Kapleau Roshi observes, nothing can replace the shaping and transforming influence of an enlightened teacher (1: 95). Similarly, Rumi says, "Wool, through the presence of a man of knowledge, becomes a carpet. Earth becomes a palace. The presence of a spiritual man creates a similar transformation" (Shah 3: 138). Underscoring the same and adding further the need for the right kind of surrender, another Sufi states that without a "Guide" you cannot realize the goal of the path. On the one hand, if you cannot surrender yourself, you cannot enter the path; on the other hand, if you surrender in the wrong way, you will be lost (Shah 2:187).

We may also feel the need to associate with a concrete example of a path before embarking on it ourselves. When we are about to begin the climb, the summit may appear unapproachable; we may doubt our abilities; the difficulties of the climb may appear overwhelming; or the summit may lose its attraction for us. In such a predicament, when we are doubtful, the master is there to demonstrate that it can be reached. When we are full of discouragement and ready to give up, he is there to teach us to have faith in ourselves, to urge us on. If we go astray or veer off course, he is there to correct our steps and set them in the right direction. If our understanding is faulty and our vision unclear, he is there to bring clarity and understanding. Above all, his role is that of reassurance. As an embodiment of the Way, he is there to assure us that we can realize the Unconditioned, since we are that already.

Recognizing the intricacies of the mind, its many moods and modes, and the subtleties of the paths and their difficulties and dangers, all the sources of experiential religion emphasize the need for an enlightened teacher. Thus, Hindu scriptures state that none but a guru can take a person out of the jungle of mental constructs and sensory stimulations that constantly trap him/her into behaving in habitual and programmed ways. Kapleau Roshi observes that, although it is possible to begin the journey on your own, progress on the path is ordinarily impossible without the teacher's guidance. For one thing, some phases of the journey being more hazardous than others, we are likely to become trapped by our conditionings, preconceived ideas, or self-deceptions, especially at such hazardous junctures. Since one who has not yet gone through these difficulties is unaware of them and their nature, without the aid of an experienced teacher s/he may fail to take the necessary steps to identify and resolve them.

Some of the initial difficulties have to do with discouragement at our inability to quiet the wandering mind, get instant results, or have our expectations met. We may doubt our ability to reach the goal or wonder whether it is worth the effort. Or we may, as Jack Engler notes about many Western students of insight meditation, become absorbed not in meditation but in psychodrama and self-therapy. At a more advanced level we may misinterpret our experiences and deceive ourselves into thinking that we are enlightened; or we may become filled with the desire for paranormal powers or with pride in our own accomplishments. The need for a teacher at this stage is illustrated by the following story told by Garma Chang (Chung-Yuan) and communicated to him by a Lama under whom he was training at that time. After five months of practice, during meditation a spider began to appear before this student. Despite his efforts to drive it away, the spider began to grow increasingly large as it drew closer to him and blocked his path. Deciding to kill it, he presented his case to his Lama. The latter, however, told him not to kill but to take a piece of chalk, and, when it appeared the next time, mark a cross on its belly. He did as he was told and then went to the Lama. Thereupon the Lama told him to lower the apron he was wearing and take a look for himself. As he did so, to his astonishment, he saw a cross mark on his belly. He realized then that had he stabbed the spider, he would have killed himself (1: 218-219).

From his own experience Eric Lerner illustrates a self-deception to which one may succumb at an advanced stage of practice. Thinking that the moment of stillness he had experienced while practicing by himself in a remote place in Sri Lanka was *Nirvana,* he went to his teachers in Burma and presented his case for confirmation. The teacher told him that he had entered the trance state and had been temporarily derailed from the path and that in order to get back on it he must maintain an uninterrupted awareness of impermanence *(anicca).* Lerner became furious at this interpretation and began to doubt the teacher's ability to know. Although Lerner realized, as he stared into her eyes, that she knew exactly the nature of his experience, he refused to accept this and kept trying to get a confirmation. He grew furious again when she told him again to keep cleaning his mind. It was only when he glanced at her again and saw his own reflection in her deep, luminous eyes and calm face that Lerner finally accepted her interpretation.

Reflecting on his behavior, Lerner concluded that it was self-deception that led him to believe that he had left ego behind and entered *Nirvana,* and made him refuse to submit to his teacher's guidance and doubt her ability to know until she shattered his pride and defenses and revealed to him that she saw everything directly. Speaking of the pride that welled up in him as a result of his ability to decipher this self-deception, Lerner states, "The most awesome aspect of understanding this deception...was the dimension, the apparent bottomlessness of the well of self. I could no longer even pride myself on my ability to penetrate the sham, because that was another layer of sham" (157). In such a situation, only a teacher who can cut through our self-deception and directly reveal the way we actually are and the exact nature of our experience, can take us out of detours, deviations, and dead ends, and put us on the right track.

If the need for enlightened teachers is evident in those traditions in which clear instructions on how to follow a method are available, it is imperative in those that work with the unconscious forces in oneself and in which the path is not clearly marked out except to initiates. Unless you have sufficient skills to harness these forces, you dare not confront them alone, lest you get lost and do harm to yourself. Such are the Tantric paths—Hindu, Buddhist, and Taoist. Their very nature and complexity, the forces of body and mind which they engage, and the absence of complete instruction prior to initiation, call for an expert who has gone through the steps and has arrived at a mature realization. Referring to the Tibetan path, Blofeld comments:

> If the purpose is merely to sample meditation, the need to find a teacher is not as imperative as when one desires to advance toward enlightenment, at which time the need becomes graver than the choice of a specialist to operate on someone hovering over the brink of life and death. With its dangerous manoeuvering of the adept's consciousness, the risk is so great that it should never be attempted without the guidance of a Lama in whom absolute faith can be placed. (2: 23)

Concurring with this observation, Tarthang Tulku says, "A qualified teacher is necessary for our intuitive inner growth, since some things are difficult to learn without the guidance of one who has attained certain understanding and realization" (1: 163). Chogyam Trungpa similarly observes: "In the Vajrayana, it is absolutely necessary to have a teacher and to trust the teacher," for, without an enlightened teacher "there is no way to realize the teachings, and so no journey, no liberation" (4: 141; 5: 61). Expressing the Taoist view, master Ko Hung insists that a good teacher is essential in making progress in "Taoist studies" (Blofeld 4: 32). And, reflecting the need in general and in Hindu Tantra in particular, Rajneesh says, "Unless you are in intimate contact with one who is awakened, it is impossible to come out of your sleep because the mind is even capable of dreaming that it is awake" (1: 100).

Qualities of an Authentic Teacher

Granted such a need, the question now is: How do you go about choosing one? How do you distinguish an enlightened from an unenlightened teacher? What are the qualities of an authentic teacher?

In reference to the third question, from what has been said so far, some characteristics of an authentic teacher should now be clear. Let me begin by saying something about those you should avoid: Avoid anyone who is on a trip of his/her own at others' expense. In the jungle of our confusion there have appeared many hungry wolves who advertise their trade and are ready to deliver what we want: painless cures, massaging of egos, instant *nirvana*. Their trip may include an entire range of greed or drives: money, sex, power, fame, identity, self-exaltation, desire to have a following or to be worshipped. If you go for such teachers, you will become deflected from the true path and become trapped in these schemes. An authentic teacher has no need or interest in any of these.

A false teacher who is on a power trip wants absolute power and control over the lives of his/her disciples. As Ken Wilber points out, such a one offers some form of primitive fusion, magical beliefs, or appeals to conformity needs. S/he poses as the absolute and permanent authority on the disciple's entire life. Claiming to be the sole arbiter of legitimacy or truth, s/he sets up rules which are to be obeyed without question. S/he wants to keep his/her disciples in complete dependency on him/her for life. The most dangerous "teachers" are those who, like Jim Jones, get their sense of identity and purpose of life from the group they control (5: 254-266).

An authentic teacher, on the other hand, does not focus attention on him/herself but on the path. S/he does not aim to keep the disciple in infantile dependency or on a prerational level of arrested development but to lead him/her to transrational levels of growth, independence, and absolute freedom. Consequently, s/he does not want to have power over you but to help you get in touch with and release the power of change and self-transcendence that resides within you. S/he wants to connect you with the power of the Spirit or the true Self. Instead of keeping you emotionally crippled for life, s/he shows you how you can throw off dependencies, free yourself from crippling situations, and be your true Self. Since s/he is already Self-realized, s/he cannot get his/her identity from anyone else but can only manifest what s/he is.

The authority an authentic teacher exercises is functional. It is not directed toward him/herself but toward the task of the disciple's Self-realization. Once that stage of development is achieved, the teacher's authority ends, for his/her sole function is to guide the disciple to that ultimate stage of growth. Thus his/her authority is temporary, and not permanent. It extends over the period of training and over those things that pertain to the path, and not over the disciple's entire life.

Since an authentic teacher is not self-centered but is centered in the Unconditioned State, if a teacher is self-centered, desires self-exaltation, worship, or adulation, avoid him/her like a plague. The same is true of self-advertisers who pose or allow their disciples to proclaim them as the perfect master; who claim they are enlightened, are the latest incarnation of God; or have the whole truth. Those who seek publicity or want to protect their image are not authentic gurus.

As already mentioned, another type you should shun is the packager. Such a one may be found giving weekend seminars, training sessions, or short self-improvement courses; organizing growth centers; propounding obscure cults; or proclaiming him/herself to be a channel, prophet, or messenger of some ascended master or other type of departed or celestial being. S/he may resort to insidious commercialism, avoiding public scrutiny until some disillusioned followers or a catastrophe brings him/her to public view. The packaging itself may be done by piecing together an assortment of teachings, fragments of various practices that leave you fragmented, confused and unsatisfied. As noted earlier, such a teacher caters to egotistical motives and infantile stages of development. S/he is motivated not so much by compassion as by compulsions of his/her own.

A truly enlightened teacher does not proclaim him/herself enlightened. S/he does not come across as having all legitimacy vested in him/her. Rather, his/her legitimacy is usually derived from a tradition of lineage, as his/her enlightenment was verified by his/her teacher whose realization was in turn authenticated by his/her teacher. Usually s/he is a chain link in the transmission of the Spirit and has received approval from his/her teacher to teach. His/her authority and legitimacy come from the path and his/her standing on it as authenticated by his/her teacher. So one of the things you should inquire about a prospective teacher is his/her credentials: Who authenticated his/her realization and sanctioned his/her teaching? Also, is his/her teaching consistent with the tradition s/he represents or has s/he watered it down to suit the fashion of the age, making it convenient and palatable to his/her followers? Thus carefully examine all prospective ones before choosing a personal teacher.

In answering the first question, each tradition gives instruction on what you should look for in an authentic teacher. Representing Hinduism and the tradition of yoga, the authors of *Yoga and Psychotherapy* suggest that you look for various behavioral clues: Is s/he restless or his/her posture poor? Such a posture reveals a lack of control over body and a dissipated, unfocused mind. Is his/her walk hurried? That may indicate a sense of being torn or under pressure. Instead, his/her walk should exhibit confidence, ease, and self-control. Is his/her speech distracted, rambling, critical, or negative about others? Is s/he dissatisfied with everything? Is his/her action self-serving, destructive, or manipulative? Is s/he playing games, trying to impress or lay a trip on you? Is s/he anxious to make you a disciple? Is s/he playing favoritism with his/her disciples? Or is s/he open to all, accepting all equally, with unconditional regard for all, shown in the feeling of sacredness displayed toward all? Does s/he radiate love, compassion, and inner peace?

As the authors of *Yoga and Psychotherapy* declare, an authentic teacher "reflects an inner peace — through a relaxed body and harmonious coordination, and through patience, confidence, clear thinking, and unselfish attention to the needs of others" (205-206). When asked how one can know whether a particular person is competent to be a guru, Ramana Maharshi likewise stated, "By the way he radiates inner peace and stillness, and by the peace of mind you feel in his presence and by the respect you feel for him" (Osborne 106).

Considering wisdom and insight as characteristics of an authentic teacher, Seung Sahn Roshi says that you should look for "a keen-eyed Zen master" (Mitchell 155). While agreeing that you should look for a deeply enlightened teacher, Kapleau Roshi adds that an authentic teacher should live by what s/he teaches, that is, his/her teaching should come from deep, personal realization, rather than from mere book learning. So you should inquire about the source of his/her teaching: Is it a result of scholarly learning, consisting of quotations from scriptures or an expression of deeply personal realization? How does s/he answer questions? Are his/her answers shallow, hesitant, unclear or anxious? Or do they reveal spontaneous, deep, intuitive insight, and a sense of peace, certainty, and truth, arising from a deep, inner pool of stillness and personal realization? (2: 34).

Another key factor, emphasized by Chogyam Trungpa and others, is the ability to communicate. Trungpa says that the criteria of an effective teacher should be not so much fame or wisdom as his/her ability to see through the student's conditionings, defenses, games, and masks, and to generate trust and confidence so that the latter is able to open him/herself completely and communicate with the teacher directly and properly (2: 40). As in psychotherapy, this ability is indeed essential for open communication and progress on the path. Agreeing with this view, Tarthang Tulku says that in selecting a teacher you should be guided by the criteria of whether s/he inspires faith and trust and is someone you can follow when the going gets tougher than you expected. He adds that the teacher should have experiential realization of the teachings, fused with compassion (1: 158).

Since the context of communication is central to the master-disciple relationship, granted the presence of other qualities noted above, a final deciding factor in choosing a teacher is whether s/he generates trust and confidence so that you can be completely open. As a fully enlightened teacher is an embodiment of a path, to be open to him/her is to be open to the path or the teachings. The teacher is a connector. S/he connects you to the teachings, and through them to the Unconditioned. The linking of the two personalities is, therefore, essential. Emphasizing confidence, Kapleau Roshi says, "A teacher may be deeply enlightened, with many followers, and yet may not be the right teacher for you, if he fails to arouse the feeling of confidence and devotion so that you cannot open yourself completely to him" (2: 34-35). Similarly, Ram Dass observes that if you meet a teacher whom everyone else loves, honors, and respects but in your heart nothing happens, instead of judging him/her or thinking that something is wrong with you, just move on. This teacher is not right for you at this moment. Advising you to trust your intuition in choosing a teacher, he continues: "Don't listen to what other people say about the Guru or even what the Guru says about the Guru, listen to what your heart says about the Guru," adding further that "for the proper transmission, the teacher, the teachings and practices should be in harmony with your needs" (1: 124).

Thus, as these factors are crucial for your ultimate development, you need to examine a prospective teacher to find out what kind of presence s/he communicates: Is it inspiring, illuminating, spontaneous, joyful, marked by deep, inner stillness? Or is it all a show? Is s/he able to see and accept everyone or is s/he seeking agreement from everyone? How do you feel in his/her presence about yourself, and about him/her? Does s/he inspire confidence in yourself and trust in him/her? Do you find that you can be completely open? Does s/he awaken a feeling that you can make the journey with him/her as your guide?

Finally, as Tarthang Tulku observes, "Ultimately, our best teacher is ourselves. When we are open, aware, and watchful, then we can guide ourselves properly" (1: 170). In all phases of the path, your surest guide — a thing you must never abandon — is your critical and discerning intelligence in tune with the deeper current in your life. You must always maintain an alertness, a clear head, a questioning attitude and an ability to differentiate what is genuine from what isn't. As Trungpa points out, "Ultimately, we can trust only in our basic intelligence" (4: 130). However, with our emotional tangles, programmed mind, and lack of prior knowledge of the path or teacher's qualifications, it is not easy to hear the voice of this intelligence. Still, it is the final deciding factor, for as Ramana Maharshi points out, the real guru is the Self, the inner Teacher (Osborne 99). If we are able to listen to that Teacher, it will lead us to the one who is its manifestation and can therefore guide us so that we ourselves can also be its manifestation to the world.

Once the question of choosing a qualified teacher is settled, related questions to be faced are whether you should go from teacher to teacher and whether you should have more than one teacher.

Here again your motive becomes the deciding factor: In going to every new teacher who appears on the scene, are you merely window-shopping, or are you doing it to find the right teacher for you? If the latter, then you should go to different teachers to find out about their teachings and teaching style, about themselves and yourself, before settling on one.

While most authorities agree that you should at first seek out different teachers, not all agree that, after you have made the choice, you should stay with one teacher to the end. Reflecting his own experience, Ram Dass says that at first you are an eclectic, going to different teachers and sampling different teachings. "But as you progress on the path, you need one guru who represents a unique and specific lineage. At the end of the path, there is a meeting of all the paths — universality" (1: 125). Somewhat agreeing with this view, Kapleau Roshi states that it is alright to go to many teachers before selecting one as your personal teacher. After the choice, however, it is not advisable to go from teacher to teacher. Since there are differences of method, personality, and depth of awakening even within one tradition, by giving conflicting advice, different teachers may create confusion in the mind of an aspirant, slowing progress, and even causing discouragement (2: 28-36). Tarthang Tulku agrees. He says that while we may at first go to many teachers, once we have a teacher, we should firmly commit ourselves to that relationship so that we can make progress on the path and stay with it until we attain complete enlightenment (1: 157-160; 2: 152-155).

Seung Sahn Roshi takes a different view. He encourages Zen students to go to different teachers, even after having chosen a personal teacher, until they find "a keen-eyed Zen master." The reason for this, he says, is that some get attached to their teacher even when s/he cannot help them. As a result, after many years of practice they do not attain enlightenment. It is difficult to get enlightened under one teacher, even if s/he is a great one (Mitchell 155-156). His advice corresponds to an ancient practice: Zen students used to travel great distances, often suffering numerous hardships, since there were no convenient modes of transportation at that time, going from teacher to teacher, until they found one under whom they felt they could realize the Truth. Sometimes their own teacher would send them to others, if they felt that that would open them up or would enable them to make greater progress or come to a deeper realization. Many Sufi masters continue this practice even today.

The Functions of a Master

Because a fully enlightened master is a living realization of the Truth, s/he is the guardian or gateway to the Unconditioned. Jesus said, "I am the Way, the Truth, and the Life." When Zen master Chao Chou was asked, "What is Chao Chou?" He replied, "East gate, west gate, north gate, south gate." Speaking of the Sufi teacher, Idries Shah says, "The Sufi teacher is the link between the disciple and the goal. He embodies and symbolizes both the 'work' itself, of which he is a product, and the continuity of the system, the 'chain of transmission'" (3: 396).

As the gateway, the master functions in six ways, which essentially involve opening, awakening, and guidance. His/her task is to open the student to two worlds: one known but not directly experienced, namely, the conditioned world or his/her actual state; the other not directly known at all—the Unconditioned.

This process begins with testing the aspirant's motive and accepting him/her as a student. Before admitting you—this was especially the case in ancient times—the teacher usually tests your aptitude for the journey; your sincerity, seriousness of intention, the aim of your search, and what you are willing to do to realize it. A story about Bodhidharma, the supposed founder of Zen, illustrates this: When a monk by the name of Shen-kuang came to visit him and most earnestly implored him to be instructed in the truth of Zen, at first Bodhidharma paid no attention. Without being discouraged by this seeming indifference, Shen-kuang stood at the entrance for days, waiting to be instructed. One day snow even buried him up to his knees. Still Bodhidharma would not instruct him. On the contrary, he tried to dissuade him by saying, "The incomparable doctrine of Buddhism cannot be grasped except after a long, hard discipline, great endurance and difficult practice. Ordinary individuals will only be wasting their time." It was only after Shen-kuang cut off his left arm with his sword and presented it to Bodhidharma as a token of his sincerity, firmness of intention, and seriousness of resolve that the master accepted him as a disciple (Suzuki 3: First Series 189-190).

Countless other stories illustrate the master testing the student's intention. Chogyam Trungpa narrates the experience of Marpa and Milarepa, two of the great early masters of Tibetan Buddhism: In his attempt to get the teachings from Naropa, Marpa exhausted every means he had, besides suffering hardships in traveling from Tibet to India. Only after he gave up collecting the teachings did Naropa accept him as a student. And Milarepa was driven to the point of despair and suicide, building and dismantling huts, which Marpa had instructed him to do, before being admitted by him as a disciple. Modern masters may not go that far, but testing the aptitude and readiness of prospective candidates is an important preliminary task of every genuine master.

Once the student is judged ready, the instruction begins. First, the master seeks to convince you, as does don Juan with Castaneda, that the world you inhabit is a description. Using various techniques, s/he will work to knock off your assumption that this description has finality. S/he will demonstrate to you that this construction is made and maintained by humans who become enslaved to it by giving it finality and inescapability, and assume it to be worthy of your allegiance. S/he will show you that once we subject ourselves to this fundamental distortion, thereafter it rules our lives, and that this is not how things are in themselves. This is most essential. Without being convinced that Reality is not the way you perceive it, and that in order to arrive at Reality you must disidentify with your construct, progress on the path is impossible. As Idries Shah observes, "The function of the teacher is to open the mind of the Seeker, so that he may become accessible to a recognition of his destiny. In order to do this, man must realize how much of his ordinary thinking is cramped with assumptions. Until this point is reached, true understanding is impossible" (3: 392).

Next the master brings you around to see yourself the way you actually are and to face your condition. S/he opens your eyes so that you are able to see that you have been formed by your programmings, and that you arrange the events of your life so as to confirm, maintain, and perpetuate your programmings, the structures of your world, consciousness, and self. S/he helps you identify the demons thus created that run your life: negative programmings, mental and emotional fixations, habits, unawareness, desires, attachments, identifications. Their identification may be done through direct teaching, assigning various exercises of self-observation, maneuvering your consciousness so that you will come around to recognize and directly observe them in operation; or indirectly, by example, by being around you. S/he awakens you to the fact that you merely react to stimuli as your programming dictates and that as long as you do so, you are not free. S/he shows you how your self has been fashioned. S/he helps you see the masks you are wearing. S/he brings you around to a palpable grasp of the fact that you are bound and ruled by these and other internal and external forces to which you have given over the control of your life and which prevent you from initiating fundamental change.

The master helps you become aware, recognize, and identify the contents of the conscious and unconscious mind through relentless self-observation not only during meditation but also throughout the day. Everything is examined in the light of awareness. Things deeply buried and long forgotten come to light. As Trupgpa observes, everything is brought to light and exposed. Nothing is left hidden. This disclosure is often very painful and hard to accept. For, at this stage you want the teacher's approval of your positive self-image; you want to hide the negative aspects of your personality. But when you discover that even this desire is exposed, you may feel discouraged, frustrated, and angry, and may begin to avoid him/her (4: 133-134).

In this attraction-repulsion, what you really do, though, is to hate yourself for having the hidden, unacceptable negative self-image exposed. Because you have an illusory self-image and are caught up in your self-importance, it is hard to see and accept things that do not conform to it. But the master does not coddle your criminal negligence of yourself. Without any interpretation, evaluation, judgment, approval or disapproval, s/he exposes all self-images and shows you the way you actually are. However, this exposure of your defenses, self-deceptions, and games is discomfiting because it does not provide the confirmation you seek. But, unless your condition is exposed, unless you are able to accept yourself just the way you are, progress on the path will be halted, and your journey to wholeness will come to an end (Trungpa 4: 134).

Ultimately, then, the aim of this exposure is to convince you that you cannot realize the teachings if you continue your present course. You must undergo a total change, a complete inner revolution. Your entire way of life, reality, consciousness, and self must be questioned, examined, disidentified with, destructured, transcended, and realigned. Toward this end, a most crucial task of the master is to drive you to a dead end state, bringing you to a direct experience of your condition as the human paradox, of your ego as a contradiction, and of the present course of your life as an impasse. The master gives you no respite from self-exposure until you come to see the very limit of your reality, consciousness, and self, until you palpably experience them as something constructed and maintained by yourself and your culture; and to see directly the impossibility of your realizing who you truly are so long as you remain within their limits. As DeMartino observes, "The master thrusts the student into the tormenting pit of the utterly raw and exposed inner contradiction. He tears away and probes into the central core of the wound. And he shows him that nothing that ego can do can resolve its contradiction, which is itself" (in Fromm et al. 148). For this reason the Zen master relentlessly urges Zen students to drive their minds to the dead end state, as does, for example, master Han Shan: "Use all your attention and strength patiently to push your mind to the very dead end; just push it on and on" (Chang 1: 113).

At this stage, your efforts to translate the teachings in terms of your familiar world so as to confirm and maintain your condition and world, and to resolve the contradiction within your reality-construct and so resolve the impasse are shown to be useless. The task of the master is to frustrate all your attempts at conceptual understanding and make you give up all efforts to grasp Reality as Such by thought and ordinary consciousness, and to help you become open to a completely new way of seeing that requires a mental revolution. As Ken Wilber observes, the essential task of the master in this respect is "to frustrate the present translations, undermine the old resistances, and encourage the new transformation by enforcing special conditions" (3: 94-95). This is so central that without stopping this category- and reality-conversion, there can be no destructuring of ordinary consciousness and reality, no self-transcendence and consequent resolution of the question in the opening of the mind to a direct experience of Reality as Such.

As Wei Wu Wei says, "The great masters invariably sought to manoeuver their disciples and pupils into turning round in the right direction, so that they might one day apprehend the truth for themselves" (1: xv). As you stop trying to translate the new in terms of the old, therefore, you reach the turning point on the road to Self-realization.

The next step is even more painful than the previous one. It consists in disidentifying with and letting go of everything with which you had hitherto identified and to which you were attached: your present constructions of self, consciousness, and reality. To this end the master helps you to dissolve negative programmings and mental and emotional fixations and blockages; and to recognize and become free of the hidden assumptions, judgments, preconceptions, habits, automatic responses, unawareness, beliefs, and values under which you operate. Since these prop up your present constructs, without this disidentification they cannot be destructured, nor can you become free of them and experience Reality. Such is the import of the following Zen story:

> Nan-in, a Japanese master, received a university professor who came to inquire about Zen. Nan-in served tea. He poured his visitor's cup full, and he kept on pouring. The professor watched the overflow until he could no longer restrain himself. "It is overfull. No more will go in." "Like this cup," Nan-in said, "you are full of your opinions and speculations. How can I show you Zen unless you first empty your cup?" (Reps 5)

Thus, the master maneuvers you to emptying yourself of everything programmed into you since childhood, so that you are able to destructure consciousness, reorganize perception, and reorder your world. As Kapleau Roshi observes, the master "cannot give you anything you don't already have [and anything that could be given to you would be useless anyway], but he can take away much that is foreign to your true-nature: the sticky beliefs, chesty opinions, petty rationalizations, illusory ideals, and deluded thoughts, all of which imprison you in a cocoon" (2: 32). Above all, as Janwillem van de Wetering tells us of his own experience, the master hammers away to knock off the core identification—the separate self: One day, as they were walking through a forest, they came to a brook. The master motioned him to sit down, and sat next to him. Drawing his attention to a piece of burnt cork floating by, the master said:

> That piece of cork is your personality. At every turn, at every change of circumstances, at every conflict, defeat or victory, a piece of it crumbles off...Till nothing is left of it. (21)

However painful this task of disidentification may appear at first, it is ultimately a strengthening and liberating experience. It makes ego strong, as only a strong, healthy, integrated, and fully developed ego is fit for the arduous journey ahead. Moreover, by removing conflict and confusion from your life and clearing the deck of unnecessary baggage, it brings freedom, buoyancy, lightness, and joy into your life. This is purification. Don Juan calls it "impeccability," which, according to him, is "proper use of energy" (4: 15). Similarly, Thoreau issued a call to simplify life. Patanjali enjoined *tapas,* which is usually translated as "austerity" but actually don Juan's "impeccability" captures its meaning exactly. Tibetans have a similar view, as Lama Govinda reports:

> I have heard a Lama say that the part of a master, adept of the 'Short Path,' is to superintend a 'clearing.' He must incite his novice to rid himself of the beliefs, ideas, acquired habits and innate tendencies which are part of his present mind, and have been developed in the course of successive lives whose origin is lost in the night of time. On the other hand, the master must warn his disciple to be on his guard against accepting new beliefs, ideas, and habits as groundless and irrational as those he shakes off. (2: 251)

This need for purification is so central that all paths or sources of experiential religion prescribe extensive practices toward this goal.

Through such purification the master helps to bring about a fundamental transformation, so that everything is at once reordered and made to fit and assume its true proportion in your life. The self shrinks as excess baggage is excised and left behind. Its concerns, drives, and desires no longer preoccupy your mind, absorb your time, or consume your life. As old programmings and habits dissolve and disappear, the present structure of consciousness changes; perception becomes reorganized; and there opens up a space of awareness in which clarity, stillness, and peace reign; in which illumination and insight flood in. As the programmed contents of the mind are cut through and cleared away, you are increasingly able to perceive the primary process directly, without the usual processing, interpretation, and bias. In the open and clear space of your awareness the desire, longing, and thoughts of the true Self blossom. The pull of the Unconditioned becomes steadier and stronger.

The task here is as critical as it is difficult. Without the prodding of a master, few would undertake such a painful task. Even a most courageous beginner — an Arjuna — is liable to feel discouraged or powerless, despondent or overwhelmed. At this stage, many are ready to quit, as Castaneda, van de Wettering and others did at first. Time and again Castaneda pleaded weakness and fear.

It was the skills of don Juan that kept him on the path, as Krishna kept Arjuna. This stage is where the patience and devotion of the master are most critically felt. Kapleau Roshi has observed:

> When the student slackens his effort he is coaxed or goaded, when he is assailed by doubt or driven to despair he is encouraged and uplifted. An accomplished roshi thus combines stern detachment with warm concern, flexibility and egolessness...But what the student responds to most keenly is the visible evidence of the roshi's liberated mind. (1: 90)

It is his example, then, that urges the student to continue down the road at this critical juncture and accomplish the task the master has laid out before him/her.

The next task of the master is to guide you in breaking free of or transcending all conditioning and constructs and experiencing the Unconditioned. Since each person must directly experience and BE the Unconditioned, neither faith nor another's experience can be a substitute; as the gateway to this realization, the master can only instruct and guide you. You must do the walking and realize the truth for yourself through personal experience. As Idries Shah observes, "As a guide he [i.e., the master] shows the Way—but the aspirant must do the walking" (3: 392). Ramana Maharshi concurs: "God and the Guru will only show the way to the release...yet, each one should by his own effort pursue the path shown by God or Guru and gain release. One can know oneself only with one's own eye of knowledge, and not with somebody else's" (Bercholz 11). So the master opens your mind to the Unconditioned, demonstrates its reality through his/her own realization, and though his/her teaching and personal example becomes a mirror and provides a map of the path, helping you enter it. How does he do this?

Once you cut through the outer and arrive at the primary construction, ready to make the most fundamental shift to pure Awareness, the master guides, goads, and checks your state of mind. S/he applies pressures where necessary so that you will let go of your hold on the familiar world, cross the boundary of the conditioned, and leap into the Unconditioned. As Kapleau Roshi observes:

> With his long years of experience and acutely discerning eye, the roshi can gauge the stage of the student's progress and give him the necessary direction and encouragement... [He will use any device he feels necessary to] arouse the student's mind from its dormant state of unawareness to the sudden realization of its true nature... [This is especially the case when he senses that the latter's mind is] hovering on the brink of

satori...In a variety of ways the roshi will prod and nudge him into making the ultimate leap into satori. (1: 87-90)

The shock techniques employed by many Zen masters, subject of so many koans, must be understood in this light. This is especially the case when, in *samadhi*, the mind arrives at the very end of all constructs but is unable to break free. All that is needed is a blow, a phrase, or some sudden action, sound, or experience to enable the mind to break free of contents and constructs and experience enlightenment. The master is always there, working relentlessly, to bring you to this point and then s/he gives you the necessary push so that you will leap over the barrier. Thus, in "The Flying Geese" incident mentioned before, Ma Tsu vigorously twisted Pai-chang's nose, which brought the latter's mind to a dead halt, while his words suddenly opened it to *satori*. In the following story Ma Tsu employed a kick for the same purpose:

> A monk called Hung Chou came to visit Ma Tsu and asked, "What is the meaning of Bodhi-dharma's coming from the West [i.e., What is the aim of Zen]?" Ma Tsu said, "Bow down to me first." As the monk prostrated himself, Ma Tsu gave him a vigorous kick in the chest. The monk was at once enlightened. He stood up, clapped his hands, and laughing loudly, cried, "Oh, how wonderful this is, how marvelous this is! Hundreds and thousands of *samadhis* and infinite wonders of the Truth are now easily realized on the tip of a single hair!" He then made obeisance to Ma Tsu. (Chang 1: 27)

Meher Baba was stuck in the state of *samadhi* for months until master Upani Maharaj threw a stone that hit him exactly in the same spot on his forehead where another master, Hazrat Babajan, had kissed him and brought him to the state of *samadhi*. Upani Maharaj's action brought Meher Baba out of *samadhi* to full realization (Needleman 1: 79-80).

Such examples illustrate how enlightened masters, seeing the disciple's mind ready for the final moment of opening, act spontaneously to give the final push that will suddenly fling open the gateway against which the latter's mind had been knocking but which he had been unable to open. Although his action may appear strange or even cruel, in his doing whatever is deemed necessary for the opening, the master's compassion is never to be doubted, for the sole aim of his action is to bring the student to realization.

When you experience enlightenment, the master's task is to test its authenticity. The importance of this function is underlined by Kapleau Roshi when he says that the neophyte may mistake various paranormal experiences, such as visions, trances, revelations, and ecstasies, for enlightenment and fall into self-deceptions. Even after enlightenment, a master is needed to dispel the subtle pride felt by the one who is enlightened (1:93).

To test the authenticity of the disciple's realization, Zen masters have devised thorough procedures, which usually involve spontaneous demonstration of the disciple's awakening. These are usually acted out. Eugene Herrigel points out that other tests may include the student's outward behavior—"the way he expresses himself, raises a bowl of tea to his mouth, the relaxed state of his mind" (56-62). Kapleau similarly observes, "What convinces the roshi are not merely the student's words, gestures, or silence (which can be equally effective), but the conviction and certainty informing them, i.e., the comprehending look in the eye, the decisiveness of the tone of his voice, and the spontaneity, freedom and thoroughness of the gestures and movements themselves" (1: 92). Other paths use different tests to authenticate the initiate's realization. But whatever the procedure and test, wherever there is the master-disciple relationship as the context for the journey, it is the task of the master to authenticate the realization.

The final function of the master is to guide you through the further stages of the path until you arrive at a state of attainment in which you are able to live and function continuously in the realm of the Unconditioned in complete naturalness, freedom, certainty, and spontaneity.

Chapter 25
The Master-Disciple Relationship

From what has been said so far, it is clear that, apart from the few exceptional individuals who came to their realization without the help of a master, the concrete experiential context of the path is the master-disciple relationship. Experiential religion has always been a context for personal experience and communication between a master and his disciples. So it was with the Buddha, Jesus, and others who followed them in successive ages. This is also true of other paths.

The state of discipleship itself is something specific and long-lasting. Not everyone who comes in contact with a master is a disciple; nor is every teacher a master. The relationship depends on personal involvement: a willingness to accept the path wholeheartedly, submit to its discipline and walk on it to the very end, and a commitment to the teacher you have chosen. As Kapleau Roshi observes, "The master-disciple relationship implies a deep, personal commitment which, unless disrupted, should last until its goal—complete enlightenment—is attained" (2: 34-35). Since it is based on mutual commitment and trust, for the relationship to work, according to Tarthang Tulku, three elements must work harmoniously: "The teacher, the teachings, and we ourselves are the foundations necessary for spiritual development. These three must be intimately linked for genuine progress to take place" (1: 162).

However, being a dynamic process, the relationship may start with some ulterior motive, such as fascination, being with friends who are disciples, curiosity or interest, a desire to belong, etc. But for the relationship to progress, such external motives must give way to inner involvement and personal commitment. As Trungpa observes, the first stage of the relationship is like going to a supermarket. You are excited and fascinated by the teacher, the practice, and the entire context of life and association with others. You come with a great deal of expectation of what the teacher and the teachings will do for you. There is a feeling of being special; and awe and admiration for the teacher. You begin with a great deal of enthusiasm (2: 42).

According to Trungpa, at the second state you feel you are being observed and judged. You discover that the teacher sees through your postures, defenses, masks, and games and asks you to give them all up. He tells you there is nothing to acquire, nothing to gain; on the contrary, you have to let go of everything and surrender yourself. This makes you want to run away or hide from him. But if you can get over this stage and open yourself, the relationship will deepen into commitment.

At the third stage, says Trungpa, the relationship assumes a matter-of-factness. As the master holds himself up like a mirror and brings you round to seeing your programmed life the way it is, you come to accept yourself as you are, recognize your conditioned reactions and begin to work creatively to transform your life. You begin to see things and yourself the way the master does — without interpreting, evaluating, judging, excusing, approving or condemning — matter-of-factly. You are able to cut through layers of programming and mental constructs and respond to people and events directly, on the primary level. This brings you closer to the master, and a meeting of minds takes place. At the fourth stage, when you come to your own mature realization, you bid farewell to the master (2: 42-45).

This suggests that, corresponding to the stages of the path, there are various stages in discipleship and kinds of disciples. Speaking of the latter, in the context of Zen, master Gattan observes, "There are three kinds of disciples: those who impart Zen to others, those who maintain temples and shrines, and then there are the rice bags and clothes-hangers" (Reps 72). This is true of every path. Jesus, for instance, had three kinds of disciples: those who were fascinated by him and wanted something from him; those who listened and accepted his teachings as long as they agreed with their own ideas and confirmed their view of the world; and those who went the whole way, who took the path to completeness and were transformed. These latter, out of whom he chose the twelve, were true disciples. Except for Judas, they were close to him and experienced the resurrection and received the transmission of the Spirit at Pentecost. Thus full discipleship entails personal commitment to the path and the teacher until the disciple receives the transmission of Mind or Spirit, experiences enlightenment, comes to a mature realization, and becomes a teacher. What are the ingredients of this discipleship?

Faith and Devotion

Faith is a foundation of the spiritual path. Without it no progress on the path is possible. That is the reason faith is emphasized by all sources of experiential religion as a basic presupposition. Zen Buddhism, for example, speaks of strong, unshakable faith as one of the three necessary requirements of the path. Similarly, Jesus spoke of strong, immovable faith—that moves mountains or apparently insurmountable obstacles. Tibetan Buddhism emphasizes the necessity of faith and devotion for the path. And, reflecting the Sufi point of view, Sheikh Mohamed Daud says, "Nothing save full submission to your teacher will carry you through the difficulties that you will meet. Complete and unswerving belief and trust in him are your only guidelines. Any hesitation or negative response will not only disturb, they will produce doubts and errors which will cloud your understanding" (Lefort 131). Early on, the Sufis have held that the disciple should be in the hands of the master "as a dead body in the hands of its washer" (Rahman 164).

Such statements seem to imply blind faith. Herrigel thinks it is required in Zen when he says that unless the disciple is able to put blind trust in the master, he cannot continue on the Zen path (27). Others disagree. From the Sufi point of view, Idries Shah says, "There are two extremes to be avoided as useless: one is being closed, which will make you stay on the periphery and become a collector of ideas; the other is compulsion to submit, throwing yourself to the will of the master. The seeker must attain some measure of balance between these two extremes before he can be said to have the capacity to learn" (3:355). Similarly, when asked whether one should unquestioningly submit to the teacher, Kapleau Roshi replied, "One must learn to think independently and rely on his intuition and life experiences. Before selecting a teacher, one should keep both eyes open—afterward only one eye" (2: 29). Blind faith, then, is useless for anything except relieving one's need to depend on another. It would be fatal on a path that leads not to blindness but to sight and absolute freedom of the Spirit, which require you not to rely on anyone else but to walk on your own two feet.

Thus we need to distinguish between blind faith, which requires you to discard your basic, critical intelligence; and strong or complete faith, which retains critical intelligence, discernment and wakefulness, but requires that you do not hold anything back. The latter does not require you to keep your eyes closed but to keep them completely open so that you can see what exactly is going on. It does entail complete trust in the master's ability to show you the way, to help you remove blinders and filtering mechanisms so that you can see clearly, directly, openly, and completely.

We need to distinguish further between faith spoken of in conventional religion and in experiential religion. Absolute faith is emphasized by both. In the former, faith is the goal or basis of religion. It is based on someone else's experience and consists of a system of beliefs, doctrines, and practices that are divorced from direct, personal experience. This is a faith in abstractions, twice removed from reality, which is not intended to be experienced. Such a faith is the final criterion for membership or belonging. And those who transmit it are not masters but preachers, teachers, or ecclesiastical functionaries who have never directly experienced, nor do they have any inclination to experience, the reality to which their abstractions are intended to refer.

On the other hand, experiential religion is concerned with the kind of faith that requires a direct, personal experience of what is believed. Here faith is not the goal but a presupposition or necessary condition for experience. It is not a substitute for, but rather something that culminates in, experience. While conventional religion may insist on keeping the doctrine pure, and this insistence becomes the more strident the more faith is divorced from experience; experiential religion emphasizes keeping the experience pure. For the latter, faith is similar to a scientific hypothesis which is tested out in experience and which becomes a guide toward experiencing the truth to which it points. This faith requires experiment, testing, and verification. The method it employs is meditation; the laboratory is your life or mind; and the experiment, testing, and verification take place in your own experience — the testing and confirmation of your realization, like the confirmation provided by other scientists, provided by the master.

As Kapleau Roshi points out, this faith has four aspects. The first is faith in the goal. Unless you believe the Unconditioned State to be real, your true nature and the goal of your life, you will never undertake the journey. This faith in Reality as Such must be absolute. Otherwise, especially when the going gets tough, you will be tempted to give up the search and settle for a substitute. That is the reason your faith cannot be in any particular idea, content, or doctrine, but in Reality as Such, beyond all concepts, contents, and constructs. Suzuki Roshi calls this kind of faith "believing in nothing," and Castaneda calls it "believing without believing."

The second aspect is faith in the path and its teachings — that following them you will be able to realize the goal. Unless you have faith in a particular path, you will not choose it. And, even if you have faith in the goal but do not believe that a particular path and its teachings will enable you to reach it, you will not choose to follow them. You will consider them useless, unworthy of your consideration, too impractical or difficult to follow. Unless the teachings become imperative and have immediacy and urgency in bringing about your self-transformation and realization of the goal, you may consider the goal sublime or beautiful but too abstract or remote from life.

The third aspect is faith in the master as the guide. Without faith in the master, you will not choose him/her as your personal guide, the master-disciple relationship will not develop; the master will not be able to guide you properly; and the opening of mind will not take place, with the result that progress on the path will be blocked. That is why Tarthang Tulku says:

> Trust in the teacher and commitment to the relationship are essential for genuine progress on the path. Some people respect the teachings and not the teacher, and this is a hindrance to progress on the path, because a fully enlightened teacher and the teachings are one. (1: 159)

Similarly, Herrigel points out that before you arrive at your own awakening, faith in the master is, indirectly, faith in the goal, and hence necessary for your realization (27).

The fourth component is faith in yourself. Without believing that you can realize the goal and without an unshakable resolve to do so, you will not embark on the journey of awakening. Even if you do choose a path, when difficulties set in, you will find it hard to continue and will give up at some point. However remote and difficult the goal may appear and however overwhelmed at times you may be by the burden of your past conditionings, the unshakable faith that you can reach the goal (which is really faith in the Self) and the undaunted determination that you must press toward it will keep you going in spite of difficulties. And, to keep you on the path, faith in the master and his encouragement and compassion prove crucial.

While devotion to the master is associated with faith, and, in this sense, considered part of the presupposition of the relationship, it is emphasized by some paths more than others. Some Hindu texts speak of "guru puja" (worship of or devotion to the guru) or meditation on the form of the guru as the form of God. This is a key practice in Tibetan Buddhism, in which the position of the teacher is more central than in others. As the living Buddha, the guru is a concrete embodiment of the Unconditioned State, or at least of the meditation into which he will initiate and empower you. So visualization and identification with the form of the guru are part of the practice. That is why an accomplished guru is necessary for the path. Unless the teacher has himself realized the reality or state of consciousness embodied in the meditation to which he is to initiate you, he cannot empower you, and visualization of his form would be useless toward attaining the goal of the meditation. Devotion is considered necessary, therefore, in awakening faith or proper motivation, in visualization and identification, and in making rapid progress on the path. And specific rules are prescribed governing your behavior toward the guru (Cf. Odier 122-124). Other paths, such as Zen and Sufism, also emphasize the need to have devotion to the master.

At this point a caution is necessary. Devotion may be a consequence of an overwhelming emotional response arising from a feeling of inadequacy in yourself, from your lack of knowledge about the path, or from awe toward the master as some sort of a god. In such a situation, the more unworthy, inadequate, or unsure and insecure you feel, the more devoted you become. This kind of devotion, so often seen in the consciousness circuit or guru cults, is not only useless but infantile and dangerous. As I have already stated, before throwing yourself at the feet of a guru, you should carefully examine your motive: Does this compulsion arise from your need to depend on him for your salvation or for instant enlightenment, to worship someone or thing, to make you feel important, or to make all your problems magically disappear without your having to do anything? Is it because of your lack of knowledge, self-confidence, developed self-identity, or uncertainty about spiritual matters that you want to devote yourself wholeheartedly to a guru as the embodiment of all knowledge? Or is your devotion based on your commitment to the path, the guru as its embodiment, and your mature and considered judgment that he has the qualities to be your guide toward the same realization he himself has experienced? Is your devotion based on respect, trust, and a meeting of minds? The first kind of devotion is useless toward spiritual progress and dangerous to emotional and sometimes even physical health; the second is the kind of devotion necessary for the path.

Initiation

All paths have some sort of initiation ceremony, marking the aspirant's formal acceptance and entrance into the path. Thus all Eastern meditative paths begin with an initiation. This is how, from the very beginning, the methods of the yogas have been communicated and transmitted from master to disciple. Before initiating him, the master tested and carefully ascertained the aptitude and ability of the aspirant: his determination, courage, endurance, physical and mental fitness, sincerity and seriousness, and desire for enlightenment as the motive for wanting to undertake the journey. It was during the initiation ceremony, performed in secret, that the master transmitted his spiritual power to the initiate and instructed him on the method of meditation and how to practice it. At initiation, he received the mantra and his chosen deity *(ishtadeva)*, on which, using the mantra, he was instructed to meditate.

Agehananda Bharati describes a typical initiation ceremony in the tantric tradition. Briefly told, it begins with the aspirant getting ready for the initiation by fasting twelve hours prior to the day of initiation. On the appointed day, the aspirant takes some fruit or other offering and presents it to the guru, who sits facing east or south. The aspirant faces the guru. The guru first invokes his own chosen deity and offers it flowers as an homage. Next, he instructs the aspirant in the preliminary rituals and devotions, and then in breathing, concentrative, and other yogic techniques. Admonishing the aspirant to keep it secret, the guru whispers the mantra in his right ear, himself repeats it three times and has him repeat it three times, first singly, then at one stretch. The main part of the initiation being over with imparting the mantra, the aspirant makes a complete prostration before the guru, rises to his feet and circles him three times, receives some sacrificed food from him, and leaves. After paying homage at the shrine, the aspirant withdraws to meditate (185-190).

With its elaborate rituals and varieties of yogas, Tibetan Buddhism requires a different initiation for each type of *tantra* (of which there are four), each presided over by a fully accomplished master of that *tantra*. Corresponding to these, there are four different types of initiation: the vase, the secret, the knowledge-wisdom, and the word initiation. The first, which is conferred with water from a vase, is given in four types of *tantras,* whereas the other three are reserved for the higher *tantras* (Cozort 34).

The Vase Initiation, which involves one of the four types of *mandalas* – the painted cloth, the colored sand, the body, and the concentration *mandala* – symbolizes and causes, or disposes and induces, the body and the psychic channels toward removing blockages caused by programming and habituation. While it is conferred, you are instructed to imagine, visualize, or sense that bliss is being generated. This initiation authorizes visualization of the deities.

The other three initiations are given only to advanced practitioners, as some of them involve unusual practices, which are reserved for the higher *tantras*. For instance, the Secret Initiation involves the fluids of consorts produced in sexual union; and the Knowledge-Wisdom Initiation uses "vagina mandala." In addition, the former is intended to cleanse speech, allow the flow of vital breath, and produce some bliss; while the latter is intended to cleanse the mind, initiate one into visualization of emptiness, and produce the experience of great bliss. The Word Initiation is intended to produce the highest enlightenment through the union of pure body and mind. It is said to produce great bliss, which is used to meditate on and arrive at emptiness *(Sunyata)* (Cozort 34-36; Blofeld 2: 143-146).

As described by Janice D. Willis, an initiation of a lower *tantra* proceeds as follows: On the day of initiation, the aspirant goes before the guru with deep faith, humility before him and the Buddha, and the desire to master the meditation. The guru blesses him/her with chants, describes the meditation, and instructs him/her on how to visualize the main deity *(yidam)* of the meditation. As he begins the main part of the initiation, the guru takes up the bell (symbolizing *Sunyata*) and the scepter (symbolizing the Awakened Mind), and, holding them in a particular form of *mudra* or hand gesture, recites the mantra. Then both recite it together. Next, the guru rings the bell and recites other protective mantras and blessings for the aspirant's successful practice. The ceremony over, the aspirant retires to begin practicing the meditation to which s/he was just initiated.

Willis says that in higher *tantras* requiring *mandala*, the initiations are much more elaborate. The *Anuttara Tantra,* for instance, requires the initiate, among other things, to keep the time and the place of the ceremony secret. At the time enjoined by the guru, in utter secrecy you go to the appointed place, where the latter had already gone in secret and carefully constructed the *mandala*, associated with the meditation, with powdered, colored sand, and with other articles of initiation: water for the mouth and feet, incense, flowers, perfume, light music, and food. After testing your sincerity, the guru allows you to enter the place, describes the meditation, instructs you on how to visualize the *mandala,* pronounces the mantra, and shows you the *mandala*. Upon seeing the *mandala,* you usually have a vision just above it. The guru then inquires of you what you have seen, and, according to your response, prescribes special practices, which you must follow as you meditate. With the initiation over, you retire into a secluded retreat to begin your practice. Willis says that at the conclusion of the first part of the ceremony, the guru sometimes gives you a short and a long reed and instructs you to sleep on them, with the long one placed under the body and the short one under the head. This induces certain dreams, which you report to the guru, who then assigns further practices based on them (38-40).

Besides such orthodox initiations, there are other, seemingly bizarre ones performed by solitary gurus who have cut themselves off from the main traditions. Bernard Bromage describes a number of such initiations, some of which have been heavily influenced by shamanistic practices and resemble American Indian rituals. Following is a glimpse into an initiation called "Devotion to the Altar."

The guru prepares himself for the initiation by resorting to solitude, self-examination, and other long and arduous practices. When he deems himself and the disciple ready, he constructs the *mandala* and places at each of its four corners and in the middle ritual vessels containing mixtures of water and milk, grain, medicinal plants, perfumes, the "three whites" — cream, cheese and butter — the "three sweets" — honey, sugar, and treacle, the "five mirrors," five pieces of rock-crystals, five images of the meditative Buddhas, arrows, variegated silks, and peacock feathers. After these are put in their proper places, the ceremony begins.

Black tea or grain liquor is set out as an offering to the deities, ritual cakes are placed in sections of the *mandala,* a bowl made from a human skull is placed in your hand, and symbolic daggers are placed at each of the four entrances of the *mandala;* four knives are driven between the bars of the doors or entrances.

After a dialogue, in which the guru ascertains your mental readiness, he ties a ring of multicolored thread to your left arm and places in turn the water pot, symbolic of purity and mastery, on the four top *chakras* or energy centers of the body — head, throat, heart and navel — signifying your participation in the sacred vows and the promise to realize your essential nature. As these proceed, the guru's assistant plays on drums made of human skin. The muffled sound of the drums is intended to put you in a proper or trance-like state, evoke the unconscious forces from within you as well as from the environment, and call to mind the primal vibrations of energy-awareness, of which all things in the universe, including yourself, are manifestations.

Next, you are blindfolded and a flower is put in your hand with instructions to throw it onto the *mandala.* The direction of the throw will determine the new name you will receive, the type of meditation you will be instructed to practice, and certain virtues and characteristics that will be revealed in your personality: For men, north will indicate a promise of complete liberation, while south will promise vital energy and abounding joy, flowing from cosmic consciousness; for women, the opposite will be true.

Toward the end of the ceremony, the blindfold is removed, signifying the removal of unawareness, whereupon you may see the guru as a beam of light and be filled with rapture (91-107).

Other Buddhist paths, too, have initiation rites. Zen, for instance, has ordination and the receiving of precepts. The latter involves shaving the head, symbolizing casting away worldly desires; repentance, symbolizing the initiate's disidentification with the former way of life and identification with Reality as Such; and the receiving of precepts, robes, and a Buddhist name, signifying a new identity (Maezumi and Glassman 1: 40-99).

As the initiation rite for Christians, baptism has many similarities with the initiation rites described above. However, because in most Christian churches baptism is administered to infants, it has lost its significance as a personal initiation into a path of Self-realization. What at present occupies a place similar to the initiation rites of other paths are the ceremonies for entrance into monastic and religious orders. As with other initiation rites, before you are admitted to these orders, your motives, intentions, aptitudes, and mental and physical fitness are tested. When you are found to have the required qualifications, you are formally admitted to the order in an initiation ceremony in which you take the vows of poverty, chastity, and obedience, and resolve to follow the rules and practices of the order. At the ceremony, you are given new clothes, symbolizing your disidentification with the former life and acceptance of the new way, and a new name, symbolizing your new identity.

Although the form may vary from Order to Order, initiation seems also to be a practice required for entrance into all Sufi Orders. One such form, used by the Nimatullahi Order, is described by Sheikh Javad Nurbakhsh, the head of the Order, as follows. The preparation for the ceremony begins with the aspirant's declaring his intention, followed by five ceremonial baths. The first bath signifies repentance for your former ways and misdeeds. The second concerns your surrendering to the will of God and becoming a Muslim, if you are not one already. (This appears to be at variance with other Sufis who claim that you do not have to be a Muslim in order to be a Sufi.) The third signifies outer and inner purity and initiation into spiritual poverty. The fourth signifies cleansing prior to appearing before the master to receive the orders of the path; while the last symbolizes your commitment to realizing the goal of the path.

The next step concerns preparation of five objects — a few yards of white cloth, a whole nutmeg, a ring, a coin, and some rock candy, which you bring to the master's presence and present to him so that he may accept and guide you on the path. Each object is symbolic. The white cloth represents your shroud and means that, like a dead body in the hands of its washer, you surrender yourself to God and to the master who represents God, and that henceforth you will consider the master's will as God's and will obey him without question. Representing your head, the nutmeg indicates your consent never to reveal divine secrets or teachings of the path confided to you. The ring represents your commitment to God alone, your assumption of spiritual poverty and letting go of your desire for and attachment to possessions. Rock candy represents rebirth. In offering it to the master, you step into the realm of spirituality and commit yourself to realizing oneness with God.

Next, you make five commitments to the master: obedience to the Islamic Law; compassion toward all creatures; keeping secret the instruction on how to meditate; following without question every order and service enjoined by the master; and self-sacrifice, signified by the meal you prepare for the dervishes. You are now initiated into the Nimatullahi Order (1: 119-125).

A quite different initiation ceremony is practiced by the Khalwatiya Order. As described by Fazlur Rahman, the ceremony begins with the master and the aspirant sitting facing each other so that their knees meet. With his face turned toward the south and hands placed in your hands, the master reads the first verse of the Quran and then says to you three times, "Say with me: 'I seek pardon of God the great.'" This is followed by a recitation of the last two verses of the Quran and the one on giving allegiance to Muhammad. Then the master prays for you, commends you to God, and instructs you to fulfill the obligations of the association and to walk on the right path.

In their similarities and differences, these initiation rites represent the first step in discipleship: entrance into the path and commitment to follow it to the very end.

Surrender

To live according to the path to which you have just been initiated is the next phase on the road to realization. Initiation is a promise and a commitment. As a result it contains everything in symbols. It does not confer enlightenment or liberation. Nor does it confer any power on you, much less the power of the path or the meditation. It is not magic. What it does at most is to dispose you, and give you the tools and techniques, to develop the skills. The most important part of it is your own preparation, the disposition you bring to it and the commitment you make to realize the goal of the path or the meditation. To realize concretely what the symbolism contains, to unpack the meaning of the symbolism in your own life, is the task of the next phase of the training, of the master-disciple relationship.

Like the daily living that follows the wedding ceremony, this is the all-important phase of submitting to the discipline and surrendering to both the path and to the master. Marking the turning point in the master-disciple relationship, surrender is what transforms you from being a student to being a disciple. It is the most important phase of self-transformation which culminates in your becoming an embodiment of the path itself. Hence masters work toward bringing the student to surrendering him/herself. Jesus does this to St. Peter in one of the climactic scenes of the Gospels. The Buddha does it to Ananda, the St. John of Buddhism. Don Juan maneuvers Castaneda to a surrender that culminates in an experience in which his ego explodes and he experiences himself to be a cluster (*skandhas* of Buddhism). What is involved in this surrender?

The answer should be clear from what has been said before. Briefly, it entails disidentification with everything with which you now identify: your self and that which supports and maintains it; and a complete break with the past, with your entire way of life. It is concerned with bringing about a total change in the way you see yourself, others, and the world; in the way you think, feel, and act. It involves a letting go of all attachments to your world and self, and freeing your life from the control of desires, drives, habits, and conditioned reactions. This clears the entire deck and leaves you completely open, with no defenses and nothing to separate your from anything. You are then able to deal directly with things as they are.

The need for this surrender arises from the fact that unless you give up your present way of life, you cannot make progress on the path. For you cannot commit yourself to it and at the same time continue to live and act as you do now, since that would imply that the path does not require any change. It would negate the very thing to which you have committed yourself at initiation. That is why Jesus said, "Anyone who puts his hands on the plough and looks back cannot be my disciple." Don Juan repeatedly tried to impress this point on Castaneda. It is what the *Tao Te Ching* means when it says, "The Way is gained by daily loss" (Blakney 1: 101). Jesus means the same when he says that you must take up your cross and follow him day after day until the separate self is completely left behind. And this is what the desert crossing means in the Sufi story, "The Tale of the Sands." Thus, surrendering is giving up your present way of life and committing yourself to the path of total change. Nothing of the present way of life must remain. It is when you let go of everything that you become identified with the path and make real progress toward your destination.

In relation to the master, surrendering means letting go of your preconceptions, points of view, ideas, judgments, fascinations, expectations and distance; dismantling the entire edifice of defenses, roles and games, and opening yourself completely. When nothing is held back and everything is let go, you arrive at a completely open space of awareness. Since the master abides in that space, a transmission of mind can then take place (Trungpa 2: 23-25).

Transmission of Mind

The third stage of discipleship is the transmission of mind. However, this is understood differently by the various traditions. While Tibetan Buddhism seems to associate transmission with initiation, Zen and other paths take it in the sense of enlightenment.

In the first sense, transmission is empowerment. In it the master communicates to the disciple the power to realize the state of consciousness at which the meditation, to which s/he has just been initiated, aims. In a wider sense, it consists in communicating the power to attain the aim of the path to which s/he has surrendered. Transmission takes place when the teachings and the path, the master and the disciple, are experienced as one. Explaining the process, Trungpa says that all stages of the path, including the transmission ceremony, are part of the process of transmission which creates a situation in which the student can mentally open himself. When the right situation is created by removing mental barriers and the distance between the teacher and the student, "the teacher acts as one entrance and the pupil acts as another, and when both doors are open there is complete Emptiness, a complete Oneness between the two...And there is a moment of silence. That is transmission" (1:33).

In the second sense, transmission takes place when, in enlightenment, All-embracing Awareness, realized by the master as his true Identity, is also experienced by the disciple as his/her Identity. At that point there is no master or disciple. There is only All-embracing Awareness, manifested in each and experienced as such by both. Thereupon the master authenticates the disciple's realization. According to Seung Sahn and Kapleau, this authentication is the transmission of the Buddha-nature (Mitchell 168). Through this transmission, as Tarthang Tulku observes, an entire lineage of past teachers and their understanding are transmitted directly to the disciple.

Such a transmission is also spoken of in other traditions. Thus, according to Idries Shah, Sufism works on this "chain of transmission." There is clear evidence that Jesus' path also worked on this chain of transmission, as he directly communicated his Mind or the Holy Spirit to his disciples by breathing, according to the Fourth Gospel, or at the Pentecost, as described by the *Acts of the Apostles*. The disciples in turn transmitted the Spirit through baptism and the laying on of hands.

The Seal of Approval

As I pointed out in Part III, enlightenment is only a beginning of the journey on the path. It is a sort of graduation. There remains further training, the deepening of enlightenment through the stages until the disciple's realization becomes complete. When that happens, or, not unlike psychotherapy, when the master judges him/her ready, the disciple receives from the master the seal of approval, signifying that s/he, too, is now an enlightened teacher and hence is certified to teach. With that approval, the disciple bids farewell to the master and shoulders the teaching, assuming the task of transmission of the Mind to others, and caring for all beings on the road to liberation.

Part V

Discovering the Way

In an instant rise from time and space.
Set the world aside,
And become a world within yourself.
— Shabistari, *Secret Garden*

Chapter 26
Meditation: The Path of Self-Realization

The overriding question, raised in the last Part but kept in abeyance until now is: Granted what has been said thus far, how do you realize the Self and thus attain liberation? In other words, how does a life open beyond its ordinary, individual, narrow self-preoccupations to the universal truth of all beings, to Being itself, to the truth of its own being? Put differently, how do you realize the Boundless, Unconditioned Reality of your own nature?

Answers to this momentous question make up the fourth essential step of experiential religion. The third step showed the possibility, reality, and nature of liberation, and the utter futility of our attempts to realize it within the present constructions of reality, consciousness, and self. It now remains for the fourth step to show how we can actually realize the Self and thus attain liberation. Constituting the core of experiential religion, this step is the actual journey of awakening and Self-realization to which the other steps are preparatory. And it is what ultimately differentiates experiential religion from conventional religion as well as from other paths similar to it. For experiential religion does not just talk about lofty things, nor does it rest content with faith, an elaborate system of belief, ritual, and organizational structure. Its distinctiveness consists in showing how you can directly experience what is recognized by conventional religion only as a matter of belief (if it is recognized at all). Experiential religion, on the other hand, is nothing, if not practical; and its fourth step is the most practical of all as it sets out the steps toward the realization of that Reality which is the goal of every human life.

As discussed in Part IV, according to experiential religion, there are essentially two ways in which the Unconditioned can reveal itself in our life: spontaneously and as a result of our actively opening ourselves to it.

For reasons already discussed in Part IV, since spontaneous revelation usually remains closed to ordinary lives, the path of deliberate, active opening is the primary avenue to Self-realization available for our time. This requires a sustained, conscious application of systematic pressures to break free of structures, mental obstacles and limits, and socio-cultural and individual life conditions. When the mind is actively brought to a still point, it is able to leap over its limit-barriers into the abyss of the Unknown, which then reveals itself as our very Self. This active opening is the way of meditation.

Although meditation has existed for perhaps over 4000 years or more, it has not won a large following, even in the East, where it appears to have originated. Why not? Why do human beings avoid what they most need in order to be truly themselves and realize their destiny?

The reasons are both socio-cultural and individual, inner as well as outer. For one thing, as the Sufis put it, humans do not know what is ultimately good for them. As Jesus said, unawareness of our unawareness prevents us from seeing the truth of our condition and, instead, makes us believe that it represents our nature. As we identify with and become attached to our condition, we become unaware of what will ultimately resolve our problems and seek to satisfy our immediate needs and desires, pursuing things which we consider good but which cannot help us in the long run. Unawareness makes us seek instant cures and magical solutions. Since we are programmed to avoid pain and seek pleasure, we tend to avoid anything that appears difficult, painful, or requires a great deal of effort; we deny its value or usefulness in our life, and then seek substitute gratifications and proceed to defend our inclinations and rationalize our behavior. So, when the way of meditation says that there is no instant nirvana, when we have to work hard on ourselves to bring about a permanent self-transformation, which is a difficult and long-range affair, it loses its appeal to us.

Furthermore, there is the fear of the unknown, the unfamiliar, which makes people cling to their situation more tightly as it becomes more empty. No small difficulty comes from the fear of facing ourselves: "Suppose I discover that I have been living a futile, empty, meaningless life; or that my life is full of illusions and I have been deceiving myself all along; or that I am phoney and hate myself. Better not open up a can of worms I cannot handle, or I will completely lose control and fall apart. Better let buried things stay buried. Let's not open up old wounds," we say and slink back to the familiar.

Moreover, people do not want total change; they want to change only those aspects that will make the system work better. Anything that advocates such a change is avoided personally, ignored or derided socially, and, when it poses a threat to the social system itself, is actively, even violently, opposed. Since the path demands a complete disidentification with everything, from within there is a tremendous resistance on the part of ego, which does not want to let go of itself and its world. It resists all change that threatens its security or survival. Since the path requires a transcendence of ego, fear of extinction makes ego resist or avoid it. Furthermore, since all of us seek confirmation of our identity and self-worth through others' acceptance, recognition or approval, when we do not get it we become afraid, depressed, or dejected at this frightening possibility and avoid the path of meditation.

Difficulties arising from people's conditioning are too numerous to mention. Once programmed to something, we become attached to it, tend to remain within its parameters, and seldom venture beyond it. When the path says that we must break free of programming altogether, we judge it impossible, too difficult, or unrealistic. We do not believe that anyone could be so completely free. Fear of losing our individuality and the massive weight of our programming keep us in line and make us trudge along our accustomed ways, believing them to be the only way that we can be ourselves.

The difficulties posed by society are almost overwhelming. Since every social system maintains itself by programming its members and having them confirm its reality-construct, if, instead of confirming, a significant number begins to follow a path that leads to questioning and abandoning it, society fights with all its might through indifference, ridicule, denunciation, threat, or outright persecution in order to discredit the path and make the members conform. At first society may spread doubt about the validity or usefulness of the path. It may pressure the individual to conform and not be weird, different, or question the meaningfulness or validity of social constructs. It may emphasize how such a pursuit is a waste of time and constitutes withdrawal from or avoidance of social or parental obligations. It may caution you that if you follow the path, you will not be able to function in the world, get ahead or succeed, or that the world will take advantage, manipulate, hurt, step on, or crush you. It may label the path illusory, fantastic, strange, or unrealistic. Even if there is no opposition from family or friends, it will become increasingly difficult for you to continue being on your own. The sheer weight and pull of society's operative structure will put doubts in the mind of a lone individual attempting to follow an altogether different vision. The weight of reality will begin to shift more and more to the side of society, and you will begin to see things according to its way; then the path may appear impractical, unworkable, or impossible.

Moreover, society neither knows of the existence of stages and states beyond the personal nor believes, when told, that they could be optimal, more functional, or a desirable way of living. Nor does it have a framework for its members to realize them. Taking ordinary consciousness to be optimal and the norm for judging the validity of all others, it usually interprets any claim of higher states to be dysfunctional, harmful, regressive, or degenerative, and thus suspect and to be avoided. Taking the separate self to be the highest stage of human development and thus the highest value, it becomes afraid and resists any talk of development beyond the personal as that would imply a dissolution of individuality and personality.

Lacking any transcendental framework, society is unable to provide any framework, structure, or method for transpersonal levels of development, or any confirmation, support, or legitimization of such a quest. As a result, anyone who embarks on it is left to him/herself. The vision of a lone individual on an isolated path can prompt a prospective seeker to give up his/her quest before setting out on the journey or making any progress.

Only those who do not listen to the voices clamoring from both within and without can keep on an even keel and continue on the path. Unless you are able to overcome such initial difficulties, you will be unable to seriously follow the Way. Only when you see the uselessness of all other ways and the futility of staying on your present course will the Way come to life for you. Then there will be no more hesitation to embark on it by choosing one of the paths, following the guidelines I have outlined in Part IV.

In this Part I shall first discuss the nature and forms of meditation and then present a generalized picture of formal meditation. I shall leave the task of describing individual paths of formal meditation to another volume.

Chapter 27
The Nature, Aims and Forms of Meditation

The Nature and Aims of Meditation

The term *meditation* is currently in vogue in the West. Over the past two decades, an influx of teachers from the East has made it a familiar, if not a household, word. Yet these teachers of diverse methods, each claiming to have the only true or effective path, have often created confusion about the nature and goals of meditation. The general bewilderment many people feel about the subject is compounded by the fact that teachers representing various traditions and methods use the same terms with different meanings. Moreover, the meanings of words may vary from East to West and according to the specific context of their use. To avoid such pitfalls, I shall approach this discussion on the nature of meditation in terms of its aims.

Although there may be as many reasons to meditate as there are meditators, there appears to be a direct correlation between the intentions of meditators and the three levels of the meditative path: the physiological level, the psychological level, and the spiritual level. Most definitions of meditation include one or more of these levels.

The Physiological Level

Many people begin to practice meditation merely as a technique for relaxation. In a high-pressure, technological society, meditation has become a means of obtaining various physiological benefits. Newspapers frequently report that management training centers are teaching meditative techniques for relaxation and stress reduction. As Daniel Goleman reports, many psychotherapists use it as a method "for patients to manage anxiety without drugs" (1: 169). He says that in 1984 the National Institute of Health issued a report that recommended meditation "above prescription drugs in the first treatment of mild hypertension" (1: 168). Many medical centers throughout the country are undertaking meditation research and teaching patients how to relax in order to reduce stress, tension, and anxiety. Goleman observes that the evidence for the effectiveness of meditation, through relaxation, in treating stress disorders has become compelling (1: 169).

In addition, by inducing relaxation, meditation has been found to lower blood pressure and cholesterol levels, improve blood flow to the heart, and increase circulation. Thus it can help prevent heart disease and stroke.

Research has shown that meditation and relaxation can strengthen the immune system by improving the levels of natural killer cells and antibody titers, warding off disease, making people less susceptible to viruses, and helping patients with their own healing (Goleman 1: 170-171). Attempting to explain this improvement of the immune system, researchers in a new discipline, called psychoneuroimmunology (PNI), have stated, as reported by Rob Wechsler, that "the brain can send signals along nerves to enhance defenses against infection and pump out chemicals that make the body fight more aggressively against disease. And since the pathways can be turned on and off by thoughts and emotions... mental states can alter the course of an illness" (52). Thus the brain and the immune system make a closed circuit and work through feeding and feedback (52-61).

In many cases of diabetes, relaxation has been shown to improve the body's ability to regulate glucose. By reducing emotional upsets and constriction of air passages, meditation also seems to relieve asthma. It can lessen the severity of angina attacks and alleviate chronic, severe pain, migraine headaches, muscular aches and pains, gastrointestinal problems, insomnia, emphysema, and skin disorders (Goleman 1: 168-171). In addition, meditation can cure psychosomatic illnesses, reduce various mental and physical malfunctioning, and increase energy and efficiency in everyday living.

As a result of the demonstrated effectiveness of meditative practice, many people have concluded that meditation is primarily a powerful relaxation technique. As impressive as the stress reduction results are (and each day an increasing number is being reported in medical journals and other periodicals), we must not likewise conclude that meditation is merely a method of achieving physiological benefits. Traditionally, such benefits have been perceived as consequences of meditation, not as goals. In the words of Roger Walsh, the goals of meditation are: to become "conscious of and familiar with our inner life;" to develop "deep insight into the nature of mental processes, consciousness, identity, and reality;" to attain "optimal states of psychological well-being and consciousness;" and, ultimately, to reach "the source of life and consciousness" (1: 18-19).

Thus meditation is ultimately concerned with bringing about a state of being that not only frees the mind from all existing programming but also does not give rise to new programming. The ultimate state realized in meditation is a state beyond ordinary consciousness. As consciousness is formed by and functions through programming, construct, content, object, or thought, and reacts to stimuli, it is subject to disturbance. Only what is programmed and reacts accordingly can be disturbed. Where there is no programming or content and no functioning through any medium, nothing can be a source of disturbance. Since only a state beyond programming can free the mind of programming, traditionally meditation has sought to bring the mind to the state beyond conditioning (to the "source of life and consciousness," as Walsh put it). The following Zen story illustrates how one can be relaxed at all times and under all circumstances in this state:

> Buddha told a parable in a Sutra: A man travelling across a field encountered a tiger. He fled, the tiger after him. Coming to a precipice, he caught hold of a wild vine and swung himself down over the edge. The tiger sniffed at him from above. Trembling, the man looked down to where, far below, another tiger was waiting to eat him. Only the vine sustained him. Two mice, one white and one black, little by little started to gnaw away the vine. The man saw a luscious strawberry near him. Grasping the vine with one hand, he plucked the strawberry with the other. How sweet it tasted. (Reps 22-23)

The Psychological Level

To arrive at such a state of continuous mental relaxation in which no external event can trigger panic, anxiety, tension, or stress is the goal of the second level of meditation. Additionally, this level is concerned with letting go of control, striving, and the effort to maintain and enhance yourself and your world, which frees you to live continuously in the open space of pure awareness and free being.

This state is not easily arrived at. Suppose you enter an elevator and a woman steps on your toe, cutting a nice slice of skin with the sharp spike of her heel. Do you feel relaxed? Do you smile and thank her for stepping on your toe? Or suppose you have an important job interview, and you are at the station waiting for the train. The station master announces that the train will be delayed an hour, and you cannot get to a phone because they are all tied up. Are you relaxed? If you have just been fired, if your son has just wrecked your car, if your wife has just announced that she is leaving you, do you feel very relaxed?

You may begin a meditation practice in order to relax, and you may feel tranquil during meditation. But as you enter your round of daily activities, you soon discover that your negative programming pulls you out of your relaxed, alert state and plunges you back into a whirlpool of anger, fear, frustration, stress, tension, or anxiety. You realize that in order to remain in relaxed awareness, you need to develop a discipline to keep your awareness free of entrapment in negative programs that create mental turmoil and emotional roller coasters. The development of such a discipline is the task of the second level of meditation. The first-level goal of relaxation is not enough. You must move beyond the physiological to the psychological level so you can free your mind of all programs that trap awareness and fill your world with tension.

At this level you begin by facing yourself and seeing yourself as you actually are. You discover that your mind is constructed with systems of programming, hemming you in, restricting you in every direction, and depriving you of a direct contact with anything. It dawns on you that your task is to free the mind of this programming by dissolving old fixations and habits, removing limits and distortions caused by dualistic constructs, clearing emotional blockages, and freeing awareness from entrapment in thoughts, objects, and mental contents. Eventually you realize that, since your consciousness is constructed of programs, unless it is completely deconstructed your awareness cannot become fully free. Working on this task enables your attention to stop darting habitually in different directions and to gather and unify around the object of meditation. This allows awareness to begin to expand, eventually transcending the personal stage and venturing out into the transpersonal, spiritual realm. It is at this second, psychological level, that you begin the process of deconstructing and transforming your consciousness, identity, and reality.

These essential tasks of the second level are clearly reflected in many discussions of meditation. For example, Tarthang Tulku has said, "Meditation is the process of self-discovery. On one level the meditation experience shows us the pattern of our lives—how we have carried on our emotional characteristics since childhood. But on another level it frees us from these patterns, making it easier for us to see our inner potential" (1: 97). Thus Tulku clearly recognizes not only the first step of the psychological level, i.e., facing yourself and seeing how your mind has been programmed; but also the second step, i.e., freeing your mind of programming and contents.

Chogyam Trungpa has observed, "Meditation is not a matter of trying to achieve ecstasy, spiritual bliss or tranquility, nor is it attempting to become a better person. It is simply the creation of a space in which we are able to expose and undo our neurotic games, our self-deceptions, our hidden fears and hopes" (4: 2). And Claudio Naranjo has defined meditation as "a persistent effort to detect and become free of all conditioning, compulsive functioning of mind and body, habitual emotional responses that may contaminate the utterly simple situation required by the participant" (Naranjo & Ornstein 9).

The process of becoming free starts with noticing and identifying your programmings. Ordinarily, they not only go unnoticed, remaining beyond your control, but they even control ordinary consciousness. Once you detect and bring them to consciousness, the next step is to become free by dissolving the negative programs and by removing the programs that limit the positive qualities. In this way meditation helps clear the mind of the fixations, distortions, filters, selective attention, limitations, and interpretations that consciousness habitually imposes on things. Void of this imposition, we can directly experience and deal with each situation without interference from conditioning. Arthur Deikman calls this destructuring process "deautomatization" and says that the very nature of meditation involves "an undoing of a psychic structure, permitting the experience of increased detail and sensation at the price of requiring more attention" (In Ornstein 2: 229).

Whereas habituation makes us unaware, deautomatization destructures consciousness and frees awareness by dissolving conditioning and habituation. To the extent that consciousness is deautomatized, awareness becomes free, to be invested in whatever is at hand. You start to see things clearly and directly; you notice what is going on in and around you.

Perceiving the centrality of the destructuring process, Robert Ornstein defines meditation as "a set of techniques designed to produce an alteration in consciousness by shifting attention away from the active, object-oriented, linear mode toward the receptive mode, and often, from an external focus of attention to an internal one" (1: 158). When understood not as a regression to the prepersonal stage but as a transcendence of the personal, this destructuring is characteristic not only of the second level of meditation, but also of all its phases. Without deconstruction, neither the continuous state of relaxation, nor freedom from negative programming and enhancement of positive states, nor attainment of higher states, nor realization of the ultimate goal of meditation is possible. So long as the mind remains fixated and operates from fixations, it will maintain the present construction, experience separation from Reality, and prevent the emergence of transpersonal states. Thus deconstruction constitutes the very heart of the second level and is the key to meditation as a whole.

Essential to this deconstruction is a reversal of the process by which ordinary consciousness is constructed, reinforced, and maintained. And essential to the reversal are disidentification with and nonattachment to external objects and mental contents. Disidentification and nonattachment are thus essential to transcendence of the personal and realization of the transpersonal states. Indeed, they are so central that meditation can be said to consist of their sustained and continuous practice until complete transcendence of all constructs, contents, and programs has been attained. At the point of complete nonattachment, you realize your identity with Reality as Such.

A recognition of this essential point has led Ken Wilber to say that meditation is nothing but a "sustained instrumental path of transcendence. And since transcendence and development are synonymous, it follows that meditation is simply *sustained development* or growth" (3: 93-99; 5: 103-117; italics his). And for Wilber, differentiation or disidentification is the principle by which an individual grows through the successive stages, from prepersonal to transpersonal, until s/he reaches the ultimate state of Consciousness as Such, which is the final goal of meditation.

Outside the period of formal meditation, in the daily activities of life, the process of deconstruction occurs through the continuous practice of disidentification and nonattachment, especially toward objects of identification, attachment, and desire. Such practice enables you to break free of fixations resulting from habitual ways of thinking, feeling, and acting. As you break free, your scattered attention becomes unified and present-centered, and awareness begins to expand and overcome its distance from things.

During the period of formal meditation itself, consciousness is deconstructed by shifting its orientation from the outside world inward, toward itself. This shift is achieved by stopping its usual mode of functioning. This cessation requires the essential step of cutting off the operations by which consciousness reinforces and maintains itself. The entire mechanism that reinforces and maintains consciousness is deactivated by cutting off external sensory stimuli and internal dialogue, and by keeping attention focused directly on the object of meditation or on the sensory stimuli or mental contents.

Ordinarily, consciousness keeps its attention focused on sensory stimuli, which prompts it to constantly scan the environment, darting from one object to another in order to stabilize and maintain itself and its separation from the world. Moreover, as we have seen, in being focused on the world, attention invariably becomes fixated, trapped, and lost. Unless the external orientation is reversed and attention is directed toward itself, toward its root and source, even a single object to which it is tied will maintain the existing constructions of reality, consciousness, and self, and prevent the emergence of higher states. One aim of keeping attention focused on the meditation object is to stop outside stimuli from reinforcing consciousness by triggering thoughts and the information-processing activities.

In addition, consciousness maintains itself and its separation from the world by triggering an incessant flow of thoughts and keeping a running commentary on everything, creating an illusion of continuity, identity, and permanence. Without stopping thoughts, programmed reactions, and the internal dialogue, the ordinary construction of consciousness will continue to be reinforced, and the crucial shift necessary for deconstruction and transcendence will be prevented. Moreover, so long as thoughts persist, attention will also remain trapped in dualistic thinking, and the shift will not occur.

In order to achieve the external and the internal shift, then, it is absolutely crucial that you keep your attention riveted directly on the primary stimulus or the first moment of impact of the meditation object and directly experience it prior to the triggering of thoughts, mental reactions, or any information-processing activities. When you are able to sustain the focus of attention for prolonged periods of time without letting your attention wander or without becoming lost in thought, the siege of the object-world upon your consciousness will begin to lift and your orientation will start to shift. As nothing intervenes at the point of immediate contact between the primary stimulus and attention, nothing will remain to reinforce or maintain the existing construction of consciousness. As a result, the latter will begin to lose its hold and awareness will begin to unify and transcend the ordinary constructions and rise to the transconscious states.

This inward shift and deconstruction, which will be explained later, proceeds from the outer to the inner, from the surface structure to the deep, inward structure, from the gross, perceptual to the symbolic, conceptual, or generalized structure. This deconstruction process is largely a reversal of the construction process. At each step of the shift, your attention breaks through yet another restriction, arriving at a more expanded and encompassing structure. A corresponding bridging of the distance between consciousness and reality also occurs. As all structures and forms become deconstructed and transcended, the separation between consciousness and reality disappears. Stopping or transcending thought is, therefore, essential to this inward turn. As Lama Govinda has observed, "In order to get to the hub of existence, into the center of our being, we must reverse the direction of our mental outlook and turn inward. This turning about in the depth of our consciousness is called *paravritti,* and is the main purpose of meditation" (2:106).

It follows that meditation cannot be equated with thinking, which can only trap awareness and reinforce the present construction. It cannot liberate the mind from itself. There is, however, a difference on this point between Eastern and Western approaches to meditation. In the West, particularly in the Catholic tradition, meditation is regarded as a discursive, sustained thought or a reflective inquiry into a subject. As a result, this tradition considers meditation as a stage preliminary to the more advanced stage of contemplation. In the East, on the other hand, essential to meditation is cutting through discursive thought and arriving at the state of awareness beyond thought. So in the East meditation is an advanced practice.

These differences arise from different goals. The East regards the ultimate aim of meditation to be a realization of the Unconditioned State. This state can be reached only by going beyond duality and discursive thought, which maintains duality. Thus the East defines meditation as a stage beyond thought. Working within the dualistic framework, however, the West does not consider discursive thought a hindrance to reaching the final goal of meditation. For the West this goal is not generally considered a realization of *identity* with God but a state of permanent *union* with "him." So the West is not adverse to viewing meditation in terms of thinking.

Nevertheless, meditation does not consist in thinking or trying not to think. Even in Christian meditation, at the advanced stage of infused contemplation, thinking falls away. The contemplative simply rests in a state of loving awareness of God's presence. So central is the need to stop thought that the ancient Indian sage Patanjali defined meditation as *chitta vritti nirodha,* that is, stopping mind-waves or deconstruction of the programmed mind(Prabhavananda and Isherwood 2: 11). The reason is that in order to bring about a complete shift in the orientation of consciousness—from the object-world toward itself—it is necessary to stop the entire range of its activities. Both the discursive thinking on the conscious level and the constant churning of the unconscious, which produces the thoughts, must cease, which will result in deconstruction.

Essentially agreeing with Patanjali, from the perspective of shamanism, Carlos Castaneda's don Juan says that stopping the internal dialogue is the key to transcending our view of the world, for the dialogue perpetuates that view and prevents transcendence. Unless attention turns away from the active face and its view of the world, its receptive face cannot be directed toward Reality. When the dialogue stops, the orientation of consciousness shifts as it pivots around and "faces" itself. As it pivots on itself, as Chuang Tzu intimated, the mind becomes empty, silent, and still; it sheds its identification with objects and consequent limitations and conditions; it experiences itself purely as itself. This process is like closing the door on the active and opening it to the receptive mode of the Janus-faced mind, with the shifts or pivoting taking place at critical junctures. Each one of these shifts consists of deconstructing a layer of programming until all layers are transcended.

In meditation, the mind is like a swinging door, swinging from doing, striving, and grasping to letting go and just Being. In this way, it transcends its fixation on things, on the limits of the objective mode, and becomes pure, limitless Awareness without contents or objects. This shift of the mind toward its essential nature is the essence of the inward turn, which is at the same time its turning directly toward Reality.

This shift from the active to the receptive mode seems to create a paradoxical situation for meditation. As Rajneesh states, "Meditation is always passive; the very essence of it is passive. It cannot be active because the very nature of it is non-doing. If you are doing something, your very doing disturbs the whole thing" (1: 16). Christian infused contemplation is likewise purely passive, as it depends solely on the action of God or All-embracing Awareness. This is true also of the advanced stages of other paths. And yet in meditation you are told to *do* something: to count or follow or observe the breath, to concentrate on an internal or external object, to chant or silently repeat a mantra, to visualize a *mandala*, to whirl *(dhikr)*, and so on. Is this not contradictory? How can you arrive at a state in which there is nowhere to go or nothing to do or to achieve—which means that there is really no arriving or going anywhere—by trying to get there? How can you arrive at not-doing *(wu wei)* by doing?

This seeming paradox can be explained by noting that meditation is an active way of deactivating the mind, of making it totally still, void of doing, so that it can purely BE. In this state there is no activity in the mind that is distinct from its being, so that doing becomes a manifestation of what is. In other words, the aim of meditation is to bring the mind to a state in which its being is its doing, and in which doing is nothing other than pure Awareness, identical with Reality as Such.

However, since our consciousness is so programmed to act, since it has been on automatic pilot for so long, it cannot simply cease doing, striving, controlling, managing, and fixing things; it cannot purely BE. Even its attempts to stop itself are expressions of striving; you cannot just take out the key of a car that has been running and make it stop instantly. As Rajneesh points out, if you have been continuously in an active mode, you cannot instantaneously stop and be nonactive (1: 18-22). If you could at will instantly stop your mind dead in its tracks, open it completely to itself, and directly experience what is, meditation would not be necessary. Since you cannot do that, at the initial phase of meditation your mind is given something to occupy itself with, to play its own game. But the nature of this activity is to undo the action mode by bringing it to a point at which all its activities cease and it becomes silent and still. This process uses doing to stop doing, arriving at not-doing through doing. The nature and aim of all meditative techniques is to use the same process by which the mind becomes programmed and fixated, and awareness trapped and lost, to unhook itself from all contents and objects, to destructure consciousness, and to arrive at absolutely free Awareness and Being.

The way the mind unhooks is by keeping its attention focused directly on the meditation object, not to create another programming, but to break free of automatic or programmed responses, habituation, and unawareness altogether. It is for this reason that you are instructed to hold your attention on the level of the primary stimulus before anything arises in the mind. This will bring the action mode to an impasse, and eventually it will cease its operation. Like a car without fuel, a mind without stimuli will stop running; its thoughts will subside, and its awareness will correspondingly increases, becoming free of conditioning and constructs. *The Lankavatara Sutra* describes this pivotal shift and deconstruction as a turning about in the deepest seat of consciousness, whereby awareness disengages from every content, object, construct, and conditioned state. Like the transformation of the caterpillar into a butterfly, this metamorphosis brings a transcendence of consciousness, and what emerges is pure, All-embracing Awareness. You cannot actively strive for or realize this transformation through any programming or construct (in fact by any means whatsoever), for it is the realm of the Unconditioned to which nothing conditioned has access.

You can see now why meditation is said to be a path without a goal, for the path *is* the goal. Because the programmed mind is tethered to obtaining results and pursuing goals, we seldom do anything except for the sake of some extrinsic reward that endows our action with value. Since a goal implies duality, a separation from what we desire, and striving only maintains it, all goal-oriented activities reinforce ordinary consciousness. As the ultimate aim of meditation is to deconstruct this consciousness and to arrive at the state beyond all duality or separation, it cannot have a goal external to itself. That is why the core of meditation does not consist in attaining any goal, but in erasing the separation from Reality created by our dualistic, goal-seeking activities. Meditation peels off all artificiality, removing all additives and preservatives deposited on us through years of conditioning, socialization, and training so that we can arrive at our natural, spontaneous, pure Self or nature.

The Spiritual Level

To arrive at this true nature or Self is the aim of the third or spiritual level of meditation. An intensification of the final phase of the psychological level naturally leads you to this third level. As attention stays focused on the meditation object for prolonged periods, awareness becomes unified; it penetrates and becomes one with the object, and, as it reverses its orientation and faces its ultimate nature, it becomes free of thought and the object-world. Thus it finally comes to experience its true nature in enlightenment.

While the second level of awakening, integration, unification, and expansion through the personal stage is concerned primarily with psychological growth, the third, spiritual, level involves growth through the transpersonal stages. While the initial steps of the second level have affinities with various psychologies and psychotherapies, at the third level these affinities are left behind. The cleaning out of negative programs, habits, and psychic debris, and karmic residue continues, however. The third level is the spirit's return journey to itself, which requires a transcendence of every barrier, limitation, and condition until only pure, Unconditioned Spirit remains as the identity of all that is.

Recognizing this ultimate aim, many experts define meditation as the path toward a realization of the Spirit, the Self, God, or Reality as Such. The classical yogas, Buddhism, Taoism, Kabbalah, Christian mysticism, Sufism, and many of their offshoots embrace this definition. As Swami Muktananda has stated, "We do not meditate to relax a little and experience some peace. We meditate to unfold our inner being...Through meditation, our inner awareness expands and our understanding of inner and outer things becomes steadily deeper...Ultimately, meditation makes us aware of our own true nature. It is this awareness which removes all suffering and delusion, and this awareness comes when we see face to face our own inner Self" (20-24).

Buddhism calls this ultimate goal a realization of *Nirvana* or Buddha-nature. As Yasutani Roshi states in the context of Zen, the highest aim of Zen meditation is "the actualization of the Supreme Way throughout our entire being and in our daily life" (Kapleau 1: 48). The aim of Taoist meditation is returning to the Source, Tao, and realizing one's oneness with it. And in the traditions of Jewish, Christian and Islamic mysticism, the ultimate aim of meditation or contemplation is union with God. Sheikh Javad Nurbakhsh may well speak on behalf of all three Western traditions when he states:

> Meditation is one of the basic conditions for the attainment of voluntary death which is the aim of the Spiritual Path. As a result of meditation, the Sufi gradually becomes estranged from the world of 'I' and 'you.' He loses even the sense of meditation with its lingering quality of duality, God causing him to die to himself and bringing him to life in Himself. (1: 80-81)

In order to realize this voluntary death, you have to transcend the personal and successively pass through the transpersonal stages. On this spiritual path awareness steadily sheds conditioning, constructs, and limitations, expanding to include more reality in its sweep while at the same time overcoming its separation from Reality.

One of the most cogent characterizations of the transpersonal stages is that of Ken Wilber. According to him, the first of these stages is the psychic, which operates beyond the ordinary causal mode, in terms of what Jung called "synchronicity." It is more intuitive, holistic, integral, inclusive, and panoramic than previous stages. Beyond the psychic is what Wilber calls the subtle level, which is characterized by the experience of union with the object of meditation, deity, or the universe. The apex of the subtle stage is union with the personal God or God-as-object. The Transcendent Other is now experienced as the immanent presence at the highest point or the deepest level of one's psyche or spirit — the archetypal self. Beyond the subtle is the causal, which is marked by the experience of identity with the Godhead or Reality as Such (6: 27-31). To be permanently established in this state and to live and act from it is the final goal of meditation.

As we have previously said, there is a difference between dualist and nondualist traditions on the final goal of the meditative path. Believing Ultimate Reality to be dualistic, traditions that conceive God as a Personal Being regard the final stage of the path as a state of permanent union between God and the individual. These dualistic traditions often describe this union in terms of the relationship between lover and beloved. On the other hand, experiencing God or Ultimate Reality to be transpersonal (and thus nondualistic), nondualist traditions, such as Vedanta Hinduism, Buddhism, and Taoism (as well as many individuals within the dualist traditions), proclaim the final goal of meditation to be identity with Ultimate Reality. In this view, meditation is essentially a process of waking up from a dream — that you are separate from all things and God — and experiencing yourself as that which IS, absolutely and unconditionally. To arrive at this identity as your permanent state is the end of the path and the goal of human existence.

Which of these views represents the final goal of meditation, the final stage of the path, the ultimate state of things?

If we follow the dualist tradition, the answer is clear: Union with God is the ultimate goal of the path. As personal God is the highest or the only form of God, so the highest relationship with "him" is the final end of the path. The claim of identity is either a sacrilege or a regression to the prepersonal stage.

Another viewpoint, that of Lawrence LeShan and others, holds that such ultimate questions pertain to models or systems of reality. Since these systems are relative to each other and our statements about them are made from within a model or system, it is impossible to stand outside all systems and adjudicate their relative truth, validity, adequacy, or finality. Since both dualism and nondualism represent alternate versions of reality, it is not possible to stand outside them and decide which is the ultimate, for any such standpoint would be another version of reality, not a neutral or transcendent ground. For LeShan, all versions are relative to one another and have equal status. Each is ultimate within its own construct. Each does something well while falling short in other respects. None is wholly useful in all matters (LeShan 2: 1-84). So all you can do is to decide pragmatically which one is ultimate for you.

According to a third view, advocated by Ken Wilber, Bernadette Roberts and others, union with God is on the relative plane, whereas identity with God represents the absolute beyond the relativity of planes and states. Thus union with God cannot be the ultimate end of the path; it must rest with identity. As Ken Wilber explains, while communion with God takes place on the subtle plane, which is the stage of "saintly religion," identity with the Godhead is experienced at the causal level, which is the stage of "sagely religion." In this state consciousness reaches Ultimate Reality as it completely transcends all relative planes and totally awakens in its original state of Consciousness as Such. In this state, "saintly communion with Spirit is transcended by sagely identity with Spirit," as "saintly revelation of God as Absolute Other is transcended by sagely revelation of God as radical and transcendental Consciousness as Such." This is the Ultimate Ground and goal of all things and of the meditative path where reigns, "asymptotic to infinity, the absolute identity of Consciousness as Such with all its manifestations" (6:33).

Which of these points of view signifies the ultimate truth? If we follow the first, the answer is clear. On the basis of the second, we cannot answer this question. Since each claim is a point of view, each is relative. So no point of view can represent the ultimate truth. Now, if nonduality is a model of reality alongside duality, then LeShan's conclusion is inescapable. There is no way that you can stand outside either view to decide which is the ultimate. However, the claim of nonduality is that it is not a model of reality, point of view, or a conceptual scheme of any kind but is a term that connotes a transcendence of all models, concepts, constructs, and frameworks, and a direct experience of reality in its Unconditioned State. As long as anything operates within a framework or construct, through models or concepts, or from a point of view, which is the case with dualism, it is on the relative plane. But if a state or experience is beyond them all, so that it cannot take place through anything but is itself the Unconditioned, then it cannot be placed alongside or be equated with relative viewpoints. As nonduality signifies this experience, it must represent the ultimate truth and the final goal of the meditative path.

Kinds of Meditation

In the broadest sense, meditation may be said to be of two kinds: spontaneous and intentional. The former is experienced when the mind suddenly stops its usual internal chatter and preoccupations with things past and future and becomes open to experiencing what is, here and now. At such moments, the distance between you and the object, be it a starry sky, a flower, a sunset, or the stillness of a forest at dawn, is lost and you experience yourself to be one with it.

Intentional meditation itself can be broadly divided into formal and informal meditation. The former requires a specific time, place, and method, while the latter does not require a special setting but can be practiced anywhere and at any time, its context being the daily activities of life.

Formal meditation itself can be divided in several ways. One is in terms of methods, such as various types of meditation based on breathing or mantra repetition. Other common types are: meditation based on sound, either chanted aloud or silently listened to; visualization; movement; focusing attention on or observing various senses or parts of the body; observation of sensations or mental contents; and various permutations or combinations of several of these types of meditation.

Others, such as Ornstein, divide formal meditation into two types: concentrative and awareness or insight. He defines the first as "an attempt to restrict awareness to a single, unchanging source of stimulation for a definite period of time" (1: 160). It involves shutting down awareness by keeping attention focused only on the object of meditation to the exclusion of all else. As attention is focused on one object, it stops its usual flitting about from one thing to another, becoming unified around the object.

Ornstein defines the second type as an attempt to open up awareness to what is, here and now, by investing attention in the ongoing stream and content of consciousness and watching it (1: 176-177). This type of meditation can be practiced either in a formal setting, as is done in Buddhism and other traditions, or carried out informally in the midst of daily activities and experiences. In the case of the latter, positive and negative programmed reactions and the ongoing flux of moment-to-moment experiences can serve as the focus of attention and observation. In formal meditation, as in *vipassana* or insight meditation, you are simply and directly aware of your bodily sensations, feelings, and mental processes and contents, cutting through their programmed configurations and attempting to arrive at a direct experience of what is. In informal meditation, on the other hand, attention is focused directly on programmed reactions so as to break free of them and arrive at a moment-to-moment awakening to what is.

Although this distinction is important, these two types of meditation are not mutually exclusive. Most fully developed paths of meditation employ both concentrative and insight meditation to arrive at enlightenment. Thus, Patanjali's *Yoga Sutras,* which is usually categorized as concentrative meditation, acknowledges and employs insight at advanced stages. This fact is also true of meditative methods in other traditions. On the other hand, paths that are considered primarily awareness meditation, such as *jnana* yoga, *vipassana,* and Zen, employ concentrative exercises at an early stage. It appears that both types are necessary to attain enlightenment. As Achaan Chah has pointed out: "Meditation is like a single log of wood. Insight and investigation is one end of the log; calm and concentration is the other end." Like a light and its switch, the two go together: "To concentrate the mind is like turning on the switch, and wisdom is the resulting light. Without the switch, there is no light. Concentration must be firmly established for wisdom to arise" (15, 90).

In the following chapter, I shall provide a generalized description of formal meditation. I shall leave a description of various meditative paths found in Hinduism, Buddhism, Taoism, Judaism, Christianity, and Islam to the companion volume.

Chapter 28
The Process of Formal Meditation

Preliminary Stages

Although each type of meditation has its own sequence, method, experiences, mental terrain, and order of progression, nevertheless a careful examination reveals a basic unity of fundamental structures and stages across meditative traditions. Such a unity strongly supports an attempt to present a generalized picture of the meditative path. Accordingly, in this chapter I shall sketch an outline of formal meditation based on this basic unity. The structures and experiences peculiar to each path or tradition will be treated in a separate volume.

In many traditions, the formal meditative path begins with the experience of what is called "conversion." It is the first step in self-awareness, in which you come to see your condition as it actually is. You see the insufficiency of your present form of life, the futility of continuing your present course, and the need for a fundamental change. Then you make a decision to enter a spiritual path to bring about self-transformation. Al-Ghazali vividly portrays his own experience of conversion to the Sufi path in the following words:

> I looked on myself as I then was. Worldly interests encompassed me on every side. Even my work as a teacher—the best thing I was engaged in—seemed unimportant and useless in view of the life hereafter... I realized I stood on the edge of a precipice and would fall into hell-fire unless I set about to mend my ways... Conscious of my helplessness and having surrendered my will entirely, I took refuge with God as a man in sore trouble who has no recourse left. God answered

my prayers and made it easy for me to turn my back on reputation and wealth and wife and children and friends. (Arberry 1:80)

This passage clearly shows that the first preliminary steps begin with awareness of and dissatisfaction with his present condition; the need to break free of its repetitive, meaningless patterns; and the decision to do so. Other paths post a similar need. Jesus issued a call to repentance. And, following him, the Eastern Orthodox Church, according to John Chirban (Wilber, Engler & Brown 298), regards conversion, or conscious commitment to a path, as the beginning of the journey. Eastern traditions emphasize similar steps in choosing a path.

The Stage of Purification

Once you make your choice and formally enter a path, the next step begins with ethical and body-mind training. The aim of ethical practice is not merely to do good and avoid evil, but to bring about a thoroughgoing inner and outer change. Concerned with the life setting of the meditator, these injunctions are designed, together with other meditative practices, in the words of Roger Walsh, to bring about "a shift in attitudes, thought, speech, and behavior aimed at the deepest possible transformation of mind, awareness, identity, lifestyle, and relationship to the world" (1: 29).

One of the body-mind trainings involves Informal Awareness Meditation (IAM). Almost every tradition of formal meditation enjoins some form of IAM to enable students to break free of their negative programmings and habits, to develop and enhance positive mental states, and to invest awareness in the daily activities that ordinarily pass in unawareness. Thus, Hinduism speaks of self-observation, in which you are instructed purely to observe your programmed states and activities without interpreting, evaluating, judging, approving or disapproving what you discover. You observe yourself and your activities neutrally, as if you were another person simply and directly witnessing what you are thinking, feeling and doing. Similarly, Krishnamurti teaches nothing but a method of self-observation, without thinking, "without condemning, judging, evaluating; just watching how you behave, your reactions; seeing without any choice; just observing so that during the day the hidden, the unconscious, is exposed" (4: 28). *Karma Yoga,* that is, acting without expecting anything in return, has the same aim.

The Buddha taught right or complete mindfulness, which can be practiced both formally and informally. In the Tibetan tradition, Chogyam Trungpa used to instruct his students to develop a feeling of space and a general acknowledgment of openness in whatever they do during the day (4: 47). The Vietnamese master Thich Nhat Hahn teaches a number of IAMs in his book *The Miracle of Mindfulness*. In one of them, called "A Day of Mindfulness," he advises devoting a day in each week to doing everything with full awareness — watching and experiencing everything with complete attention (27-31). Tarthang Tulku instructs the beginner to develop a quality of openness in each situation by maintaining continuous awareness. Even when you forget, as a beginner invariably does, you are to bring the attention back and focus it on the present moment. And, for the ordinary person, who does not engage in formal meditation for prolonged periods, Tulku rightly considers this form of meditation more important than the formal type (1: 87, 132).

In order to correct deficiencies in personality, before initiating the student into formal meditation, the Kabbalah teaches specific methods of self-development. One such exercise, designed for both self-discovery and moment-to-moment awakening, consists of keeping attention focused on the present moment as completely as possible. This is similar to Buddhist mindfulness meditation. Another exercise involves meditating on one negative program at a time and then ruthlessly confronting it through self-examination until it loses its control over the practitioner. Other forms of self-examination are also taught (Hoffman 96-111).

In a real sense, all the teachings of Jesus are nothing but forms of IAM, designed to free the mind of all conditioning, positive and negative. Thus freed, you are able to experience the natural state of unconditional love, which opens the way to realizing your oneness with God. In this realization, you attain that Perfection of Being which is God "himself." "Be perfect as your Heavenly Father is perfect," sums up the goal of this path. Since God is the perfection of each thing just as it is, to touch this perfection within yourself is to touch God.

Jesus taught two basic approaches to freeing ourselves from negative and positive programmings and experiencing perfection. The first consists in ceasing to react according to the dictates of our programming and doing the polar opposite or acting according to the promptings of our true Self. This strategy shifts the action to an altogether different plane and helps us break free of the programming. The second consists in ceaselessly practicing present-centered consciousness. By so doing we are able to be awake from moment to moment and see perfection as the ever-present nature of our true Self. His teachings on turning the other cheek and loving our enemies aim to free us from negative and positive programs, respectively; and his counsel on developing a nonjudgmental mind and present-centered consciousness are intended for moment-to-moment awakening.

The Sufis practice various IAMs that have similar aims. Thus, Sheikh Javad Nurbakhsh quotes Abu Osman Maghrebi as saying that the noblest action on the path is self-examination designed to eliminate negative programmings. Since actions that are selfish and contrary to the path are considered vicious and must be eliminated, the initiates are taught first to know what they are. They must constantly examine their mental states and their actions by continuously observing whatever arises in the mind, positive or negative. Next, the initiates must analyze weaknesses or negative programmings and strive to eliminate them; they must assess positive qualities and try to develop them. At the end of each day they must examine themselves and take account of their positive and negative behavior, resolving to rectify the imbalance the next day if the negative outnumbers the positive. If the positive outnumbers the negative, they must redouble their efforts to eliminate the negative programs. Thus they should undertake to resolve psychological conflicts and lessen the control of the self until they reach a state of psychological balance, harmony, and peace of mind (1: 18, 56-97).

Learning from the Sufis, Gurdjieff adopted the practice of assigning his students similar exercises. In order to develop moment-to-moment awareness, he instructed them to maintain a continuous awareness of a part of the body. For the same purpose, he taught them to remember "I am" by focusing attention on and being aware of the "I am" in whatever they were doing (Rajneesh 2: 144-149).

In addition, ethical and devotional practices and various disciplines are prescribed by all meditative traditions. Their aims are to purify and unify consciousness; rearrange your life according to new, ultimate priorities; help you to gain mastery over your bodily and mental powers, free them from external control, and shift your attention inward. Thus, the first two steps of *Yoga Sutras* of Patanjali involve ethical and devotional precepts, while the next three steps concern body-mind training that prepare the initiate for formal meditation. Of the Eightfold Path the Buddha taught, the first six steps are devoted to similar training. Taoism assigns similar practices. The Kabbalah insists on the observance of the Torah. Christian mysticism and Sufism emphasize a well-ordered moral life and ascetic practices as requirements for meditation. Such training awakens, strengthens, and unifies motivation, thus preparing you for the arduous journey ahead.

Some writers regard mastery of these ethical practices and body-mind training as preliminary to formal meditation (cf. Brown 1: 226). Were this the case, no one could begin formal meditation, since such a mastery would require at least a lifetime. Actually, these practices encompass the entire life of the meditator and are meant to be carried out into the daily activities outside the period of formal meditation.

The Stage of Concentration

After learning the preliminaries of posture, breathing, and directing the attention inward by cutting off external stimuli, you begin formal meditation with concentration. By whatever name it is called and whatever method or object is used, concentration is essential for all forms of formal meditation. You cannot make progress in meditation without developing it. This is obviously true of concentrative meditation, in which it serves as the point of entry into the meditative states. It is no less true, as already noted, of insight meditation. Without developing the calmness and clarity that concentration provides, you will not be able to observe physical sensations and mental phenomena at their immediate point of contact with attention. Only when your mind is, as master Achaan Chah puts it, "like a clear forest pool," which is the result of the advanced state of concentration, will the nature of conditioned existence be reflected in it. You will then be able to gain the insights that will blossom into enlightenment. Reflecting this double-edged process, Achaan Chah has stated, "Concentration must be firmly established for wisdom to rise" (Kornfield & Breiter 90).

Essential to concentration is shifting attention away from the world and one's programmed responses and directing it inward by holding it on one object. This shift of the orientation of consciousness toward its source frees and unifies attention. It makes the mind "one-pointed." The key to achieving these steps is to hold attention focused directly on one object prior to triggering the perceptual information-processing activity or any movement in the mind. For this reason, in concentrative meditation you are instructed to hold the attention on one object and become unified with it. The object may be chanting or repeating a mantra; watching, counting, or following the breath; gazing at a flame, a *yantra*, a picture of the guru, or an icon; visualizing a deity or a *mandala;* whirling or walking. In awareness meditation, you may be instructed to observe the sensation of the breath, slowly scan your body from head to foot, and observe your sensations with bare attention and clear comprehension of their nature. Or you may observe each mental event at the exact moment it arises, watch its duration, and notice the exact moment it ceases.

As you begin concentrating, you may start where you are, with a consciousness that experiences itself as separate from everything, including the object of concentration. Scattered among a multitude of objects of identification, attachment, and desire, your attention is getting constantly trapped and lost as it restlessly pursues one thing, then another. Or, like a butterfly going from flower to flower, your attention flits from one thing to another, never resting anywhere nor becoming occupied with anything for long, but ever preoccupied with what your programming dictates.

At other times your attention takes a dive and completely disappears from view, only to reemerge minutes, perhaps hours, later. Moreover, as it gets trapped and lost, the mind automatically responds to familiar things, people, and situations without being aware of them. And then, like a radar antenna, it searches for new, different, important, or exciting things to make it feel alive, to give pleasure; or it avoids those things that pose a threat to survival or become potential sources of pain. As a result, not only does your mind exhibit these same characteristics toward the object of concentration, but because it is not an object of identification, attachment, or desire, you find it extremely hard to stay focused. Finding the object of concentration dry, abstract, dull, unfamiliar, and unappealing, your mind runs away and plunges into its habitual preoccupations.

Moreover, in focusing attention on the object of concentration, you have shifted your mind's habitual orientation from the outside inward. Because of a change in its structural orientation and its habitual, constantly shifting field of attention, the mind will not and cannot keep its attention focused on the object for long.

Cut off from external stimuli and turned away from its orientation toward the object world, the mind triggers the only other source of stimuli with which it can maintain itself. It opens up the seemingly inexhaustible reservoir of programmings and impressions, stored up as a result of identification, attachment, and desire. These stimuli now crowd upon the brow of consciousness demanding attention and release. The fountain of inner dialogue now opens up and the stream gushes out in the form of fantasies, arguments, plans, exhortations, admonitions. Like "a drunken monkey," in the words of Swami Vivekananda, the mind jumps from one thing to another. Or one thought triggers a chain reaction, and, through association, builds up a fantasy world. Images seen on TV or movies; images of people, places, and things; memories, opportunities, hurts, or pleasures missed, enjoyed, desired, or anticipated leap into view.

Thus, as you begin to meditate, everything floats up into view, clamoring for attention and absorbing it like parched earth soaking up spring rain. When external stimuli are turned off, the mind turns on its internal juices to keep itself going. The programmed tapes begin to play over and over again like a broken record. Unable to find satisfaction in the unreality of its inner circuitry, the mind keeps repeatedly playing its programmed tapes to create an illusion of reality, permanence, continuity, and satisfaction in order to assure itself of its existence or self-worth. But as unreality and dissatisfaction continue, the mind keeps running them along the habitual grooves of its inner circuitry, as if the frequency of their occurrence will overcome the lack. A thousand and one things pull it away from the present and plunge it into the merry-go-round of existence. In the process, attention keeps drifting in and out, resulting in the scattering and entrapment of awareness and loss of concentration. Such is the infinite distractability of the programmed mind with which you have to deal as you begin to concentrate.

Faced with this situation, your immediate reaction may be to become frustrated, agitated, distracted, or discouraged. You want the mind to stop wandering, but it does not cooperate. So what do you do? You may try to force your mind to stop thinking and become quiet. But as soon as you try this approach, you find that it doesn't work. In fact, the opposite happens. Instead of quieting down, your mind gets more disturbed, giving rise to more thoughts. By forcing the mind to do your bidding, you only add conflict, confusion, or tension to a volatile situation. The effect is like first putting a tiger in a cage and then, wanting it to stop pacing up and down, you place it in a smaller cage, which disturbs it even more. The tension caused by the struggle may even give you a headache. Frustrated, disturbed, discouraged or exhausted, you may be tempted to give up meditating.

If you want to progress in meditation, you must remember never to force your mind to stop thinking or wandering. The mind does what it has been programmed to do. None of the usual tactics will work to quiet it; they will only reinforce its programmed behavior, giving rise to more thoughts and wanderings, with added complications.

Rather, essential to making the mind stop is doing something that does not reinforce, but cuts through its programmed reaction and brings it to a direct contact with the primary stimulus of the object. In the absence of reinforcement, the mind will wind down by itself, just as when the electric current is turned off, the record player comes to a stop by itself. You must never forcibly try to stop your mind from thinking; nor must you allow your attention to be carried off by the wind of every thought that pops into your head. Either action will give rise to more thoughts and trap your awareness further. When you do not choose either alternative but hold your attention focused directly on the primary stimulus, you stop reinforcing your consciousness and begin destructuring it. In addition, you must never pay any attention to whatever arises in your mind, unless, of course, that is the object of concentration. Your attitude toward thoughts must be one of noninvolvement or nonattachment. Simply leave them alone. Allow them to rise and disappear, without trapping your attention. When it slips away, as it invariably will in the beginning, simply bring it back and refocus it on the object of concentration. This nonattachment is to be practiced even when the contents of consciousness are the object of meditation.

The initial stage of concentration, then, consists of constantly bringing attention back to the object of concentration, back to the present, back to itself from its endless wanderings, from its habitual tendency to get immersed and lost in the objects of desire and preoccupation, much like a child let loose in a toy store. Since the mind will not become still overnight, you must be patient and gentle toward it as a loving mother is toward her child. As the mind has been programmed to behave in this way since infancy, its programming is not going to disappear overnight. When you stop trying to control or manage your mind and, instead, stop reinforcing it by practicing ceaseless and unflagging disidentification and nonattachment toward whatever arises, you will discover that it gradually becomes still by itself.

Your mind may also trigger all kinds of defensive maneuvers. It may tell you that you are too busy to meditate, or that right now you are not in the mood. It may point out that you could meditate if only others did not disturb you, if there were no distractions. Giving in to these promptings will only reinforce and strengthen your programming, confirming your belief that meditation does not work, is too difficult, or that you cannot do it. So it is imperative that you not give in to the frustration or discouragement you may feel. Again, by seeing these frustrations as part of the programmed reactions of your mind, you can begin to break free of the programming and quiet your restless mind.

Another problem may crop up at this stage: Unable to find its usual reinforcement, your mind may start triggering all kinds of expectation-reactions. You probably began meditating with all kinds of expectations: You wanted meditation to make all your problems magically disappear; you expected it to be fun, exciting, or exotic. You thought you would see all kinds of images, colors, lights, visions; you thought you would gain paranormal powers. You may even have anticipated world-shattering insights, instant enlightenment, or immediate tranquility. But when you discover that meditation does not reinforce any of your expectations, that nothing spectacular happens, or that for all your efforts you have only pain in your ankles, legs, knees, and thighs, you may be tempted to lose interest, feeling cheated, bored, disgusted, angry, or frustrated. Your hopes and expectations are dashed to pieces, doubts creep into your mind, and you begin to think that meditation is a waste of time.

Not finding any of its expectations met, within a few seconds after you begin to concentrate, the mind may drift off into fantasies or reveries. It may run after sensory stimuli, thoughts, or experiences, or may become preoccupied with self-therapy. Or it may take a dive into the turbid sea of unawareness, becoming dull, languid, and murky. When it resurfaces, your mind appears heavy, unclear, and disoriented. As you struggle to refocus, your meditation period comes to an end in a state of frustration or confusion.

Progress in meditation does not take place until the mind becomes disenchanted with a forest of illusory desires, goals, hopes, dreams, and expectations for fulfillment and happiness. Again, the paradox is that when you give up your desires, goals, and expectations, what you wanted begins to happen. So, sit in meditation with no expectation of anything happening, of gaining anything, or getting somewhere, but with the firm intention of being nowhere other than the present. Begin with the conviction that since there is only the present and you are already in it, there is nowhere else to go and nothing to do, attain, gain or lose. The only thing lacking in you is the awakening that brings the realization that you lack nothing. When you are able to just sit and be here now, you will have overcome the initial difficulties, and your progress on the path will be assured. You will discover that real progress is slow, subtle, and cumulative.

At the initial stage, especially of insight meditation, as you begin to focus attention on your mental contents, you will come to experience what makes you tick. You will discover discontinuities in your stream of consciousness, and you will see that what was continuous and automatic is made up of thousands of momentary stimuli rapidly succeeding one another. As you directly observe the inner workings of your mind and watch the tangles of your thoughts, fantasies, emotions, desires, and attachments, you will discover how they spin out of your mind and create your world.

In concentrative as well as insight meditation, as you get involved in a process of constantly bringing your attention back from its wanderings, you will begin to become aware of how unaware you are of your unawareness. You will discover what the Buddha meant when he said, "Ignorance is the condition of all conditioned things." You will see how unawareness envelops the states and activities of the programmed mind and the entire span of conditioned existence as your mind dives into thoughts and fantasies, and is carried along by a current of unawareness, sweeping over your life and carrying you into oblivion. Suddenly your mind pops its head into the fresh air of awareness and sees what it has been doing, only to plunge and get lost again. How different is this unawareness, this wandering of the mind, from that of sleep and dream states? Not much, according to Roger Walsh, who points out how, as we become identified with and lost in mental contents, awareness becomes reduced and distorted, so that we spend much of our life in a hypnotic, trance state or *maya*. And he observes what every meditator has discovered, that even in meditation, at the initial stage, well over ninety percent of our time is spent lost in fantasies (1: 23-38). If this is the case when we try to wake up, what can we say of our *normal* waking hours?

Along with unawareness and unreality or illusoriness, you also gain insights into other characteristics of your present condition. For instance, as you focus attention on the primary stimulus, you discover how in its usual state, consciousness perceives things through such filters as emotions, wants, desires, attachments, judgments, and so on, which are projected onto the primary stimulus. As the stimulus becomes coated with layers of these filters, what you perceive as objects or things are largely a product of your own mind. You discover how from moment to moment you are constantly evaluating and making judgments and thus distorting the primary process. This brings insight into the illusory character of what you believe to be real.

As you find how little control you have over your mental process, you come to see how, as Ram Dass puts it, you are a prisoner of your own mind. You come to experience how your life is a product of programming, which reduces it to a state of bondage. You see how the framework of your consciousness is fashioned largely out of these programmed states, which cause it to function automatically, putting out repetitive patterns of thought, feeling, and behavior. These patterns make you blindly respond to stimuli, obey their commands, and willingly or helplessly subject yourself to their tyranny.

You discover that what you thought to be yourself, your identity, consists mostly of patterns of learned responses that were programmed as a result of past experiences. Like alien intruders, these patterns came to occupy the vacant territory called "you." Other insights follow as the mind keeps exposing the web it spins to create your world and self.

Such insights and torrential release of thoughts, fantasies, and images must not be thought to be negative or detrimental. On the contrary, they are a necessary part of meditation. Unless they are released, you cannot wake up. Their release means that many of the defenses, blinders, and filters that restrict, distort, interpret, and create your distance from reality are beginning to be removed, deconstructing consciousness.

At this stage people usually experience release of negative emotional fixations or blockages, tensions, and energies that may have physiological manifestations. As Patricia Carrington observes, some people experience a sudden lightness or weightlessness, as if floating in air; others may feel a heaviness of the body, like sinking through the floor; yet others may feel that their body has disappeared. During deep relaxation, some feel intense heat, icy cold, or a burning or tingling sensation, a sudden itch, a temporary numbness in some part of the body, or even a pulsation throughout the body or on top of the head. Sometimes people perspire profusely, tremble, shiver, or if the energy release is particularly intense, they may experience a pounding heart or rapid breathing. Sometimes the body or some part of it may feel enlarged. At other times it may seem very tiny. Some may experience momentary discomfort, pain or a headache; others may sigh, yawn, or make automatic sucking sounds, experience muscle twitches, jerks, or involuntary movements. Some people experience all kinds of smells; others hear various sounds, such as humming, rushing, or ringing; yet others see different images, such as sparks, spirals, whirls, vivid colors, or bright lights. It is not uncommon to experience periods of restlessness or to have strong emotional reactions. Some people burst into laughter or tears, some feel intense rage, sexual sensations, or even experience orgasm (93-95).

During the first few weeks of practice, you may experience one or more of these phenomena; others may experience none at all, depending on the intensity of the meditation practice and the psychological state of each individual. Carrington observes that each person's pattern of stress/energy release may vary, paralleling their preoccupations, their mental fixations, emotional blockages, conflicts, or, in unusually intense cases, traumatic or unusual experiences. It is not necessary to have such side effects to benefit from meditation. You should neither expect them nor be surprised or disturbed if they occur.

When the repressed contents of the unconscious begin to come to the surface of consciousness, one tendency among many meditators, especially in the West, is to do self-therapy. As Jack Engler observes, many meditators in the West, upon discovering the hidden motives, fears, neurotic tendencies, emotionally charged thoughts, and other mental contents, become fascinated by them, give up meditating, and proceed to analyze them and figure out their causes (1: 27-290). Such self-analysis not only fixates one on the "psychodynamic level of experience" (Engler 1: 27), it derails him/her from meditation. That is the reason all traditions consider this preoccupation a hindrance to meditation. As Abbott Thomas Keating observes, the nature of unloading the unconscious is such that it does not focus on any particular content but loosens up all the psychological rubbish. The best thing to do if that happens is "to throw everything out together in one big garbage bag" (97), that is, practice nonattachment toward all things that arise. Just acknowledge them and let them be or simply observe them. They will clear up when all tensions and energies are released.

If they do not disappear, however, Patricia Carrington suggests various strategies to clear them up. If you suddenly feel restless during meditation, for instance, she suggests that you recognize it as normal, continue to meditate, and periodically make it the focus of attention until it disappears. If you have a pain that will not go away, make it the focus of attention, move into it, and keep the focus on it until it dissolves and disappears. Anxiety can be handled by deep abdominal breathing. If none of these strategies works, reduce meditation time or suspend meditation for several days until the anxiety disappears, and then return to your regular practice (98-106).

The more tension and energy are released, the more the mind quiets down, the more attention remains focused on the object of concentration. Instead of scattering attention among a multitude of objects and becoming fragmented as it darts from one thing to another, an undivided, prolonged focus on one object enables attention to shift its focus, and gather and unify around it. This unification is sometimes called "one-pointedness of mind." The longer it remains thus focused, the less scattered, and more unified it will become, and the more it will shift its focus from the external world to the internal object. This one-pointedness cannot be attained without the shift and unification of attention, which are key steps in the development of formal meditation.

This unification is expansion of awareness. The more awareness is freed, the more it will lose its ordinary, narrow, constricted, and distorted focus, its distance from things. It will begin to include within its embrace more events of the day, mental states, and activities that we usually pass in unawareness. It will become more inclusive, wide-ranging, stable, and present-centered. In terms of the object of concentration, the mind will be able to stay directly on it or on the primary stimulus without being sidetracked by outside goings-on, inside thought processes, or blankness of mind.

This does not mean that thoughts disappear at this stage. Rather, as you stop reinforcing the action mode and begin to disidentify, the object-world begins to lift its siege and the mind cuts loose from it. Cut off at their roots, thoughts at first decrease in frequency and intensity, and gradually drift off. As the clamor of thoughts begins to subside, the mind slows down, jumps around less, and becomes very calm. Fewer thoughts arise, and those that do, do not easily disturb or break concentration. You are able to notice them arise and sail by without sticking in your mind. Being aware of your thoughts as they arise, you are usually able to let them come and go without getting trapped and lost in them.

As you keep attention focused on the object, you will notice subtler levels of thought and subliminal mental chatter. They represent the mind's tendency to label, categorize, or conceptualize experience. In spite of their presence, your mind will now settle down and remain calm. Occasionally it will become completely calm. More and more gaps will appear in which no thought is present. Your breath will become very gentle, regular, rhythmic, sometimes imperceptible. However, you will need to keep your attention sharp and clear by holding it focused directly on the object or the primary stimulus. Otherwise your mind, without being fed by thoughts or external stimuli, may go blank or play dead (i.e., experience sensory deprivation), a phenomenon the Tibetans call "the sinking mind," as a kind of ultimate protest.

Meditation/Contemplation: Penetration of Duality

At this stage of meditation or initial contemplation, the flow of attention toward the object of concentration or observation becomes fairly uniform and uninterrupted. If concentration was begun with an external object, the focus now shifts to an internal representation. As you continue to make the representation the focus of meditation for prolonged periods, various processes of transformation and deconstruction begin to occur both in the object and in consciousness.

One of these may be called "the displacement effect." A prolonged focus of attention will cause the object to begin to displace all other thoughts and contents, which were still present during concentration, and begin to flood and occupy the mind during meditation. Assuming center stage, the object will push everything else to the periphery. Increasingly, even throughout the day, the meditation object will break through the barrier of ordinary preoccupations, activities, automatic responses, defenses, and unawareness, and erupt into and occupy your mind, as if the meditation were continuing uninterruptedly during waking hours.

This phenomenon occurs especially when the object of concentration is simultaneously experienced on various sensory levels and becomes, in effect, a condensation of the entire perceptual field. Reduced to one point, which the Hindu and Buddhist traditions call "the seed" ("synesthesia" in psychology), it emits sensory information pertaining to various fields, such as light, sound, patterns of vibration, and images (Brown 1: 237). In Western traditions, such as Christian mysticism, Sufism and Kabbalah, this stage is known as the stage of illumination. In its advanced form it also covers what Christian writers call "acquired contemplation."

As you carry the focus of attention on perceptual objects outside the meditation period, which is an essential feature of every path of formal meditation, you will experience a greater clarity and immediacy. You will be aware of and respond to things, people, and situations at the primary level of stimuli. As you do so, it will appear that you are perceiving things with new sensory awareness, as if for the first time. For instance, as you focus attention on the sound of crickets, you will notice discrete tones or sounds succeeding one another and creating the continuity which we ordinarily perceive. The same thing will happen with other sensory awareness. Things will just be there for you in all their nakedness and truth. You will be aware of other people's motivation and subtle behavior, together with your programmed affective or mental reactions as they arise.

And you will be aware of similar processes in yourself. Your hidden thoughts, motivations, drives, and compulsions will now surface and come to focus in the clarity of your awareness. In walking meditation, for instance, you will notice how the continuous process of walking is composed of innumerable discrete moments of decision the brain makes in rapid succession. This is true of everything we do automatically, usually in unawareness. Thus you will be aware from moment to moment how your mind continuously makes judgments and decisions in terms of likes, dislikes, desires, fears, etc. You will also notice more things in your environment. Things in nature, especially things for which hitherto you had no time or which did not hold your interest, will now appear before you in their immediacy, bathed in delight.

Furthermore, as the first phase of the shift of attention away from outer objects and toward inner thoughts and programmings occurs, you will begin to disidentify and become nonattached to the outer realms of things, people, situations, and familiar constructs. As the mind begins to become free of the control exercised by desire, attachment, and identification, you will be less driven to seek identity outside yourself and will correspondingly experience less need to wander among the world of objects, trying to make ego Real. The need to go galloping after possessions, achievements, power, success, or relationships to give you identity or self-worth, to find acceptance or approval in order to be yourself or be happy will diminish. You will be less compelled to seek others' company in order to overcome loneliness or your inability to be by yourself. Instead, a sense of self-confirmation and a feeling of well-being will rise up from within and will be supported by your environment.

In the same measure, the compulsion to fulfill others' or society's expectations will lose its hold over you. You will become increasingly disenchanted with the merry-go-round of life and disensnared by things, thoughts, situations, and relationships that are not growth-producing. Disillusioned with the illusions, fantasies, or deceptions surrounding life, your mind will begin to become reality-based, responding to people and situations directly, rather than in socially accepted ways, imposed categories, or value judgments. Increasingly finding satisfaction in being in the present, your mind will begin to be present-centered. As you become more relaxed and at peace with yourself, you will increasingly discover that just being is enough. Lightness and buoyancy will increase as the feeling of separation from people and things begins to decrease.

Union of Samadhi: Oneness with the Object

Beyond the meditative is the state of union or *samadhi*. At this stage, like a laser beam, unified attention cuts through the object-construction and experiences unity with the reality that it ordinarily symbolizes or represents. As attention penetrates its construction, the object begins to dissolve into the primary process of reality. At the same time it cuts through the programming and construction of consciousness and arrives at the primary process of awareness beyond. As both boundaries dissolve, there remains no medium, framework, form, construction, or limitation to keep them separate. The object expands, as does awareness. The two become one process of reality and awareness at the same time. As the construction of a separate subject and a separate object is transcended, the gap dividing them is simultaneously bridged. There remains no mind separate from the object and no object separate from the mind. Rather, what you experience is the reality manifesting itself in the form of the object. So the mind's journey toward the reality of the object is at the same time its journey toward its own reality, leading to their convergence, whereupon they are experienced as one.

This process happens in several stages. The first phase in the deconstruction of ordinary consciousness occurs when attention remains fixed directly on the object for prolonged periods. This deconstruction concerns the outer layers of programming and object-construction. Exclusively focused on the object, like a sperm encircling and penetrating an ovum, attention begins to penetrate and cut through the outer layers of programming: cultural associations, emotional reactions, the verbal layer, categorization or linguistic codification, and interpretation, evaluation, and judgment. Next it penetrates the symbolic construction, the model formed in the brain from single or repeated experiences. As this happens, the ordinary distance between attention and object is bridged. As the outer construction falls away, the object is no longer experienced as a solid, fixed, separate entity but a process of constant change in which no specific perceptual pattern is discerned. Things pass in and out of each other and appear as a mass of light (Brown 1: 237-238).

This movement of attention toward the center of the object is at the same time its journey toward its own center. The core of the journey is this simultaneous penetration and destructuring of reality and consciousness. As the deconstruction of verbal (or category) and symbolic layers (which are the layers of meaning) takes place at this stage and the onset of the next stage of meditation, many meditators report that they experience the world in its nakedness, void of meaning. Speaking of his own experience, Roger Walsh says, "I could be looking at something completely familiar, such as a tree, a building, or the sky, and yet without an accompanying internal dialogue to label and categorize it, it felt totally strange and devoid of meaning. It seems that what made something familiar, and hence secure, was not simply its recognition, but the actual cognitive process of matching, categorizing, and labeling it, and that once this was done, more attention and reactivity was focused on the label and labeling process than on the stimulus itself" (1: 42).

Since the focus of attention now is not on the reaction but the primary process of the stimulus itself, the world no longer appears as familiar or meaning-laden. For instance, if you focus attention on music, it is not music that you hear, but one discrete sound succeeding another. In your daily activities, you will experience people and situations without the normal restrictions, defenses, labels, or value judgments. You will feel as though layers of defenses, limits, and familiar associations that create or give meaning to things in the ordinary world have been peeled off. Instead of responding to programmed reactions, you will relate to people and things in terms of the immediate point of contact between awareness and stimulus. Pointing this out and speaking of his own experience, Roger Walsh says, "The experience feels like having a faint but discernible veil removed from my eyes, and that veil is made up of hundreds of subtle thoughts and feelings" (1: 43).

Such an experience may appear painful and cause anxiety or disorientation at first, as Walsh, Bernadette Roberts, and others report. But it is something you have to experience and pass through at this transitional stage in which the old reality-construct is being dismantled and the new Reality has not yet emerged. In terms of the Christian stage-differentiation, this contemplative journey is part of the process of passing though "the dark night of the senses."

On the positive side, the process is part of the removal of ordinary restrictions imposed by programming and our habitual way of dealing with the world, which creates what Roger Walsh calls "an unseen prison" (1: 42). Its removal ushers in an expansion of reality and awareness and brings clarity to life and immediate contact with things.

Penetrating further, attention arrives at the second major transpersonal stage — at what Ken Wilber calls the lower subtle level. At this stage, staying continuously on the object, attention penetrates and deconstructs or transcends the inner stages of the perceptual process and the construction of the world we ordinarily perceive (Brown 1: 240). This is the second stage of emptying the mind and stopping the world. As the inner dialogue stops, attention transcends the ordinary perceptual object-construction. Such deconstruction takes awareness beyond the ordinary world where causality reigns. Events are perceived more in terms of simultaneity or "synchronicity" than discreteness. As a result, awareness emerges as predominantly intuitive, holistic, integral, inclusive, and panoramic (Wilber 6: 27-29).

At the next major transpersonal stage, called "subtle" by Ken Wilber, the object of meditation retains only the subtle form or the primary process in which solidity is replaced by fluidity. As no thought, concept, idea, or perceptual model is present, the separate self is deactivated. Meditation continues without any effort, activity, or interference on your part. You enter into a passive or purely receptive state, in which the object appears as a constantly changing process. As meditation proceeds and you learn to balance the flow, the construction of focal attention and the sense of separation generated by it are transcended; and you come to experience a oneness with the object, which alone now remains in awareness (Brown 1: 241-245).

This stage of *samadhi,* in which you reach the first phase of oneness, may be called "subjective oneness." As primary duality still remains, this relative oneness is achieved with the object and remains limited to its subtle form and to the framework of meditation. Hence in many Eastern traditions it is called "*samadhi* with support" or "seed" *samadhi.* At this stage, there remains only the primary duality or polar principles that constitute the universe as well as the individual. Because both awareness and object arrive at their primary level of construction, both are experienced in their universal, archetypal form. As only the object remains in awareness, it is at this stage that you experience the universal or "cosmic consciousness."

In Christian stage-differentiation, this stage of *samadhi* is the stage of infused contemplation in which all activity on your part ceases and God or the object of contemplation becomes active and dominant. It spans what is called "the prayer of simple union" and full union with God.

At this stage, not only do you experience oneness with the object during meditation, but you carry this absorption over into everything throughout the day. Eruption of the object into consciousness, its assumption of the center stage, and displacement of everything else now become continuous. Remaining at the center, the object now does everything in you, as you. Whatever you do, you experience it as the object doing. Thus, reflecting the Zen experience, Yasutani Roshi says that when you become absorbed in the object of the koan, whatever you experience, it is the object experiencing it: Your hearing, seeing, touching, tasting, smelling, thinking, and being are nothing but the object experiencing itself in and as you (Kapleau 1: 110). Similarly, Koryu Osaka Roshi observes, "At this point there is no distinction between inside and outside. You totally become one with the object, from morning to night, even in sleep or dreams. At this stage the object becomes your whole universe" (Maezumi and

Glassman 1: 86-87). Confirming this, the author of *The Cloud of Unknowing* says:

> It stays with you all day long so that it goes to bed with you, gets up with you the next day, follows you around all day long, whatever you may be doing, pulls you away from your usual daily exercise that comes between it and you, accompanies or follows your desire so that it seems to you either that it is all the same desire or that you do not know what it is which has altered your demeanor and made you cheerful (Colledge 180).

According to Ken Wilber, this stage is the seat of archetypal or divine forms, subtle sounds, audible illuminations, transcendent insight, and absorption into or union with the divine forms or the object of meditation. In Hinduism this state is known as *savikapla samadhi;* in Theravada Buddhism it spans the end of the fourth and the beginning of the sixth *jhana* or state of absorption; in insight meditation this is the pseudo-nirvana of subtle form; in Zen it is experienced as absorption in the koan; and in Tibetan Buddhism it constitutes the experience of identity with the deity of the meditation or with the meditative Buddhas (5: 91-97; 6: 29-30). While according to Eastern traditions, this is the god realm, Western traditions speak of it as the angelic (lower subtle) and divine (higher subtle) realms. The lower subtle is also the realm of prophetic vision and revelation, biblical and quranic, as is evidenced by prophetic visions, illumination and clairaudience, such as those experienced by Moses, Isaiah, Muhammad, and Jesus at his baptism.

Thus, because of this unitive mode, various psychic phenomena are likely to manifest themselves at this stage. Not everyone who reaches this stage experiences these paranormal or psychic powers, but they tend to be characteristics of this stage, although some of them may appear earlier or later. Such powers include: telepathy, clairvoyance, clairaudience, out-of-the-body experiences or astral travel, foreknowledge, reading other people's minds, healing, levitation, rapture, ecstasy, visions of God, Christ, the Buddha, etc.

In most cases, these experiences appear spontaneously. Blofeld reports that telepathy is common among advanced Tibetan yogis. Ram Dass intimates that his teacher, Guru Maharaj-ji, was able to perceive events from a distance without being there. And we have stories of Christian saints, such as Teresa of Avila and John of the Cross, experiencing ecstasy and levitation. Some authorities, such as Patanjali in his *Yoga Sutras,* claim that you can even consciously strive to attain such powers.

All major traditions agree, however, that you should not be deceived that attaining such powers is the goal of meditation, or that they constitute enlightenment. In fact, these powers can become obstacles if you get caught in pursuing them for themselves, for gaining power over others, or for recognition and self-enhancement. That is why these traditions warn you to stay clear of them. Thus, after describing how to attain these powers, Patanjali advises avoidance of them since they are obstacles to *nirvikalpa samadhi*. Zen calls them *makyo*, or illusions, and admonishes you not to pay attention to them if they arise. This admonition is the source of the famous Zen saying, "If you see the Buddha on the road, kill him." Similar warnings are issued by other traditions. So, if you happen to experience any paranormal power, do not attach importance to it, but set your sight on the next stage of the path.

According to both Eastern and Western traditions, the subtle stage culminates in union with the personal God of theism. The self with which this union takes place is the archetypal self, described by many Western mystics as the highest or deepest point in ourselves. Beyond the psyche, it is the realm of the spirit, sometimes spoken of as the "divine spark" in us. Thus union takes place between two primal or ultimate forms: the ultimate form in the individual and in reality or God as the ultimate form, as the Transcendent Other. These forms constitute the primary polarity of the primal duality, which are the ultimate forms in which Reality as Such or the Unconditioned State manifests itself. Most Jewish, Christian, and Islamic mystics describe their experience of union with this ultimate divine form. A realization of this union in its permanent form is considered the highest state of consciousness attainable in this life.

Absolute Oneness or Identity: Enlightenment

In many traditions, the onset of the next major stage begins with insight meditation or infused contemplation. Its aim is to cut through the subtle form, the residual contents, programming, and form of consciousness. Using various perspectives, you first cut through the "seed" or subtle form and arrive at what Patanjali calls "seedless *samadhi*," in which no contents, only impressions, remain in awareness. Further refinement leads to a transcendence of the method, object, and framework of the meditation, that is, transcendence of the path itself. From this perspective you are first able to observe and then transcend the structure of space and time. This enables you to experience the simultaneous origin, cessation, and interdependence of all phenomena in the universe as movements in absolute Oneness. You are able to observe the very process whereby forms, objects, and events—or the phenomena of the world—are constructed and maintained, and pass out of existence. From this Oneness you are able to experience the undivided wholeness of the universe in which each thing is seen to interconnect, interpenetrate, and inhere in all and all in each (Brown 1: 246-256).

As attention cuts through even this universal process and the corresponding residual programming on the unconscious level, it experiences a pivotal shift away from contents and turns toward itself and its Source. Thereby it becomes empty, silent, and still. In this void state, only the original, natural activity of the primordial state, to which even the ordinary meditation becomes a hindrance, remains. Everything else drops off. There is now only the elemental state of awareness itself (Brown 1: 260).

When this state matures or reaches a critical mass, the final breakthrough occurs as absorption in the void is broken up. Thereupon the structural limits of consciousness and object, forms, and events are broken through and transcended; and Awareness emerges in the pure state of itself beyond programming, content, and construct. With nothing other than itself left to create a separation or distance from anything, Awareness experiences its true nature to be pure, unconditioned, undifferentiated, and formless, identical with Reality in its Unconditioned State of itself. Thus it experiences its nature to be the nature and reality of all things in their Unconditioned State. We see then that as the mind comes to experience itself in its ultimate state beyond any form, content, condition, or construct, it experiences nothing to be excluded from it (all-embracing), nothing to be separate from it (nondual), nothing to be other than it (absolutely one or identical). This is enlightenment – the experience of the Supreme Identity: the identity of Awareness and Reality, which is the identity of each thing just as it is, and consequently, your own true identity. The paradox is that only when you disidentify, become empty of, and transcend all contents, objects, programming, conditions, and constructs – everything you believe to be real but which in fact separates your from Reality – do you discover yourself to be no other than that very Reality.

This experience of enlightenment is described differently by different traditions. But every tradition that is a witness to it speaks of it in ontological terms as the experience of identity beyond union. This is the ontological revelation in which is laid bare not any form of God, but the very nature of God beyond form, spoken of as *Brahman, Nirvana* or Buddha-nature, Tao, and the Godhead by the sources of experiential religion. And the stage in which it occurs is variously described by these sources: for Hinduism it is *nirvikalpa samadhi;* for Theravada Buddhism "path-enlightenment;" for Zen the eighth of the Ten Ox-herding Stages; for Taoism returning to the Source; for Eckhart, Roberts, and other Christian mystics, it is the experience of God's "is-ness" or essence and identity beyond union; and for Kabbalah and Sufism as passing away into the being of God, which alone remains and is revealed everywhere to be That other than which nothing exists.

Realization of the Unconditioned State

Although enlightenment is the direct experience of the Ultimate as itself, it is not its ultimate realization. As already discussed in Part III, to arrive at it you have to pass through progressive stages of enlightenment, which are mapped out in greater or lesser detail by the various sources of experiential religion.

Those who depict these stages agree that your supreme life-journey begins with enlightenment, which is both an end and a beginning of the meditative path. It is the end of the process of arriving at Self-realization and the beginning of the realized life. Enlightenment opens up the boundless, eternal life, but it does not give you a permanent hold on it. Being a transitory experience, it provides a glimpse into your real identity and center but not a realization of it as the permanent, natural, and only state in which you continuously and effortlessly dwell. For this to occur, as we already said, you need to burn up all traces, roots, residues, and consequences of conditionings and constructs from your conscious and unconscious mind. This is the integrative process, the stages of transcendence following the experience of enlightenment.

Finally, in the ultimate state of transcendence, there is a permanent shift of the center of your being and consciousness to the Unconditioned State, which then emerges as the new identity and permanent center from which you think, feel, live, and act. Any trace of duality between ordinary consciousness and All-embracing Awareness is then completely transcended; no distinction between enlightenment and nonenlightenment, between conditioned and unconditioned, remains in your consciousness. All-embracing Awareness alone remains as your normal, ordinary, natural, and permanent state, in which all conditioned things and states appear as its manifestation, so that everywhere and everything you encounter is revealed as its embodiment.

As we have said, the sources of experiential religion describe this end-state in various ways from their own perspectives. Hinduism calls it *sahaja samadhi* and *Turiya;* to Theravada Buddhism it is fruition or final enlightenment or *Nirvana;* Zen calls it Buddhahood, attained at the ninth and tenth of the Ox-herding Stages. A similar view is presented by Tibetan Buddhism, which considers it the ultimate end of the path, beyond the Nine Stages of Tranquility. Taoism calls it becoming the Source, Tao. This is the divine state in which all things are at all times, because beyond or other than it there literally is nothing.

It is the incarnational state in which the individual is revealed to be a full embodiment of the Unconditioned in conditioned existence, as exemplified by the Buddha, the great sages of the Upanishads, Jesus, and the great sages manifested throughout history, East and West. This is the fullest dimension of humanity and the complete realization of what we truly are.

Conclusion

With this portrayal of the ultimate state of realization, which is the ascent of the manifest to the Unmanifest and the revelation of the Unmanifest as the manifest, the path of experiential religion reaches its termination. As this state is the realization of the ultimate purpose of existence, nothing more remains to be said other than to urge you to realize and live the life of the Unconditioned in this very world and help others to do the same, so that each of us can become a manifestation of the All.

Bibliography

Ajaya, Swami. *Yoga Psychology.* Honesdale, PA.: Himalayan International Institute, 1978.
Al-Ghazali. *The Faith and Practice of Al-Ghazali.* Translated by W. Montgomery Watt. Chicago: Kazi Publications, 1982.
Allport, Gordon W. *Pattern and Growth in Personality.* New York: Holt, Reinhart & Winston, 1937.
_____. *Personality.* New York: Holt, Reinhart & Winston, 1937.
Arabi, Ibn al. *The Bezels of Wisdom.* Translated by R.W.J. Austin. New York: Paulist Press, 1980.
Arberry, A.J. *Sufism.* New York: Harper & Row, 1970.
Attar, Farid ud-din. *The Conference of the Birds.* Translated by Afkham Darbandhi and Dick Davis. New York: Penguin Books, 1984.
Balsekar, Ramesh S. *Pointers from Nishargadatta Maharaj.* Durham, NC: Acorn Press, 1982.
Barrett, William, ed. *Zen Buddhism.* Garden City, NY: A Doubleday Anchor Book, 1965.
Bercholz, Samuel, ed. *The Spiritual Teachings of Ramana Maharshi.* Boulder: Shambhala Publications, Inc., 1972.
Berger, Raoul and Thomas Luckmann. *The Social Construction of Reality.* New York: Doubleday & Company, Inc., 1972.
Bharati, Agehananda. *The Tantric Tradition.* New York: Samuel Weiser, Inc., 1975.
Blakney, Raymond B., trans. *Meister Eckhart.* New York: Harper & Row, Publishers, Inc., 1941.
_____, trans. *The Way of Life: Tao Te Ching.* New York: New American Library, Inc., 1955.
Blofeld, John, trans. *The Zen Teaching of Huang Po.* New York: Grove Press, Inc., 1958.
_____. *The Tantric Mysticism of Tibet.* New York: E.P. Dutton Publishing Company, Inc., 1970.
_____. *The Secret and the Sublime.* New York: E.P. Dutton, 1973.
_____. *Taoism.* Boulder: Shambhala Publications, Inc., 1978.

Bohm, David. *Wholeness and Implicate Order*. London: Routledge & Kegan Paul, 1982.
Bromage, Bernard. *Tibetan Yoga*. Willingborough, England: The Aquarian Press, 1979.
Brown, Daniel P. "The Stages of Meditation in Cross-Cultural Perspective." In *Transformations of Consciousness*. Edited by Ken Wilber, Jack Engler, and Daniel P. Brown. Boston & London: Shambhala, 1986.
_____ and Jack Engler. "The Stages of Mindfulness Meditation: A Validation Study I-II." In *Transformations of Consciousness*.
Brown, Norman O. *Life Against Death*. Middletown, Ohio: Wesleyan Press, 1959.
_____. *Love's Body*. New York: Random House, Inc., 1966.
Bruner, Jerome. *Actual Minds, Possible Worlds*. Cambridge, MA: Harvard University Press, 1986.
Brunton, Paul. *The Quest of the Overself*. York Beach, ME: Samuel Weiser, Inc., 1970.
Burke, Omar Michael. *Among the Dervishes*. New York: Dutton, 1975.
Burtt, Edwin A., ed. *The Teachings of the Compassionate Buddha*. New York: New American Library, Inc., 1955.
Camus, Albert. *The Stranger*. Translated by Gilbert Stuart. New York: Random House, Inc., 1946.
_____. *The Plague*. Translated by Gilbert Stuart. New York: The Modern Library, Random House, 1948.
Capra, Fritjof. *The Tao of Physics*. Berkeley: Shambhala Publications, Inc., 1975.
_____. "Holonomy and Bootstrap." In *The Holographic Paradigm and Other Paradoxes*. Edited by Ken Wilber. Boulder: Shambhala Publications, 1982.
Carrington, Patricia. *Freedom in Meditation*. Garden City, NY: A Doubleday Anchor Book, 1978.
Castaneda, Carlos. *A Separate Reality*. New York: Simon & Schuster, 1971.
_____. *Journey to Ixtlan*. New York: Simon & Schuster, 1972.
_____. *Tales of Power*. New York: Simon & Schuster, 1974.
_____. *The Fire From Within*. New York: Pocket Books, 1984.
Chan, Wing-tsit, ed. *A Source Book in Chinese Philosophy*. Princeton, NJ: Princeton University Press, 1972.
Chang (Chung-Yuan), Garma C.C. *The Practice of Zen*. New York: Harper & Row, 1970.
_____. *The Buddhist Teaching of Totality*. University Park and London: The Pennsylvania State University Press, 1971.
_____, trans. *Teachings of Tibetan Yoga*. Secaucus, NJ: The Citadel Press, 1974.

_____, trans. *Original Teachings of Ch'an Buddhism*. New York: Grove Press, Inc., 1982.

Cleary, Thomas, trans. and ed. *The Original Face*. New York: Grove Press, 1978.

Cole, K.C. "A Theory of Everything." *The New York Times Magazine*, 18 October, 1987, pp. 20-28.

Colledge, Eric, trans. *The Book of Privy Counselling*. In *Medieval Mystics of England*. Edited by David Knowles. New York: Harper & Row Publishers, 1961.

Conze, Edward et al. *Buddhist Texts Through the Ages*. New York: Harper & Row, 1954.

_____. *Buddhist Meditation*. New York: Harper & Row, 1956.

_____. *Buddhist Wisdom Books*. New York: Harper & Row, 1958.

David-Neel, Alexandra and Lama Yongden. *The Secret Oral Teaching in Tibetan Buddhist Sects*. San Francisco: City Lights Books, 1967.

Dawood, N.J., trans. *The Koran*. Baltimore: Penguin Books, 1974.

De Bary, William Theodore et al., ed. *The Buddhist Tradition*. New York: Random House, Inc., 1972.

Deikman, Arthur. *Personal Freedom*. New York: Grossman Publishers, 1976.

_____. "Bimodal Consciousness." In *The Nature of Human Consciousness*. Edited by Robert Ornstein. San Francisco: W.B. Freeman Press, 1973.

_____. "Deautomatization and the Mystic Experience." In *The Nature of Human Consciousness*.

De Riencourt, Amory. *The Eye of Shiva*. New York: William Morrow & Company, Inc., 1981.

Deutsch, Eliot. *Advaita Vedanta: A Philosophical Reconstruction*. Honolulu: The University of Hawaii Press, 1985.

Drumond, Richard H. *Gautama the Buddha*. Grand Rapids: William B. Eerdmans, 1974.

Dunne John S. *The Way of All the Earth*. New York: The Macmillan Company, Inc., 1972.

Egan, Harvey D. *Christian Mysticism*. New York: Pueblo Publishing Company, Inc., 1984.

Eliade, Mircea. *Yoga: Immortality and Freedom*. Princeton, NJ: Princeton University Press, 1969.

Embree, Ainslee T., ed. *The Hindu Tradition*. New York: Random House, Inc., 1972.

Emerson, Victor F. "Research on Meditation." In *What Is Meditation?* Edited by John White. Garden City, NY: Doubleday & Company, Inc., 1974.

Engler, Jack. "Therapeutic Aims in Psychotherapy and Meditation." In *Transformations of Consciousness*. Edited by Ken Wilber, Jack Engler, and Daniel P. Brown. Boston: Shambhala, 1986.

Epstein, Perle. *Kabbalah*. Boston & London: Shambhala Publications, Inc., 1988.

Erikson, Erik H. *Childhood and Society*. New York: W.W. Norton & Company, Inc., 1983.

Evans-Wentz, Y.W., trans. *The Tibetan Book of the Great Liberation*. New York: Oxford University Press, 1968.

_____, trans. *Tibetan Yoga and Secret Doctrines*. New York: Oxford University Press, 1978.

Ferguson, Marilyn. "Karl Pribram's Changing Reality." In *The Holographic Paradigm and Other Paradoxes*. Edited by Ken Wilber. Boulder: Shambhala, 1982.

Fox, Matthew. *Breakthrough. Meister Eckhart's Creation Spirituality in New Translation*. New York: Doubleday, 1980.

Franck, Frederick, ed. *The Buddha Eye*. New York: The Crossroad Publishing Company, 1982.

Free John, Da. *The Dawn Horse Testament*. San Raphael, CA: The Dawn Horse Press, 1985.

Fromm, Eric et al. *Zen Buddhism and Psychoanalysis*. New York: Harper & Row, 1970.

Gendlin, Eugene T. *Focusing*. New York: Everest House Publishers, 1978.

Goldstein, Joseph and Jack Kornfield. *Seeking the Heart of Wisdom*. Boston & London: Shambhala, 1987.

Goleman, Daniel. *The Meditative Mind*. Los Angeles: Jeremy P. Tarcher, Inc., 1988.

_____. "Relaxation: Surprising Benefits Detected." *New York Times* 4, July 1986: C 1, 11.

Gordon, Chad and Kenneth J. Gergen, eds. *The Self in Social Interaction*. New York: John Wiley & Sons, 1968.

Govinda, Lama Anagarika. *Foundations of Tibetan Mysticism*. New York: Samuel Weiser, Inc., 1973.

_____. *Creative Meditation and Multi-Dimensional Consciousness*. Wheaton, IL: Quest Books, 1976.

Groeschel, Benedict J. *Spiritual Passages*. New York: The Crossroad Publishing Company, 1984.

Gyatso, Geshe Kelsang. *Clear Light of Bliss*. Translated by Tenzing Norbu. London: Wisdom Publications, 1982.

Hakeda, Y.S., trans. *The Awakening of Faith*. New York: Columbia University Press, 1967.
Halevi, Z'ev ben Shimon. *The Way of Kabbalah*. New York: Samuel Weiser, Inc., 1976.
Hanson, Virginia, ed. *Approaches to Meditation*. Wheaton, IL: A Quest Book, 1976.
Harrison, Edward. *Masks of the Universe*. New York and London: The Macmillan Publishing Company, 1985.
Hesse, Hermann. *Demian*. Translated by Michael Roloff and Michael Lebeck. New York: Bantam Books, Inc., 1970.
Hixon, Lex. *Coming Home*. Garden City, NY: Doubleday, 1978.
Hoffman, Edward. *The Way of Splendor*. Boulder: Shambhala, 1981.
Ibsen, Henrik, authorized trans. *An Enemy of the People*. In *Plays of Henrik Ibsen*. New York, Tudor Publishing Co., 1934.
Idel, Moshe. *Kabbalah*. New Haven & London: Yale University Press, 1988.
Janis, Irving L. et al. *Personality*. New York: Harcourt, Brace, & World, 1969.
Johnson, Clive, ed. *Vedanta*. New York: Bantam Books, 1974.
Johnston, William. *Silent Music*. San Francisco: Harper & Row, 1979.
_____, trans. and ed. *The Cloud of Unknowing*. Garden City, NY: Doubleday Image Books, 1973.
Kapleau, Philip. *The Three Pillars of Zen*. New York: Doubleday & Company, 1972.
_____. *Zen: Dawn in the West*. Garden City, NY: Doubleday & Company, 1979.
Keyes, Ken. *Handbook to Higher Consciousness*. Berkeley: Living Love Center, 1974.
_____. *How to Enjoy Your Life In Spite of It All*. St. Mary's, KY: Living Love Publications, 1980.
Kornfield, Jack and Paul Breiter, comps. and eds. *A Still Forest Pool. The Insight Meditation of Achaan Chah*. Wheaton, IL: A Quest Book, 1986.
Krishnamurti, Jiddu. *The First and the Last Freedom*. New York: Harper & Row, Inc., 1954.
_____. *Commentaries on the Living*. Series I-III. Wheaton, IL: A Quest Book, 1968.
_____. *Think on These Things*. New York: Harper & Row, 1970.
_____. *The Flight of the Eagle*. New York: Harper & Row, 1971.
_____. *Talks and Dialogues*. New York: Avon Books, 1972.
_____. *You Are the World*. New York: Harper & Row, 1972.
Laing, R.D. *The Divided Self*. Baltimore: Penguin Books 1965.
Lawrence, H.D. "The Man Who Died." In *St. Mawr and The Man Who Died*. New York: Random House, Inc., 1953.

Lefort, Raphael. *The Teachers of Gurdjieff.* New York: Samuel Weiser, 1975.
LeShan, Lawrence. *How to Meditate.* New York: Bantam Books, 1975.
_____. *Alternate Realities.* New York: Ballantine Books, 1976.
Levine, Stephen. *A Gradual Enlightenment.* Garden City, NY: Doubleday & Company, 1979.
Lings, Martin. *What Is Sufism?* Berkeley: University of California Press, 1976.
Maezumi, Teizan, Roshi. "Receiving the Precepts." In *On Zen Practice II.* Edited by Teizan Maezumi and Bernard Glassman. Los Angeles: Zen Center of Los Angeles, 1977.
Maezumi, Teizan and Bernard T. Glassman. *The Hazy Moon of Enlightenment.* Los Angeles: Zen Center of Los Angeles, 1978.
Mascaro, Juan, trans. *The Upanishads.* Baltimore: Penguin Books, 1973.
May, Rollo. *Love and Will.* New York: Norton & Simon, 1969.
Merril-Wolff, Franklin. *Pathways Through to Space.* New York: Julian Press, 1973.
Merton, Thomas. *Mystics and Zen Masters.* New York: Farrar, Strauss & Giroux, 1967.
_____. *The Way of Chuang Tzu.* New York: New Directions, 1965.
Miller, Barbara S. trans. *The Bhagavad-Gita.* New York: Bantam, 1986.
Mishima, Yukio. *The Sailor Who Fell from Grace with the Sea.* Translated by John Nathan. New York: Alfred A. Knopf, Inc., 1965.
Mitchell, Stephen, comp. and ed. *Dropping Ashes on the Buddha. The Teaching of Zen Master Seung Sahn.* New York: Grove Press, Inc., 1976.
Monks, Ramakrishna Order. *Meditation.* Hollywood: Vedanta Press, 1984.
Mountain, Marion. *The Zen Environment.* New York: Bantam Books, 1983.
Muktananda, Swami. *Meditate.* Albany: The State University of New York Press, 1980.
Murti, T.R.V. *The Central Philosophy of Buddhism.* London: George Allen & Unwin, 1960.
Nagarjuna. *The Philosophy of the Middle Way.* Translated and annotated by David J. Kalupahana. Albany: State University of New York Press, 1986.
Naranjo, Claudio and Robert Ornstein. *On the Psychology of Meditation.* New York: Viking Press, 1973.
Needleman, Jacob. *The New Religions.* New York: Pocket Books, 1972.
_____. *A Sense of the Cosmos.* New York: E.P. Dutton, 1976.
_____. *Consciousness and Tradition.* New York: Crossroad, 1982.
Neisser, Ulrich. *Cognitive Psychology.* New York: Appleton-Century-Crofts, 1966.
Nicholas of Cusa. *The Vision of God.* Translated by Emma Gurney Salter. New York: Frederick Unger Publishing Co., 1960.

Nicholson, Reynold A. *The Mystics of Islam*. London: Routledge & Kegan Paul, 1963.

Nurbakhsh, Javad. *In the Paradise of the Sufis*. New York: Khaniqahi-Nimatullahi Publications, 1979.

_____. *Sufism*. New York: Khaniqahi-Nimatullahi Publications, 1982.

Odier, Daniel. *Nirvana Tao*. Translated by John Mahoney. New York: Inner Tradition International, Ltd., 1986.

Ornstein, Robert, ed. *The Nature of Human Consciousness*. San Francisco: W.H. Freeman & Company, 1973.

_____. *The Psychology of Consciousness*. 2d. ed. New York: Harcourt, Brace & Jovanovich, 1977.

_____. *The Mind Field*. New York: Pocket Books, 1978.

_____. "Contemporary Sufism." In *Transpersonal Psychologies*. Edited by Charles T. Tart. New York: Harper & Row, 1975.

Osborne, Arthur, ed. *The Teachings of Ramana Maharshi*. New York: Samuel Weiser, Inc., 1962.

Otto, Rudolf. *Mysticism East and West*. New York: Macmillan, 1972.

Pearce, Joseph Chilton. *Exploring the Crack in the Cosmic Egg*. New York: Pocket Books, 1975.

_____. *The Bond of Power*. New York: E.P. Dutton, 1981.

Piaget, Jean. *The Construction of Reality in the Child*. Translated by Margaret Cook. New York: Ballantine Books, 1974.

Prabhavananda, Swami, trans. *Srimad Bhagavatam: The Wisdom of God*. New York: Capricorn Books, 1968.

Prabhavananda, Swami and Christopher Isherwood, trans. *The Song of God: Bhagavad-Gita*. New York: New American Library, Inc., 1951.

_____. trans. *How to Know God: The Yoga Aphorisms of Patanjali*. New York: New American Library, 1969.

Prabhavananda, Swami and Frederick Manchester, trans. *The Upanishads: Breath of the Eternal*. New York: New American Library, 1957.

Prem, Krishna. *The Yoga of the Bhagavad Gita*. Baltimore: Penguin Books, 1973.

Pribram, Karl. "What the Fuss Is All About." In *The Holographic Paradigm and Other Paradoxes*. Edited by Ken Wilber. Boulder: Shambhala, 1982.

Pseudo-Dionysius. *The Complete Works*. Translated by Colm Luibheid. New York: Paulist Press, 1987.

Quine, Willard van Orman. *From A Logical Point of View*. New York: Harper & Row, 1963.

Rahman, Fazlur. *Islam*. Garden City, New York: Doubleday, 1968.

Rahula, Walpola. *What the Buddha Taught*. New York: Grove Press, 1974.

Rajneesh, B.S. *Meditation: The Art of Ecstasy*. New York: Harper & Row, 1976.

Rama, Swami et al. *Yoga and Psychotherapy.* Glenview, IL: Himalayan International Institute, 1976.
Ram Dass. *Journey of Awakening.* New York: Bantam Books, 1978.
_____. *Grist for the Mill.* New York: Bantam Books, 1979.
Reps, Paul, comp. *Zen Flesh, Zen Bones.* Garden City, NY: Doubleday Anchor, n.d.
Rieker, Hans-Ulrich. *The Secret of Meditation.* New York: Samuel Weiser, 1975.
_____. *The Yoga of Light. Hatha Yoga Pradipika.* Translated by Elsy Becherer. Middletown, CA: The Dawn Horse Press, 1978.
Rinboshay, Lati and Napier, Elizabeth. *The Mind in Tibetan Buddhism.* Valois, NY: Gabriel/Snow Lion, 1981.
Rinboshay, Lati and Locho. *Meditative States in Tibetan Buddhism.* Translated by Jeffrey Hopkins. London: Cameron Printing Co. Ltd., 1983.
Roberts, Bernadette. *The Experience of No-Self.* Boulder: Shambhala Publications, Inc., 1984.
_____. *The Path to No-Self.* Boulder: Shambhala, 1985.
Riordan, Kathleen. "Gurdjieff." In *Transpersonal Psychologies.* Edited by Charles T. Tart. New York: Harper & Row, 1975.
Ruysbroeck, Jan Van (John Ruusbroec). *The Spiritual Espousals and Other Works.* Translated by James A. Wiseman. New York: Paulist Press, 1985.
Saddhatissa, H. *The Buddha's Way.* New York: George Braziller, Inc., 1971.
St. Bonaventure. *The Soul's Journey into God.* Translated by Ewert Cousins. New York: Paulist Press, 1978.
St. Gregory Palamas. *The Triads.* Translated by Nicholas Gendle. New York: Paulist Press, 1980.
St. Gregory of Sinai. "Instructions to Hesychasts." In *The Fire and the Cloud.* Edited by David A. Fleming. New York: Paulist Press, 1978.
St. Ignatius Loyola. "The Spiritual Exercises." In *The Fire and the Cloud.* Edited by David A. Fleming. New York: Paulist Press, 1978.
St. John Climacus. *The Ladder of Divine Ascent.* Translated by Colm Luibheid and Norman Russell. New York: Paulist Press, 1982.
St. John of the Cross. *Ascent of Mount Carmel.* Translated by E. Allison Peers. Garden City, NY: Doubleday, 1958.
_____. *Selected Writings.* Edited by Ernest E. Larkin. New York: Paulist Press, 1987.
St. Simeon the New Theologian. *The Discourses.* Translated by C.J. de Catanzaro. New York: Paulist Press, 1980.
St. Teresa of Avila. *The Interior Castle.* Translated by Kiernan Kavanaugh and Otilio Rodriguez. New York: Paulist Press, 1979.

Sangharashita, M.S. *The Three Jewels.* Surrey, England: Windhorse Publications, 1977.
Sartre, Jean-Paul. *Being and Nothingness.* Translated by Hazel E. Barnes. New York: Washington Square Press, 1968.
Schimmel, Annemarie. *Mystical Dimensions of Islam.* Chapel Hill: University of North Carolina Press, 1975.
Schlosser, Edith. "Christian Mysticism." In *Approaches to Meditation.* Edited by Virginia Hanson. Wheaton, IL: A Quest Book, 1973.
Schumann, Hans W. *Buddhism.* Translated by Georg Feuerstein. Wheaton, IL: A Quest Book, 1974.
Schuon, Fritof. *The Transcendent Unity of Religions.* New York: Harper & Row, 1975.
Sekida, Katsuki. *Zen Training.* New York: John Weatherhill, Inc., 1975.
Shah, Idries. *Tales of the Dervishes.* New York: E.P. Dutton, 1970.
_____. *The Way of the Sufi.* New York: E.P. Dutton, 1970.
_____. *The Sufis.* Garden City, NY: Doubleday & Co., 1971.
Shankara. *Crest-Jewel of Discrimination.* Translated by Swami Prabhavananda and Christopher Isherwood. Hollywood: Vedanta Press, 1978.
Shapiro, Deane. *Meditation: Self-Regulation Strategy and Altered States of Consciousness.* New York: Aldine Publishing Company, 1980.
Shapiro, Deane and Roger Walsh, eds. *Meditation: Classic and Contemporary Perspectives.* New York: Aldine, 1984.
Shaya, Leo. *The Universal Meaning of the Kabbalah.* Baltimore: Penguin Books, 1973.
Slater. Philip. *The Pursuit of Loneliness.* Boston: Beacon Press, 1968.
_____. *Earthwalk.* Garden City, NY: Doubleday Anchor, 1974.
Smith, Adam. *Powers of Mind.* New York: Ballantine Books, 1975.
Smith, Huston. *Forgotten Truth.* New York: Harper & Row, 1976.
_____. *Beyond the Post-Modern Mind.* New York: Crossroad, 1982.
Sohl, Robert and Audrey Carr. *The Gospel According to Zen.* New York: New American Library, 1970.
Spencer, Sidney. *Mysticism in World Religion.* South Brunswick, NJ: A.S. Barner & Company, Inc., 1963.
Spencer-Brown, G.S. *Laws of Form.* New York: Julian Press, 1972.
Spiegelberg, Frederick. *Spiritual Practices of India.* New York: The Citadel Press, 1962.
Suzuki, Deisetz Teitaro. *Manual of Zen Buddhism.* New York: Grove Press, 1960.
_____, trans. *The Lankavatara Sutra.* London: Routledge & Kegan Paul, 1968.
_____. *Essays in Zen Buddhism.* First Series. New York: Grove Press, Inc., 1961.

_____. *Essays in Zen Buddhism.* Second Series. London: Luzac & Company, 1933.
_____. *Essays in Zen Buddhism.* Third Series. New York: Samuel Weiser, 1971.
_____. *Mysticism, Christian and Buddhist.* New York: Harper, 1971.
Suzuki, Shunryu, Roshi. *Zen Mind, Beginner's Mind.* New York: Weatherhill, Inc., 1973.
Tart, Charles T. *States of Consciousness.* New York: Dutton, 1975.
_____, ed. *Transpersonal Psychologies.* New York: Harper, 1975.
Thoreau, Henry David. *Walden.* In *The Portable Thoreau.* Edited by Carl Bode. New York: Penguin Books, 1984.
Trungpa, Chogyam. *Meditation in Action.* Berkeley, Shambhala, 1970.
_____. *Cutting Through Spiritual Materialism.* Berkeley: Shambhala Publications, Inc., 1973.
_____. *The Foundations of Mindfulness.* Berkeley: Shambhala, 1976.
_____. *The Myth of Freedom and the Way of Meditation.* Boulder: Shambhala Publications, Inc., 1976.
_____. *Journey Without Goal.* Boulder: Prajna Press, 1981.
Tsong-ka-pa. *Tantra in Tibet.* Vols. 1-3. Translated and edited by Jeffrey Hopkins. London: George Allen & Unwin, 1980.
Tulku, Tarthang. *Gesture of Balance.* Emeryville, CA: Dharma Publishing, 1977.
_____. *Openness Mind.* Emeryville, CA: Dharma Publishing, 1978.
_____. *Time, Space, and Knowledge.* Emeryville, CA: Dharma Publishing, 1977.
Underhill, Evelyn. *Mysticism.* New York: E.P. Dutton, 1961.
Van de Wettering, Janwillem. *A Glimpse of Nothingness.* Boston: Houghton Mifflin Company, 1975.
Waldenfels, Hans. *Absolute Nothingness.* New York: Paulist Press, 1976.
Walker, Kenneth. *A Study of Gurdjieff's Teaching.* New York: Samuel Weiser, 1974.
Walsh, Roger. "Meditation Practice and Research." *Journal of Humanistic Psychology* 23 (Winter 1983): 18-50.
_____. "The Consciousness Discipline." *Journal of Humanistic Psychology* 23 (Spring 1983): 28-30.
_____. "Journey Beyond Belief." *Journal of Humanistic Psychology* 24 (Spring 1984): 30-65.
Walsh, Roger and Deane Shapiro, eds. *Beyond Health and Normality.* New York: Van Norstand Reinhold Company, 1983.
Walsh, Roger and Frances Vaughan, eds. *Beyond Ego.* Los Angeles: J.P. Tarcher, Inc., 1980.
Washburn, Michael. *The Ego and the Dynamic Ground.* Albany: State University of New York Press, 1988.

Watson, Burton, trans. *Chuang Tzu: Basic Writings*. New York: Columbia University Press, 1964.
Weber, Renee. "The Enfolding-Unfolding Universe: A Conversation with David Bohm." In *Holographic Paradigm and Other Paradoxes*. Edited by Ken Wilber. Boulder: Shambhala Publications, 1982.
_____. "The Physicist and the Mystic — Is A Dialogue Between Them Possible? A Conversation with David Bohm." In *The Holographic Paradigm*.
_____. "The Tao of Physics Revisited: A Conversation with Fritjof Capra." In *The Holographic Paradigm*.
Wei Wu Wei. *Ask the Awakened*. Boston: Little, Brown & Co., 1963.
_____. *Open Secret*. Hong Kong: The Hong Kong University Press, 1965.
White, John. *Everything You Wanted to Know About TM*. New York: Pocket Books, 1976.
_____, ed. *The Highest State of Consciousness*. Garden City, NY: Doubleday Anchor, 1972.
_____, ed. *What Is Meditation?* Garden City, NY: Doubleday Anchor, 1974.
Wilber, Ken. *The Spectrum of Consciousness*. Wheaton, IL: A Quest Book, 1977.
_____. *No Boundary*. Los Angeles: Center Publications, Inc., 1979.
_____. *The Atman Project*. Wheaton, IL: A Quest Book, 1980.
_____, ed. *The Holographic Paradigm and Other Paradoxes*. Boulder: Shambhala, 1982.
_____. *Eye to Eye*. Garden City, NY: Doubleday Anchor, 1983.
_____. *A Sociable God*. New York: McGraw-Hill Book Co., 1983.
Wilber, Ken, Jack Engler and Daniel P. Brown, eds. *Transformations of Consciousness*. Boston & London: Shambhala, 1986.
Willis, Janice D. *The Diamond Light*. New York: Simon & Schuster, 1972.
Wood, Ernest. *Concentration: An Approach to Meditation*. Wheaton, IL: A Quest Book, 1952.
_____. *Seven Schools of Yoga: An Introduction*. Wheaton, IL: A Quest Book, 1973.
Yu, Lu K'uan. *Chan and Zen Training*. First Series. Berkeley: Shambhala Publications, 1970.
_____. *The Secret of Chinese Meditation*. New York: Samuel Weiser, 1971.
_____. *Taoist Yoga*. New York: Weiser, 1977.
Zimmer, Heinrich. *Philosophies of India*. London: Routledge & Kegan Paul, 1969.

Index

A

Abbasi, el Mahdi, 36
Absolute, 203-204, 206, 231, 260, 265
Absolute Oneness, 158, 211-232, 233, 255-256, 269, 279, 281, 284, 287
   three characteristics of, 216-232
Adequate evidence, 112-113
Advaita (nondualist) Vedanta, 22, 218, 254-255, 266, 364
Ahankara, 197
Aitareya Upanishad, 235
Ajaya, Swami, 132
Al-Ghazali (Sufi philosopher), 209, 241, 369
Al-Junaid (Sufi master), 188
Allegory of the Cave, x, 23, 107, 115
All-embracing Awareness, 69, 199, 200-201, 218, 233-247, 256-258, 262-265, 272-273, 275, 345, 361-362, 380-390
Allport, Gordon, 119, 122-123
Al-Nuri (Sufi master), 230
Anicca (impermanence), 57, 70
Animal state, 52
Annihilation, 187-189, 224, 268, 273-274
Ansari (Sufi master), 188
Anuttara Tantra, 340
Arabi, Ibn (Sufi master), 188, 231
Arberry, A.J., 188, 230
Archetypal Self, 40, 345
Arica, 143, 311
Arjuna, 30, 148, 329-330
Arnold, Edwin, 193, 196
Asceticism, 48, 148
Ashtavakra Gita, 40, 76, 150, 181, 275
Asura (giant) state, 51
Atman (the Self), 10, 131, 195-196, 198-200, 233, 254
Attachment, 12, 17, 33, 40, 44, 47-48, 65, 72, 74-75, 96-98, 120, 149, 155, 157, 160, 174, 176, 185, 257-258, 263-264, 267, 276-277, 280, 282, 294, 306, 315, 317, 326, 344, 358, 373-374, 377-378, 382, *passim*
Attar, Farid ud-din (Sufi master), 83, 166, 194, 209, 231
Attention, 94, 358-360, 362, 366, 373-381, *passim*
Automatization, 94-95
Avalokitesvara, Bodhisattva, 175
Avatamsaka Sutra, 220-221, 261
Aversion/Avoidance, 72, 136
Awareness, 4, 12, 36, 93-94, 132, 146, 173, 237-238, 241-246, 355, 360-62, 370, 375, *passim*
   definition of, 4-5
Awakening of Faith, The, 73, 237
Ayer, A.J., 120

B

Baba, Meher, 331

Baqa, 274
Basic assumptions, 63-67
Bassui (Zen master), 182, 239
Bawa, Guru, 209, 244
Becker, Ernest, 34, 87
Behaviorism, 43
Berger, Raoul, 102
Bhagavad Gita, 30, 35, 42, 147-148, 152-153, 158, 163, 198, 200, 217, 276, 279
Bhakti Yoga, 255
Bharati, Agehananda, 339
Bible, 267, 297
Bistami, Bayazid (Sufi master), 230-231, 273
Blofeld, John, 50, 159, 201, 222, 238, 240, 267, 319, 340, 386
Bodhidharma, 325
Bodhisattva ideal, 283, 286
Bohm, David, 109, 111, 114, 172, 214-215
Bondage, 37-44, 48, 51, 53, 59, 74, 81, 103, 127, 135, 144, 149, 157, 179, 181, 183, 267, 275, 277, *passim*
Brahman, 10, 22, 69, 153, 158, 198-200, 217, 226-227, 234-235, 244, 254-256, 388
Bromage, Bernard, 340-341
Brown, Daniel P., 257, 372, 381, 383-389
Brown, Norman O., 71, 184
Bruner, Jerome, 93, 116
Buddha, ix, 12, 31-34, 39, 42, 45, 57, 70, 76, 93, 95, 120, 133, 147, 150, 158, 160, 166, 173, 181, 185, 193, 202, 205, 236, 262, 280, 292-296, 298-299, 314, 333, 340, 343, 355, 370, 372, 377, 387, 390
Buddhahood, 158-159, 202, 236, 263, 266, 389

Buddha-nature, 202, 209, 227, 259-260, 262-263, 265, 363, 388
Buddhism, ix, 2, 9-13, 16, 21-23, 49-50, 57, 71, 75, 81, 85, 87, 125, 132, 158-159, 164-165, 173, 181, 203, 236, 250, 256-266, 296, 363-364, 366-367
Burke, Omar Michael, 18, 210

C

Camus, Albert, 14, 26, 45, 64, 142
Capra, Fritjof, 92, 109, 112, 214
Carrington, Patricia, 378-379
Castaneda, Carlos, 15, 24-25, 29, 100, 104, 111, 152, 155, 178, 310, 325, 329, 335-336, 343-344, 360
Catholicism, ix
Cause of the Human Condition, 69-89
Chah, Achaan, 29, 367, 373
Chakra, 341
Chandogya Upanishad, 69, 217, 244
Chang, Garma (Chung-Yuan), 175, 220-222, 279, 317
Chao Chou (Joshu: Zen master), 167, 324
Chirban, John, 270, 370
Choosing a path, 305-310
Choosing a teacher, 314-319
Chosen deity *(ishta deva),* 339-340
Christ (Jesus), 184, 210, 262, 285, 311, 386
Christianity, ix, 9, 16, 168, 274, 285, 299, 341, 367
Christ-nature, 207, 209, 269, 270
Christ-self, 183-185, 209
Christian mysticism, 269-273, 363, 372, 381, 388

Index

affirmative way, 224
negative way, 225
Chuang Tzu, 13, 16-17, 24, 26, 48-49, 57, 70, 79, 88, 133-134, 147, 154, 160, 167, 175-176, 203-205, 216, 222-223, 266, 360
Cleaving, 223, 268
Cloud of forgetting, 177, 184
Cloud of Unknowing, The, 177, 184, 386
Cognitive psychology, 25
Compassion, 38, 265, 279, 280-286, 342
Completed/Perfected Man, 149, 209-210, 273-274
Completeness, 136, 158, 187, 189, 249-278, 279, 310
Concentration (stage of), 373-381
Concentrative meditation, 366-367, 373, 377
Condition of absolute naturalness, 264-265
Conditioned existence, 13, 22, 32, 50, 56-57, 77, 81, 141, 166, 173, 193, 256, 258, 267, 295, 330, *passim*
Conditioning, 37-47, 49, 183, 275, 355, 357, 363
Consciousness, 4, 10, 12-13, 18, 23, 25, 32, 38, 42, 51, 56, 64, 75, 93, 108, 126, 141, 152-153, 155, 169, 185, 193, 199, 233, 310, 355-360, 362, *passim*
construction of, 66, 91-106, 120, 183, 271, 349, 359, 383
definition of, 4-5
frames of, 91-106
stream of, 38, 377
Consciousness as Such, 156, 255, 358, 365

Construction of reality, 107-118, 176, 183, 271, 349
Construction of self, 119-128, 183, 271, 349
Contemplation, 360, 363, 381-382
Conventional religion, 1-3, 5, 336, 349
Cosmic consciousness, 385
Cozort, Daniel, 339-340
Craving, 76, 78, 136, 257, 276, 362
Cross, 182-184

D

Daikaku (Zen master), 202, 265
Dark night of the senses, 384
Daud, Sheikh Mohamed (Sufi master), 306, 335
Death instinct, 75, 95
Deautomatization, 357
De Blois, Louis, 208
Deconstruction of consciousness, 148, 171-172, 177, 179, 271, 295, 356-357, 359-360, 362, 378, 381, *passim*
of reality, 383-385; of self, 385
Deikman, Arthur, 34, 94, 99, 121-123, 143-144, 152, 249, 357
De Leon, Luis, 225
Delusion, 38, 47, 52, 64, 79, 136, 252, 316
DeMartino, Richard, 126, 327
Dependent coarising, 71, 295
Desire, 12, 15, 17, 21, 33, 38, 40, 47-48, 51, 64, 72, 75-85, 96, 98-99, 120, 124, 129, 132-133, 145, 155, 163, 169, 257-258, 263, 280, 294, 326, 344, 350, 358, 362, 373-374, 377-378, 382, *passim*

Desiringness, 76-84, 145, 164-165, 276-277
Desiringlessness, 145, 163-169
Devekut, 268
Devotion, 335, 337-338, 340
Dharma-maya, 203, 261
Dhikr, 192, 361
Dhyani (meditative) Buddhas, 386
Direct experience, 5, 63-64, 186, 211-212, 241, 293, 297, 306, 349, 361, 389
Disidentification, 143, 153, 155, 157, 159, 181-185, 189, 257, 271, 341, 343, 350, 358
Displacement effect, 381
Dissatisfaction, 30, 32, 34, 48, 50-51, 53, 77, 80, 88, 99, 103, 131-132, 374
Dogen (Zen master), 174
Don Juan, 24-26, 29, 104, 111, 147, 152, 155, 178, 310, 325, 329, 343-344, 360
Dov Baer, Rabbi, 206
Dualism/duality, 65, 69-70, 166, 198, 214-216, 223, 249, 256, 258, 276, 294, 360, 364-365, 387
Dualistic structure, 87, 93-94, 145, 174, 181, 356
Dualistic thinking, 149, 158, 177, 359
Dukkha, 31-34, 51, 54, 57, 72, 77, 81, 87, 133, 150, 158, 173-174, 181, 199, 256-258, 292-295, 310, *passim*
Dunne, John S., 279-280

E

Eastern Orthodox Church, 270, 370
Eastern religions, ix, 284-286

Eckhart, Meister, 159, 165-166, 177, 184, 208-209, 227-229, 240, 244, 272, 388
Eddington, Arthur, 107, 110
Effortless Being, xi, 264
Ego, 3, 11, 52, 82, 84-89, 124-127, 153, 155, 164, 181-185, 194, 209, 256, 258, 277, 298, 307, 311, 329, 350, *passim*
Egolessness, 187-189, 280
Eightfold Path, 257, 372
Ein Sof, 206, 223-224, 268
Eliade, Mircea, 56, 255-256, 277
Emptiness, 53, 88, 236-237, 345
Emptiness is form, 219, 228, 265, 274
Emptying the mind, 145-146, 171-178, 384
Enfolding-unfolding universe, 109
Enlightenment, 31, 222, 246, 259-260, 262, 265, 284, 294-296, 305-307, 309-310, 324, 332, 334, 338-339, 343-345, 363, 367, 388-389
Enlightened teacher, 314, 316-317
Entering the stream, 257
Erikson, Erik H., 34, 156
EST, 143-144, 306
Eternal/eternity, 244-245, 251, 273
Experiential religion, x, 1-6, 9-10, 19, 37, 63-64, 66, 69, 71, 96, 116, 120, 131, 137, 141, 143-144, 161, 171, 181, 232, 251-253, 278, 290-291, 303, 317, 333, 335-336, 349, 389-390
Explanation (structure of), 113
Explicate order, 109

F

Faith, 3, 330, 335-338, 349

Index

Fana, 188-190, 273-274
Ferguson, Marilyn, 108
Five ranks (of Tozan), 262-265
Fixations (mental and emotional), 38, 72, 149, 153, 160, 263, 267, 273, 282, 306, 326, 328, 356, 378, *passim*
Form is emptiness, 219, 228, 264, 274
Formless, 191, 268
Formless Ground, 203, 206, 229, 234, 264, 274
Formless State, 158, 269
Freud, Sigmund, 30, 34, 75, 123, 142, 199, 311
Fromm, Erich, 18, 25, 327
Functions of a Master, 324-332

G

Gattan (Zen master), 334
Gautama (Buddha), 295
God, 3, 14, 16, 35-36, 67, 69, 70-71, 80, 125, 165, 168, 177, 185, 187, 195, 208, 223, 225-226, 228-229, 231, 252, 272, 281, 297-298, 301, 311, 330, 342-343, 358, 360-361, 363, 386-388, *passim*
  as Transcendent Other, 3, 213, 297, 300, 387
  as Personal Being, 195, 250, 364
God-as-object, 209, 229, 250, 364
God-as-subject, 209, 229
Godel, Kurt, 130
Godhead, 165, 198-199, 206, 208-209, 223, 226-228, 231, 240, 252, 268-272, 281, 297-298, 301, 311, 330, 342-343, 358, 360-361, 363, 386-388
God state, 51

Goleman, Daniel, 144, 257-258, 353-354
Goodman, Nelson, 116
Gospel According to John, The, 15, 26, 35, 210, 345
Govinda, Lama Anagarika, 23, 25, 50, 87, 175, 193, 260, 262, 329, 359
Grasping, 33, 88, 121, 257
Greed, 12, 24, 38, 88, 121, 136, 257, 312
St. Gregory Palamas, 210
Gurdjieff, G.I., 18, 274, 309, 372
Guru, 314, 317, 319-321, 323, 330, 337-340, 373, *passim*

H

Habits, 15, 17, 38, 149, 263, 273, 326, 344, 370
Habituation, 38, 43, 50, 94, 169, 275, 339, 357, 362
Hahn, Thich Nhat (Vietnamese master), 370
Hakuin (Zen master), 159, 263, 282-283
Halevi, Z'ev ben Shimon, 14-15, 40, 50, 52, 206
Han Shan (Zen master), 175, 242, 244, 327
Happiness, 31-32, 39, 99, 132-134
Harada Roshi, 265
Hare Krishna Movement, 143
Harrison, Edward, 110-111
Hasidic masters, 187
Heart Sutra, 218-222, 264-265, 274
Heisenberg, Werner, 214
Hell state, 53
Herrigel, Eugene, 332, 335, 337
Hesse, Hermann, 124

Hinduism, ix, 9-11, 13, 16, 21-24, 39-40, 49, 56, 71, 74, 78, 84, 125, 132, 149, 171, 173, 181, 195, 197, 200, 203, 217, 250, 254-256, 265-266, 274, 307, 317, 321, 337, 367, 370, 389, *passim*
Hixon, Lex, 206-207,. 209, 224, 274
Hoffman, Edward, 15, 26, 35, 148
Holographic paradigm, 108-109
Holonomic theory, 109-110, 214
Holy Spirit, 345
Hsueh Yen (Zen master), 244
Hua Yen School of Buddhism, 218, 220-221, 239, 261, 267
Huang Po (Zen master), 159, 166, 175, 201, 238-239, 242, 259-260
Hui-neng (the sixth patriarch), 158-159, 174-175, 178, 202, 242, 259
Hujwiri (Sufi master), 188
Hululi, Dil Bar Khan (Sufi master), 309
Human condition, 9, 21-22, 30, 37, 39, 49, 58-59, 69-71, 85, 96, 132, 141-142, 145, 181
Human paradox, 129-137
Human Potential Movement, 249
Human state, 52
Hung, Ko (Taoist master), 319
Hungry ghost state, 52
Huxley, Aldous, 137

I

Ibsen, Henrik, 17
Idel, Moshe, 188, 206, 224, 268
Identification, 23, 47, 71-74, 86-87, 93, 96-97, 120, 149, 151, 154-155, 157, 160, 176, 185, 276, 280, 294, 309, 326, 337-338, 341, 358, 360, 373-374, 382, *passim*

Identity, 24, 67, 125, 132, 164, 167, 173, 183, 186, 189-190, 213, 239, 255, 260, 356, 359, *passim*
Identity with God, 208-209, 224-231, 268-275, 360, 364, 365
Ignorance, 10-11, 95, 377
Illumination, 270, 293, 296, 298, 386
Illusion, 21-25, 27, 31, 38, 53, 56, 74, 79, 87, 103, 182, 193, 212, 250, 316, 382
Impasse, 56, 127, 129, 137, 192, 327, 362
Impermanence, 57, 81, 86, 93, 295
Implicate order, 109
Incompleteness, 76, 102, 127, 179, 181, 189, 249, 250, 255
Incompleteness Theorem, 114, 130
Indwelling/Inherence (mutual), 216-223 *passim*, 239, 295
Inertia, 52, 136
Infinite/Infinity, 224, 251, 259-260, 262, 268
Informal Awareness Meditation (IAM), 37-71
Infused contemplation, 360-361, 385, 387
Initiation, 338-344
Isa Upanishad, 217
Insight meditation, 317, 366-367, 373, 377, 387
Insufficiency, 32-33, 51, 77-78, 369
Interconnected, 113-114, 216, 239, 268, 295, *passim*
Internal dialogue, 104, 145, 171, 358-360
Interpenetration, 216-223, 239, 268, 295
St. Isaac the Syrian, 270
Islam, ix, 9, 16, 299, 367

J

Jeans, Sir James, 107
Jesus, 15-16, 27, 64, 150-51, 182, 185, 190, 202, 207, 224, 269, 280, 22, 297-299, 303, 324, 333-334, 335, 344-345, 350, 371, 386, 390
St. John of the Cross, 168, 185, 225, 386
Jones, Jim, 320
Judaism, 9, 16, 267-268, 299, 367
Julian of Norwich, 208-209
Jung, Carl, 303

K

Kabbalah, 14, 26, 35, 40, 48, 50, 73-74, 148, 186-187, 206, 223, 267-268, 285, 363, 371-372, 381, 388
Kagan, Jerome, 100
Kaivalya Upanishad, 196-197, 217
Kant, Immanuel, 116
Kapleau, Philip Roshi, 11, 222, 237, 260, 265, 315-317, 322, 324, 328, 330-333, 335-336, 345, 363, 385
Karma, 42-43, 72, 133, 135, 153, 257-258, 263, 275, 315
Karma Yoga, 152, 279, 370
Kashani, Ezzuddin (Sufi master), 188
Keating, Abbott Thomas, 379
Khahwatiya Order (Sufis), 343
Kingdom of God, 151, 206-208, 298
Koan, 185, 202, 205, 245, 265, 385
Korzybski, Alfred, 214
Krishna, 148, 152, 330
Krishnamurti, J., 34, 370

L

Language, 99-102, 123

Lankavatara Sutra, The, 72-73, 75, 174-175, 187, 258, 362
Lao-tzu, 79, 167, 203-204, 222, 227
Law of Conservation of Programming, 96
Law of Construction/Structural Law, 81, 114, 130
Lawrence, D.H., 54, 280
Laws of Manu, 78
Leaving self behind, 146, 181-194, *passim*
Lefort, Raphael, 149, 306, 309, 315, 335
Lerner, Eric, 318
LeShan, Lawrence, 101, 107, 114, 364-365
Letting go, 182, 184-188, 364-365
Levine, Stephen, 33, 76-77, 85, 87
Liberation, 136, 141-144, 146, 151, 171, 173-174, 181-182, 199, 232, 246, 253-280, 283-284, 286, 289, 294, 296, 305, 307, 309, 314, 319, 341, 343, 345, 349
Life instinct, 75
Lin-chi (Zen master), 159, 167, 175, 178, 260
Lings, Martin, 209
Logic, 114-115
Logos, 35, 199, 202, 207, 210, 240
Love, 38, 48, 281
Love and compassion, 266, 279-286
Love your enemies, 151, 371
Luckmann, Thomas, 102-105

M

Madhyamika School of Buddhism, 201, 218, 220, 236, 239
Maezumi, Teizan Roshi, 260
Mahabharata, 78

Maharaj-ji, Guru, 386
Maitri Upanishad, 39, 70, 171
Makyo, 22, 387
Mandala, 268, 339-341, 361, 373
Mandukya Upanishad, 233
Mann, Thomas, 41
Mantra, 239, 338-340, 361
Marpa (Tibetan Buddhist master), 282, 325
Master-disciple relationship, 333-345
Mathematics, 114
Ma-tsu (Baso: Zen master), 202, 245, 282, 331
Maximos the Confessor, 270
May, Rollo, 41, 53
Maya, 22-23, 25, 27, 56, 79, 103, 144, 195, 198, 377
Meditation, 2, 173, 192, 293, 303, 308, 314, 337-338, 340, 343-344, 349-367, 369-372, 375-379, 381-383
nature and aims of, 353-366
kinds of, 366-367
Mercy, 281
Middle Path, 294
Milarepa (Tibetan Buddhist master), 282, 325
Mindfulness, 370-71
Mishima, Yokio, 63, 275
Moksha, 277
Moment-to-moment awakening, 367, 371-372, 382
Moses, 296-299, 386
Motives for choosing a path, 310-314
Mudra, 340
Muhammed, 298-299, 343, 386
Muktananda, Swami, 304, 363
Mundakya Upanishad, 211
Muslim, 342
Mystical marriage, 270

Mysticism, x, 206

N

Nagarjuna (Buddhist philosopher), 181, 237-239
Nameless, 203, 226
Nan Chuan (Zen master), 167
Naranjo, Claudio, 357
Naropa (Tibetan Buddhist master), 325
Needleman, Jacob, 331
Negative programming, 82, 88, 263, 273, 311, 326, 328, 357, 366, 370-372
Neisser, Ulrich, 93
New Age Movement, 143, 305
New Creation, 269
New Man, 269
New Testament, 35, 41, 58, 81, 133, 165, 176, 182, 206-207, 224, 281, 297
Newton's First Law, 43
Nicholas of Cusa, 240
Nicholson, Reynold A., 274
Nietzsche, Friedrich, 30, 143
Nimatullahi Order (Sufis), 342
Nirmana-kaya, 203, 261
Nirvana, 150, 158, 199, 200-201, 219, 236, 256-259, 295, 318, 363, 388-389
Nirvikalpa samadhi, 255, 273, 287-388
Nishargadatta Maharaj, 4, 56, 70, 187
Nonattachment, 145, 147-161, 265, 268, 276, 358, 375-377, 379
Nondualism/nonduality, 66-67, 114, 193, 203, 226, 266, 364-366, *passim*
Nonjudgmental mind, 371

Nonreturner, 257
Not-doing *(wu wei)*, 153-155, 361
Not-enough *(dukkha)*, 32
Nurbakhsh, Javad (Sufi master), 188, 230, 274, 342, 363, 371

O

Objectless, 235
Object-pole, 108, 120-121, 124-125, 153, 172, 235
Oblivion of time, 55-56, 127, 137
Odier, Daniel, 338
Old Testament, 14, 25, 35, 58, 70, 73, 79, 81, 133, 207
Once returner, 257
Oneness, absolute, 223-232 *passim*
 relative, 223-232 *passim*
One-pointedness of mind, 380
Original face, 202
Ornstein, Robert, 56, 80, 92-94, 104, 155, 161, 306, 312, 357, 366
Osaka, Koryu Roshi, 385
Otto, Rudolph, 218
Ouspenski, P.D., 18
Ox-herding stages, 258-262, 274, 388-389

P

Pai-chang (Zen master), 245, 282, 331
Paradox, 183, 192, 194, 284, 361, 377
Paranormal powers, 313, 317, 376, 386
Patanjali, 149, 173, 254-255, 329, 360, 372, 386, 387
St. Paul, 35, 41-42, 58, 81-83, 133, 176, 207-209, 269, 285
Pearce, Joseph Chilton, 53, 100-105

Perfected/Completed Man, 149, 209-210
Personhood, 14
Personal stage (of development), 2, 155, 183, 356, 363
Philosophy, 58, 9}, 107, 193
Physics, 91, 107
Piaget, Jean, 93
Pirsig, Robert, 21
Plato, x, 23, 107, 115-116
Pribram, Karl, 108-109
Primal revelation, 292-304
Primordial state, 266
Programming (of consciousness), 11-12, 15, 21, 25, 32, 37-40, 42-44, 50, 75, 83, 92, 95-96, 102, 108, 120, 144-145, 169, 171, 176, 179, 233, 235, 267, 275, 315-316, 326, 339, 351, 355-356, 362, 371-376, 383-384, *passim*
Pseudo-Dionysius, 226, 270-272
Psychology, 2, 91, 96, 107, 285, 363
Psychotherapy, 143, 353, 363
Pure Subjectivity, 209, 229, 234
Purification, 148, 270, 329, 370
Purusha, 254

Q

Qoheleth, 25, 50, 58, 133, 289
Qualities of an authentic teacher, 319-324
Quandary, 56, 127, 194
Quantum mechanics, 109-111
Quantum theory, 107, 112, 214
Quine, William van Orman, 116
Quran, 298, 343

R

Rahman, Fazler, 298, 335, 343

Rajneesh, B.S., 143, 166, 319, 361
Ram Dass, 75, 79, 190, 307-308, 322-323, 378
Rama, Swami, 75, 119, 121, 156
Ramana Maharshi, 22, 70, 148, 158, 189, 195, 197, 212, 235, 241, 255-256, 275, 303, 309, 314, 321, 323, 330
Ramanuja, 255
Rank, Otto, 34
Reality as Such, 3, 22, 30-34, 45, 64-65, 69, 70-71, 73-74, 77-78, 91, 114-116, 125-126, 129, 131-132, 136, 145-156, 150, 155, 1732, 182, 187-188, 194-195, 201, 203, 209, 211-213, 216, 218, 220, 227, 233-234, 236, 238-241, 243, 246, 249-250, 252, 255-260, 275-276, 278, 294-295, 300, 327, 336, 341, 358, 361, 363, 387, *passim*
Relativity, theory of, 109, 214
Relaxation, 353-354, 357
Restlessness, 51, 53, 88, *passim*
Resurrection, 184, 273, 285
Return to the Source, 264, 268, 274, 388-389
Revelation, 132, 178, 266, 290-305, 307
    relative, 299-301, 365
    absolute, 232, 265, 277, 300, 365
Roberts, Bernadette, 26, 184-185, 187-188, 194, 208-209, 229-234, 245, 272, 276, 365, 384, 388
Roszak, Theodore, x
Rumi, Jalal al-din, 133-134, 178, 230-231, 316
Russell, Bertrand, 215
Rustam, Sheikh Daggash (Sufi master), 149, 309

Ruysbroeck, Jan van, 208-209, 225, 240

S

Sabbath, Linda, 39
Salvation, 48, 285
Samadhi, 255, 263, 294, 331, 383-389 *passim*
    Savikalpa (*samadhi* with support), 385-386
    Nirvikalpa, 255, 273, 287-288
    Dharmamegha, 255
    Sahaja, 255, 265, 274, 389
Sambhoga-kaya, 203, 261
Samkhya Yoga (philosophy), 199
Samsara, 32, 49-50, 72, 166, 219, 258
Sanai, Hakim (Sufi master), 18, 74
Saraha, 265, 280
Sarbin, Theodore, 119, 121
Sartre, Jean-Paul, 16-17, 45, 125
Sat, chit, ananda, 199
Satori, 331
Schimmel, Annemarie, 149, 188
Schroedinger, Erwin, 107, 214
Schumann, Hans Wolfgang, 32
Sefirotic Tree, 268
Sekida, Katsuki, 262
Self-realization, 149-150, 171, 181, 211-212, 254-255, 320, 328, 349-350, 389
Self-transformation, 67, 306, 312, 350, 369
Self-transparency (of All-embracing Awareness), 242-244
Seng T'san (Zen master), 182
Separate self (ego), 5, 84-89, 117, 119-120, 125, 127, 144, 182, 192, 209
    construction of, 119-127

deconstruction of, 181-194, *passim* 362, 385
Seung Sahn, Roshi, 85, 159, 265, 314, 322-323, 345
Shabistari (Sufi master), 177-178
Shah, Idries, 17, 26-27, 36-37, 73, 80, 134, 149, 151-152, 177-178, 186, 230, 313, 316-317, 324-325, 330, 335, 345
Shankara (Hindu philosopher), 22, 218, 256
Shakespeare, William, 104
Shaya, Leo, 187, 206, 223
Shen Hui (Zen master), 113, 239
Shibili (Sufi master), 186
Shimano, Eido Roshi, 265
Skandhas, 11, 31, 33, 85
Skinner, B.F., 47
Slater, Philip, 13, 134, 249
Sleepwalking state, 14-15
Smith, Adam, 143
Social construction of reality, 101-105
Sociology, 91
Socrates, 13
Source (Ultimate Reality as), 16, 29, 191, 207, 222-223, 246, 264-265, 267, 363, 388-389
Spencer-Brown, G., 110, 215
Sperry, Roger, 93
Srimad Bhagavatam, 39-40, 69, 75, 132, 171, 173, 181, 193, 197, 253, 276
Stage of concentration, 373-381
Stopping the world, 146, 171-172, 178-179, 384
Stress reduction, 353-354
Structural Law, 81
Subjectless (All-embracing Awareness as), 234

Subject-pole, 108, 120, 125, 235
Subtle state, 364
Suchness, 223, 256, 264, 272
Suffering, 12, 31, 37-38, 56, 73, 80, 83, 87-88, 133, 137, 165, 181-183, 256, 276-277, 284, 286, 310, *passim*
Sufism/Sufis, 16-17, 26, 36, 71, 149, 151, 166, 177, 185, 188-190, 209, 230, 241, 273-275, 307, 315-317, 324, 338, 345, 350, 363, 369, 371-372, 381, 388
Sunyata, 158, 167, 175, 201, 203, 218-220, 227, 236, 238-239, 279, 340
Supernatural, 66
Supreme Identity, 156, 158, 193, 206, 208-210, 218, 220, 228-230, 235, 237, 258, 264, 272, 274, 295, 300, 388
Surangama Sutra, 236
Surawardi (Sufi master), 188
Surrender, 310, 343-344
Suzuki, D.T., 73, 86, 119, 220, 260, 325
Suzuki, Shunryu Roshi, 87, 202

T

Taittiriya Upanishad, 173
Takuan (Zen master), 159, 174
Tanha, 76-85
Tantra (Hindu), 255, 309, 318-319, 339
Tao, 13, 70, 79, 154, 167-168, 175, 203-205, 222-223, 227, 240, 266-267, 363, 388-389
Taoism, 9, 13, 16, 79, 88, 133, 153, 167, 175, 203, 222, 240, 250, 266-267, 274, 319, 363, 364, 372, 389

Tao Te Ching, 70, 79, 88, 153, 159, 167-168, 181, 189, 344
Taoist Yoga, 173, 222, 267, 309, 318
Tapas, 329
Tarski, Alfred, 115
Tart, Charles T., 92, 100, 103
Tathagata, 258, 295
Theory of implication, 113
Theravada Buddhism, 258, 386, 388-389
St. Theresa of Avila, 208, 225, 270, 386
St. Thomas Aquinas, 227-228
Thomas, Dylan, 29, 142
Thoreau, Henry David, 18, 23, 74, 329
Tibetan Buddhism, 203, 222, 242, 260, 266, 307, 309, 318, 325, 335, 337, 339-340, 344, 370, 386, 389
Tibetan *Tantras,* 337-340
Tov, Baal Shem, 15, 26, 186-187
Tozan (Zen master), 203, 262, 266
Transcendence, 59, 63, 113, 146, 173, 183, 187-188, 192-194, 231, 239, 246, 255-258, 264, 266, 272-273, 275-276, 279, 312, 358, 362-363, *passim;* of ego, 187-189, 192, 199, 306, 351, 357, *passim*
Transcendent Unity, 204
Transformation, 17, 70, 169, 176, 183, 269, 272, 285, 308, 310, 316, 356, 362, 370, *passim*
Transforming union, 270
Transmission of mind, 344-345
Transpersonal Reality, 195
Transpersonal stages, 1-3, 155, 157, 183, 363-364, 384
Transpersonal states, 182, 189, 301, 356-357, 359
Tree of Life, 268

Tri-kaya, 203, 261
Trinity, 199
Triple terror (of ego),% 52
True nature, 66
True Self, 11, 17, 36, 82, 84, 151, 164, 182, 185, 195-210, 371
Trungpa, Chogyam, 50-51, 53, 76, 86, 266, 282, 294, 312-313, 319, 322-323, 325-326, 333-334, 356, 370
Tseng Lao-weng (Taoist master), 259
Tseng-tsan (Zen master), 259
Tsung Kao (Zen master), 174-175, 242
Tsung-mi (Zen master), 73
Tulku, Tarthang, 33, 76, 87, 239, 249, 282, 319, 322-324, 333, 337, 345, 356, 371
Turiya, 389
Turning the other cheek, 151, 371
Tu Shun (Hua Yen master), 221

U

Ultimate Reality, 56, 175, 189, 235, 254, 256, 260, 300, 364-365
Ultimate transcendence, 194
Unawareness, 9-18, 23, 26, 35-36, 44, 52, 64, 71, 79, 84, 88, 95, 105, 136, 149, 295, 303, 306, 326, 328, 350, 362, 370, 376-378, 380-382, *passim*
Unconditioned Reality, 3, 66, 199, 202-203, 206, 210, 212-213, 238, 278, 349
Unconditioned, the, 32, 37, 67, 132, 141, 175, 185, 189, 203, 207, 212-213, 217, 219, 256-258, 263-264, 266, 278, 282, 295, 297, 300, 302,

Index

317, 324-325, 329-330, 332, 349, 362, 365, 390
Unconditioned State, 22, 43, 66, 131, 145, 150, 158-159, 171, 174, 199, 200, 202-203, 217-218, 232-233, 252, 255, 259, 264, 278-279, 320, 336-337, 360, 365, 387-389
Unconscious, 36, 39, 43, 182, 234, 263, 290, 370
Undifferentiated, 197, 388
Undifferentiated Unity, 224
Undivided wholeness, 113-114, 222, 268
Unfolding-enfolding universe, 109-110
Unification of attention, 380
Union with God, 268, 270, 360, 363-365, 385
Union with meditation object, 383-387 *passim*
Unreality, 127, 378
Unreality - Illusion, 21-27
Upanishads, 42, 173, 195, 197, 200, 217, 231, 235, 242, 254, 390

V

Vajrayana (Tibetan Buddhism), 319
Van de Wetering, Janwillem, 192, 328
Vedanta, 22, 254-256, 266, 364
Vipassana (insight meditation), 366-367
Visualization, 307, 337-340, 361, 373
Visuddhimagga, 256
Vivekananda, Swami, 104, 194, 374
Void, 205
Void-nature, 159, 203
Vonnegut, Kurt, 141

W

Walker, Kenneth, 18
Walsh, Roger, 18, 25, 354-355, 370, 377, 384
Weber, Renee, 109, 112, 214
Wechler, Rob, 354
Wei Wu Wei, 39, 87, 235, 327
Western religions, ix, 285-286
Wheel of Life, 47, 50-51, 53-54, 70, 72, 75-76, 80, 96, 103, 127, 132, 135, 148, 164, 166, 169, 179, 275, 286
Wigner, Eugene, 110
Wilber, Ken, 71, 110, 119, 122, 125, 131, 135, 143, 156, 196, 206, 214-215, 244, 255, 264, 320, 327, 358, 364-365, 384-386
Willis, Janice D., 340
Wittgenstein, Ludwig, 101, 135, 215
Wolfe, Thomas, 142
Wu wei, 153-154, 167

Y

Yahweh, 297
Yamada Roshi, 260
Yantra, 373
Yasutani Roshi, 11, 22, 182, 222, 260, 363, 385
Yoga, 173, 339
Yogachara School of Buddhism, 201, 218, 220, 236-239
Yoga Sutras, 149, 254-255, 367, 372, 386
Yu, Lu K'uan, 222
Yung-chia Ta-shih (Zen master), 242, 259
Yung Ming (Hua Yen master), 239

Z

Zen Buddhism, 161, 166-167, 177, 189, 192, 202, 205, 238, 259, 262, 279, 282, 307, 324-325, 327, 334-335, 338, 344, 355, 363, 367, 385-389

Zen master(s), 158, 167, 174, 176, 192, 242, 259-260, 314, 322, 324, 327, 332